Physical Setting:

EARTH SCIENCE

STAREVIEW

"Strategic Test Achievement Review"

Authors
Wayne Garnsey & Virginia Page

Graphics
Eugene Fairbanks & Wayne Garnsey

Artwork
Eugene B. Fairbanks

N&N Publishing Company, Inc.
18 Montgomery Street   Middletown, New York 10940-5116

For Ordering & Information
1-800-NN 4 TEXT
Internet: www.nn4text.com   email: nn4text@nandnpublishing.com

TO THE TEACHER

N&N's Physical Setting – Earth Science is structured according to the new Earth science standards and assessments. It is a comprehensive review and supplement for a one-year general introduction to Earth Science on the secondary (commencement) school level.

This book is centered on Earth's "natural" processes, and environmental awareness is an integral part of the presentation. Therefore, the effects on Earth systems and landscape produced by humankind is discussed in relation to the Earth's own dynamic processes.

If you are familiar with other books by N&N in *Biology*, *Chemistry*, *Physics*, and *Earth Science* (traditional and modified program), you are aware of our narrative writing philosophy (that is, tutorial – one-on-one). Our hundreds of illustrations are basic and easy to understand, just as a teacher illustrates a point – avoiding the superfluous. Topical questions are asked to stimulate and direct the student's attention and encourage thinking. Hundreds of multiple-choice, constructed response questions, and practice exams challenge the student's learning and provide extended practice for the final exam.

Vocabulary is always a part of our books. After all, how can the student read for comprehension when she/he does not understand "the language?" To help, our glossary and index are combined. The glossary is comprehensive and provides concise definitions, explanations, and examples. And, if the student needs more understanding of the term, the text page references are provided right there – with the term, not in a separate index.

Beginning on page 4 is *Your Construction Guide to "Tri-Sense(able) Learning"* – AN INFORMAL CONVERSATION WITH THE STUDENT. Encourage your students to read and make the *"Tri-Sense(able) Learning"* a part of their study program. It's not magical – just common sense, and it works.

All of your colleagues at N&N wish for your students, as well as ours, good learning, good grades, and good application of the knowledge and processes studied here. If you have criticisms, comments, and/or suggestions, we want to hear from you.

Send us a letter, email us at *nn4text@nandnpublishing.com*, or call us at *1-800 NN 4 TEXT*.

DEDICATED TO OUR STUDENTS

WITH THE SINCERE HOPE THAT THIS BOOK WILL FURTHER ENHANCE THEIR EDUCATION AND BETTER PREPARE THEM WITH AN APPRECIATION AND UNDERSTANDING OF THE SCIENTIFIC PRINCIPLES THAT SHAPE OUR WORLD.

Our sincere thanks to the many teachers and their students who contributed their knowledge, skills, experience, and assistance in the preparation of this manuscript.

Special thanks to Fran Harrison and Paul Stich for their editorial assistance.

© Copyright 2001, **Revised 2013**

N&N Publishing Company, Inc.

Internet: www.nn4text.com   phone: 1-800-NN 4 TEXT   email: nn4text@nandnpublishing.com

SAN # - 216-4221   Item Code # - 530   ISBN # 978-0-935487-74-9

11 12 13 14 15 Bang Printing 2016 2015 2014 2013

Printed in the United States of America, Brainerd, MN

TABLE OF CONTENTS

A CONVERSATION WITH THE STUDENT: YOUR CONSTRUCTION GUIDE TO
"TRI-SENSE(ABLE) LEARNING"

So, you don't like to read directions. You like to "cut to the chase," "skip the boring stuff," and "can't be bothered with details."

However, can you agree that if something can save you hours of tedious effort, it is worth a few minutes of your valuable time?

Well, if you have "wisdom beyond your years," you just agreed. Great, you are ready to begin *Tri-Sense(able) Learning*.

Agree or Disagree: "A mind is a terrible thing to waste." Whether you want to or not, common sense tells you that you have to agree. So, let's utilize your best asset in life – your brain. What follows will help you succeed not only in this course, but in all of life's situations.

Try it. There's "no cost or obligation." Nothing additional to buy. (You already have the book.) Nothing to lose – everything to gain!

If you "can't talk the talk, you can't walk the walk." It's true, you must be able to communicate, and to do that, you must know the words. So, start your learning with the **Vocabulary Words** at the beginning of each Unit. Look up words that you don't know or you can't use in a sentence that others will understand. Use the glossary at the end of this book.

Once you are satisfied that you understand the key words of the Unit, begin reading the material. Read to learn (comprehension), but understand that this kind of reading is different than reading for pure pleasure.

You may be one who enjoys learning about the Earth, or you may have very little interest in Earth Science. In either case, becoming proficient in your knowledge of Earth Science or any other school subject is work. Learning requires you to study. Studying requires **concentration**, **planning**, **time**, and **hard work**. So, if you want to be "the most that you can be," you must make the commitment.

At sometime in your life, you've been deep into something of real interest. Just as you're getting to "the good part," you are interrupted. You get angry. Why? Your concentration was broken. When the irritation was gone, what did you have to do? That's right! You started all over again – from the beginning! So, you ask, "What's that got to do with anything?"

You won't like this, but studying with the television on, boom-box blasting, or another distraction just doesn't work. You need a quiet place where you can "talk it through" to yourself – even out loud. Commit yourself to a study time without interruptions such as the phone. Concentration needs quiet. Even a computer's CPU, at 500+MHz, becomes confused and corrupted and freezes when conflicts *interrupt its thinking!*

Did you know that you have an Intranet (similar to the Internet) within yourself? Sounds radical, perhaps silly, but remember that it is your senses that input into your brain –

your massive, unlimited hard drive. It's a fact that Intel's Pentium® "megahertz brains" can't come close to the computing abilities of your brain – your memory center. Think of using your brain much like using your home or school computer. Inputting the information is easy. Remembering where you put it, and getting it back out, is difficult. On the Internet, you use the *search engines* into which you put "key words" or descriptions. Yahoo®, Excite®, and WebCrawler® do the rest.

Your brain is already equipped with an excellent *search engine*, called *recollection*. Your brain's search engine works much the same way as the computer's does with AOL® "key words." If you organize how you store information, it becomes easy to retrieve it when needed, such as on a test.

For example, suppose you want a certain CD. You head for the mall, then to a particular store in that mall. If you don't know where the store is located, you check the mall's directory. Once inside the music store, you search for a sign with your category of music on it. Then you search for another sign with music type or artist. You have the idea. It's not at all unlike using the computer with hard drives, partitions, folders, and files.

With your study environment (no distractions) and determination to learn ("just do it") in good shape, let's get down to it. Here's how ***Tri-Sense(able) Learning*** works.

First, use your eyes. Start by telling your brain what it is that you are going to read about. Don't skip headings – skim over them so you know what you will be reading about. Then, read the material, one paragraph at a time. STOP! Tell your brain what you just read – the topic and brief description of the information in the paragraph.

Give this a try: read the paragraph in the following box using the procedure suggested above. See if your results are similar to mine.

A. WEATHERING

The physical and chemical processes that change the characteristics of rocks on the Earth's surface are called **weathering**. In order for weathering to occur, the physical environment of the rocks must change and the rocks must be exposed to the air, water in some form (ice, snow, or liquid), or the acts of humans or other living things. Therefore, weathering is the response of rocks to the change in their environment.

Now tell yourself what you read without looking back at the paragraph.

Topic of paragraph – "Weathering"
Paragraph talked about – "change causes weathering"
What causes change? – "physical and chemical processes"
What are physical processes? – "exposure to air, water, humans, and others"
KEY WORDS – "weathering, physical process, chemical process, environment, rocks, exposure, change"

Couldn't do it? Don't quit, try another ***Tri-Sense(able) Learning*** tool – using your fingers to write! That's right, take notes as you read. DO NOT WRITE DOWN SENTENCES – just the "key words."

Don't worry, your brain will put the words together right, IF you have imputed the words to the brain.

That's the secret. *Tri-Sense(able) Learning* follows the old "KISS" principle, "**K**eep **I**t **S**imple **S**tudent."

"Just the facts, M'am," said *Dragnet's* Sergeant Friday, "Just the facts." But, how do you get the facts? ... Ask! You can easily learn what a paragraph is telling you. When you finish reading the paragraph, ask, How? What? Where? When? and Why? questions of the paragraph's topic – in this case, "Weathering."

Examples:

A HOW question? – "How does weathering occur?"
  Answer – "By exposing rocks to air, water, and acts of man or living things."
A WHAT question? – "What causes weathering?"
  Answer – "physical and chemical processes."
A WHERE question? – "Where does weathering happen?"
  Answer – "On rocks on the Earth's surface."
A WHEN question? – "When does weathering take place?"
  Answer – "When rocks respond to a change in their environment."
A WHY question? – "Why do processes cause weathering?"
  Answer – "Physical and chemical processes change the characteristics of rocks on the Earth's surface."

Still not sure? Try yet another addition to the *Tri-Sense(able) Learning* input routine. Now, this really sounds foolish, perhaps even embarrassing, but try using your ears!

If you study the paragraph as above and still cannot tell yourself what you just read, then adjust your input by adding sound. In other words, read out loud! Add to sight and touch, go with the "surround sound!" By doing this, your brain will consider the incoming information very important.

Why? (Get ready, this is a six part explanation.)

When you read out loud, you must (1) *input* the words through your eyes, (2) *process* the data within your brain, (3) *convert* this processed data from vision to audio, (4) *coordinate* nerves and muscles for speech, (5) use your ears to **input** the sound, and finally, (6) *re-process* the data within your brain.

This more than triples the input of data in the brain – as three senses are utilized, seeing, touching, and hearing. The resulting complex brain function makes the information "more important" to your memory center, allowing you to more easily learn and, <u>most</u> <u>importantly</u>, *recall* the information studied.

Put it all together, and what do you get? *Tri-Sense(able) Learning* with fantastic results – success! Sight (vision input/processing), touch (processing/writing output), and speaking/hearing (sound output/re-input) work together in a marvelous way – by the Rule of Squares (2x – 4x – 16x). That is, **vision** input and processing gives you twice the data input/retrieval. Add **touch** processing and writing and you square the result to four times the learning power. But, if you add the third, **sound** output and re-input, you square the 4 times to 16 times. Now that's human MEGA-HERTZ power. Like the odds? You should, because 1 gets you 2, 2 gets you 4, but 3 gets you 16!

Now, put this constructive learning into practice.

Turn to The Prologue. Begin reading. First, use the Tri-sense approach to read and study each Unit, then answer the questions. You'll be absolutely amazed at the benefits of practicing this simple but guaranteed to succeed, *Tri-sense(able) Learning* technique.

VOCABULARY

classification	instruments	phases of matter
conclusion (hypothesis)	interface	sensory perception
cyclic change	inverse relationship	time
density (mass/volume)	mass	variables
dynamic equilibrium	measurements	volume
energy flow	observation	weight
events	percent error	
inferences (interpretations)	pressure	

A. EVIDENCE & FACTS

Observations involve the interaction of a person's senses, such as sight, hearing, taste, touch, and smell, with the environment (surroundings). Observations directly involve **sensory perception**. Since our powers of observation are limited by our senses, it is often necessary for an observer to use **instruments** to extend his or her ability to observe and collect data. Any piece of information determined directly through the senses is called an **observation**.

How can the local environment be observed?

Instruments are used to improve upon one's powers of observation. For example, it is possible to observe the moon with the human eye, but a telescope increases the amount of detail that can be observed.

Instruments are used to extend one's ability to collect data which cannot be detected by human senses. For example, the human body has no sense receptors that can determine the presence of potentially dangerous radiation, such as x-rays and atomic radiation. However, using a detection device like the Geiger counter allows a person to make observations beyond the capabilities of human senses.

Inferences are interpretations based on observable properties. In other words, an inference is an **interpretation** or a **conclusion** (**hypothesis** or "educated guess") based on observations. For example, students observe a smooth stone along a stream. They infer that the smoothness is caused by the eroding action of water on the stone. This inference *may* or *may not* be a fact.

In the study of science, inferences may become "facts" because of the discovery of additional collaborating evidence. The same scientist, or another scientist, may make observations which prove that the water did cause the stone to become smooth.

It is important to understand the difference between an observation (what is discovered with the senses) and an inference (what is interpreted by the mind). Without sufficient observations, inferences may be incorrect.

A **system of classification** is based on the properties of an observed event or object. Events or objects that are similar in their properties are generally grouped (organized) together, allowing for more meaningful study. For example, all naturally formed solid objects composed of one or more minerals may be classified as rocks. This helps to organize the study of Earth materials. However, it does not accurately describe all rock types. Therefore, rocks are "sub-classified" into many other groups, such as sedimentary, igneous, and metamorphic rocks. In turn, these rock types are again "sub-classified" into further, more distinct groups. For example, sedimentary rocks may be classified as clastics, evaporites, or organic rocks.

How can observations within the environment be classified?

B. PROPERTIES OF OBJECTS

UNITS OF MEASUREMENTS

Measurements contain at least one basic dimensional quantity and describe the properties of objects numerically. These include quantities such as mass, length, or time.

> *How can properties of the environment be measured?*

Mass is the amount (quantity) of matter which an object contains and is usually measured in **grams** (1/1000 kilogram). Mass is distinguished from weight and should not be confused with it.

Weight of an object is determined by the pull of gravity on the mass of the object. Therefore, the object's (e.g., dog's) mass remains constant regardless of the amount of gravitation acting upon it; whereas, the weight of the object (e.g., dog) varies according to the gravitational force.

Length is the distance between the ends or sections of an object, or the total distance between two determined points of that object and is usually measured in **meters**, **centimeters** (1/100 meter), or **millimeters** (1/1000 meter).

Time is the measurable period during which an action, process, or condition exists, continues, or occurred. It may be a measurement such as a second, or a season, a schedule, an age, or a generation. Time may be a less definite measurement since it is often a relative event.

DIMENSIONAL QUANTITIES & COMPARISONS

Some properties of matter cannot be measured by basic, single units of measurement. Instead, mathematical combinations of the basic dimensional quantities must be used. Examples include:

> **Density** is a measurement involving the mass (quantity) of a substance or material per unit of volume.
>
> **Pressure** is the amount of force compared to the surface area.
>
> **Volume** is space occupied, expressed in cubic units. It is a combination of three dimensions, including length, width, and height.

ERRORS

Since all measurements are made by senses or by extensions of senses (instruments) and are actually approximations, measurements cannot be expected to be "exact." Therefore, a small margin of error is expected. For example, a centimeter scale may be used to measure the length of an object. The actual length of the object may be slightly more or less than the centimeter increments on the scale. Therefore, a slight error may occur when the measurement is taken.

Percent Error

$$\text{percent error} = \frac{\text{difference from accepted value}}{\text{accepted value}} \times 100$$

Percent Error is obtained when mathematical calculations are used to solve problems involving measured and accepted values (see bottom of previous page).

For example, if a student using a balance determines the mass of an object to be 95 grams, but the mass of that object is actually 100 grams, there is an error. To determine the percent error, the student compares the observed mass and the actual mass, then finds the difference between them (subtraction).

$$\underset{\text{(accepted value)}}{100 \text{ grams}} - \underset{\text{(measured mass)}}{95 \text{ grams}} = \underset{\text{(difference)}}{5 \text{ grams}}$$

The percentage error is determined as follows:

$$\text{percent error} = \frac{5 \text{ grams}}{100 \text{ grams}} \times 100 = 5\%$$

SAMPLE PROBLEMS

1   A student's measurement of the mass of a rock is 30 grams. If the accepted value for the mass of the rock is 33 grams, what is the percent error of the student's measurement?

   (1) 9%   (3) 30%
   (2) 11%   (4) 91%

2   A student determines that the density of an aluminum sample is 2.9 grams per cubic centimeter. If the accepted value for the density of aluminum is 2.7 grams per cubic centimeter, what is the student's approximate percent error?

   (1) 0.70%   (3) 7.4%
   (2) 0.20%   (4) 20%

Density is the concentration of the matter found within an object and is independent (does not depend) of the size and the shape of the material. Density is the mass of the object divided by the volume of the object, which is usually given in **g/cm³**:

$$\text{density} = \frac{\text{mass}}{\text{volume}}$$

PHASES OF MATTER

Earth materials may exist in three main forms: solid, liquid, or gas. These three states or phases of matter are dependent on the pressure or temperature conditions in which the material is placed. Generally, the material will change from a gas to a liquid to a solid as the temperature is lowered or as pressure is increased. As the temperature is increased or the pressure is lowered, the material will change state from a solid to a liquid to a gas.

There are several factors which affect the density, therefore the state (or phase), of a substance. Factors include:

• ***The density of a gas varies with pressure and temperature.*** For example, in a weather system, warmer air rises through cooler air, because the warmer air molecules are farther apart (less dense). The cooler air is more compressed (air molecules are closer together, having greater density, because of the higher pressure).

Compared to the cool air, warm air has lower pressure. Therefore, the less dense warm air is pushed up by the more dense cool air which is sinking. Increasing the pressure on a gas causes the gas to contract (molecules move closer together). Decreasing the pressure produces the opposite effect. This principle also applies to liquids and solids, but to a lesser extent.

• ***The maximum density of most materials occurs in the solid phase***. For example, a granite rock will sink in a melt of granitic magma (liquid rock).

However, water is a noted exception to the above. Water has its maximum density at a temperature of approximately 4°C, when it is a liquid. Therefore, the solid form of water, ice, will float on liquid water. When water freezes to form ice, it expands. The water molecules move farther apart, making ice less dense than liquid water.

> *What are some characteristics of the properties of the environment?*

C. Nature Of Change

Characteristics Of Change

The Earth environment is in a constant state of change. Any change in an Earth system or object can be described as the occurrence of an **event**. This event (change) may occur suddenly (such as lightning during a thunderstorm). Change may also be observed to take very long periods of time (for example, the formation of a mountain).

Graphing – A Way To Show Data

Factors involved in change are called **variables**. For example, if the temperature was measured and recorded every hour for twelve hours, time and temperature would be the variables.

How can changes be described?

Graphing of data (the variables) is often used to show the kind and rate of change that occurs between the variables. The variable you know before you begin (in this case, time in months) is plotted on the horizontal axis of the graph.

The shape of the graph line shows what kind of change occurred. The steepness of the graph line indicates the rate of change. The steeper the line, the faster the rate of change. In this case, the graph illustrates a rapid increase of temperature during the months of March, April, and May, then a slowing in June and basically no change in July. In August there is a slow decrease in temperature, followed by a rapid decrease from September to November.

If both variables change in the same direction, the graph will show a **direct relationship**. The graph at the right, comparing stream velocity and particle suspension, illustrates this. The direct relationship, according to the graph is, *as stream velocity increases, the amount of suspended particles it can carry increases, as well.*

If one variable increases as the other variable decreases, the graph will show an **inverse relationship**. The graph at the right, comparing stream velocity and particle deposition, illustrates this. The inverse relationship, according to the graph is, *as stream velocity increases, the amount of particles settling decreases.*

Graphs showing repeating patterns indicate **cyclic changes** in the variables. The graph below compares time of day with height of the tide. The relationship between the variables represents a cyclic change. As time increases, the height of the tide increases, then decreases, then increases, and so on. Graphing data in this way helps make accurate predictions.

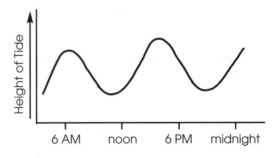

In addition to line graphs, pie graphs and bar graphs may also be used to show data.

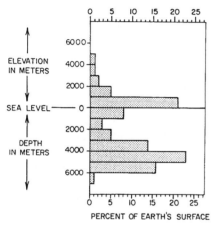

Sources of Nitrogen Emissions (24.5 million tons/yr.)

Sources of Sulfur Dioxide Emissions (29.7 million tons/yr.)

The pie graphs above compare the sources (in percent) of Nitrogen and Sulfur Dioxide emissions.

The bar graph below shows the percentage (%) distribution of the Earth's surface elevation above and depth below sea level.

Graphs can also be used to compare more than one factor using the same variables. The graph below from the *Earth Science Reference Tables* compares the travel

time for earthquake *P*– and *S*–waves. Note that the variables, Travel Time (vertical axis) and Epicenter Distance (horizontal axis), are used for both waves.

CYCLIC & NON-CYCLIC CHANGES

Most changes in the environment are cyclic. **Cyclic changes** involve events that repeat in time and space, usually in an orderly manner. For example:

- Through alternating changes in state (phase) (e.g., evaporation and condensation), water is cycled and purified between the ground, water reservoirs, and the atmosphere.

- Seasonal changes (also cycles), such as freezing and thawing, produce predictable changes such as the primary type of weathering that is dominant.

- The Sun, Moon, stars, planets, and other celestial objects have definite cyclic motions.

General weather patterns repeat in an orderly manner. However, not all changes are cyclic. There are "one-direction" events, such as the radioactive decay of certain elements, the extinction of a species, or the impact of a meteorite on the Moon.

D. ENERGY & CHANGE

ENERGY FLOW & EXCHANGE

When environmental change occurs, energy is lost by one part (source) of the environment and gained in another part (sink). This change occurs *simultaneously* (at the same time). For example, as the energy of the Sun (the source) strikes the Earth's crust (the sink) and is absorbed, the radiant energy produces heat to warm the surface of the Earth. The energy within the high speed winds (the **source**) of a hurricane or tornado is absorbed by trees, buildings, and other things (the **sink**), causing destruction and erosion.

What is the relationship of energy to change?

This exchange of energy (loss or gain) occurs at an **interface** (boundary) between the affected parts of the environment. Change in the environment occurs at an interface between materials, such as air to rock. Rocks weather on the outside where they come in contact with moisture and gases in the air.

PREDICTABILITY OF CHANGE

If there is sufficient evidence and knowledge of the nature of the environmental change, it may be possible to predict the scope (type and amount) and direction that future changes will take.

Meteorologists are able to predict general storm tracks and astronomers are able to predict eclipses because of the many years of collecting data. It should be noted that general events are fairly predictable (such as the sunrise/sunset), whereas individual occurrences are much more difficult to precisely predict (such as the weather).

It is usually easier to make accurate predictions when there are many observations and few variables involved in the change.

ENVIRONMENTAL BALANCE

Our environment is in a **state of equilibrium** that tends to remain unchanged because, when equilibrium is disturbed nature works to establish a new one. Change is also constant, so what appears to be unchanged, may indeed be slowly changing. For example, if a stream is eroding and depositing sediment at the same rate in a stream bed, there appears to be no change at that location. The erosional-depositional rate of the stream is said to be in **dynamic equilibrium** or balance.

Should there be a sudden change in the climatic or weather conditions, such as severe rainfall causing flooding, there could be a vast change in the stream. Erosion could change the stream's banks, its course, and its contents.

QUESTIONS FOR PROLOGUE

1   In order to make observations, an observer must always use
   1   experiments
   2   the senses
   3   proportions
   4   mathematical calculations

2   While in the classroom during a visual inspection of a rock, a student recorded four statements about the rock. Which statement about the rock is an observation?
   1   The rock formed deep in the Earth's interior.
   2   The rock cooled very rapidly.
   3   The rock dates from the Precambrian Era.
   4   The rock is black and shiny.

3   A person observes a sediment consisting of clay, sand, and pebbles and then states that this material was transported and deposited by an agent of erosion. This statement is
   1   a fact
   2   a measurement
   3   an inference
   4   an observation

4   Which statement made during a weather report is most likely an inference?
   1   The record low temperature for this date was set in 1957.
   2   Hot and humid conditions will continue throughout the week.
   3   The high temperature for the day was recorded at 2 p.m.
   4   The current barometric pressure is 29.97 in.

5   A predication of next winter's weather is an example of
   1   a measurement
   2   a classification
   3   an observation
   4   an inference

6   Using a ruler to measure the length of a stick is an example of
   1   extending the sense of sight by using an instrument
   2   calculating the percent of error by using a proportion
   3   measuring the rate of change of the stick by making inferences
   4   predicting the length of the stick by guessing

7   The diagram at the right shows a rock and a standard mass on a double pan balance. Which statement about the rock is best supported by the diagram?

   1   The rock has a smaller volume than the standard mass.
   2   The rock has less mass than the standard mass.
   3   The rock has a greater force of gravity than the standard mass.
   4   The rock has a greater density than the standard mass.

8 If each side of the cube shown at the right has the same length as the measured side, what is the approximate volume of the cube?
(1) 2.20 cm³
(2) 4.84 cm³
(3) 6.60 cm³
(4) 10.65 cm³

9 A classification system is based on the use of
1 human senses to observe properties of objects
2 instruments to observe properties of objects
3 observed properties to group objects with similar characteristics
4 inferences and conclusions

10 Which property was probably used to classify the substances in the chart below?

Group A	Group B	Group C
water	aluminum	water vapor
gasoline	ice	air
alcohol	iron	oxygen

1 chemical composition
2 state (phase) of matter
3 specific heat
4 abundance within the Earth

11 The table at the right identifies four density groups. According to this classification system, a sample of quartz with a mass of 27 grams and a volume of 10 cubic centimeters should be placed in group
1 A
2 B
3 C
4 D

Group	Density (g/cm³)
A	1.0-3.9
B	4.0-7.9
C	8.0-11.9
D	12.0-15.9

12 Student A finds the density of a piece of quartz to be 2.50 grams per cubic centimeter. Student B finds the density to be 2.80 grams per cubic centimeter. The actual density of quartz is 2.65 grams per cubic centimeter. Which is a true statement about student A's percent of error?
1 It is less than student B's percent of error.
2 It is greater than student B's percent of error.
3 It is the same as student B's percent of error.
4 It cannot be determined.

13 A student determines the density of a rock to be 2.2 grams per cubic centimeter. If the accepted density of the rock is 2.5 grams per cubic centimeter, what is the percent error from the accepted value?
(1) 8.8%
(2) 12.0%
(3) 13.6%
(4) 30.0%

14 A student calculates the period of Saturn's revolution to be 31.33 years. What is the student's approximate percentage of error? [refer to *Earth Science Reference Tables*]
(1) 1.9%
(2) 5.9%
(3) 6.3%
(4) 19.0%

15 Which factor can be predicted most accurately from day to day?
1 chance of precipitation
2 direction of the wind
3 chance of an earthquake occurring
4 altitude of the Sun at noon

16 Over a 30-day period, an observer would have the most difficulty measuring the
1 rotation of the Earth
2 discharge of a river
3 changing phases of the Moon
4 weathering of a mountain

17 The diameter through the equator of Jupiter is about 143,000 kilometers. What is this distance written in scientific notation [powers of 10]?
(1) 143×10^2 km
(2) 1.43×10^3 km
(3) 1.43×10^5 km
(4) 143×10^5 km

Note: Question 18 has only three choices.

18 In which phase (state) do most Earth materials have their greatest density?
1 solid
2 liquid
3 gas

19 At which temperature does water have its greatest density?
(1) −7°C
(2) 0°C
(3) 96°C
(4) 4°C

20 The diagrams below represent two solid objects, *A* and *B*, with different densities.

Object A (Density = 0.8 g/cm³)   Object B (Density = 1.2 g/cm³)

What will happen when the objects are placed in a container of water (water temperature = 4°C)?
1 Both objects will sink.
2 Both objects will float.
3 Object *A* will float, and object *B* will sink.
4 Object *B* will float, and object *A* will sink.

21 The diagrams below represent two differently shaped blocks of ice floating in water. Which diagram most accurately shows the blocks of ice as they would actually float in water?

22 Compared to the density of liquid water, the density of an ice cube is
1 always less
2 always greater
3 always the same
4 sometimes less and sometimes greater

Note: Question 18 has only three choices.

23 If a wooden block were cut into eight identical pieces, the density of each piece compared to the density of the original block would be
1 less
2 greater
3 the same

24 The graph at the right shows the relationship between the mass and volume of a mineral.

What is the density of this mineral?
(1) 6.0 g/cm³
(2) 9.0 g/cm³
(3) 3.0 g/cm³
(4) 4.5 g/cm³

25 During a laboratory activity, four students each determined the density of the same piece of granite. The results are shown in the table at the right.

Student	Density Determined
1	2.69 g/cm³
2	2.71 g/cm³
3	2.72 g/cm³
4	2.69 g/cm³

The accepted value for the density of granite is 2.70 grams per cubic centimeter. Therefore, the results of this activity indicate that
1 the accepted density of granite is incorrect
2 the balance used by student 3 was broken
3 each student determined the exact accepted value for the density of granite
4 the density determined by each student contains a small error

26 As shown at the right, an empty 1,000.-milliliter container has a mass of 250.0 grams. When filled with a liquid, the container and the liquid have a combined mass of 1,300. grams.

What is the density of the liquid? [refer to the *Reference Tables*]

(1) 1.00 g/mL
(2) 1.05 g/mL
(3) 1.30 g/mL
(4) 0.95 g/mL

27 A mineral expands when heated. Which graph best represents the relationship between change in density and change in temperature when that mineral is heated?

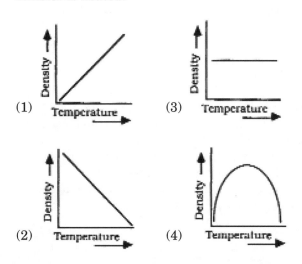

28 A student calculates the densities of five different pieces of aluminum, each having a different volume. Which graph best represents this relationship?

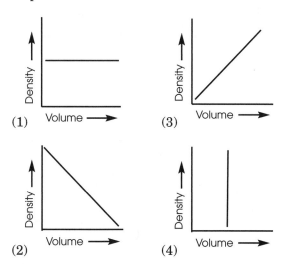

(1)   (3)

(2)   (4)

29 Generally, what is the correct relationship between pressure and temperature when a material changes from a gas to a liquid to a solid?
1 temperature increases, only
2 temperature lowers and/or pressure increases
3 both temperature and pressure decrease
4 both temperature and pressure increase

30 When the amounts of water entering and leaving a lake are balanced, the volume of the lake remains the same. This balance is called
1 saturation
2 transpiration
3 equilibrium
4 permeability

31 An interface can best be described as
1 a zone of contact between different substances across which energy is exchanged
2 a region in the environment with unchanging properties
3 a process that results in changes in the environment
4 a region beneath the surface of the Earth where change is not occurring

32 Which line best identifies the interface between the lithosphere and the troposphere?

[Not to Scale]

1 line A
2 line B
3 line C
4 line D

33 Future changes in the environment can best be predicted from data that are
1 highly variable and collected over short period of time
2 highly variable and collected over long periods of time
3 cyclic and collected over short periods of time
4 cyclic and collected over long periods of time

34 Which graph most likely illustrates a cyclic change?

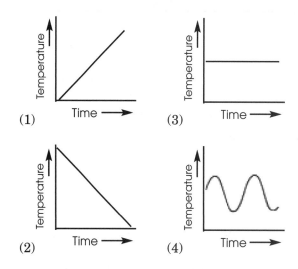

(1)   (3)

(2)   (4)

35 Which statement best explains why some cyclic Earth changes may not appear to be cyclic?
1 Most Earth changes are caused by human activities.
2 Most Earth changes are caused by the occurrence of a major catastrophe.
3 Most Earth changes occur over such a long period of time that they are difficult to measure.
4 No Earth changes can be observed because the Earth is always in equilibrium.

36 During a ten year period, which is a noncyclic change?
1 the Moon's phases as seen from the Earth
2 the Earth's orbital velocity around the Sun
3 the impact of a meteorite on the Earth
4 the apparent path of the Sun as seen from the Earth

CONSTRUCTED RESPONSE

Base your answers to questions 1 through 10 on your knowledge of Earth science, the *Reference Tables* and the data in Tables I and II below. Tables I and II show the volume and mass of three samples of mineral *A* and three samples of mineral *B*.

Table I: Mineral *A*

Sample No.	Volume	Mass
1	2.0 cm^3	5.0 g
2	5.0 cm^3	12.5 g
3	10.0 cm^3	25.0 g

Table II: Mineral *B*

Sample No.	Volume	Mass
1	3.0 cm^3	12.0 g
2	5.0 cm^3	20.0 g
3	7.0 cm^3	28.0 g

Use the data to construct a graph on the grid provided below.

1   Mark an appropriate scale on the axis labeled "Mass (in grams)."

2   Plot a line graph for mineral *A* and label the line "Mineral *A*."

3   Plot a line graph for mineral *B* and label the line "Mineral *B*."

MASS v. VOLUME

4   Write the formula for density:

5   Substitute the data for sample 3 of mineral *A* into the formula and determine the density of mineral *A*.

Density of *A*:

6   Substitute the data for sample 3 of mineral *B* into the formula and determine the density of mineral *B*.

Density of *B*:

7   In one sentence, tell what sample 2 of minerals *A* and *B* have in common.

8   In a sentence, explain what happens to the masses of these minerals if their volume increases.

9   Predict the mass of a same amount of mineral *A* with a volume of 12.0 cm^3.

10   Explain what would happen to the density of sample 1 of mineral *B* if it is heated until it melts.

Base your answers to questions 11 through 15 on the diagram and information below and on your knowledge of Earth science.

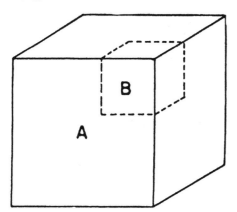

In the diagram, object *A* represents a solid cube of uniform material having a mass of 192.0 grams and a side that is 4.0 cm long. Cube *B* is a part of cube *A*.

11 Substitute the appropriate data into the formula for density and calculate the density of cube *A*

12 If cube *B* is removed from cube *A*, what will be the value of the remaining part of cube *A*?

13 What is the density of cube *B* apart from cube *A*?

14 If pressure is applied to cube *A* until its volume is one-half of its original volume, what will its new density be?

15 A student measured the mass of cube *B* in order to calculate its density. The cube had water on it while its mass was measured. In one sentence, predict how the calculated value for density would compare with the actual density.

16 A student finds the mass of an igneous rock sample to be 48.0 grams. Its actual mass is 52.0 grams. What is the student's percent error?

17 Devise a classification system for the following rocks: rock salt, dolostone, rhyolite, sandstone, basalt, rock gypsum, conglomerate, shale, and granite.

In one sentence, tell what property you used.

18 In one sentence, tell what property is used to classify the land-derived sedimentary rocks listed in the *Earth Science Reference Tables*.

19 The diagram below represents the scale of a triple beam balance. What mass is indicated by this scale?

20 A 10.0-milliliter sample of a substance has a mass of 20.0 grams.
What would be the mass of a 200.-milliliter sample of the same substance?

UNIT ONE

EARTH DIMENSIONS

VOCABULARY

oblate spheroid	stratified (layered)	Prime Meridian	isobars
altitude	zones	International Dateline	isotherms
latitude	troposphere	Greenwich Mean Time	iso-surface
gravity	stratosphere	(GMT)	gradient
centrifugal effect	mesosphere	GPS (Global Positioning	contour lines
coordinates	thermosphere	System)	(topographic)
axes	tropopause	field	Polaris (North Star)
parallels	hydrosphere	models	
meridians	lithosphere	isolines	

Knowing the shape of the Earth and the properties and characteristics resulting from this shape is important to the overall understanding of the Earth and its systems.

A. EARTH'S SHAPE

The Earth appears to be the shape of a sphere (round in circumference), when observed from space or scaled down to a model, such as a classroom globe. However, by actual measurement, the Earth is not a perfect sphere. Instead, it has an oblate shape, having a larger circumference around the equator (0° latitude), than through the poles (degrees longitude).

The circumference of the Earth at the equator is 40,076 kilometers, and the equatorial diameter is 12,757 kilometers. The circumference of the Earth through the poles is 40,008 kilometers, and the polar diameter is 12,714 kilometers. Therefore, the Earth is slightly "bulged" at the equator and slightly "flattened" at the poles. Thus, the true shape of the Earth is best defined as an **oblate spheroid**.

over the geographic North Pole of the Earth. To understand why Polaris can be used to help determine the Earth's shape, it is necessary to understand the "geometry of a sphere" and the terms latitude and altitude.

> *How can Earth's shape be determined?*

When observing an object in the atmosphere or space, the object's **altitude** refers to its angle (measured in degrees) above the horizon. When locating a point on the Earth's surface, the term **latitude** describes the point's position (measured as an angle in degrees) north or south of the Earth's equator.

According to a principle of the "**geometry of a sphere**," as a sphere is rotated, the angle of a fixed point outside of a sphere as compared to the surface of that sphere, is equal to the angle of the sphere's rotation. Therefore, if a sphere is rotated 45°, a fixed point outside of that sphere will be at an angle of 45° from its original point, before the sphere's rotation. (Note the illustration on the next page.)

Considering Polaris to be a fixed point above the North Pole, its angle (altitude) to the Earth's polar axis should be the same as the angle of the Earth's tilt on that same axis. Indeed, the altitude of Polaris corresponds very closely with an observer's latitude. But,

POLARIS AS EVIDENCE

Observations of the North Star (Polaris). If a straight line passed from the South Pole, through the center of the Earth (polar axis) to the North Pole, and continued into space, it would very nearly pass through Polaris as well. Therefore, the star **Polaris** is called the **North Star**, as it lies in space practically

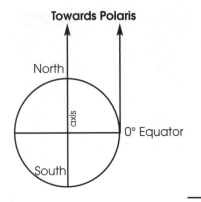

Towards Polaris

North

axis

0° Equator

South

Towards Polaris

45° North Latitude

North

45°

0° Equator

45°

axis

South

Disproving That Earth is a Perfect Sphere

As seen in these illustrations, the altitude of Polaris should be the same as the observer's latitude on the Earth, if the Earth is a perfect sphere.

---

when the angles are measured with precise instruments, the accurately measured altitude of Polaris is *not exactly* the same as the observer's latitude on Earth. Therefore, Polaris gives evidence that the Earth is not a *perfect* sphere; instead, it is *slightly* out of round, or **oblate**.

Photographs of the Earth from space. With the exploration of space, came the ability to take photographs of the Earth from great distances in space. When precisely measured, these photographs show the Earth to be larger at the equator and flatter at the geographic poles. However, the shape of the Earth, when drawn to scale on a sheet of paper, appears to be perfectly round.

Gravimetric (gravity) measurements. Gravity is the force of attraction between any two objects. Since the Earth has such a large mass, smaller objects with less mass are attracted (pulled) towards the Earth. If the Earth were a perfect sphere, it would be expected to exert an equal pull on objects anywhere on or above the Earth's surface at equal distances from the center of the Earth.

The **law of gravitation** states that a *gravitational force is proportional to the square of the distance between the two centers of attracted objects*. In other words, the weight of an object moved anywhere on the surface of the Earth (assuming Earth is a perfect sphere), should remain the same. However, precise measurements of objects indicate that the same object weighs more at the poles than at the equator of the Earth. Even accounting for the **centrifugal effect** produced by the Earth's rotation, there is still a greater gravitational pull at the poles than at the

equator. (Note, the Earth's oblateness in the left illustration below is greatly exaggerated.)

B. EARTH'S "SPHERES"

ATMOSPHERE

The atmosphere of the Earth is composed of the materials (solids, liquids, and gases) that form a thin envelope surrounding the Earth, held in place by gravitation and rotating with the Earth. The atmosphere extends several hundred kilometers above the Earth's surface into space and is the least dense of the Earth's three spheres: atmosphere, hydrosphere, and lithosphere.

> *What is the extent of the atmosphere, hydrosphere, and lithosphere?*

The atmosphere is **stratified** (layered) into **zones**, each having distinct characteristics, including temperature and pressure ranges, composition, and effects produced on the Earth's surface (see Earth's Atmospheric Zones on the next page). These zones include (from the Earth's surface towards space):

- **Troposphere**. Lowest region of the atmosphere between the Earth's surface and the **tropopause**, characterized by decreasing temperature with increasing altitude.

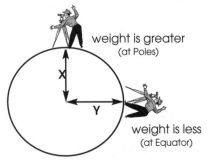

weight is greater (at Poles)

X

Y

weight is less (at Equator)

Earth Model (left)
Y greater distance than X; therefore, X has greater force of gravity.

Sphere Model (right)
Y and X are equal distances; therefore, Y and X have equal forces of gravity.

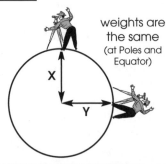

weights are the same (at Poles and Equator)

X

Y

- **Stratosphere**. Region above the troposphere and below the mesosphere, where temperature increases with altitude because of the presence of ozone.

- **Mesosphere**. Portion of the atmosphere from about 30 to 80 kilometers above the Earth's surface, characterized by temperatures that decrease from 10°C to -90°C with increasing altitude.

- **Thermosphere**. Outermost shell between the mesosphere and outer space, where temperatures increase steadily with altitude.

North Pole View   South Pole View

Earth's Hydrosphere (Oceans)

HYDROSPHERE

Almost three quarters (approximately 71%) of the Earth's surface is covered with a relatively thin film of water. Compared to the other zones of the Earth, it is very thin, only averaging 3.5 to 4.0 kilometers thick, much like the skin on an apple.

The **hydrosphere** includes all bodies of water, marine (salt-containing oceans) and fresh (inland lakes and rivers).

LITHOSPHERE

The most solid portion of the Earth is the rock near the Earth's surface and is a continuous solid shell, often under the hydrosphere. It accounts for the general underwater features of the Earth, including mountains, valleys, and the ocean floor.

Earth's Atmospheric Zones

outer space

Distance (measured in Kilometers)

600

500

300
Thermosphere

200

100
Mesosphere

Stratosphere
0 sea level   Troposphere

C. EARTH POSITIONS
COORDINATE SYSTEMS

There are many reference systems that can be used to determine positions on the Earth. A coordinate system uses a **grid** of imaginary lines and two points, called **coordinates**, to locate a particular position on the surface of the Earth (see illustration below). A fixed point can be located on a graph by identifying **axes** (the intersecting point of two lines).

How can a position on the Earth's surface be determined?

LATITUDE – LONGITUDE COORDINATE SYSTEM

The most commonly used coordinate system for the Earth is the **latitude – longitude system**, which is based on observations of the Sun and other stars. Since the Earth is an oblate sphere, it is not practical to use a flat graph. Although the principle of locating a fixed point remains the same, the axes are imaginary lines called **parallels** and **meridians** circling the Earth.

PARALLELS OF LATITUDE

The rotation of the Earth determines the position of the geographic poles. Located halfway between the North (90° N latitude) and South (90° S latitude) Poles is the Equator (0° latitude).

MERIDIANS OF LONGITUDE

The lines running between the North Pole and the South Pole are called **meridians**. The

Locating a Fixed Point on a Graph (Coordinate System)

1st - read along the horizontal axis from the dot to the intersecting vertical line, x = d.

2nd - read along the vertical axis from the dot to the intersecting horizontal line, y = 2.

The location of the point is at the intersection of the horizontal (x) and vertical (Y) lines, d,2.

Prime Meridian runs through Greenwich, England and has a longitude of 0°. Longitude is measured using the meridians east or west of the Prime Meridian (0°) to a maximum longitude of 180° (**International Dateline**).

LATITUDE & LONGITUDE MEASUREMENTS

Both latitude and longitude are measured in degrees. Latitude is distance measured in degrees north or south of the equator (0° to 90° North, 0° to 90° South). Longitude is distance measured in degrees east or west of the Prime Meridian (0° to 180° meridian).

Latitude. The altitude of Polaris above the horizon is often used to determine a particular latitudinal position in the Northern Hemisphere. In the Southern Hemisphere other stars are used. Since travel in space, in air, and on the water require very precise navigation, astronomical tables (as found in *Reed's Almanac*) are also used. They account for variations in the positions of celestial bodies based on time and date.

Longitude. The Earth rotates from west to east, 360° in a 24 hour period of time, or a distance of 15° of longitude per hour. Comparing your local time with the time at Greenwich, England (0°), enables you to determine your longitude. For every hour difference in time between an observer and **Greenwich Mean Time** (**GMT**) or universal time (**UT**), the observer is 15° away from the Prime Meridian.

If the Sun is on the Prime Meridian, it is 12 noon at Greenwich, England. Since the Earth rotates west to east, the Sun has not yet reached it highest point (noon time) to the west of Greenwich; therefore, time is earlier to the west. However, to the east of Greenwich, the Sun has already passed its highest point; therefore, time is later to the east of Greenwich.

For example, a ship sailing in the Atlantic Ocean maintains a clock (chronometer) with Greenwich Mean Time. If a time comparison is taken when the Sun is at its highest point over the ship (the ship's "local noon") and found to be 3 hours earlier than Greenwich Mean Time; then we know that the ship is at 45° West Longitude, since the ship's local time is 3 hours earlier than the same time in Greenwich (3 x 15° = 45°).

Modern navigational techniques such as **GPS** (**Global Positioning System**) used on land, air, and sea, employ the use of signals from both Earth and orbiting satellites.

D. POSITION CHARACTERISTICS

FIELDS

A **field** is a region of space that contains a measurable quantity at every point. For example, every point in a region would have a temperature. Other examples of fields include: gravity, magnetism, relative humidity, and atmospheric pressures.

> *How can the characteristics of a position be measured and described?*

ISOLINES

In order to visualize field quantities **models** may be used. Models are simplified representations of objects, structures or systems. Models may be used to

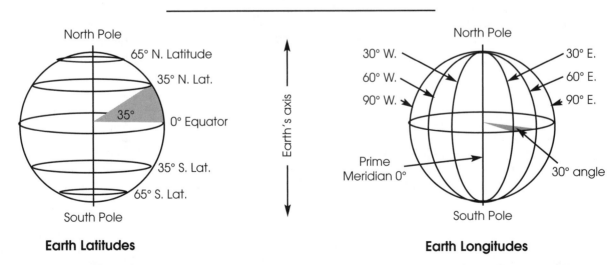

Earth Latitudes   **Earth Longitudes**

analyze, explain, interpret or to design. One kind of model is a map using **isolines**. Isolines connect points that have the same field value. Models using isolines represent field characteristics in two-dimensions.

Map models showing the elevation, shape, and steepness of the land may be drawn using isolines called **contour lines**. Contour lines connect places of the same elevation. A 3-dimensional model of a mountain might be designed from a 2-dimensional isoline map of the land surface. The same map model could also be used to construct a profile of the land surface to interpret.

There are many different kinds of isolines which may be used to make models. Isolines always connect places of the same value. Isolines on a weather map connecting places with the same air pressure are called **isobars**; those connecting places of the same temperature are called **isotherms**.

ISO-SURFACES

Isolines can only show quantities on a two-dimensional surface, but **iso-surfaces** are models representing field characteristics in three dimensions, such as a magnetic field or a contour map of varying elevations, temperatures, or pressures. Note that all of the points on an iso-surface must have the same field value.

FIELD CHANGES

Fields are generally not *static* (unchanging). The characteristics of fields are usually *dynamic*. They change with the passage of time.

For example, the temperatures and air pressures over the surface of the Earth are in a constant state of change. Therefore, a weather map shows only those field conditions occurring during a specific time and date. Also, a contour map made several years ago of a particular landscape would have to be updated from time to time to remain accurate because of the changes produced by the forces of nature and humankind.

GRADIENT

A **gradient** or average slope within the field expresses the rate of change of the field quantity from one place to another place. The following formula is used to determine the rate of change:

$$\text{gradient} = \frac{\text{change in the field value}}{\text{change of distance}}$$

Example: If a weather map shows a change in atmospheric pressure from 996 mb to 1004 mb between towns that are 400 kilometers apart, then the rate of change (gradient) is 8 mb per 400 kilometers or 0.02 mb/km.

SAMPLE PROBLEMS

1 A stream in New York State begins at a location 350 meters above sea level and flows into a swamp 225 meters above sea level. The length of the stream is 25 kilometers. What is the gradient of the stream?

2 A contour map shows two locations, *X* and *Y*, 5 kilometers apart. The elevation at location *X* is 800 meters and the elevation at location *Y* is 600 meters. What is the gradient between the two locations?

CONTOUR (TOPOGRAPHIC) MAP

One advantage the topographic map has over the typical road map is the ability to show the terrain or land surface by using isolines. Called **contour lines**, these isolines connect places of the same elevation (usually based on sea level measurements). Generally, every 5th line is an **index contour line**. It is printed darker and is interrupted to give the elevation.

The difference in elevation between two consecutive contour lines is the **contour interval**. Common intervals are 5, 10, 20, 50, and 100 meters. Enclosed

Isolines Indicating a Gradient
Note: Gradient on the east side of the LOW is steep; whereas, the gradient on the west side is gentle.

depressions are shown with hachured contour lines (the hachure marks ┬┬┬┬ pointing down-slope.)

The map legend gives distance scales along with a key of symbols representing natural and cultural (man-made) features of the field, such as cities, roads, buildings, marshes, and forests.

Comparing topographic maps over time may be used to show changes in the Earth's surface.

PROFILE

A vertical cross section of the land surface between two points on a topographic (contour) map may be shown by constructing a profile. To construct a profile, place the straight edge of a sheet of paper between the two points on the map. Wherever a contour line meets the edge of the paper, place a mark on the paper and note the elevation of that point. When all the points have been marked, place the edge of the paper against a vertical scale and graph the points vertically. When you connect the points with a smooth line, you will see the profile of the surface between those two map locations.

QUESTIONS FOR UNIT 1

1 An observer watching a sailing ship at sea notes that the ship appears to be "sinking" as it moves away. Which statement best explains this observation?
1 The surface of the ocean has depressions.
2 The Earth has a curved surface.
3 The Earth is rotating.
4 The Earth is revolving.

2 The true shape of the Earth is best described as a
1 perfect sphere
2 perfect ellipse
3 slightly oblate sphere
4 highly eccentric ellipse

3 According to the *Earth Science Reference Tables*, the radius of the Earth is approximately
(1) 637 km
(2) 6,370 km
(3) 63,700 km
(4) 637,000 km

4 At sea level, which location would be closest to the center of the Earth?
(1) 45° South latitude
(2) the Equator
(3) 23° North latitude
(4) the North Pole

5 At which location would an observer find the greatest force caused by the Earth's gravity?
1 North Pole
2 New York State
3 Tropic of Cancer (23½°N.)
4 Equator

6 Which statement provides the best evidence that the Earth has a nearly spherical shape?
1 The Sun has a spherical shape.
2 The altitude of Polaris changes in a definite pattern as an observer's latitude changes.
3 Star trails photographed over a period of time show a circular path.
4 The length of noontime shadows change throughout the year.

7 Which diagram most accurately shows the cross-sectional shape of the Earth drawn to scale?

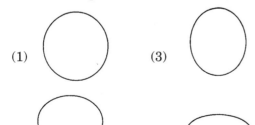

8 Which object best represents a true scale model of the shape of the Earth?
1 a Ping-Pong ball
2 a football
3 an egg
4 a pear

9 The best evidence that the Earth has a spherical shape would be provided by
1 the prevailing wind direction at many locations on the Earth's surface
2 the change in the time of sunrise and sunset at the single location during 1 year
3 the time the Earth takes to rotate on its axis at different times of the year
4 photographs of the Earth taken from space

10 The polar circumference of the Earth is 40,008 kilometers. What is the equatorial circumference?
(1) 12,740 km
(2) 25,000 km
(3) 40,008 km
(4) 40,076 km

11 The diagram at the right shows an instrument made from a drinking straw, protractor, string, and rock. This instrument was most likely used to measure the

1 distance to a star
2 altitude of a star
3 mass of the Earth
4 mass of the suspended weight

12 The Big Dipper, part of the star constellation Ursa Major, is shown below.

Which letter represents Polaris (the North Star)?
(1) A
(2) B
(3) C
(4) D

13 An observer in New York State measures the altitude of Polaris to be 44°. According to the *Reference Tables*, the location of the observer is nearest to
1 Watertown   3 Buffalo
2 Elmira   4 Kingston

14 As an observer travels northward from New York State, the altitude of the North Star
1 increases directly with the latitude
2 decreases directly with the latitude
3 increases directly with the longitude
4 decreases directly with the longitude

15 To an observer on a ship at sea, at which latitude does the North Star appear closest to the horizon?
(1) 5° N   (3) 50° N
(2) 20° N   (4) 85° N

16 A large earthquake occurred at 45° N. 75° W. on September 5, 1994. Which location in New York State was closest to the epicenter of the earthquake? [Use the *Reference Tables*.]
1 Buffalo   3 Albany
2 Massena   4 New York City

17 As a ship crosses the Prime Meridian, the altitude of Polaris is 65°. What is the location of the ship?
1 65° South latitude, 0° longitude
2 65° North latitude, 0° longitude
3 0° latitude, 65° West longitude
4 0° latitude, 65° East longitude

18 The shaded area of the map below represents large areas of surface basaltic bedrock in the northwestern United States.

Which location is in the shaded area of surface basaltic bedrock?
(1) 40° N 120° W   (3) 46° N 120° W
(2) 44° N 122° W   (4) 48° N 116° W

19 What is the elevation of the highest contour line shown on the map?
(1) 10,000 feet
(2) 10,688 feet
(3) 10,700 feet
(4) 10,788 feet

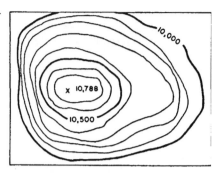

20 Isolines on the topographic map below show elevations above sea level, measured in meters. What could be the highest possible elevation represented on this map?
(1) 39 m
(2) 41 m
(3) 45 m
(4) 49 m

Base your answers to questions 21 and 22 on the diagram below which represents a contour map of a hill.

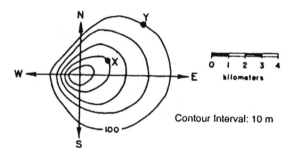

Contour Interval: 10 m

21 On which side of the hill does the land have the steepest slope?
1 north   3 east
2 south   4 west

22 What is the approximate gradient of the hill between points *X* and *Y*?
(1) 1 m/km   (3) 3 m/km
(2) 10 m/km   (4) 30 m/km

Base your answers to questions 23 through 27 on the topographic map below and on your knowledge of Earth science. Points A, B, C, D, E, F, X, and Y are locations on the map. Elevation is measured in meters.

26 The gradient between points A and B is closest to
(1) 20 m/km (3) 80 m/km
(2) 40 m/km (4) 200 m/km

27 Which diagram best represents the profile along a straight line between points X and Y?

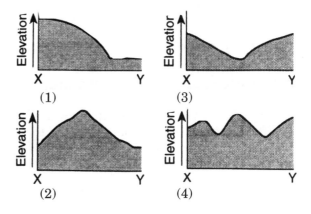

23 What is the contour interval used on this map?
(1) 20 m (3) 100 m
(2) 50 m (4) 200 m

24 Which locations have the greatest difference in elevation?
(1) A and D (3) C and F
(2) B and X (4) E and Y

25 Between points C and D, Rush Creek flows toward the
1 north 3 east
2 south 4 west

Base your answers to questions 28 through 30 on the outline map of the state of Washington below, the *Reference Tables*, and your knowledge of Earth science. The map shows isolines of ash-fall depths covering a portion of the State of Washington which resulted from a volcanic eruption of Mount St. Helens.

28 Which two towns received the same depth of volcanic ash?
1 Pasco and Wenatchee
2 Yakima and Ephrata
3 Centralia and Ritzville
4 Spokane and Ellensburg

29 Which equation should be used to determine the ash-fall gradient in millimeters per kilometer between Spokane and Ritzville?

(1) Gradient = $\dfrac{55 \text{ mm} - 15 \text{ mm}}{75 \text{ km}}$

(2) Gradient = $\dfrac{75 \text{ km}}{55 \text{ mm} - 15 \text{ mm}}$

(3) Gradient = $\dfrac{55 \text{ mm} - 15 \text{ mm}}{100 \text{ km}}$

(4) Gradient = $\dfrac{100 \text{ km}}{55 \text{ mm} - 15 \text{ mm}}$

30 If some of the ash was blown by the prevailing wind from the western edge of the ash-fall to the northeastern border of Washington, what was the approximate maximum distance that it traveled?

(1) 150 km   (3) 500 km
(2) 250 km   (4) 740 km

CONSTRUCTED RESPONSE

Base your answers to questions 1 through 5 on the topographic map of Cottonwood, Colorado, below.

Cottonwood, Colorado

1 What is the contour interval of this map?

2 State the general direction in which Cottonwood Creek is flowing.

3 State the highest possible elevation, to the *nearest meter*, for point *B* on the topographic map.

4 On the grid below, draw a profile of the topography along line *AB* shown on the map.

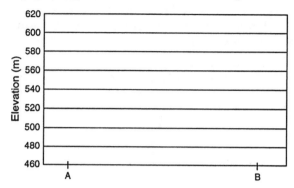

5 Calculate the gradient of the slope between points *X* and *Y* on the topographic map, following the directions below.

a   Write the equation for gradient.

b   Substitute data from the map into the equation.

c   Calculate the gradient and label it with the proper units.

Base your answers to questions 6 through 9 on the latitude-longitude system shown on the map. The map represents a part of the Earth's surface and its coordinate (grid) system. Point *A* through *F* represent locations in this area.

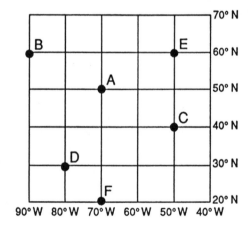

6 What is the latitude and longitude of point *A*?

7 What is the compass direction from point *D* toward point *E*?

8 In a sentence or two, explain where this map is located in relation to the Equator and Prime Meridian.

9 As a person travels from location *E* to location *C*, what will happen to the observed altitude of Polaris?

Base your answers to questions 10 through 12 on the information and the field map below.

Pesticide Concentrations In Ground Water (ppb)

A water-soluble pesticide was applied to the ground surface at location *A* as shown on the map. Precipitation occurred and some of the pesticide that was carried into the ground dissolved in the water. As the ground water moved through the ground, it distributed the pesticide. A scientist took samples of the ground water and determined the concentration of the pesticide in parts per billion (ppb). The field map shows the concentrations of the pesticide.

10 Draw an accurate isoline map, following the directions below.

a Use an interval of 50 ppb.

b Begin your drawing with the 200-ppb isoline.

11 Using one or more complete sentences, briefly describe the general pattern of pesticide concentration as the distance from location *A* increases.

12 Use the isoline map you have made to determine the gradient of pesticide concentration in ppb between point *B* and point *C*, following the directions below.

a Write the formula for the gradient.

b Substitute data into the formula.

c Calculate the gradient.

d Label your answer with proper units.

Base your answers to questions 13 through 16 on the diagram below which represents elevation data for a certain landscape region. Points *A*, *B*, *C*, and *D* are specific locations on the surface of this landscape.

13 The steepest slopes in this landscape are located along a straight line between which two lettered points?

14 There is a lake in this landscape region. Place the letter "*L*" on the map where the lake would most likely be located and explain why you chose that location.

15 A radio tower is located on the top of the highest hill on this map. Place the letter "*R*" where this tower is likely located.

16 A person hiking from the radio tower to the lake would walk in what compass direction?

Base your answers to questions 17 through 20 on the topographic map below represents a coastal landscape. The contour lines show the elevation in meters.

17 What is the contour interval of the map?

18 What is the distance along the dirt road from point *G* to *H*?

19 In what compass direction does the river flow between points *E* and *F*? Explain *one* way you can determine the direction of flow.

20 Show your work and label with appropriate units.

  a   Write the equation used to determine gradient

  b   Determine the gradient from point *C* to point *D*.

Base your answers to questions 21 and 22 on the temperature field map below. The map shows 25 measurements (in °C) that were made in a temperature field and recorded as shown. The dots represent the exact locations of the measurements. *A* and *B* are locations within the field.

Temperature Field Map (°C)

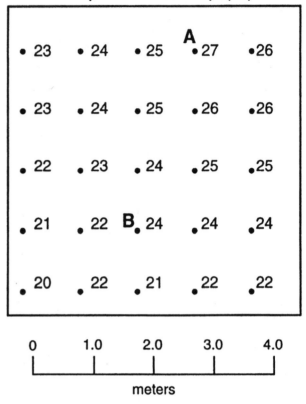

meters

21 On the temperature field map, draw three isotherms: the 23°C isotherm, the 24°C isotherm, and the 25°C isotherm.

22 In the space provided, calculate the temperature gradient between locations *A* and *B* on the temperature field map, following the directions below.

  a   Write the equation for gradient.

  b   Substitute data from the map into the equation.

  c   Calculate the gradient and label it with the proper units.

ROCKS, MINERALS, & RESOURCES

VOCABULARY

lithosphere	streak	magma	precipitation	contact & thermal
rock	luster	vesicles	evaporites	metamorphism
monomineralic	cleavage	lava	organic sediments	regional metamor-
mineral	fracture	extrusion & intrusion	bioclastic	phism
rock-formers	crystal	felsic & mafic miner-	fossil	orogeny
elements	specific gravity	als	metamorphic rocks	rock cycle
physical & chemical	crystalline	sedimentary rocks	recrystallization	quarry
properties	silicate	compression &	parent rock	fossil fuels
hardness	igneous rock	cementation	weathering & erosion	nonrenewable
Mohs' Scale of	solidification	transporting agent	foliation & banding	resources
Hardness	crystallization	evaporation	distorted structure	recycle & reuse

The solid portion of the Earth's crust, the **lithosphere**, is composed of naturally formed material made of one or more minerals, called **rock**. All rocks are composed of minerals. When only one mineral is found in a rock, the rock is said to be **monomineralic**. When a rock is composed of more than one mineral type, the rock is said to be **polymineralic**. Most rocks have a number of minerals in common.

A. MINERALS

Minerals are naturally occurring, inorganic, crystalline, solid materials with definite chemical composition, molecular structure, and specific physical properties. Of the more than 2,400 minerals on the Earth, about a dozen of them are so abundant that they comprise more than 90% of the lithosphere. These common minerals are called the "**rock-formers**."

CHARACTERISTICS OF MINERALS IN ROCKS

Minerals may be composed of single elements or compounds of two or more **elements**. Although there are more than 2,400 minerals, most of the Earth's crust is made of a relatively few common elements (composed of atoms which cannot be reduced to simpler substances). The most abundant element is oxygen (O_2 = 46.6% total Earth mass, 93.8% total Earth volume), and the second most abundant element is Silicon (Si = 27.7% total Earth mass, 0.9% total Earth volume). The other major elements are Aluminum (Al), Iron (Fe), Calcium (Ca), Sodium (Na), Potassium (K), and Magnesium (Mg).

PHYSICAL & CHEMICAL PROPERTIES

Minerals are identified on the basis of well-defined physical and chemical properties such as color, hardness, streak, luster, cleavage and fracture, crystal form and a variety of special properties such as odor, magnetism, and optical properties.

Color may be used for mineral identification. Whereas a few minerals have a distinctive color, many minerals have the same color. Also, one mineral may have many colors because of traces of other elements. A good example is the mineral quartz, which may be white, pink, green, yellow, or purple.

Hardness is the resistance of a mineral to being scratched. Scratch two pieces of different minerals together. The harder mineral will make a scratch on the softer one. **Mohs' Scale of Hardness** lists ten minerals in order of hardness with #1 (talc) being the softest and #10 (diamond) being the hardest. By using one of these minerals of known hardness to scratch an unknown mineral, the relative hardness of the unknown mineral may be determined. Mineral hardness may also be compared to common objects like a fingernail, copper penny, or glass (see chart below).

MINERAL HARDNESS

Moh's Hardness Scale		Approximate Hardness of Common Objects
Talc	1	
Gypsum	2	Fingernail (2.5)
Calcite	3	Copper penny (3.5)
Fluorite	4	Iron nail (4.5)
Apatite	5	Glass (5.5)
Feldspar	6	Steel file (6.5)
Quartz	7	Streak plate (7.0)
Topaz	8	
Corundum	9	
Diamond	10	

Streak is the color of the powder of a mineral when crushed or scratched across a streak plate (a piece of unglazed porcelain). The color of a mineral may look very different than the color of its streak.

Luster is the appearance of light reflected from a mineral's surface. A mineral might shine like metal having a metallic luster. If a mineral does not look like a metal (nonmetallic) it might look glassy, waxy, greasy, pearly, earthy, or dull.

Some minerals tend to break along one or more smooth planes or surfaces. These minerals are said to have **cleavage**.

If a mineral has no well-defined cleavage it is said to have **fracture**. Minerals that have fracture usually break with uneven, splintery, or jagged surfaces.

The **crystal** form of a mineral is the external geometric form that results from the internal atomic structure of the mineral. Minerals similar in color may be distinguished by their difference in crystal form.

Specific gravity, the ratio of the weight of a mineral sample to the weight of an equal volume of water, is another property used to identify minerals. A mineral with a specific gravity of 3.0 would be 3.0 times as heavy as equal volume of water. The specific gravity of a mineral is numerically equal to its density, because the **density** of pure water is 1 g/cm^3.

Some minerals have **special properties** such as calcite which will give off bubbles of carbon dioxide when a drop of cold, dilute hydrochloric acid is placed on it. The mineral halite tastes salty, magnetite is magnetic, and talc feels slippery.

MINERAL PROPERTIES

Minerals are said to be **crystalline** which means the atoms inside are bonded in a particular structure or pattern. Two minerals with the same chemical composition may have very different properties. A good example is diamond and graphite which are both made of carbon. Graphite is made of weakly bonded layers of carbon atoms and is very soft. Diamond is formed at great depths where extreme pressure causes the carbon atoms to have a compact structure so that diamond is the hardest mineral.

Minerals may be grouped according to the elements of which they are made, or the compounds which they can form. For example, the **oxide** group is made of compounds of oxygen and one other element. The **carbonate** group is made of one or more metals combined with a carbon and three oxygen atoms (CO_3).

Since oxygen and silicon are the two most abundant elements in the Earth's crust, it is not surprising that the **silicates**, minerals containing both oxygen and silicon, are the largest group of minerals.

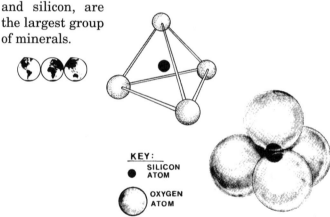

KEY:
● SILICON ATOM
○ OXYGEN ATOM

B. ROCKS

Rocks are classified by origin as igneous, sedimentary, or metamorphic, depending on their mineral composition and their texture which is determined by the environment in which they form. The visible characteristics of rocks give clues to the processes and conditions of their formation.

B1. IGNEOUS ROCKS

Igneous rocks are formed from the solidification and crystallization of molten rock, making the rocks solid, compact, and/or hard.

Beneath the Earth's surface, molten rock material is called **magma**. When the magma reaches the Earth's surface, it is called **lava**. When magma or lava cools and solidifies, it forms igneous rock. As the liquid rock solidifies and becomes hard, mineral crystals may form, resulting in the igneous rock having a crystalline texture. Usually, there are many different minerals within this kind of rock.

The **texture** of the igneous rocks is dependent upon the rate of cooling. Slow cooling produces large crystals – rocks with a coarse texture (**phaneritic**). Rapid cooling produces small crystals – rocks with a fine texture (**aphanitic**). When bubbles of gas are in solidifying lava, holes called **vesicles**, are formed. Igneous rocks like scoria, that contain these holes are said to be **vesicular**.

Cooling is related to both temperature and pressure. Rapid cooling produces small crystals or a grainy texture. Very rapid cooling results in no crystal formation or a glassy texture. This is the result of a rapid drop in temperature or a pressure decrease. These conditions would exist near the surface of the Earth or when the molten material (lava) breaks through the surface, as during a volcanic eruption. When lava flows out and hardens on the Earth's surface, it is called an **extrusion**. The rock formed is called **extrusive igneous rock**.

However, deep within the Earth both temperature and pressure are much higher than at the surface. Therefore, cooling is slower and crystal size is larger. When magma hardens in the Earth, it is called an **intrusion**. The rock formed is called **intrusive igneous** rock. By looking at the size of the crystals in igneous rocks, the relative cooling rates of the rocks may be estimated.

Igneous rocks form by solidification and crystallization from magma or lava. To form magma, minerals must be melted. Some minerals, like quartz and mus-

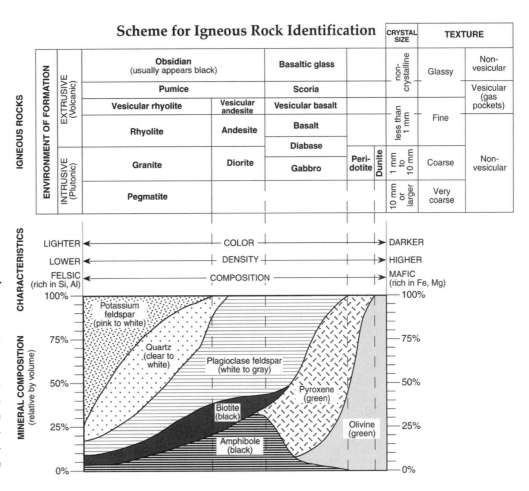

covite mica, melt and solidify at relatively low temperatures. Others, like olivine and pyroxene, melt and solidify at much higher temperatures. In a body of cooling magma, the minerals that melt at high temperatures crystallize first and settle out of the melt. Those that melt at relatively low temperatures crystallize last, separating them from the minerals that crystallized first.

This is why igneous rocks of different composition form from the same body of magma. This is the reason that igneous rocks containing olivine do not usually contain quartz.

The *Scheme for Igneous Rock Identification Chart* shows that texture, color, density, and mineral composition are used to identify igneous rocks. The light colored rocks are made primarily of the felsic minerals which are high in aluminum. Therefore, these rocks are lower in density than the dark colored mafic minerals, high in iron and magnesium.

An exception to the normal density identification is the glassy igneous rock, obsidian. A sample of obsidian may appear black, but is felsic in composition.

Igneous rocks are common in both the continental and oceanic crust of the Earth. Low density, felsic, granitic igneous rock is common in the continental land masses while the ocean basins are made primarily of high density, mafic, basaltic igneous rock.

B2. SEDIMENTARY ROCKS

The weathering processes break rock and produce inorganic sediments, which are transported by water, wind, and glaciers and deposited in different locations on land or under water. **Sedimentary rocks** usually contain rounded grains cemented in layers because running water is the major **transporting agent** of sediment. Many of the sedimentary rocks form under large bodies of water in the following ways.

COMPRESSION & CEMENTATION

Some sedimentary rocks form when the pressure of water and other overlying sediments compress very small particles (clay and colloids) that have settled from the transporting agent (deposition). The pressure may itself be sufficient to form these fine sediments into rock. An example of a compressed (constricted, squeezed) sedimentary rock is shale, although cementing (binding particles and fragments of rocks) may occur also. In fact, some shales are layers made totally of natural cement.

Some sediments are combined with mineral cements that **precipitate** out of (separated from solution) the ground water and result in cementation. Common mineral cements are iron, silica, and lime. Usually, cementation occurs with the larger sediments, such as sand, pebbles, and small rocks.

Sandstone is an example of a sedimentary rock in which the cemented particles are sorted in a uniform size. Most conglomerates are formed when the pebble sized particles are unsorted and cemented together. Frequently, the color of the rock is determined by the cementing agent.

CHEMICAL PROCESSES

Some sedimentary rocks form as a result of chemical processes, such as the **evaporation** and **precipitation** of a dissolved mineral out of evaporating water.

The precipitation of one mineral from solution forms monomineralic rocks, called **evaporites** (such as limestone, dolostone, gypsum, and rock salt).

BIOLOGICAL PROCESSES

Some sedimentary rocks form as a result of biologic processes. **Organic sediments** include the remains of any living thing, including plants and animals. Coal forms from plant remains which are deposited in water, decayed, and then compressed.

Scheme for Sedimentary Rock Identification

INORGANIC LAND-DERIVED SEDIMENTARY ROCKS					
TEXTURE	GRAIN SIZE	COMPOSITION	COMMENTS	ROCK NAME	MAP SYMBOL
Clastic (fragmental)	Pebbles, cobbles, and/or boulders embedded in sand, silt, and/or clay	Mostly quartz, feldspar, and clay minerals; may contain fragments of other rocks and minerals	Rounded fragments	Conglomerate	
			Angular fragments	Breccia	
	Sand (0.006 to 0.2 cm)		Fine to coarse	Sandstone	
	Silt (0.0004 to 0.006 cm)		Very fine grain	Siltstone	
	Clay (less than 0.0004 cm)		Compact; may split easily	Shale	
CHEMICALLY AND/OR ORGANICALLY FORMED SEDIMENTARY ROCKS					
TEXTURE	GRAIN SIZE	COMPOSITION	COMMENTS	ROCK NAME	MAP SYMBOL
Crystalline	Fine to coarse crystals	Halite	Crystals from chemical precipitates and evaporites	Rock salt	
		Gypsum		Rock gypsum	
		Dolomite		Dolostone	
Crystalline or bioclastic	Microscopic to very coarse	Calcite	Precipitates of biologic origin or cemented shell fragments	Limestone	
Bioclastic		Carbon	Compacted plant remains	Bituminous coal	

Some water animals, such as coral, use minerals to form their shells. When they die, the minerals (often calcium and sea salts) are left behind, compress, and form sedimentary rocks (limestone). Fossil evidence is found nearly exclusively in sedimentary rocks.

Sedimentary rocks are classified as **fragmental** (**clastic**), **chemical**, or **organic** depending upon how they were formed. The **fragmental sedimentary rocks** are composed of various sediments which have been compacted and cemented together. This kind of sedimentary rock is classified on the basis of grain size. As shown on the *Reference Tables*, if the particles range in size from 0.006 to 0.2 cm, the rock is sandstone.

The particle size in sedimentary rocks is related to the agent that transported and deposited the particles. The most important agent is running water which deposits sediment in **horizontal layers**. These horizontal layers are an important identifying characteristic of many sedimentary rocks.

A range of particle sizes, often resembling a stream bed or delta deposit, has larger, denser particles on the bottom and decreasing particle size and density towards the top of the rock. A predominance of one particle size in a layer indicates the deposition of one type, size, and density of sediment.

Chemically and **organically formed sedimentary rocks** are identified by composition and texture. The chemical sedimentary rocks tend to be made of one mineral such as rock salt made of the mineral halite. These rocks have a crystalline texture. Although limestone is the most abundant chemically formed rock, nearly 90% of limestone is formed organically. Made of cemented shells, shell fragments, and skeletal remains. Rocks, such as these, are **bioclastic**.

Fossils found in sedimentary rocks provide evidence of the environment in which the rocks formed. Sedimentary rocks containing fossils of fish were formed in a marine environment whereas, fossilized impressions of land plants were not.

B3. METAMORPHIC ROCKS

Metamorphic rocks are igneous, sedimentary, and other metamorphic rocks that have been changed in form usually deep within the Earth. The high pressures, temperatures, and chemical solutions deep in the Earth cause changes in the existing rocks, forming them into metamorphic rocks.

Metamorphism is the result of the **recrystallization** of *unmelted* minerals under high temperature and pressure. These extreme conditions cause the mineral crystals to grow and new minerals to form without melting (a solid state reaction). The original rock from which a metamorphic rock forms is called the **parent rock**. Parent rock may be igneous, sedimentary, or metamorphic. The **weathering** and **erosion** of the Earth's surface eventually exposes the metamorphic rocks.

Metamorphic rocks are usually harder and more dense than the rocks from which they were formed. Original layers frequently become bent or distorted. The metamorphic rock may also show **foliation**, an alignment of minerals or the separation of minerals into platy (flaky) layers or light and dark bands.

The presence or absence of foliation provides the basis for classifying metamorphic rocks. The nonfoliated metamorphic rocks are classified by composition.

Banding of different minerals give some metamorphic rocks a striped appearance, involving the segregation of light and dark minerals into layers. Generally, the more intense the temperature and pressure conditions, the thicker the mineral bands that are formed. Thick banding indicates a high degree of metamorphism.

Distorted structure is the folding and bending of rock layers, brought about by very strong Earth forces, causing the rock to have deformed structural appearance.

Contact metamorphism occurs where molten magma or lava comes in contact with other rocks and changes them. Since the change is caused by heat, this process is also called **thermal metamorphism**. There is no specific point that exists between the changed and unchanged rock; however, a transition zone from altered to unaltered rock may form. Any rock may be altered by the action of molten material passing over or through it.

Scheme for Metamorphic Rock Identification

TEXTURE		GRAIN SIZE	COMPOSITION	TYPE OF METAMORPHISM	COMMENTS	ROCK NAME	MAP SYMBOL
FOLIATED	MINERAL ALIGNMENT	Fine	MICA / QUARTZ / FELDSPAR / AMPHIBOLE / GARNET / PYROXENE	Regional (Heat and pressure increases)	Low-grade metamorphism of shale	Slate	
FOLIATED	MINERAL ALIGNMENT	Fine to medium			Foliation surfaces shiny from microscopic mica crystals	Phyllite	
FOLIATED	MINERAL ALIGNMENT	Fine to medium			Platy mica crystals visible from metamorphism of clay or feldspars	Schist	
FOLIATED	BAND-ING	Medium to coarse			High-grade metamorphism; mineral types segregated into bands	Gneiss	
NONFOLIATED		Fine	Carbon	Regional	Metamorphism of bituminous coal	Anthracite coal	
NONFOLIATED		Fine	Various minerals	Contact (heat)	Various rocks changed by heat from nearby magma/lava	Hornfels	
NONFOLIATED		Fine to coarse	Quartz	Regional or contact	Metamorphism of quartz sandstone	Quartzite	
NONFOLIATED		Fine to coarse	Calcite and/or dolomite	Regional or contact	Metamorphism of limestone or dolostone	Marble	
NONFOLIATED		Coarse	Various minerals	Regional or contact	Pebbles may be distorted or stretched	Metaconglomerate	

The largest amount of metamorphic rock is produced by **regional metamorphism** associated with the extreme pressures that accompany **orogeny** or mountain building.

Different metamorphic rocks may be formed from the same parent rock depending upon the pressure/ temperature environment in which it forms. For example, if a piece of shale (sedimentary) is metamorphosed, it progressively would form slate → phyllite → schist → gneiss as the **degree of metamorphism** increased.

DISTRIBUTION

Sedimentary rocks are found usually as a thin layer, or veneer, over large areas of continents. Igneous rocks, at or near the surface, are found in regions of volcanoes or mountains where **intrusion** (forced while molten into cracks or between other layers of rock) and **extrusion** (ejected at the Earth's surface) have occurred. Where intrusive igneous and metamorphic rocks are found exposed on the surface of the Earth, it is usually caused by removing of over-lying rock through millions of years of weathering and erosion by water, wind, and glaciers.

C. THE ROCK CYCLE

The **rock cycle** is a model to show how closely the rock types are related. With the exception of meteorite material from space, the amount of rock material on Earth remains constant. The rocks themselves, however, gradually change responding to changes in their environment

Generally, igneous rock is considered to be the primary or parent rock of the Earth's crust. As rocks are attacked by the forces of weathering and erosion, the sediments formed are deposited, cemented, and formed into sedimentary rocks.

Rock Cycle in Earth's Crust

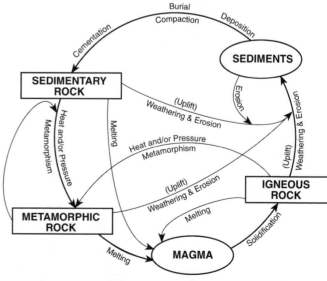

If these rocks are exposed to pressure and temperature extremes, they may be changed into metamorphic rocks. These rocks may then be subjected to additional Earth forces, melting them into magma and eventually solidifying into igneous rock. The rock cycle is then completed.

Any type rock, igneous, sedimentary, or metamorphic, may be changed into any other type depending upon the environment to which it is subjected. There is no preferred or predictable path that a rock will take within the environment.

EVIDENCE FOR THE ROCK CYCLE

The composition of some sedimentary rocks suggests that the components (sediments or rock particles and fragments) had varied origins. As previously discussed, sedimentary rocks may develop from a combination of sediments and organic remains that may have been transported great distances from several sources and deposited in one place. Then, the forces of the environment change these varied sediments into compacted and cemented rock.

The composition of some rocks suggests that the materials have undergone multiple transformations as part of the rock cycle. The Model of the Rock Cycle (from the *Earth Science Reference Tables*) shows how one form of rock can be processed into any number of other forms of rock. For example, starting with igneous rocks and following the outside pathway counterclockwise, igneous rock may be eroded – deposited – buried – cemented into sedimentary rock. That rock can be transformed by heat and pressure into metamorphic rock, and then be melted and solidify into igneous rock again. However, there are many other possible pathways in the rock cycle model.

The igneous rock may be recrystallized, forming metamorphic rock, which could then be eroded – deposited – buried – cemented into sedimentary rock. It is possible that sedimentary rock originally formed on the surface, could take a pathway through the rock cycle model, and eventually be part of a molten rock extrusion and finally become an extrusive igneous rock.

D. ENVIRONMENT OF ROCK FORMATION & USE

The composition, structure, and texture of a rock depends on the environment (formation location) in which the rock forms.

Just as the conditions under which rocks form determine many of their properties, the properties determine how the rocks are used. For example, the igneous rock granite has the ability to take a high polish and therefore is used for monuments and ornamental building stone. Gabbro, which is also igneous, has a hard intergrown crystaline structure of mafic minerals. This rock is often crushed and used as road metal (broken stones used in building and repairing roads) or as railroad ballast.

The sedimentary rock sandstone is used mainly for building construction because its layers make it relatively easy to quarry (cut from the ground) in large identical slabs. Brownstone buildings, like those found in New York City are built from red-brown Triassic sandstone.

The foliated metamorphic rock slate with its slaty cleavage makes it easy to cut into roofing tiles and flagstone. Marble, the nonfoliated metamorphic rock is also an important industrial material. Marble of all colors is used for statuary and many architectural and ornamental purposes.

E. RESOURCE CONSERVATION

With the Earth's population rapidly increasing, the demand for energy and products is rapidly increasing as well. At the present time, fossil fuels are the primary source of energy. **Fossil fuels** – coal, oil, and natural gas – were formed from organic matter in the ancient past and are **nonrenewable resources**. They are nonrenewable, because they are being used much faster and in greater amounts than they can form. In addition to producing energy, petroleum derivatives are used in making plastics, medicines, cosmetics, fabrics, and many other products. Much of the global economy depends upon the availability of these resources. Uneven distribution of resources and increasing demand for dwindling resources results in higher prices, a decrease in the standard of living for many and in the past has even resulted in wars.

Like the fossil fuels, most minerals are nonrenewable resources. In addition to using alternative energy sources where possible (solar, hydropower, wind, wave, geothermal, and nuclear energy), we must practice the *four "R's" of conservation* – **Reduce**, **Reuse**, **Recycle**, and **Reclaim**. We must find ways to reduce our need, reuse what we can (less packaging and fewer disposables), use materials that can be recycled, and reclaim usable material from things that have already been discarded.

QUESTIONS FOR UNIT 2

1 The data table below gives information on mineral hardness.

MINERAL HARDNESS

Moh's scale would be most useful for
1 identifying a mineral sample
2 finding the mass of a mineral sample
3 finding the density of a mineral sample
4 counting the number of cleavage surfaces of a mineral sample

2 The physical properties of a mineral are largely caused by its
1 volume
2 melting point
3 organic composition
4 internal arrangement of atoms

3 A student crushes a small sample of mineral to see the color of its powder. The student is trying to determine the mineral's
1 density
2 luster
3 chemical composition
4 streak

4 To identify a mineral sample embedded in a block of plastic, which of the following physical properties could not be used?
1 crystal shape   3 color
2 hardness   4 luster

5 According to the *Reference Tables*, the most abundant element in the Earth's crust is
1 oxygen   3 aluminum
2 silicon   4 magnesium

Base your answers to questions 6 through 9 on your knowledge of Earth science, the *Reference Tables*, and the table of minerals (below) which shows the physical properties of nine minerals.

6 Which mineral has a different color in its powdered form than in its original form?
1 pyrite   3 kaolinite
2 graphite   4 magnetite

Mineral	Color	Luster	Streak	Hard-ness	Density (g/mL)	Chemical Composition
biotite mica	black	glassy	white	soft	2.8	$K(Mg,Fe)_3(AlSi_3O_{10})(OH_2)$
diamond	varies	glassy	colorless	hard	3.5	C
galena	gray	metallic	gray-black	soft	7.5	PbS
graphite	black	dull	black	soft	2.3	C
kaolinite	white	earthy	white	soft	2.6	$Al_4(Si_4O_{10})(OH)_8$
magnetite	black	metallic	black	hard	5.2	Fe_3O_4
olivine	green	glassy	white	hard	3.4	$(Fe,Mg)_2SiO_4$
pyrite	brass yellow	metallic	greenish-black	hard	5.0	FeS_2
quartz	varies	glassy	colorless	hard	2.7	SiO_2

Definitions

    Luster: the way a mineral's surface reflects light
    Streak: color of a powdered form of the mineral
    Hardness: resistance of a mineral to being scratched
        (soft — easily scratched; hard — not easily scratched)

Chemical Symbols

Al	— Aluminum	Pb	— Lead
C	— Carbon	Si	— Silicon
Fe	— Iron	K	— Potassium
H	— Hydrogen	S	— Sulfur
Mg	— Magnesium	O	— Oxygen

7 Which mineral contains iron, has a metallic luster, is hard, and has the same color and streak?
1 biotite mica 3 kaolinite
2 galena 4 magnetite

8 What do the minerals quartz, olivine, and biotite mica have in common with diamond?
1 hardness 3 color
2 luster 4 composition

9 Which mineral would be best to use in the manufacture of sandpaper?
1 quartz 3 kaolinite
2 graphite 4 biotite mica

10 The diagrams below represent samples of five different minerals found in the rocks of the Earth's crust.

Which physical property of minerals is represented by the flat surfaces in the diagrams?
1 magnetism 3 cleavage
2 hardness 4 crystal size

11 The relative hardness of a mineral can best be tested by
1 scratching the mineral across a glass plate
2 squeezing the mineral with calibrated pliers
3 determining the density of the mineral
4 breaking the mineral with a hammer

12 Quartz mineral samples are best identified by their
1 hardness 3 size
2 color 4 mass

13 What causes the characteristic crystal shape and cleavage of the mineral halite as shown in the diagram at the right?

HALITE (salt)

1 metamorphism of the halite
2 the internal arrangement of the atoms in halite
3 the amount of erosion the halite has undergone
4 the shape of other minerals located where the halite formed

14 When dilute hydrochloric acid is placed on the sedimentary rock limestone and the nonsedimentary rock marble, a bubbling reaction occurs with both. What would this indicate?

1 The minerals of these two rocks have similar chemical composition.
2 The molecular structures of these two rocks have been changed by heat and pressure.
3 The physical properties of these two rocks are identical.
4 The two rocks originated at the same location.

15 The data table at the right shows the composition of six common rock-forming minerals.

Mineral	Composition
Mica	$KAl_3Si_3O_{10}$
Olivine	$(FeMg)_2SiO_4$
Orthoclase	$KAlSi_3O_8$
Plagioclase	$NaAlSi_3O_8$
Pyroxene	$CaMgSi_2O_6$
Quartz	SiO_2

The data table provides evidence that

1 the same elements are found in all minerals
2 a few elements are found in many minerals
3 all elements are found in only a few minerals
4 all elements are found in all minerals

16 Why do diamond and graphite have different physical properties, even though they are both composed entirely of the element carbon?
1 Only diamond contains radioactive carbon.
2 Only graphite consists of organic material.
3 The minerals have different arrangements of carbon atoms.
4 The minerals have undergone different amounts of weathering.

17 Which statement best describes a general property of rocks?

1 Most rocks have a number of minerals in common.
2 Most rocks are composed of a single mineral.
3 All rocks contain fossils.
4 All rocks contain minerals formed by compression and cementation.

18 Nine rock samples were classified into three groups as shown in the table below.

Group A	Group B	Group C
Granite	Shale	Marble
Rhyolite	Sandstone	Schist
Gabbro	Conglomerate	Gneiss

This classification system was most likely based on the
1 age of the minerals in the rock
2 size of the crystals in the rock
3 way in which the rock formed
4 color of the rock

19 Which two processes result in the formation of igneous rocks?
1 solidification and evaporation
2 melting and solidification
3 crystallization and cementation
4 compression and precipitation

20 According to the *Reference Tables*, which property would be most useful for identifying igneous rocks?
1 kind of cement
2 mineral composition
3 number of mineral present
4 types of fossils present

21 The diagram at the right shows a sample of rock material that contains coarse-grained intergrown crystals of several minerals. [Mineral crystals are shown actual size.]

This rock sample should be identified as
1 rhyolite
2 granite
3 scoria
4 basalt

22 Which granite sample most likely formed from magma that cooled and solidified at the slowest rate?

(1)

(3)

(2)

(4)

Base your answers to questions 23 through 26 on the diagram below which represents a geologic cross section.

23 In which location is a geologist most likely to find rock composed of intergrown crystals?
(1) A   (3) C
(2) B   (4) D

24 The rock at B most likely contains
1 quartz, only
2 quartz and potassium feldspar, only
3 potassium feldspar, pyroxene, and olivine
4 plagioclase feldspar, pyroxene, and olivine

25 Which rock is most likely organic in origin?
1 limestone   3 basalt
2 sandstone   4 conglomerate

26 At which location would quartzite most likely be found?
(1) A   (3) E
(2) B   (4) D

27 Which two igneous rocks could have the same mineral composition?
1 rhyolite and diorite
2 pumice and scoria
3 peridotite and andesite
4 gabbro and basalt

28 The diagram at the right represents the percentage by volume of each mineral found in a sample of basalt.

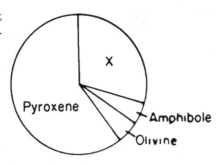

Which mineral is represented by the letter *X* in the diagram?
1 orthoclase feldspar
2 plagioclase feldspar
3 quartz
4 mica

29 In the diagram below, each angle of the triangle represents a 100 percent composition of the mineral named at that angle. The percentage of the mineral decreases toward 0 percent as either of the other angles of the triangle is approached. Letter *A* represents the mineral composition of igneous rock.

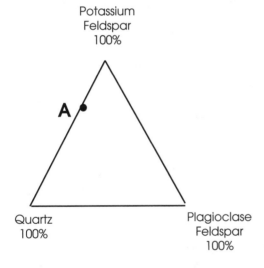

Rock *A* is a coarse-grained igneous rock that can best be identified as
1 rhyolite   3 granite
2 pumice   4 gabbro

30 Which property is common to most dark-colored igneous rocks?
1 high density
2 intrusive formation
3 abundant felsic minerals
4 coarse-grained texture

31 Which rock has cooled most rapidly from a molten state?
1 gabbro   3 quartzite
2 granite   4 obsidian

Base your answers to questions 32 and 33 on the diagram below which represents the formation of a sedimentary rock. [Sediments are drawn actual size.]

Sediments   Sedimentary Rock

32 The formation of which sedimentary rock is shown in the diagram?
1 conglomerate   3 siltstone
2 sandstone   4 shale

33 Which two processes formed this rock?
1 folding and faulting
2 melting and solidification
3 compaction and cementation
4 heating and application of pressure

34 A conglomerate contains pebbles of limestone, sandstone, and granite. Based on this information, which inference about the pebbles in the conglomerate is most accurate?
1 They had various origins.
2 They came from other conglomerates.
3 They are all the same age.
4 They were eroded quickly.

35 According to the *Reference Tables*, which sedimentary rock most likely formed as an evaporite?
1 siltstone   3 gypsum
2 conglomerate   4 shale

36 What rock is formed by the compression and cementation of sediments with particle sizes ranging from 0.08 to 0.1 centimeter?
1 basalt   3 granite
2 conglomerate   4 sandstone

37 Most of the surface bedrock of New York State formed as a direct result of
1 volcanic activity
2 spreading of the ocean floor
3 melting and solidification
4 compaction and cementation

38 Which characteristic of a sedimentary rock would furnish the greatest amount of information about the environment in which the rock was deposited?
1 hardness   3 density
2 color   4 texture

39 The diagram below represents a conglomerate rock. Some of the rock fragments are labeled.

Which conclusion is best made about the rock particles?
1 They are the same age.
2 They originated from a larger mass of igneous rock.
3 They all contain the same minerals.
4 They have different origins.

40 According to the *Reference Tables*, which characteristic determines whether a rock is classified as a shale, a siltstone, a sandstone, or a conglomerate?
1 the absolute age of the sediments within the rock
2 the mineral composition of the sediments within the rock
3 the particle size of the sediments within the rock
4 the density of the sediments within the rock

41 Metamorphic rocks result from the
1 erosion of rocks
2 recrystallization of rocks
3 cooling and solidification of molten magma
4 compression and cementation of soil particles

42 While a geology student was walking along several outcrops, she found a rock specimen that showed the following characteristics:

Grain Size – Coarse
Texture – Foliated
Composition – Quartz, feldspar, amphibole, garnet, and pyroxene

This specimen should be identified as
1 hornfels   3 gneiss
2 slate   4 anthracite

43 The metamorphism of a sandstone rock will cause the rock to
1 be melted
2 contain more fossils
3 become more dense
4 occupy a greater volume

44 Which rock is most likely a metamorphic rock?
1 a rock showing mud cracks
2 a rock containing dinosaur bones
3 a rock consisting of layers of rounded sand grains
4 a rock composed of distorted light-colored and dark-colored mineral bands

45 Which diagram best represents a sample of the metamorphic rock gneiss? [Diagrams show actual size.]

46 Which characteristics are most useful for identifying the conditions under which a metamorphic rock was formed?

1 color and luster
2 shape and mass
3 hardness and size
4 composition and structure

47 Refer to the Rock Cycle diagram below.

Rock Cycle in Earth's Crust

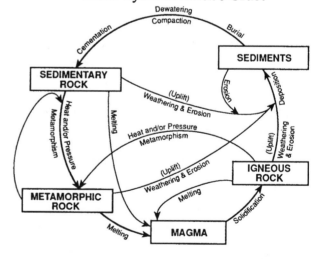

Which type(s) of rock can be the source of deposited sediments?
1 igneous and metamorphic rocks, only
2 metamorphic and sedimentary rocks, only
3 sedimentary rocks, only
4 igneous, metamorphic, and sedimentary rocks

48 Which statement about the formation of a rock is best supported by the rock cycle?

1 Magma must be weathered before it can change to metamorphic rock.
2 Sediment must be compacted and cemented before it can change to sedimentary rock.
3 Sedimentary rock must melt before it can change to metamorphic rock.
4 Metamorphic rock must melt before it can change to sedimentary rock.

49 Heat and pressure because of magma intrusions may result in
1 vertical sorting
2 graded bedding
3 contact metamorphism
4 chemical evaporites

50 What is one difference between the metamorphic rocks quartzite and hornfels?
1 Hornfels is foliated; quartzite is nonfoliated.
2 Hornfels contains plagioclase; quartzite does not contain plagioclase.
3 Hornfels is produced by regional metamorphism, quartzite is produced by contact metamorphism.
4 Hornfels is medium grained; quartzite is fine grained.

51 Which statement is best supported by the graph shown below?

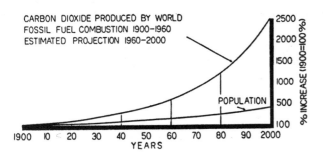

1 From 1960 to 2000 it is anticipated that there will be a decrease in the use of fossil fuels.
2 From 1900 to 1960, the average person continuously used a greater quantity of fossil fuel.
3 By 1980 the world population was approximately 400 million.
4 From 1970 to 2000 the world population will remain relatively constant.

Base your answers to questions 52 and 53 on the world map and graph below. The graph shows the relationship between average annual income and average annual energy used per person for several countries.

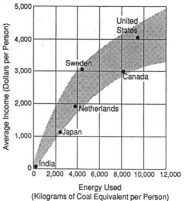

52 In which country is the average energy used per person the greatest?
1 India
2 Netherlands
3 United States
4 Japan

53 According to the graph, the average income of a person in Sweden is about the same as the average income of a person in Canada, but the average energy used per person in Sweden is about half the amount used per person in Canada. What is the most likely reason for this difference in energy use?

1 Sweden has more daylight per year than Canada and uses less energy for lighting.
2 Since Sweden's climate is much warmer than Canada's, Sweden uses less energy for heating.
3 Homes in Canada are better insulated than homes in Sweden and require less energy for heating.
4 People in Canada travel more and for longer distances by automobile than people in Sweden.

54 According to the *Earth Science Reference Tables,* in which New York State landscape region was most of the surface bedrock formed by regional metamorphism?
1 Atlantic Coastal Lowlands
2 Appalachian Uplands
3 Tug Hill Plateau
4 Adirondack Highlands

55 According to the *Earth Science Reference Tables,* much of the surface bedrock of the Adirondack Mountains consists of
1 slate and dolostone
2 gneiss and quartzite
3 limestone and sandstone
4 conglomerate and red shale

Base your answers to questions 56 through 58 on the cross section below. The cross section shows the surface and subsurface rock formations near New York City.

56 The portion of the Palisades sill that contains large crystals of plagioclase feldspar and pyroxene is considered to be similar in texture and composition to
1 obsidian
2 granite
3 basalt glass
4 gabbro

57 Which rock formation was originally limestone?
1 Palisades sill
2 Fordham gneiss
3 Inwood marble
4 Manhattan schist

58 The rock types shown on the left side of this geologic cross section were mainly the result of
1 heat and pressure exerted on previously existing rock.
2 melting and solidification of crustal rocks at great depths
3 tectonic plate boundaries diverging at the mid-ocean ridge
4 compaction and cementation of sediments under ocean waters

CONSTRUCTED RESPONSE

Base your answers to questions 1-4 on your knowledge of Earth science, the *Reference Tables* and the data below for five different rock samples.

Data Table

ROCK SAMPLE	ORIGIN	CRYSTAL SIZE OR GRAIN SIZE	OTHER CHARACTERISTIC
1	igneous	no crystals	glassy
2	igneous	coarse	light color
3	igneous	fine	dark color
4	sedimentary	0.0003 cm in diameter	contains dinosaur footprints
5	metamorphic	coarse	shows banding

Geologic Section Across the Hudson River

Palisades Sill Intrusion

Hudson River

Manhattan Schist

River Silt

Newark Group of Sandstones and Shales

Inwood Marble

Manhattan Schist

Fordham Gneiss

1 What sedimentary rock is represented by sample 4? During what geologic era was it likely to have been formed?

2 In a sentence, explain why rock sample one (1) has a glassy texture.

3 In a short paragraph, explain the probable cause of the banding characteristic seen in rock sample five (5).

4 Which rock sample is granite? Explain how you know.

Base your answers to questions 5 and 6 on the six illustrations below which represent six different rock types.

ROCK A: cemented sand and rounded pebbles

ROCK B: uniform smooth sand grains firmly cemented together

ROCK C: a matrix of fine colloidal-sized particles with shell fossils

ROCK D: large intergrown mineral crystals

ROCK E: crumpled, distorted bands of different minerals

ROCK F: cemented sand and angular rock fragments

5 Classify each rock sample as igneous, sedimentary or metamorphic.

Rock A _____

Rock B _____

Rock C _____

Rock D _____

Rock E _____

Rock F _____

6 In one or two sentences, explain what characteristic(s) of the rock led to your classification.

Base your answers to questions 7 through 9 on the data table below. The data table shows the relationship between the amount of aluminum in a type of rock and the energy needed to extract aluminum from that rock.

Amount of Aluminum in Rock (percent)	Amount of Energy needed to produce one ton of Aluminum (thousands of kilowatt-hours)
3	220
5	140
10	90
20	65
30	54
40	49
50	48

7 Mark an appropriate scale on the axis labeled "Amount of Aluminum in Rock." Plot a line graph using the data in the table above.

8 Based upon the graph you constructed, how much energy is needed to produce aluminum from rock that is 15 percent aluminum?

_____ thousands of kilowatt-hours

9 Using one or more complete sentences, describe how the amount of aluminum in a rock is related to the amount of energy needed to extract the aluminum from the rock.

Base your answer to questions 10 through 13 on the table below provides data about the texture and mineral composition of four different igneous rocks having the same volume.

Rock	Texture	Orthoclase feldspar	Quartz	Plagioclase feldspar	Mica	Amphibole	Pyroxene
A	coarse	62%	20%	7%	7%	4%	0%
B	coarse	24%	40%	19%	10%	7%	0%
C	fine	6%	16%	41%	14%	23%	0%
D	fine	0%	0%	50%	0%	6%	44%

10 According to the rock cycle diagram in the reference Tables, all four rock samples have undergone what process?

11 Which two igneous rocks on the chart most likely formed closest to the surface of the earth? Explain how you can tell.

12 Which rock sample is probably basalt?

13 Which rock sample contains the most magnesium and has the greatest density?

Base your answer to question 14 on the two rock samples shown below.

Granite   Basalt

14 Make a chart or use sentences to compare and contrast the rock samples shown above. Include rock type, environment of formation, texture and density in your comparison. Suggest how each rock type might be used.

Base your answer to question 15 on the two rock samples shown below.

Sandstone   Conglomerate

15 In one or more sentences state one way the rock types pictured above are similar and one way they differ.

Base your answers to questions 16 through 19 on your knowledge of Earth science and the *Properties of Common Minerals* chart in the *Reference Tables*.

16 A company decides to expand its business by manufacturing sandpaper. What mineral listed on the *Common properties of Common Minerals* chart would be a good one to use? Explain why?

17 A student puts a drop of cold, dilute hydrochloric acid on a mineral. But, no reaction occurs. When a piece of this same mineral is ground into a powder and a drop of the same acid is applied, a bubbling reaction occurs. According to the *Properties of Common Minerals* chart, what might this mineral be?

18 Describe two ways galena and pyrite are similar and two ways they are different.

19 A student with no special equipment to use is given two colorless crystals. One of the crystals is the mineral halite and the other is calcite. How could the student identify which mineral is which?

VOCABULARY

crust	focus & epicenter	shadow zone	mid-ocean ridges
fault zone	seismograph	mantle	magnetic polarity
strata	compressional wave	inner & outer cores	boundaries (convergent,
displaced fossil	long or *L-wave*	continental & oceanic	divergent & transform)
subsidence	primary or *P-wave*	crusts	subduction zone
displaced strata	secondary or *S-wave*	Mohorovicic Discontinuity	island arc
bench mark	Modified Mercalli Scale	or Moho	San Andreas Fault, CA
crustal plate	Richter Scale	plate tectonics	mantle convection cells
earthquake	volcanoes	continental drift	asthenosphere
seismic wave	tsunamis	sea floor spreading	hot spots

A. CRUSTAL ACTIVITIES

The solid rock outer zone of the Earth is known as the **crust**. This crust is in a constant state of change, and there is much evidence to support the idea that the Earth's surface has always been changing.

Some of these changes can be directly observed, such as the results of earthquakes, crustal movements (both horizontal and vertical) along **fault zones** (and volcanoes on the surface of the Earth. Other evidence indicates that parts of the Earth's crust have been moving to different locations for billions of years.

DYNAMIC LITHOSPHERE

Earth's lithosphere is in a constant state of change in order to maintain a state of dynamic equilibrium. The minor crustal changes include the deformation and displacement of strata and fossils.

DEFORMED ROCK STRATA

Sedimentary rocks appear to form in horizontal layers. However, observations of the Earth's surface indicate that the original formations of rock have changed through past Earth movements. These changes include **tilting**, **folding**, **faulting**, and the **displacement** of these layers of rock or **strata**.

Displaced Fossils. Marine fossils, the remains or imprints of once living ocean organisms such as corals, fish, and other marine animals are found in layers of sedimentary rock in mountains, often thousands of feet above sea level. These marine fossils found at high elevations above sea level suggest the past **uplift of rock strata**.

Subsidence is the sinking or settling of rock strata. Observations at great depths in the oceans suggest that subsidence has occurred in the past, since fossils of shallow water organisms, marine animals that once lived near the ocean surface, have been found in the rocks of the ocean floor.

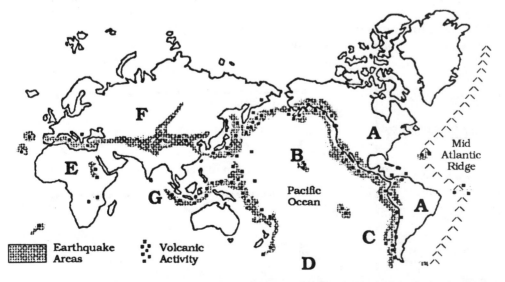

Key
Major Plate Areas:

A – American
B – Pacific
C – Nazca
D – Antarctic
E – African
F – Eurasian
G – Indian

Displaced Strata. The displacement of strata provides direct evidence of crustal movement. These crustal movements may be either horizontal or vertical or a combination of both.

Horizontal Displacement (faulting) occurs when the Earth's surface shifts sideways along a transform fault or crack in the crust. **Vertical displacement** (faulting) occurs when a portion of the Earth's surface is either uplifted or subsides, also along a fault. For example, in California, where earthquakes are fairly common result of crustal activity, both types of displacement can be observed along the San Andreas Fault Zone.

During the San Fernando earthquake of 1971, the horizontal displacement along the fault zones caused portions of roads to be displaced so that one road was separated into two. Because of the uplift and subsidence of adjacent land, cliffs and ravines were formed. The actual amount of movement can be calculated by comparing bench marks.

A **bench mark** is a permanent cement or brass marker in the ground indicating elevation above mean sea level and the latitude and longitude of that particular location. Following the San Fernando earthquake some bench marks were displaced several meters vertically and horizontally.

AREAS OF CRUSTAL ACTIVITY

Crustal activities, such as earthquakes and volcanoes, occur for the most part in specific zones or regions of the Earth. Generally, they are along the borders of continents and oceans. The most active zones usually follow the continental borders of the Pacific Ocean, mid-ocean ridges, and across southern Europe and the Middle East into Asia. These zones mark the boundaries or edges of large pieces of the Earth's crust called **crustal plates**.

An **earthquake** is the sudden trembling or shaking of the ground, usually caused by movement along a break or fault in rock layers, releasing stress that has built up in the ground. When an earthquake occurs, **seismic waves** are generated and move out in all directions from the **focus** (point of origin). The point on the surface of the Earth directly above the focus is known as the **epicenter** of the earthquake. These seismic waves are detected and registered on delicate sensing instruments called **seismographs**.

B. EARTHQUAKES

Earthquakes generate several kinds of waves. Two types of earthquake waves that travel through the Earth are **compressional** and **shear** waves. **Compressional waves**, also called **Primary** or *P-waves*, cause the material through which they pass to vibrate in the same direction as the wave is traveling. **Shear waves**, also called **Secondary** or *S-waves*, cause the material through which they pass to vibrate at right angles to the direction in which the wave is traveling.

L-waves (long period waves) or surface waves are Rayleigh and Love waves that ripple the surface of the Earth causing the damage associated with earthquakes.

VELOCITIES OF WAVES

When traveling in the same material, primary waves travel at a greater velocity than secondary waves. Therefore, a seismograph records the primary waves before the secondary waves arrive. A single seismogram showing the arrival times of the primary and secondary waves may be used to determine the distance to the earthquake and its time of origin. By calculating the difference in arrival time between the primary and secondary waves on the travel-time graph in the *Earth Science Reference Tables*, the distance from the seismographic station to the epicenter may be determined.

The larger the difference in arrival times of the primary and secondary waves, the greater the distance to the earthquake epicenter. Additional information is needed to determine the direction to the epicenter.

ORIGIN OF THE TIME OF AN EARTHQUAKE

The origin time of an earthquake can be inferred from the evidence of the epicenter distance and the travel time of the *P-waves* and *S-waves* (see the *Earthquake S-wave and P-wave Time Travel* graph below). The farther the recording station is from the epicenter, the longer it takes for the *P-waves* to reach the station. For example, a recording station receives the *P-wave* at 7:10 a.m. and the *S-wave* 5 minutes and 30 seconds later. If the epicenter distance has been determined to be 4,000 kilometers (determined by the difference – 5.5 minutes – in the arrival time of the *P-* and *S-waves*), then the travel time for the *P-wave* was 7 minutes. The earthquake's time of origin was 7:03 a.m. (7:10 less 07 minutes *P-wave* travel time).

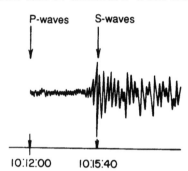

EPICENTER LOCATION

By using the distance to the epicenter from a minimum of three seismograms (*A*, *B*, and *C*), the location of the earthquake's epicenter (*E*) can be calculated. On a map, the distance to each epicenter is drawn as the radius of a circle around each seismographic station. The epicenter (*E*) is located where the three circles intersect.

Modified Mercalli Scale of Earthquake Intensity

Intensity Value	Description of Effects
I	Usually detected only by instruments
II	Felt by a few persons at rest, especially on upper floors
III	Hanging objects swing; vibration like passing truck; noticeable indoors
IV	Felt indoors by many, outdoors by few; sensation like heavy truck striking building; parked automobiles rock
V	Felt by nearly everyone; sleepers awakened; liquids disturbed; unstable objects overturned; some dishes and windows broken
VI	Felt by all; many frightened and run outdoors; some heavy furniture moved; glassware broken; books off shelves; damage slight
VII	Difficult to stand; noticed in moving automobiles; damage to some masonry; weak chimneys broken at roofline
VIII	Partial collapse of masonry; chimneys, factory stacks, columns fall; heavy furniture overturned; frame houses moved on foundations

MEASURING EARTHQUAKE STRENGTH

The strength of earthquakes is estimated in a variety of ways. The **Modified Mercalli Scale** is based upon the damage inflicted by the earthquake. This **intensity scale** ranges from I to XII with I being felt by few people to XII resulting in total devastation to nearly all structures. Although this scale is still used to help locate the centers of earthquakes, it is not very precise, because building design and the nature of the surface materials may cause great variations in the resulting damage.

The **Richter Scale** is a **magnitude scale** used to describe the amount of energy released by an earthquake. Richter scale magnitudes range from 0 to 9. Those that are less than 2.5 are not usually felt by people. Each step up the magnitude scale indicates a release of 32 times more energy than the previous step.

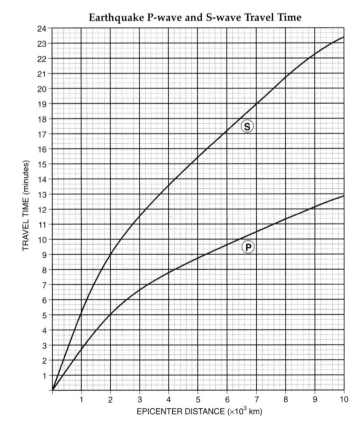

Earthquake P-wave and S-wave Travel Time

A magnitude 6 earthquake releases 32 times more energy than a magnitude 5 earthquake. A magnitude 6 earthquake may cause significant destruction if it occurs in a populated area. Approximately 20 major earthquakes in the magnitude 7.0-7.9 range occur each year and about once every 5-10 years an earthquake of 8.0 or more will devastate a region.

Both earthquakes and **volcanoes** present geologic hazards to people. Most people are killed or injured in an earthquake by falling debris or collapsing buildings. Unless they have been designed to withstand earthquakes, most buildings cannot withstand the side-to-side shaking resulting from earthquake waves. If the ground beneath the building is made of loose sediment, the shaking causes the sediment to break up and move, causing the building to fall over.

Fire is a big danger in the aftermath of an earthquake since fires often result from ruptured gas pipes. Firefighting equipment often cannot reach the fires because the streets are blocked with fallen debris and water lines supplying the hydrants have been broken by the shaking ground.

Large submarine earthquakes or those that occur along a coastline may result in **tsunamis** or **seismic sea waves**, which come in series. Small tsunamis at one part of the coast can be giants a few miles away. After an earthquake never go to a beach to watch for a tsunami. If you can see a big tsunami, you are too close to escape it! These giant waves have been known to completely destroy communities along low-lying coasts.

Although lava from volcanic eruptions may produce new land whose surface will weather into fertile soil, people living in actively volcanic areas are subjected to potential dangers. Flowing lava may destroy developed property, and violent explosions of ash and poisonous gases are an ever present danger.

TRANSMISSION OF WAVES

Studying the transmission of earthquake waves as they travel through the Earth allows scientists to make inferences about the composition and interior structure of the Earth.

The velocity of earthquake waves varies according to the density and elastic properties of the material through which they are traveling. The greater the density and rigidity of the material, the greater their velocity. As they travel through materials of varying density and rigidity, the variation in their velocity causes the

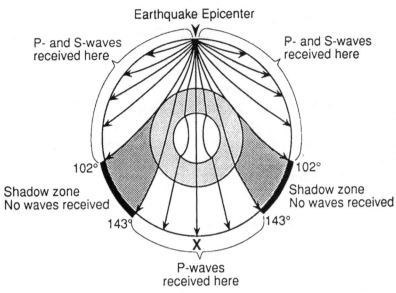

waves to be bent or refracted. Since the density of the Earth gradually increases with depth, earthquake waves tend to increase in their velocity and are continually refracted as they travel down into the Earth.

Compressional or *P-waves* are transmitted through solids, liquids and gases, but *S-waves* are only transmitted through solids. This difference provides valuable information for scientists about the interior structure of the Earth. *S-waves* that penetrate the Earth to the depth of the outer core (2900 km) disappear. Since these waves are not transmitted by the outer core, the material of the outer core is assumed to be liquid.

Earthquakes generate *P-* and *S-waves* that move out from the earthquake focus in all directions. The seismographs that are located within 102° from the epicenter record both the *P-* and *S-waves*. Those seismographs that are farther away do not record the *S-waves* because they are not transmitted through the core. In a region known as the **shadow zone**, a band that runs from approximately 102° to 143° away from the earthquakes' epicenter (the opposite side of the Earth) neither the *P-* nor the *S-waves* are recorded. This is caused by the refraction of the *P-waves* out of that region.

C. CRUST & INTERIOR PROPERTIES

There are four major Earth zones, three solid zones, and one liquid zone. The **crust**, the **mantle**, and the **inner core** are solid zones. The only liquid zone is the **outer core**.

Crustal Thickness. The crust of the Earth compared to the other zones is relatively thin, only a few kilometers in average depth. The average thickness of the **continental crust** is greater than the average

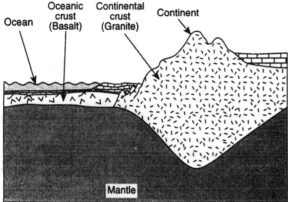

Ocean / Oceanic crust (Basalt) / Continental crust (Granite) / Continent / Mantle

thickness of the **oceanic crust** (under the ocean).

Crustal and Interior Composition. The oceanic and continental crusts have different compositions. The continental crust of the Earth is mainly composed of a low density felsic granitic material; whereas, the ocean crust is mafic or basaltic in nature. The mantle, on which the Earth's crust rests, accounts for the greatest part of the volume of the Earth. The crust-mantle boundary is called the **Mohorovicic Discontinuity** or the **Moho.**

Below the mantle is the liquid outer core and the solid inner core. Evidence from the behavior of seismic waves composition of and the presence of metallic meteorites, suggests that the inner portion of the Earth is mainly a high density combination of the metallic elements iron (Fe) and Nickel (Ni).

Interior Characteristics. The density, temperature, and pressure of the Earth's interior increase with depth (see figure on the Inferred Properties of the Earth's Interior, from the *Earth Science Reference Tables* above).

Inferred Properties of Earth's Interior

DENSITY (g/cm³)
2.7 granitic continental crust
3.0 basaltic oceanic crust
MOHO
3.4–5.6
9.9–12.2
12.8–13.1
EARTH'S CENTER

D. PLATE TECTONICS

Plate tectonics is the theory that the Earth's lithosphere is made of a number of solid pieces, called **plates**, and these plates move in relation to each other. The term "tectonics" refers to the forces that deform the Earth's crust.

The **lithosphere** is made of the crust and the rigid upper part of the mantle. Although plate tectonics is a recent idea, it incorporates the earlier idea of **continental drift** put forth by Alfred Wegener in 1915. Wegener noted that the present continents appear to fit together as fragments of an originally larger landmass, much the same way the pieces of a jigsaw puzzle fit together. This is especially true if the edge of the continental shelves are used as the boundaries.

ORDOVICIAN	458 million years ago
DEVONIAN/MISSISSIPPIAN	363 million years ago
PENNSYLVANIAN	306 million years ago
TRIASSIC	232 million years ago
CRETACEOUS	119 million years ago
TERTIARY	59 million years ago

PLATE MOTION

Evidence to support the idea that the continents were together as one large landmass includes more than the shapes of the continents. For example:

- Rock layers and fossils may be correlated across ocean basins. Many of the same rock types and their mineral composition, as well as the fossil types found in the rocks along the eastern coastline of South America match those along the western coastline of Africa.

- Some mountain chains appear to be continuous from continent to continent (example, Appalachians and Caledonian).

- Rock and fossil evidence indicates ancient climates much different from those of today (example, glacial deposits in tropical regions; coal deposits in the Arctic).

- Rocks of the ocean basins are much younger than continental rocks. Note: the most conclusive evidence comes from the ocean basins.

Tectonic Plates

Key

→ Relative motion at plate boundary	
⇄ Transform plate boundary (transform fault)	
Divergent plate boundary (usually broken by transform faults along mid-ocean ridges)	
Convergent plate boundary (subduction zone) — overriding plate, subducting plate	
- - - - Complex or uncertain plate boundary	
☆ Mantle hot spot	

Continent

Continent

Direction of Movement

Movement of the Mid-Atlantic Ocean Ridge

SEA (OCEAN) FLOOR SPREADING

There is much evidence to indicate that the ocean floors are spreading out from the mountain regions of the oceans (mid-ocean ridges). The two major pieces of evidence are related to the **age of igneous ocean materials** and the **reversal of magnetic polarity**.

Igneous Ocean Rocks. The ocean crust is primarily composed of basaltic rocks that are formed when molten rock (magma) rises, solidifies, and crystallizes into the igneous rocks of the mid-ocean ridges (mountains). Evidence shows that igneous material along the center of the oceanic ridges is younger (more recently formed) than the igneous material farther from the ridges. Note that the age of rocks can be accurately determined by using radioactive dating techniques. Therefore, as new ocean crust is generated at mid-ocean ridges, the ocean floor widens.

Reversal of Magnetic Polarity. The strips of igneous (basaltic) rock which lie parallel to the mid-ocean ridges show matched patterns of magnetic reversals. Over the period of thousands of years, the magnetic poles of the Earth reverse (switch) their polarities (the north magnetic pole changes to the south magnetic pole and vice versa). When the basaltic magma flows up in the middle of the ridge and begins to cool, crystals of magnetic minerals align themselves with the Earth's magnetic field like tiny compass needles, thus recording magnetic polarity at the time of formation. Therefore, when the magnetic field is reversed, the new igneous rocks formed during the reversed polarity period have a reversed magnetic orientation from the previously formed rocks. These changes in magnetic orientation are found on both sides of the mid-ocean ridges, indicating that the development of the ocean floor is from the center of mid-ocean ridges outwards.

Rocks found in vastly different locations in the Earth's crust have recorded the position of the Earth's magnetic poles. This strongly supports the continental growth and mountain building concepts that are related to plate tectonics.

CORE

The movement of lithospheric plates throughout geologic time has resulted in changes in geography, climate, and evolution of life.

The lithospheric plates are various sizes, with some made only of ocean crust and others carrying continents on them. Three kinds of plate motion are associated with plate boundaries, **convergent**, **divergent**, and **transform**. The compressional forces at convergent boundaries, tensional forces at divergent boundaries, and shearing forces at transform boundaries result in a variety of surface features (see illustration on the next page).

At convergent plate boundaries, plates collide with each other. Where an ocean plate collides with a continental plate, the denser ocean plate, made of basaltic material, dives down (subducts) into the mantle forming a **subduction zone**. Here an ocean trench forms on the surface and below old crust is consumed by the mantle. The overriding continental plate is crumpled up to form a chain of mountains like the Andes of South America.

In areas where two ocean plates converge, the older, denser plate will subduct, also forming a trench on the surface along with a chain of island, called an **island arc**. Many of these may be seen along the northern and western boundaries of the Pacific Ocean.

If a continental plate collides with another continental plate, the edges of both plates are crumpled up forming folded mountains like the Himalayas of India.

At **divergent** plate boundaries, the plates move apart are allow heat and magma to flow up from below forming parallel ridges made of new crustal material. This can clearly be seen in the Mid-Atlantic Ridge. When divergence occurs within a land mass, such as in Africa, the tension results in the formation of a large rift valley which eventually develops into an arm of the sea.

Heat and pressure conditions sufficient to result in the formation of magma are found along plate boundaries in areas where subduction or rifting

Divergent Boundary

Transform Boundary

Plate Boundaries
Movement of crustal sections (plates) is indicated by arrows. The locations of frequent earthquakes are indicated by symbols as shown in the key. (Diagrams are not drawn to scale.)

(KEY)

[CONTINENTAL CRUST (GRANITE)]

[OCEANIC CRUST (BASALT)]

[MANTLE]

★ EARTHQUAKE FOCUS

➤ DIRECTION OF PLATE MOVEMENT

Convergent Boundary

Convergent Boundary

(divergence) occur. The magma will eventually result in the formation of new igneous rocks and may metamorphose other rocks with which it has contact. The heat and pressure generated at subduction zones is also associated with regional metamorphism in areas of mountain building. The downwarping of the crust at these same areas provides basins where both ocean and continental sediment may be deposited.

In places like the San Andreas Fault of California, the shearing forces cause plates to grind slowly past each other. This is called a **transform plate boundary**. At this type of boundary crust is neither formed nor consumed, however, shallow focus earthquakes are very common.

Although plate motion is only a few centimeters per year, the interactions of the boundaries result in earthquakes, volcanism, and mountain building on a grand scale showing that the Earth is a dynamic (changing) system.

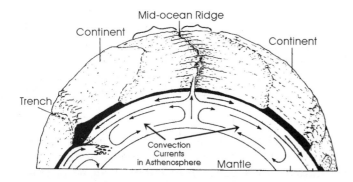

MANTLE CONVECTION CELLS

In the past, scientists discounted Wegener's idea of continental drift, because they could not explain a mechanism that could move continents. However, over the years new evidence has been collected that indicates that approximately 200 million years ago, the major continents were connected, and that since that time they have been moving

Although forces exist within the Earth that are powerful enough to move the lithospheric plates, the scientific community has not been in total agreement on the specific mechanism involved.

A **convection cell** is a stream of heated material that is moving because of density differences. Evidence suggests that convection cells exist within a part of the mantle called the **asthenosphere** because of the occurrence of heat flow highs in areas of mountain building and heat flow lows in areas of shallow subsiding basins. Residual heat from the formation of the Earth plus heat generated by radioactive decay are two sources of energy to drive this mechanism. These convection cells are likely a part of the driving force which causes the continents to move.

HOT SPOTS

Hot Spots are places on the Earth's surface with unusually high heat flow. Most of these occur along active plate margins, but some are found within the plates. The cause of these hot spots is thought to be plumes of magma rising up from the mantle producing sites of active volcanism. As a plate passes over a hot spot, a chain volcanic mountains forms, like the Hawaiian Islands. The only mountain that remains active is the mountain located directly over the hot spot.

QUESTIONS FOR UNIT 3

1   A large belt of mountain ranges and volcanoes surrounds the Pacific Ocean. Which events are most closely associated with these mountains and volcanoes?
1   hurricanes   3   tornadoes
2   sandstorms   4   earthquakes

2   Which best describes a major characteristic of both volcanoes and earthquakes?
1   They are centered at the poles.
2   They are located in the same geographic areas.
3   They are related to the formation of glaciers.
4   They are restricted to the Southern Hemisphere.

3   Recent volcanic activity in different parts of the world support the inference that volcanoes are located mainly in
1   the centers of landscape regions
2   the central regions of continents
3   zones of crustal activity
4   zones in late stages of erosion

4   Which graph best represents the relationship between volcanic activity and earthquake activity in an area?

(1)

(3)

(2)

(4)

5   The immediate result of a sudden slippage of rocks within the Earth's crust will be
1   a convergent plate boundary
2   an earthquake
3   erosion
4   the formation of convection currents

6   Earthquakes generally occur
1   in belts or zones of activity
2   uniformly over the earth
3   only under the oceans
4   mostly in North America

7 Which evidence has led to the inference that solid zones and liquid zones exist within the Earth?
1 analysis of seismic wave data
2 the Earth's rotational speed during the different seasons
3 direct temperature measurements of the Earth's interior
4 gravitational measurements made at the Earth's surface

8 The place where an earthquake appears to originate is called the
1 epicenter
2 core
3 focus
4 zenith

9 Placing a seismograph on the Moon has enabled scientists to determine if the Moon has
1 water
2 an atmosphere
3 radioactive rocks
4 crustal movements

10 Seismic studies of the Moon have helped scientists to make inferences about
1 water erosion on the Moon
2 weathering on the Moon's surface
3 radioactivity of the Moon's surface rocks
4 the Moon's interior

11 Useful information regarding the composition of the interior of the Earth can be derived from earthquakes because earthquake waves
1 release materials from within the Earth
2 travel through the Earth at constant velocity
3 travel at different rates through different materials
4 change radioactive decay rates of rocks\

Note: Question 12 has only 3 choices.

12 The behavior of earthquake waves indicate that as depth in the Earth increases, the density generally
1 decreases
2 increases
3 remains the same

13 The most destructive aspect of submarine earthquakes is the production of
1 offshore trenches
2 longshore currents
3 giant sea waves along shores
4 rip tides

14 After a large earthquake in the Yakutat Bay, several coastal communities in Alaska suffered much damage when struck by seismic sea waves called
1 breakers
2 surf
3 ground swell
4 tsunamis

15 An abrupt change in the speed of seismic waves is an indication that the
1 seismic waves are colliding
2 shear wave overtakes the compressional wave
3 waves are going into a material with different properties
4 waves are passing through material of the same density

16 When the seafloor moves as a result of an underwater earthquake and a large tsunami develops, what will most likely occur?
1 Deep-ocean sediments will be transported over great distances.
2 No destruction will occur near the origin of the earthquake.
3 The direction of the tsunami will be determined by the magnitude of the earthquake.
4 Severe destruction will occur in coastal areas.

17 The landscape shown in the diagram is an area of frequent earthquakes.

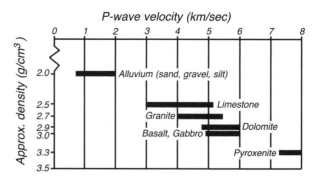

This landscape provides evidence for
1 converging convection cells within the rocks of the mantle
2 movement and displacement of the rocks of the crust
3 density differences in the rocks of the mantle
4 differential erosion of hard and soft rocks of the crust

18 The graph below shows the average velocities of *P-waves* traveling through various rock materials.

The graph indicates that *P-waves* generally travel faster through rock materials that
1 have greater density
2 have undergone metamorphism
3 are unconsolidated sediments
4 are formed from marine-derived sediments

19 The epicenter of an earthquake is located near Massena, New York. According to the *Reference Tables*, the greatest difference in arrival times of the *P-* and *S-waves* for this earthquake would be recorded in
1 Albany, NY
2 Utica, NY
3 Plattsburgh, NY
4 Binghamton, NY

Base your answers to questions 20 through 23 on the *Earth Science Reference Tables*, the table below, and your knowledge of Earth science. The table shows some of the data collected at two seismic stations, *A* and *B*. Some data have been omitted.

Station	Arrival Time of *P*-Wave	Arrival Time of *S*-Wave	Difference in Arrival Times of *P*- and *S*-Waves	Distance to Epicenter
A	6:02:00 p.m.	6:07:30 p.m.	5 min 30 sec	— km
B	— p.m.	6:11:20 p.m.	7 min 20 sec	5,700 km

20 Which seismogram most accurately represents the arrival of the *P-* and *S-waves* at station *A*?

(1)

(2)

(3)

(4)

21 What is the approximate distance from the epicenter to station A?
(1) 1,400 km
(2) 1,900 km
(3) 3,000 km
(4) 4,000 km

22 Which statement best describes the seismic waves received at station *B*?
1 The *P-wave* arrived at 6:12 p.m.
2 The *S-wave* arrived before the *P-wave*.
3 The *P-wave* had the greater velocity.
4 The *S-wave* passed through a fluid before reaching station *B*.

23 What is the minimum number of *additional* stations from which scientists must collect data in order to locate the epicenter of this earthquake?
(1) 1
(2) 2
(3) 3
(4) 0

Base your answers to questions 24 and 25 on the diagram of the Earth showing the observed pattern of waves recorded after an earthquake.

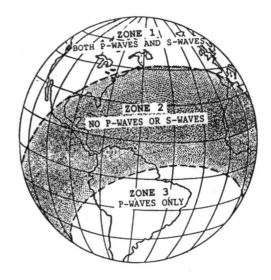

24 The lack of *S-waves* in Zone 3 can best be explained by the presence within the Earth of

1 density changes
2 mantle convection cells
3 a liquid outer core
4 a solid inner core

25 The location of the epicenter of the earthquake that produced the observed wave pattern most likely is in the
1 crust in Zone 1
2 mantle in Zone 2
3 crust in Zone 3
4 core of the Earth

26 The circles on the map show the distances from three seismic stations, *X*, *Y*, and *Z*, to the epicenter of an earthquake.

Which location is closest to the earthquake epicenter?
(1) *A*   (3) *C*
(2) *B*   (4) *D*

Base your answers to questions 27 and 28 on your knowledge of Earth science, the *Reference Tables*, and the map which shows three circles used to locate an earthquake epicenter. Five lettered locations, *A*, *B*, *C*, *D*, and *E*, are shown as reference points. Epicenter distances from three locations are represented by r$_1$, r$_2$, and r$_3$.

27 Location *D* is about 3,600 kilometers from the epicenter. What was the *S-wave* travel time to location *D*?
(1) 5 minutes 10 seconds
(2) 6 minutes 20 seconds
(3) 7 minutes 30 seconds
(4) 11 minutes 40 seconds

28 At which location could the seismogram at the right have been recorded?

(1) *A*   (3) *C*
(2) *B*   (4) *D*

29 The map below represents intensity values of an earthquake according to the *Modified Mercalli Scale of Earthquake Activity*.

Modified Mercalli Scale of Earthquake Intensity

Intensity Value	Description of Effects
I	Usually detected only by instruments
II	Felt by a few persons at rest, especially on upper floors
III	Hanging objects swing; vibration like passing truck; noticeable indoors
IV	Felt indoors by many, outdoors by few; sensation like heavy truck striking building; parked automobiles rock
V	Felt by nearly everyone; sleepers awakened; liquids disturbed; unstable objects overturned; some dishes and windows broken
VI	Felt by all; many frightened and run outdoors; some heavy furniture moved; glassware broken; books off shelves; damage slight
VII	Difficult to stand; noticed in moving automobiles; damage to some masonry; weak chimneys broken at roofline
VIII	Partial collapse of masonry; chimneys, factory stacks, columns fall; heavy furniture overturned; frame houses moved on foundations

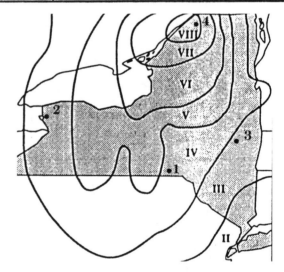

The epicenter of this earthquake is most likely located closest to
1   Binghamton (1)   3   Albany (3)
2   Niagara Falls (2)   4   Mt. Marcy (4)

30 The Mercalli-scale intensity of an earthquake that occurred before the invention of the seismograph can be inferred by
1   observing the local topography
2   reading historical observations of the event
3   measuring the rate at which heat escapes from the Earth
4   measuring the strength of the Earth's gravitational field

31 The cross-sectional diagram below of the Earth shows the paths of seismic waves from an earthquake. Letter *X* represents the location of a seismic station.

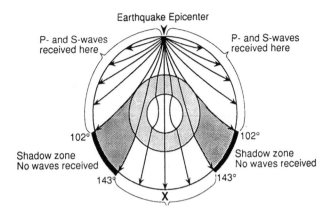

Earthquake Epicenter

P- and S-waves received here

P- and S-waves received here

102°

102°

Shadow zone No waves received

Shadow zone No waves received

143°

143°

X

Which statement best explains why station *X* received only *P-waves*?
1 *S-wave* traveled too slowly for seismographs to detect them.
2 Station *X* is too far from the focus for *S-waves* to reach.
3 A liquid zone within the Earth stops *S-waves*.
4 *P-waves* and *S-waves* are refracted by the Earth's core.

32 Which information would be most useful for predicting the occurrence of an earthquake at a particular location?
1 elevation
2 climate
3 seismic history
4 number of nearby seismic station

33 Which characteristic of metallic meteorites would give the most useful information about the Earth's core?
1 mass and volume
2 reflectivity and color
3 composition and density
4 temperature and state of matter

34 According to the *Earth Science Reference Tables*, the rock located 1,000 kilometers below the Earth's surface is believed to be
1 liquid at approximately 1,800°C
2 solid at approximately 3200°C
3 liquid at approximately 4,000°C
4 solid at approximately 4,500°C

35 The primary cause of convection currents in the Earth's mantle is believed to be the
1 differences in densities of Earth materials
2 subsidence of the crust
3 occurrence of earthquakes
4 rotation of the Earth

36 Two geologic surveys of the same area, made 50-years apart, showed that the area had been uplifting 5 centimeters during the interval. If the rate of uplift remains constant, how many years will it take before there is a 50 centimeter change?
(1) 250 years   (3) 500 years
(2) 350 years   (4) 700 years

37 Which of the following provides evidence for the theory of continental drift?
1 The shapes of the continents suggest that they could "fit together."
2 All the continents contain igneous rocks.
3 There is a close correspondence between zones of earthquake and volcanic activity.
4 Rocks at the Earth's surface are constantly being eroded.

38 Contact zones between tectonic plates may produce trenches. According to the *Earth Science Reference Tables*, one of these trenches is located at the boundary between which plates?
1 Australian and Pacific
2 South American and African
3 Australian and Antarctic
4 North American and Eurasian

39 The theory of plate tectonics suggest that
1 the continents moved because of changes in the Earth's orbital velocity
2 the continent's movements were caused by the Earth's rotation
3 the present-day continents of South America and Africa once fit together like puzzle parts
4 the present-day continents of South America and Africa are moving toward each other

Base your answers to questions 40 through 44 on the map below and your knowledge of Earth science. The map shows crustal plate boundaries located along the pacific coastline of the United States. The arrows show the general directions in which some of the plates appear to be moving slowly.

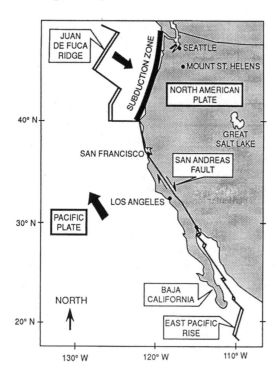

43 What would a study of the East Pacific rise (a mid-ocean ridge) indicate about the age of the basaltic bedrock in this area?
1 The bedrock is youngest at the ridge.
2 The bedrock is oldest at the ridge.
3 The bedrock at the ridge is the same age as the bedrock next to the continent.
4 The bedrock at the ridge is the same age as the bedrock at the San Andreas fault.

44 The best way to find the direction of crustal movement along the San Andreas fault is to
1 study the Earth's present magnetic field
2 observe erosion along the continental coastline
3 measure gravitational strength on opposite sides of the fault
4 match displaced rock types from opposite sides of the fault

Base your answers to questions 45 and 46 on your knowledge of Earth science, the *Reference Tables*, and the diagrams which represent geologic cross sections of the upper mantle and crust at four different Earth locations. In each diagram, the movement of the crustal sections (plates) is indicated by arrows and the locations of frequent earthquakes are indicated by symbols as shown in the key. [Diagrams are not drawn to scale.]

40 Which feature is located at 20° North latitude and 109° West longitude?
1 San Andreas fault
2 East Pacific rise
3 Baja, California
4 Juan de Fuca Ridge

41 Geologic studies of the San Andreas fault indicate that
1 many earthquakes occur along the San Andreas fault
2 the North American plate and the Pacific plate are locked in dynamic equilibrium
3 the subduction zone is the boundary at which the crustal plates are drifting apart
4 the age of the bedrock increases as distance from the fault increases

42 Which features are most often found at crustal plate boundaries like those shown on the map?
1 meandering rivers and warm-water lakes
2 plains and plateaus
3 geysers and glaciers
4 faulted bedrock and volcanoes

45 Which location best represents the boundary between the African plate and the South American plate?
(1) A   (3) C
(2) B   (4) D

46 Which diagram represents plate movement associated with transform faults such as those causing California earthquakes?
(1) *A* (3) *C*
(2) *B* (4) *D*

Base your answers to questions 47 through 50 on the diagram below. The diagram shows a portion of the Earth's oceanic crust in the vicinity of the mid-Atlantic ridge. The stripes in the diagram represent magnetic bands of igneous rock formed in the oceanic crust. The orientation of the Earth's magnetic field at the time of rock formation is shown as arrows within each band. Letters *A*, *B*, *C*, *D*, and *E* represent locations on the seafloor.

47 According to the diagram, which two locations have rock with the same magnetic orientation?
(1) *A* and *B* (3) *B* and *E*
(2) *A* and *E* (4) *D* and *E*

48 Heat flow measurements are made at locations *A* through *E*. Which graph best represents these measurements?

(1)

(3)

(2)

(4)

49 According to the *Theory of Plate Tectonics* the crust in this area is formed by convection currents in the asthenosphere below the mid-Atlantic ridge. Which cross-sectional diagram best represents the currents that formed the ridge?

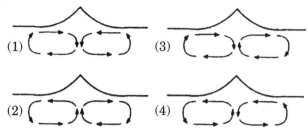

50 Along a line drawn from location *A* to location *E*, the relative age of the oceanic crust would most likely
1 decrease from *A* to *E*
2 increase from *A* to *E*
3 decrease from *A* to *C* and increase from *C* to *E*
4 increase from *A* to *C* and decrease from *C* to *E*

Base your answers to questions 51 through 53 on the *Earth Science Reference Tables*, the map and information below, and your knowledge of Earth science.

The map shows the location of major islands and coral reefs in the Hawaiian Island chain. Their ages are given in millions of years.

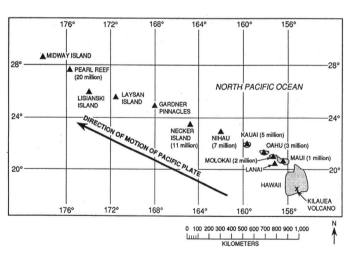

The islands of the Hawaiian chain formed from the same source of molten rock, called a hot plume. The movement of the Pacific Plate over the Hawaiian hot plume created a trail of extinct volcanoes that make up the Hawaiian Islands. The island of Hawaii (lower right) is the most recent island formed. Kilauea is an active volcano located over the plume on the island of Hawaii.

51 Approximately how far has the Pacific Plate moved since Necker Island was located over the hot plume at *X*?
   (1) 300 km   (3) 1,900 km
   (2) 1,100 km   (4) 2,600 km

52 Approximately how long will it take the noon Sun to appear to move from Kauai to Pearl Reef?
   (1) 1 hour
   (2) 2 hours
   (3) 15 minutes
   (4) 45 minutes

53 Which graph shows the general relationship between the age of individual islands in the Hawaiian chain and their distance from the hot plume?

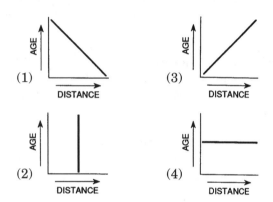

54 Hot springs on the ocean floor near the mid ocean ridges provide evidence that
   1 climate change has melted huge glaciers
   2 marine fossils have been uplifted to high elevations
   3 meteor craters are found beneath the oceans
   4 convection currents exist in the asthenosphere

55 Evidence of subduction exists at the boundary between the
   1 African and South American plates
   2 Australian and Antarctic plates
   3 Pacific and Antarctic plates
   4 Nazca and South American plates

56 The diagram below represents a cross section of a portion of the Earth's crust.

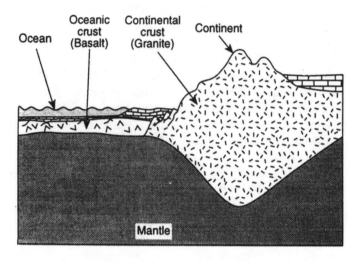

Which statement about the Earth's crust is best supported by the diagram?
   1 The oceanic crust is thicker than the mantle.
   2 The continental crust is thicker than the oceanic crust.
   3 The continental crust is composed primarily of sedimentary rock.
   4 The crust is composed of denser rock than the mantle is.

57 The scale below shows the age of rocks in relation to their distance from the Mid-Atlantic Ridge.

Some igneous rocks that originally formed at the Mid-Atlantic Ridge are now 37 kilometers from the ridge. Approximately how long ago did these rocks form?
   (1) 1.8 million years ago
   (2) 2.0 million years ago
   (3) 3.0 million years ago
   (4) 45.0 million years ago

Constructed Response

Base your answers to questions 1 through 4 on the information and map below and on your knowledge of Earth science.

An earthquake occurred in the southwestern part of the United States. Mercalli-scale intensities were plotted for selected locations on a map, as shown at below. (As the numerical value of Mercalli ratings increases, the damaging effects of the earthquake waves also increase.)

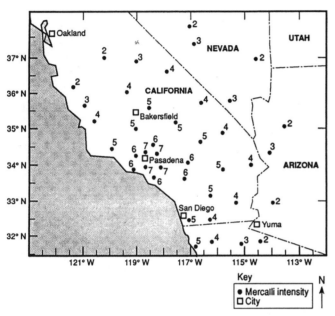

1 Using an interval of 2 Mercalli units and starting with an isoline representing 2 Mercalli units, draw an accurate isoline map of earthquake intensity.

2 State the name of the city that is closest to the earthquake epicenter.

3 State the latitude and longitude of Bakersfield.

4 Using one or more complete sentences, identify the most likely cause of earthquakes that occur in the area shown on the map.

Base your answers to questions 5 through 10 on your knowledge of Earth science, the *Reference Tables*, and the three seismograms shown below. The seismograms were recorded at earthquake recording stations *A*, *B*, and *C*. The letters *P* and *S* on each seismogram indicate the arrival times of the compressional (primary) and shear (secondary) seismic waves.

5 Tell which station is farthest from the epicenter and explain how that can be determined.

6 How far is station *B* from the epicenter?

7 Explain how the speeds of *P*- and *S*-waves enable a seismologist to determine the distance to an epicenter.

8 The radius of each circle on the map at the right represents the distance from each seismographic station to the epicenter. Label the points representing the three recording stations (*A*, *B*, *C*) to correctly illustrate the position of the seismographic stations relative to the earthquake epicenter.

9 A fourth station recorded the same earthquake. The *P*-wave arrived, but the *S*-wave did not arrive. What is a possible explanation for the absence of the *S*-wave?

10 The epicenter distance from station *A* was calculated to be 7,600 kilometers. Approximately how long did the *P*-wave take to get to station *A*?

Base your answers to questions 11 through 14 on your knowledge of Earth science, the *Reference Tables*, and the four seismograms shown below. The seismograms were recorded at earthquake recording stations *A*, *B*, *C*, and *D*. The letters *P* and *S* on each seismogram indicate the arrival times of the compressional (primary) and shear (secondary) seismic waves.

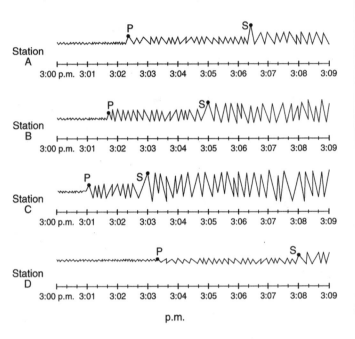

Base your answers to questions 15 through 18 on the *Earth Science Reference Tables*, the map below, and your knowledge of Earth Science. The map shows mid-ocean ridges and trenches in the Pacific Ocean. Specific areas *A*, *B*, *C*, and *D* are indicated by shaded rectangles.

11 Which seismogram was recorded closest to the epicenter? Explain one way you can tell.

12 How many kilometers is Station *A* from the epicenter?

13 List the stations in order of distance from the epicenter beginning with the closest.

14 More property damage occurred near the station second in distance from the epicenter than at the closest station. State one reason this might have occurred.

15 In one or more sentences, state the likely cause of the movement of the crustal plates.

16 The East Pacific Rise is an area of mid-ocean ridge. The crust at this location is composed mainly of what rock?

17 On the map, draw arrows on both sides of the East Pacific Rise indicating the direction of plate motion.

18 In one or more sentences, compare the plate motion in shaded rectangular Area *C* with the motion in Area *D*.

Base your answers to questions 19 through 22 on your knowledge of Earth science, the *Reference Tables*, and the diagrams which represent geologic cross sections of the upper mantle and crust at four different Earth locations. In each diagram, the movement of the crustal sections (plates) is indicated by arrows and the locations of frequent earthquakes are indicated by symbols as shown in the key. [Diagrams are not drawn to scale.]

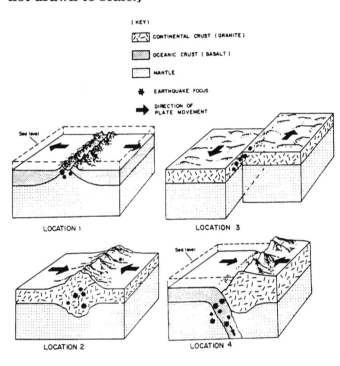

LOCATION 1

LOCATION 3

LOCATION 2

LOCATION 4

19 Explain why *Location 1* has primarily shallow focus earthquakes.

20 Which location would have some deep focus earthquakes? What is happening at this location that results in these deep focus earthquakes?

21 Which of the four locations most likely represents formation *X* in the profile shown below?

22 On the diagram below, draw arrows illustrating the motion of the convection currents in the mantle at this location.

UNIT FOUR

SURFACE PROCESSES & LANDSCAPES

VOCABULARY

weathering	erosion & gravity	fetch	graded & cross bed-	glacial till
sediment	transported sediment	wavelength	ding	erratics, moraines
physical weathering	residual sediment	crest & trough	mountain, plateau &	eskers, kames &
chemical weathering	transporting agent	surf and current	plain	drumlins
oxidation	abrasion	groins, jetties &	uplifting forces	kettle holes
carbonation	running water	beaches	leveling forces	outwash plain
hydration	stream channel	wave refraction	isostasy	rock resistance
weathering rate	discharge	mass wasting	The Great Ice Age	competent rocks
soil & soil association	meandering stream	colloid	arid & humid	incompetent rocks
soil composition	deposition	horizontal & vertical	glaciers	escarpment
parent material	dynamic equilibrium	sorting	Alpine glaciers	faults, folds, & joints
soil conservation	solution & suspension	landscape	Continental glaciers	drainage

A. WEATHERING

The physical and chemical processes that change the characteristics of rocks on the Earth's surface are called **weathering**. In order for weathering to occur, the physical environment of the rocks must change and the rocks must be exposed to the air, water in some form (ice, snow, or liquid), or the acts of humans or other living things. Therefore, weathering is the response of rocks to the change in their environment. Note: The longer the rocks are exposed to these weathering agents, the greater the degree of weathering.

EVIDENCE OF WEATHERING

Weathering Processes. When rocks are exposed to the hydrosphere and the atmosphere (water, air, and the substances within them), the physical and/or chemical composition and characteristics of the rocks can change. The end products of weathering are generally called **sediments** and are classified as boulders, cobbles, pebbles, sand, silt, clay, colloids, and dissolved particles (ionic minerals).

How is the Earth's crust affected by the environment?

Physical Weathering
Action of Freezing on Rocks

Physical Weathering. In physical weathering, rocks are broken into smaller pieces without changing the chemical nature of the rock. For example, a section of the surface of a mountain may break off because water freezes in a crack in the rock surface, expanding and splitting the rock. The falling rock mass may shatter into boulders and rocks of various sizes. Even though the rock has changed in physical form, it has not changed chemically and still maintains its original composition. The action of wind or water-carried sediment (erosion) may further abrade (wear away by rubbing) the surface of the rocks forming fine particles.

Chemical Weathering. In chemical weathering, rocks are broken, and the rock material itself is also changed. Examples of chemical weathering include:

- **oxidation** occurs when oxygen from the air combines with the minerals of the rock to form oxides (for example, iron and oxygen form iron oxide, rust).

Weathering Agents and **Erosional Processes**
tend to form caves in Limestone

Weathering Determined by Climate

- **carbonation** occurs when water containing carbonic acid dissolves the minerals of the rock (for example, the action of carbonic acid on limestone).

- **hydration** occurs when minerals, such as mica or feldspar, absorb water, weaken, and crumble to form clay.

CLIMATE AFFECTS WEATHERING

Climate affects both physical and chemical weathering. The chart above shows that climate tends to determine the amount, types, and/or rate of weathering. In cold and moist climates, physical weathering is dominant. In warm and humid climates, chemical weathering is dominant. In general, the more moisture available, the more weathering occurs.

WEATHERING RATES

Rock particles will weather at different rates depending on their mineral composition and its resistance to weathering agents. The harder the mineral, the slower the weathering. The softer the mineral, the faster the weathering.

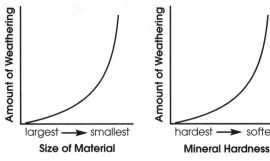

SOIL FORMATION

Soil is a combination of particles of rocks, minerals, and organic matter produced through weathering processes. Soil contains the materials necessary to support various plant and animal life.

As a result of the weathering processes and biologic activity, **soil horizons** (**layers**) develop. These soil horizons vary in depth depending on the amount of weathering, the time over which the weathering occurs, and the climate. Normally, the longer the weathering occurs, the greater the depth of the soil formation.

What are the products of weathering?

In addition to weathering, the complex interrelationships of living organisms are significant factors in soil formation. For example, the breakdown and decay of leaves from plants and the life activities of earthworms and other small animals aid in the formation of soil. In addition, the effects caused by frost, rain, and air add to the process of weathering.

Soil Formation Diagram of Immature Soil to Mature Soil

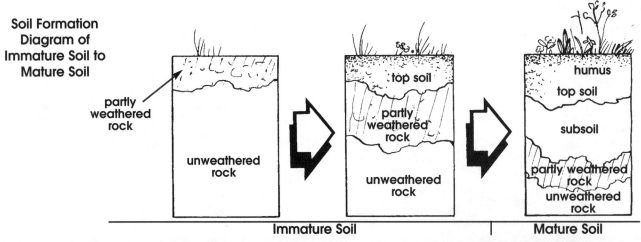

Immature Soil · Mature Soil

Soil associations differ in composition depending on the climate. The lack of large amounts of water in arid regions causes a general decrease in the vegetation and animal populations, thereby decreasing organic materials in the soil and producing only thin or poorly developed soils. Arid soils are often high in mineral salts since they are not dissolved and carried away (leached) by water. The soil of a humid region is usually high in organic materials, low in mineral salts, less sandy, and better capable of supporting large populations of plants and animals.

Different bedrock composition produces different **soil composition**. Although climate is the most important factor in the determination of soil type, soils formed from parent material of different minerals will have different chemical compositions.

Good soil is more valuable than gold, because fertile soil enables the production of food to support the Earth's growing population. Each year billions of tons of soil are eroded away or spoiled by human activities. Soils may be contaminated by salt from roads and the use of herbicides or other toxic chemicals. Construction, mining, and poor agricultural practices may cause rapid erosion. Since it frequently takes several hundred years to form one centimeter of soil, it is necessary for everyone to protect this essential resource by practicing proven methods of **soil conservation**.

B. Erosion

Erosion refers to the transportation of rock, soil, and mineral particles from one location to another by the action of water, wind, or ice. The motive power behind all of the agents of erosion is **gravity**. It is very important to note that a transporting system includes all of the agents involved in erosion and weathering, the transporting agent, energy, and the material moved.

> *What evidence suggests that rock materials are transported?*

Displaced Sediments

The major evidence of erosion is the displacement of sediments from their source to another location. The beaches that border the coastlines of the United States are the result of **transported sediment** (sand) from inland mountains, by streams and rivers, to the oceans. The mineral composition of sediments and organic remains (fossils) found with the sediments are often indications of the sources of the erosional products.

Residual sediment is the material that remains at the location of the weathering, and transported sediment is the erosional product that has been moved from the source of weathering to another location. In New York State, there are far more transported sediments than there are residual sediments.

Properties Of Transported Materials

The actions that affect erosion and move sediments from one place to another are called **transporting agents**. Transported materials often possess properties distinctive of their transporting medium. Therefore, it is often possible to determine what eroding force and transporting agent moved the sediment.

For example, water generally tends to smooth and round the rock particles. Cobblestones, often used in Colonial times as road beds because of their round and smooth characteristics, were the results of abrasion in streams.

The longer the water or wind action, the smoother and rounder the sediment becomes. Sediments moved by winds are often pitted, or "frosted," as a result of abrasion during their travel.

Glacial products often have surface scratches caused by being pushed and scraped by ice. When the action of gravity alone causes erosion, the sediments are sharp edged and angular. This evidence can be observed along highway road cuts and at the base of mountains.

Erosional and Transporting Agents

Factors Affecting Transportation

Gravity, water, wind, ice, and human activities are the main factors affecting the transportation of the sediments of weathering.

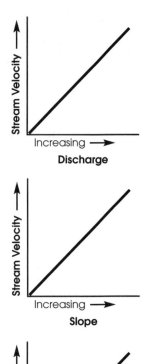

How are the products of weathering transported?

Gravity. Most all transporting systems are caused by gravity. Gravity may also act alone, such as when loose pieces of rock on the side of a slope break away and fall down hill. Gravity also acts with other transporting agents, such as when water transports sediments in a stream.

Water. Running water (stream) is the predominant agent of erosion on the Earth. As streams downcut the underlying bedrock, they initially carve V-shaped valleys. There are a number of factors which affect the way in which the running water of a stream transports sediment.

Water Velocity & Sediments

In a **stream channel**, the average velocity of the running water increases with an increase in the discharge. The **discharge** is the volume of water in the stream at any given location during a specific amount of time. Velocity and discharge of a stream are interdependent. In the spring, the streams usually move faster, because of the greater amount of water volume from melting snow and runoff.

The velocity of the water in a stream is directly proportional to the slope of a stream channel. As the slope of a stream increases, the velocity of the stream increases.

The fastest water flowing in a stream with a straight course is in the center just below the surface where friction is the least. However, in a meandering stream, the fastest water is on the outside of the curve or **meander** (such as A and C on the diagram below left), so that erosion is greatest on the outside of the meanders (again points A and C). Deposition takes place in the slower water on the inside of the meanders (such as at point D). Between the meanders is a "change-over" between erosion and deposition (such as point B).

Boundaries between erosion and deposition occur at various locations throughout the length of a stream. These interfaces are often found midstream in meanders and where changes in velocity occur near the mouths of streams. Where neither the process of erosion nor deposition is dominant, a state of dynamic equilibrium exists.

The greater the amount of friction a stream has with its bed or channel, the slower the water will flow. The most efficient channel is one that is smooth and has a semicircular shape.

Stream Velocity
Relationship between Stream Velocity and
(1) Water Discharge,
(2) Slope of the Stream Bed, and
(3) the Size of Particles carried by the stream.

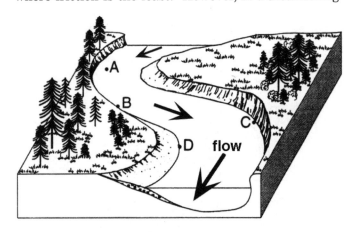

Relationship of Transported Particle Size to Water Velocity

As the velocity of the stream water increases, the size of the particles that can be moved by the stream also increases. Streams carry material in **solution** (dissolved), in **suspension** (colloids, clay, silt, and sand), and by rolling, bouncing, or dragging along the stream bed (pebbles, cobbles, and boulders).

WIND & ICE EROSION

Wind (such as a desert sand storm) and ice (such as a glacier) act as transporting agents for rock materials. The factors involved in wind and ice erosion are similar to the factors which affect running water erosion. The steeper the slope of a mountain, the faster a glacier will move. This enables it to carry larger erosional materials. Glaciers can transport the largest sized sediments (boulders). Light winds move only the smallest sediments, but strong winds may carry heavier and larger materials, such as sand, but rarely more than a meter or so above the ground.

OCEAN WAVES

Most of the ocean's surface waves are caused by the wind. The size of the waves is determined by wind speed, the length of time the wind blows in one direction and the distance the wind has blown across the water. This distance is known as the **fetch**.

Submarine earthquakes or landslides may generate **tsunamis**. Although these giant waves are often called "tidal waves," they are unrelated to tidal effects. Tsunamis can cause catastrophic loss of life and property damage.

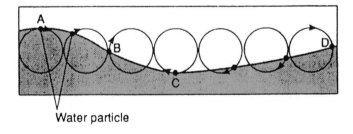

Water particle

Water Particles Rotate in Circular Paths in Waves

COASTAL PROCESSES

The top of a wave in open water is known as its **crest**, and the low point is the **trough**. **Wavelength** is the distance from one crest to the next and wave height is the vertical distance from the crest to the trough. As a wave moves through water, the water particles rise and fall in circular paths with little forward movement of the water until the wave gets close to shore.

When a wave reaches shallow water along the shore, friction causes the bottom of the wave to move more slowly than the crest, which falls over on the shore forming a breaker resulting in the foaming water called **surf**. The water from the breaking wave washes up on the shore as swash moving sand forward. As gravity pulls the water back, the backwash rolls beach materials toward the ocean.

As waves strike the shoreline at an angle, they form a **longshore current** in the **surf zone** which moves sediment parallel to the coast. The sands transported by these currents are deposited farther along the coast. Coastal communities may build walls, called **groins**, perpendicular to the shore to prevent the longshore currents from removing sand from their beaches. **Jetties**, much like groins, are rock barriers built on both sides of a harbor entrance to slow down sedimentation which would clog the entrance to the harbor.

Beaches vary in size, shape, and composition. Although a majority of beaches are made of sand, there are gravel, pebble, cobble and boulder beaches, named for the size of the particles. Beaches vary in color depending upon the parent material forming the sand. Black sand beaches may form and are made from basaltic lava. Pink and very white sand beaches are formed from shells and coral.

WAVE REFRACTION

As a line of waves approaches the shore it tends to bend and strike the shore "head on." The greatest force of the water strikes the headlands extending out into the water. The force of the waves striking the headlands breaks the rocks straightening the coastline. Erosion and deposition are constantly changing coastlines. Several meters of material may be removed by one violent storm.

MASS MOVEMENT

Mass movement or **mass wasting** occurs when soil and/or pieces of rock are pulled downslope. The movement may be rapid like a landslide or mudslide or slow like soil creep. Factors such as gradient, available moisture, and temperature variations all play a part in mass movement.

EFFECT OF HUMANS

Humans add greatly to the natural processes of land erosion through activities, such as highway and industrial construction, destruction of forests from the careless setting of forest fires and uncontrolled tree cutting without reforestation, strip mining, poor landfill projects, and other such activities.

C. DEPOSITION

Deposition is a part of the erosional-depositional system, in which sediments carried by a transporting agent are dropped from the medium because the system loses energy. Deposition is also called **sedimentation**. Since water is the predominant transporting agent, final deposition often occurs at the end of a stream, where the stream flows into a larger body of water, such as a lake or an ocean. Dissolved ionic minerals and colloids are released by the process of precipitation, and larger particles settle out of the transporting medium.

How are eroded materials deposited?

Density. Two particles of the same size and shape, but of different densities will settle at different rates. A high density particle will settle faster than a low density particle, since a high density particle is heavier.

Rapid Deposition in a Quiet Medium

Velocity. As the velocity of a **sediment laden flow** decreases, the particles of greater weight and density settle out first. This decreasing velocity results in **horizontal sorting** (see the illustration below). When a stream enters another body of water such as the ocean, the heavier particles settle out first, and the lighter particles settle farther out into the ocean.

FACTORS AFFECTING DEPOSITION

The major factors that affect the rate of deposition are particle size, shape and density, and the velocity of the transporting medium.

Size. The smaller particles settle more slowly than the larger particles, because as the velocity of a stream slows, the larger and usually heavier particles drop the fastest pulled down by gravity. The smaller particles tend to remain in suspension for longer periods of time, settling more slowly.

Sorting in a Quiet Medium

Colloids, particles approximately 10^{-4} to 10^{-6} millimeters across, generally remain in suspension indefinitely as long as there is even the slightest movement of the transporting medium.

When there is little or no movement in the transporting medium, sorting in a quiet medium (such as still-water or air) produces horizontal layers.

Graded Bedding in a Series of Depositions

If deposition is rapid, **graded bedding**, or **vertical sorting** occurs. The heavier, larger, and more dense particles settle first, followed by the smaller, lighter, and less dense particles. In general, the bottom of the stream bed will have the larger particles and the particle size will decrease toward the top of the stream bed.

The particles in a moving medium do not necessarily move at the same velocity as the transporting medium. Particle movement is usually slower than the transporting medium movement.

Colloidal particles in suspension tend to move at the same velocity as the stream, but particles that are more dense (heavier) or have a greater resistance (larger and flatter) often move at a slower velocity than the fluid transporting medium. Pebbles rolling along a stream bed travel slower than the water.

Shape. The other factors affecting deposition being equal, a round (spherical) shaped sediment particle will settle out of the transporting medium faster than a flat (disk) shaped particle. The greater the resistance of a flat particle causes it to settle more slowly.

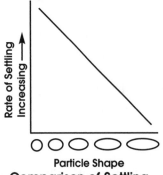

Comparison of Settling Rate & Particle Size

Horizontal Sorting

The cross section of the stream illustrates horizontal sorting showing that larger, rounder, high density particles settle out of decreasing water velocity the fastest.

Wind deposited sediments are most common in regions with arid or dry climates and along coastlines where sand dunes may form. Although the range of particle sizes deposited by the wind is smaller than those of other agents of erosion, the sediments still show the characteristic of sorting. Changes in direction of the wind may result in the layers or beds of sediment being deposited at different angles. This is called **crossbedding**.

In areas where strong winds carry sediment, rock formations, buildings, and other structures may show the effects of sandblasting.

Deposition made by gravity acting alone or by glacial ice is unsorted, since sediments of all sizes, shapes and densities are deposited together. Outwash, sediment deposited by the meltwaters of a glacier shows characteristics similar to stream deposits.

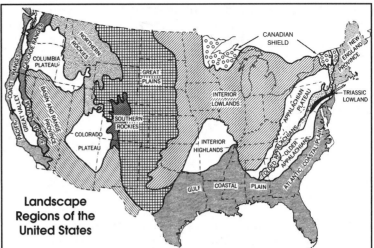

Landscape Regions of the United States

D. LANDSCAPE CHARACTERISTICS

Earth's landscapes are the results of the interaction of crustal materials, forces, climate, humans, and time.

How is the Earth's surface shaped by weathering, erosion, and deposition?

LANDSCAPE REGIONS

Distinctive landscape regions can be identified by sets of **landscape characteristics** that seem to occur together. Obviously, the landscape characteristics of Long Island (lowlands) region are expected to be different from the landscape of the Adirondack (mountains) region.

Generally, the boundaries between landscape regions are well defined. Landscape regions tend to be separated by mountains, large bodies of water, and other natural boundaries.

Since the continents are so large and usually bordering on oceans, they have several distinctive types of landscape regions. For example, the North American continent has regions that represent all of the major landscape regions of the Earth.

The major landscape regions of the continental United States include (west to east) the Pacific Mountain System, Intermountain Plateaus, Northern and Southern Rockies, Interior (Great) Plains, Interior Highlands and Lowlands, Laurentian Uplands, Appalachian Highlands, and Atlantic Coastal Plain.

The surface of New York State has many distinctive landscape regions because of a large number of bedrock variations. These include (north to south) Saint Lawrence Lowlands, Champlain Lowlands, Adirondack

Mountains – Landscape Regions

Landscapes may be classified as mountains, plains or plateaus. They may be distinguished from each other by their relief and internal rock structure. **Mountains** have high relief and deformed rock structures. **Plateaus** have moderate relief, high elevation, and horizontal rock structures. **Plains** are characterized by low relief and horizontal rock layers.

Generalized Landscape Regions of New York State

Key
— Major geographic province boundary
— Landscape region boundary
— · — State boundary
— · · — International boundary

Highlands (mountains), Tug Hill Plateau, Erie-Ontario Lowlands (plains), Allegheny Plateau, Hudson-Mohawk Lowlands, Taconic and New England Highlands, and the Atlantic Coastal Lowlands (plains).

ENVIRONMENTAL FACTORS

The **environmental factors** involved in landscape development, include uplifting and leveling forces (constructive and destructive, respectively), climate, bedrock characteristics, time, and human activities (positive and negative). There is a delicate balance between the multiple environmental factors in all landscapes. Any change in these factors results in a modification of the landscape and the establishment of a new equilibrium.

UPLIFTING & LEVELING FORCES

The two major forces which oppose each other in the formation of landscapes are the forces of uplifting and leveling– also called the constructional and destructional forces.

Uplifting forces are referred to as **constructional forces** because their affect is to build mountains, enlarge the continents, and increase the elevation of some landscape. The forces originate from within the Earth and include the forces of **diastrophism** (folding and faulting), earthquakes, volcanoes, and **isostasy**. The **forces of destruction**, **leveling forces**, include the processes of the erosional-depositional system, weathering, and subsidence. These are forces found working on the surface of the Earth which operate primarily because of gravity, removing, and transporting materials from higher elevations and depositing them at lower elevations.

In any particular landscape or at any specific time in the Earth's history, either the force of leveling or uplifting may be dominant in a region, depending on the rate at which the uplifting or leveling occurs. The rate of uplift or subsidence may result in a modification of landscape by altering hill slopes, the drainage patterns of mountain and river regions, or orographic wind patterns over various landscape regions.

What forces modify landscapes?

During the building of the Appalachian Mountains in the eastern United States, the force of uplifting was dominant. However, today the forces of leveling are dominant in that region since the elevation is decreasing. This change is because of weathering and erosion which are occurring faster than uplifting. In general, the uplifting forces are dominant where landscapes are increasing in elevation, and the forces of leveling are dominant when landscapes are becoming lower.

CLIMATIC EFFECTS ON LANDSCAPE DEVELOPMENT

The **climatic factors** of temperature and moisture greatly affect the rate of the change in characteristics of landscapes. A change in climate may result in a modification of the landscape. For example, some scientists are concerned over the effects caused by a build up of carbon dioxide in the atmosphere. They suggest that this increase may bring about an increase in the Earth's average temperatures, resulting in a general warming of the Earth's surface. This could cause the melting of the polar ice regions, raising the sea level, thereby flooding low lying continental regions. A change in moisture from arid to humid would increase the rate of weathering and erosion and cause an angular landscape to become more rounded.

The steepness of hill slopes in an area is affected by the balance between weathering and the removal of materials. This can be observed in the hill slopes of arid and humid regions. Since arid regions have less water erosion, the hill slopes are generally more steep

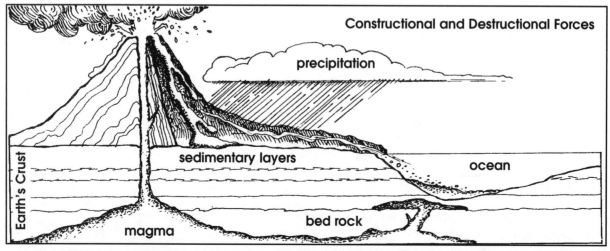

Constructional and Destructional Forces

precipitation

sedimentary layers

ocean

Earth's Crust

magma

bed rock

HUMID

ARID

Sea level

Climatic Effects on Landscapes

and angular, showing fewer signs of erosion. But in humid regions, there is more weathering, erosion, and deposition of materials causing rounded hills and less steep hill slopes **The Great Ice Age** is an example of an extreme climatic change modifying the landscape.

Stream characteristics are affected by the climate. If the climate is dry (**arid**), the streams are intermittent (seasonal) and the water is usually collected in basins, remaining in the region. In wet (**humid**) climates, the streams are permanent, usually flowing into rivers and eventually into large bodies of water. Therefore, in arid regions most of the weathered sediment remains near the source, but in humid regions the sediment is often transported far from the source of the weathering.

Glaciers are found at high altitudes and in the high latitudes, because these are the locations where more snow falls during the winter season than melts during the summer season. The snow accumulates and compaction and recrystallization changes it to glacial ice. The ice flows slowly out of these centers of accumulation or snow fields because of the force of gravity and weight of the ice. The ice always has a forward motion. The fastest ice flow occurs in the center of the glacier where there is the least friction with the valley walls. If the front of the ice appears to move backward or retreat, it is because the glacier is melting faster than it is moving forward.

Glaciers found in high mountains are called **Alpine glaciers**. These glaciers tend to make a rough, jagged landscape gouging out bowl-shaped **cirques** and u-shaped valleys and leaving **arêtes** (sharp ridges) and **horns** (pyramid-shaped mountains), as they move out of a snow field.

Continental glaciers are large ice sheets like those found in Antarctica and Greenland. As they move out from the center of accumulation, the tremendous weight of the thick ice tends to depress, scour, and round the land surface.

Striations on Limestone Bedrock
(Exposed in New York State)

As glaciers move, they carry, push, and drag huge amounts of **glacial till** (unsorted sediment). The sediment ranges in size from enormous boulders to the finest clay. Sediment frozen in the bottom of the glacial ice (the cutting tools) abrades the surface over which the glacier passes. Large fragments form parallel striations or grooves in the surface indicating the direction the glacier was moving. Finer sediment polishes the rock surface. The rounding of rock surfaces and glacial striations in both the Catskills and Adirondacks shows that the glacial ice that covered New York State buried the land at least one mile deep.

The melting ice left large boulders, called **erratics** scattered over the landscape. The rock type of an erratic may be so distinct as to enable scientists to trace the rock to its point of origin giving evidence of the direction of ice flow.

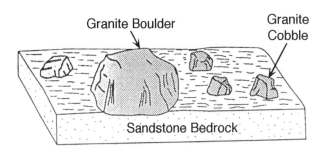

Granite Boulder

Granite Cobble

Sandstone Bedrock

Glacial Erratics

Glaciers have greatly altered the landscapes of New York State. In some areas glacial landscapes have many erosional features. These have been formed by the weight of the moving ice scraping, polishing, rounding, and depressing the land. Other areas are covered with depositional features made of sediment transported and deposited directly by the glacial ice or the meltwaters of the glacier.

River valleys through which glaciers have passed have been rounded into the characteristic U-shape of a **glacial valley**.

Glacial Valley

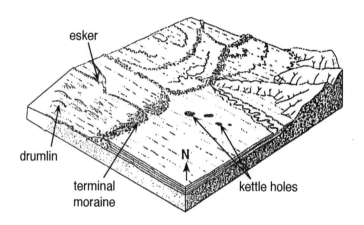

Glacial Features

Depositional features are made of unsorted glacial material called till or outwash which is sorted and deposited by glacial streams. Features made of till are called **moraines**. Often the surface is covered with ground moraine which has been deposited under the glacier. A ridge marking the farthest advance of the ice is called a terminal moraine. Winding ridges of glacial material deposited in streams within or below the ice are **eskers**. **Kames** are cone-shaped hills formed along the ice front while drumlins are elongated hills shaped like the back of a spoon.

A broad area in front of the **terminal moraine** deposited by water from the melting glacier is an outwash plain. **Kettle holes** are depressions resulting from melting blocks of ice that were buried in either the moraine or outwash.

GLACIAL HISTORY

Layers of weathered till, buried under other layers of weathered till, show that there have been several periods of glaciation during the Pleistocene Epoch. New York State experienced a series of glacial and interglacial periods.

Features resulting from glacial erosion and deposition may be seen over most of Northeast United States. The north-south trending valleys of the Finger Lakes show river valleys widened by glacial erosion and dammed up by the deposition of moraine.

Swarms of **drumlins**, hills shaped like the back of a spoon, are found on the Lake Ontario Plain. The alignment of these drumlins indicates the direction of ice movement.

The northern ridge forming Long Island is terminal moraine, marking the farthest advance of the glacier. The southern part of Long Island is composed of outwash plain made from layers of horizontally deposited sorted material left behind by the water from the melting ice front. Lake Ronkonkoma is an example of a kettle lake left by a large mass of melting ice buried in the glacial sediment.

Almost all of New York State was covered by the ice sheet originating in Labrador. The water from this melting ice deposited gravel and sand in large sorted and layered deposits. These deposits are an important geological resource in the economy of New York State.

In addition to changing the landscape, the ice age in the northern United States caused the migration of animals and changes in the animal and plant communities. Most of the soils found in New York State and Pennsylvania are thin, rocky, and poorly developed, made of weathered glacial till.

As glaciers grew and the ice advanced, sea level dropped because of the increased amount of water being held as ice. Pleistocene fossil evidence shows that, during this time, the continental shelf off Long Island was exposed and was inhabited by terrestrial (land) organisms. As the ice gradually melted during the interglacial periods, sea level rose again returning the continental shelf to a marine environment.

Clues to prehistoric conditions on Earth are gathered by studying cores of glacial ice collected from deep within glaciers. Some of this ice formed centuries ago trapping air, dust, and pollen from the distant past.

Glacial Erosion
New York State Finger Lakes Result of Glacial Erosion of River Valleys

BEDROCK EFFECT
ON LANDSCAPE DEVELOPMENT

The rate at which landscape development occurs may be influenced by the bedrock of the region. Different landscape regions have various kinds of bedrock. Rock resistance is the ability of different rock types to resist the forces of weathering and erosion. For example, where hard bedrock is exposed to the environment, only a small amount of weathering and erosion occurs. This is because the hard bedrock is more resistant to the forces of weathering and erosion than softer kinds of bedrock.

Samples Of Bed Rock Resistance

Nonsedimentary Bedrock
Mountain Building (non-existent leveling)

Bedrock
Varying Resistance (escarpments)

Sedimentary Bedrock
(plateau)

Complex Bedrock
(faulting and variations of leveling)

Where bedrock with varying degrees of rock resistance occur together, the softer bed rocks are weathered and eroded at a faster rate than the more resistant bedrock. The landscape surface is less regular than when there is a rock with a consistent resistance to weathering.

The shape and steepness of hills are affected by the local bedrock composition. **Competent rocks** (resistant to weathering and erosion) are responsible for the development of plateaus (high, stable landscapes with little or no distortion), mountains, and escarpments. These areas often have slow rates of change.

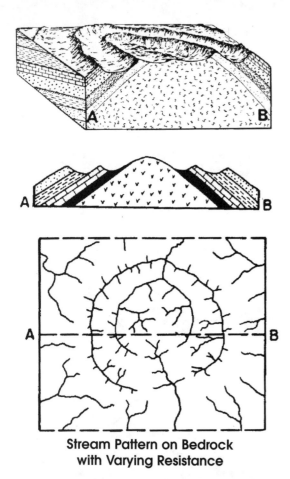

Stream Pattern on Bedrock
with Varying Resistance

Weak or **incompetent rocks** (poor resistance to weathering and erosion) usually underlie valleys and other low level areas. Meandering streams, thick soil horizons, and deep layering usually characterize weak rock areas.

The difference between competent and weak areas can be observed in an **escarpment**, which is a steep slope separating two gently sloping surfaces. Many escarpments are the result of weathering forces on slopes with rocks of different resistance.

Structural features in bedrock, such as **faults**, **folds**, and **joints**, frequently affect the development of hill slopes. Generally, the more distortion in the rock mass of the hill slope, the greater the variety of changes occurring in the surface. The weathering effect is varied, since faults, folds, and joints expose rocks with different resistance to the forces of change.

Annular
Drainage

Radial
Drainage

Stream characteristics, including gradient (slope), width and depth, and drainage pattern and direction of flow, are controlled by bedrock characteristics. When the resistance of the bedrock over which the stream flows is consistent, a random drainage pattern forms, called dendritic drainage. Trellis drainage forms in regions of parallel folds and/or faults, whereas radial drainage is associated with volcanic cones and young domes. Annular (ring-shaped) drainage develops on domes as they become eroded.

Dendritic
Drainage

Trellis
Drainage

TIME AFFECT ON LANDSCAPE DEVELOPMENT

The stage of development of a landscape is determined by the duration of time during which environmental factors have been active. Older landscapes generally show more effects of weathering and erosion than do younger landscapes.

AFFECT ON LANDSCAPE DEVELOPMENT

The activities of humans have altered the landscapes in many areas. Humans have modified landscapes both in negative and positive ways.

NEGATIVE AFFECTS BY HUMANS ON THE LANDSCAPE

Both intentional and unintentional technological oversights have brought about unplanned consequences that have destroyed or reduced the quality of life in many landscape regions. In some cases, technological advances have produced waste products which humans do not know how to dispose of safely. In other cases, industrial wastes are disposed of carelessly and/or criminally.

Agricultural lands, water sources, grazing grasslands for livestock, and forests have been so badly misused as to have resulted in the starvation and extinction of total populations of plants and animals.

High population density areas are the most affected regions because of the concentration of the landscape pollution or the misuse of the landscape.

POSITIVE AFFECTS BY HUMANS ON LANDSCAPE

Positive affects of human activities on landscapes have come through an increased awareness of various ecological and landscape interactions. Humans have begun to intervene in the widespread destruction, through the efforts of individuals, community groups, and conservation clubs. There are attempts to clean up toxic waste dumps, reclaim wasted lands, and prevent continued disruption of the environment.

QUESTIONS FOR UNIT 4

1 The principal cause of the chemical weathering of rocks on the Earth's surface is
   1 rock abrasion
   2 the heating and cooling of surface rock
   3 mineral reactions with air and water
   4 the expansion of water as it freezes

2 Which type of climate causes the fastest chemical weathering?
   1 cold and dry   3 hot and dry
   2 cold and humid   4 hot and humid

3 Which factor has the least effect on the weathering of a rock?
   1 climatic conditions
   2 composition of the rock
   3 exposure of the rock to the atmosphere
   4 the number of fossils found in the rock

4 Water is a major agent of chemical weathering because water
   1 cools the surroundings when it evaporates
   2 dissolves many of the minerals that make up rocks
   3 has a density of about one gram per cubic centimeter
   4 has the highest specific heat of all common earth materials

5 The diagram below represents a geologic cross section.

Which rock type appears to have weathered and eroded the most?

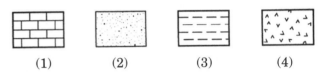

    (1)   (2)   (3)   (4)

6 The diagram below shows a process of weathering called frost wedging.

Frost wedging breaks rocks because as water freezes it increases in
   1 density
   2 specific heat
   3 mass
   4 volume

Note: Question 7 has only 3 choices.

7 As the humidity of a region decreases, the amount of weathering taking place usually
   1 decreases
   2 increases
   3 remains the same

8　According to the *Reference Tables*, which stream velocity would transport cobbles, but would not transport boulders?
(1) 50 cm/sec (3) 200 cm/sec
(2) 100 cm/sec (4) 400 cm/sec

9　A river transports material by suspension, rolling, and
1　solution 3　evaporation
2　sublimation 4　transpiration

10　Which is the best evidence that erosion has occurred?
1　a soil rich in lime on top of a limestone bedrock
2　a layer of basalt found on the floor of the ocean
3　a large number of fossils embedded in limestone
4　sediments found in a sand bar of a river

11　In the diagram below, the arrow shows the direction of stream flow around a bend.

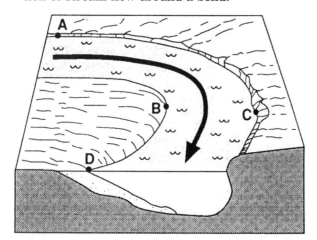

At which point does the greatest stream erosion occur?
(1) A (3) C
(2) B (4) D

12　The composition of sediments on the Earth's surface usually is quite different from the composition of the underlying bedrock. This observation suggests that most
1　bedrock is formed from sediments
2　bedrock is resistant to weathering
3　sediments are residual
4　sediments are transported

13　Which change would cause the topsoil in New York State to increase in thickness?
1　an increase in slope
2　a decrease in rainfall
3　an increase in biologic activity
4　a decrease in air temperature

14　The diagram below shows a soil profile formed in an area of granite bedrock. Four different soil horizons (layers), *A*, *B*, *C*, and *D*, are shown.

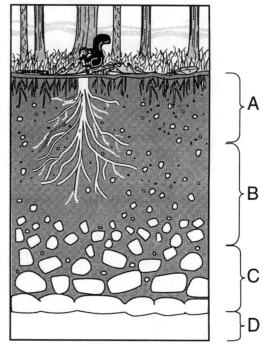

Which soil horizon contains the greatest amount of material formed by biological activity?

(1) *A*　(2) *B*　(3) *C*　(4) *D*

15　The cross section below shows residual soils that developed on rock outcrops of metamorphic quartzite and sedimentary limestone.

Which statement best explains why the soil is thicker above the limestone than it is above the quartzite?
1　The quartzite formed from molten magma.
2　The limestone is thicker than the quartzite.
3　The quartzite is older than the limestone.
4　The limestone is less resistant to weathering than the quartzite.

16　Which statement best describes a stream with a steep gradient?
1　It flows slowly, producing a V-shaped valley.
2　It flows slowly, producing a U-shaped valley.
3　It flows rapidly, producing a V-shaped valley.
4　It flows rapidly, producing a U-shaped valley.

17 The cartoon above presents a humorous view of Earth science. The cartoon character on the right realizes that the sand castle will eventually be
1   compacted into solid bedrock
2   removed by agents of erosion
3   preserved as fossil evidence
4   deformed during metamorphic change

18 The graph below shows how environmental temperatures affect the amount of organic material (humus) added to and removed from soils in humid regions.

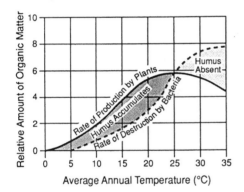

The graph supports the conclusion that soils in regions with average annual temperatures above 25° C have
1   little humus present
2   the highest production of humus
3   a low breakdown of humus
4   the same amount of humus as soils in cooler regions

19 What change will a pebble usually undergo when it is transported a great distance by streams?
1   It will become jagged and its mass will decrease.
2   It will become jagged and its volume will increase.
3   It will become rounded and its mass will increase.
4   It will become rounded and its volume will decrease.

20 The map at the right represents a river as it enters a lake. At which locations is the amount of deposition greater than the amount of erosion?

(1) A, C, and E   (3) B, D, and F
(2) B, C, and F   (4) A, D, and E

21 A stream is entering the calm waters of a large lake. Which diagram best illustrates the pattern of sediments being deposited in the lake from the stream flow?

(1)

(2)

(3)

(4)

22 If all the particles illustrated have the same mass and density, which particle will settle fastest in quiet water? [Assume settling takes place as shown by arrows.]

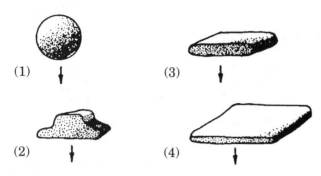

(1) (2) (3) (4)

23 Why do particles carried by a river settle to the bottom as the river enters the ocean?
 1 The density of the ocean water is greater than the density of the river water.
 2 The kinetic energy of the particles increases as the particles enter the ocean.
 3 The velocity of the river water decreases as it enters the ocean.
 4 The large particles have a greater surface area than the small particles.

24 The velocity of a stream is decreasing. As the velocity approaches zero, which size particle will most likely remain in suspension?

 1 pebble   3 clay
 2 sand   4 boulder

25 Small spheres that are identical in shape and size are composed of one of four different kinds of substances: A, B, C, or D. The spheres are mixed together and poured into a clear plastic tube filled with water.

Which property of the spheres caused them to settle in the tube as shown in the diagram?

 1 their shape
 2 their size
 3 their density
 4 their hardness

Base your answers to questions 26 and 27 on the diagram and your knowledge of Earth science.

Equipment used to measure settling times of the particles illustrated

26 Which graph below best represents the effect of particle size on settling time if the particle densities are the same?

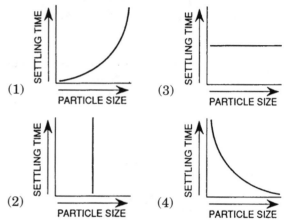

(1) (2) (3) (4)

27 All three sediments in the diagram are placed in the cylinder with water, the mixture is shaken, and the particles are allowed to settle. Which diagram best represents the order in which the particles settled?

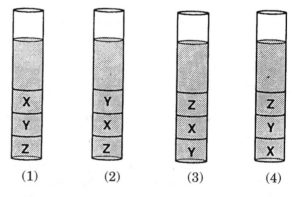

(1) (2) (3) (4)

28 Which is the most common source of energy for surface ocean waves?
 1 the Earth's rotation
 2 disturbances of the ocean bottom
 3 planetary winds
 4 heat flow and seafloor spreading

Base your answers to questions 29 and 30 on the diagram which shows the movement of water particles in ocean waves. The particles are represented by black dots. Letters *A*, *B*, *C*, and *D* are points of reference.

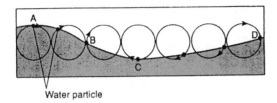

Water particle

29 The passage of a wave will cause a particle of water at the surface to
1   move horizontally, only
2   move vertically, only
3   move in a circular path
4   remain stationary

30 The wave pattern shown in the diagram would occur most often in
1   a longshore current parallel to a coastline
2   shallow water in the breaker zone of a beach
3   a turbidity current
4   deep water

Base your answers to questions 31 through 34 on the profile below. Four zones within the profile are labeled. The profile shows ocean waves approaching a beach. The circles show the motion of water beneath the wave.

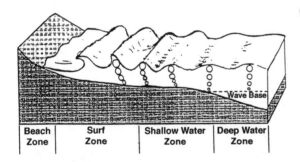

| Beach Zone | Surf Zone | Shallow Water Zone | Deep Water Zone |

31 In which zone is sand most likely to be moving along the shore?
1   deep water zone
2   shallow water zone
3   surf zone
4   beach zone

Note: Question 32 has only 3 choices.

32 If a strong coastal storm with high wind speed moves into the region, the wave heights are likely to
1   increase
2   decrease
3   remain the same

33 The sand on this beach has its origin from the weathering of granite bedrock. According to the *Earth Science Reference Tables*, a mineral that is likely to be found in the sand is
1   quartz   3   halite
2   calcite   4   olivine

34 The major source of sediments found on the deep ocean bottom is
1   erosion of continental rocks
2   submarine landslides from the mid-ocean ridges
3   icebergs that have broken off glaciers
4   submarine volcanic eruptions

35 Which diagram best represents a cross section of a valley which was glaciated and then eroded by a stream?

  (1)   (3)

  (2)   (4)

Base your answers to questions 36 through 38 on the diagram, the *Reference Tables*, and your knowledge of Earth science. The diagram represents a glacier moving out of a mountain valley. The water from the melting glacier is flowing into a lake. Letters *A* through *F* identify points within the erosional-depositional system.

36 Deposits of unsorted sediments would probably be found at location
(1) *E*   (3) *C*
(2) *F*   (4) *D*

37 An interface between erosion and deposition by the ice is most likely located between points
(1) *A* and *B*   (3) *C* and *D*
(2) *B* and *C*   (4) *D* and *E*

38 Colloidal-sized sediment particles carried by water are most probably being deposited at point
(1) *F*　　　　　(3) *C*
(2) *B*　　　　　(4) *D*

39 Four samples of aluminum, *A*, *B*, *C*, and *D*, have identical volumes and densities, but different shapes. Each piece is dropped into a long tube filled with water. The time each sample takes to settle to the bottom of the tube is shown in the table.

Sample	Time to Settle (sec)
A	2.5
B	3.7
C	4.0
D	5.2

Which diagram most likely represents the shape of sample *A*?

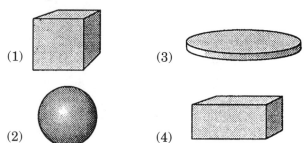

(1)　　　　　(3)

(2)　　　　　(4)

40 One characteristic used to classify landscape regions as plains, plateaus, or mountains is
1　type of soil
2　amount of stream discharge
3　weathering rate
4　underlying bedrock structure

41 Which cross-sectional diagram best represents a landscape region that resulted from faulting?

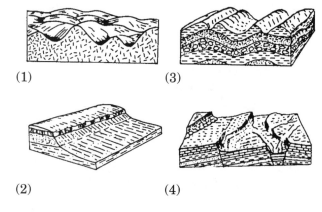

(1)　　　　　(3)

(2)　　　　　(4)

42 An area of gentle slopes and rounded mountaintops is most likely because of
1　climatic conditions
2　earthquakes
3　the age of the bedrock
4　the amount of folding

43 The diagram below represents the surface topography of a mountain valley.

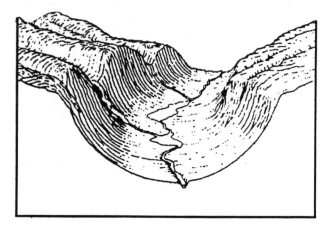

Which agent of erosion most likely created the shape of the valley shown in the diagram?
1　wind　　　　　3　ocean waves
2　glaciers　　　4　running water

Base your answers to questions 44 through 48 on your knowledge of Earth science and the diagram which represents a geologic cross section in which no overturning has occurred. The letters identify regions in the cross section.

44 The surface features in region *A* were produced primarily as a result of the process of
1　folding　　　　3　erosion
2　faulting　　　4　glaciation

45 Which type of crustal movement is shown in region B?
1　faulting　　　　3　jointing
2　volcanic eruption　4　folding

46 Which region shows the typical characteristics of plateau
(1) *A*　　　　　(3) *C*
(2) *B*　　　　　(4) *D*

47 Which region is least likely to have fossils in the surface bedrock?
(1) *A*　　　　　(3) *C*
(2) *B*　　　　　(4) *D*

48 Which stream drainage pattern would most likely be found on the surface of region C?

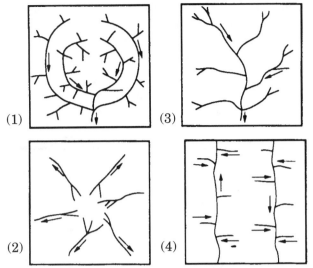

(1) (3)

(2) (4)

49 Which kind of stream pattern would most likely be found on the type of landscape shown in the diagram?

(1) (3)

(2) (4)

Base your answers to question 50 on the diagram below that shows the surface landscape features and the internal rock structure of a cross section of the Earth's crust.

50 How would this region most likely appear immediately after undergoing a period of glaciation?

(1) (3)

(2) (4)

51 The diagrams below represent geologic cross sections from two widely separated regions.

The layers of rock appear very similar, but the hillslopes and shapes are different. These differences are most likely the result of
1   volcanic eruptions
2   earthquake activity
3   soil formation
4   climate variations

52 Which change is most likely to occur in a landscape region that is uplifted rapidly by folding?
1   The climate will become warmer.
2   The stream drainage patterns will change.
3   The composition of the bedrock will change.
4   The hillslopes will become less steep.

53 The diagram below represents a cross section showing glacial deposition on top of solid bedrock.

The evidence suggests that the maximum elevation of glacial deposition prior to erosion by the stream is
(1)   100 ft   (3)   300 ft
(2)   200 ft   (4)   700 ft

54 The diagrams below represent profiles of four different landscapes, *A*, *B*, *C*, and *D*.

KEY

Base your answers to questions 57 through 59 on the *Earth Science Reference Tables*, the diagram below, and your knowledge of Earth science. The diagram shows a cross section of the Grand Canyon. The rock type of layer *X* has been purposely left blank.

Which landscape is most likely to have a noticeable change in its profile after a heavy rainstorm?

(1) *A* (3) *C*
(2) *B* (4) *D*

55 The block diagrams below show a river and its landscape during four stages of erosion.

In which order should the diagrams be placed to show the most likely sequence of river and landscape development?

(1) *A, D, B, C* (3) *C, B, A, D*
(2) *B, D, C, A* (4) *D, A, C, B*

56 In which type of landscape are meandering streams most likely found?
1 gently sloping plains
2 regions of waterfalls
3 steeply sloping hills
4 V-shaped valleys

57 The Grand Canyon is primarily the result of erosion caused by
1 wind
2 volcanic activity
3 glaciers
4 running water

58 The most probable explanation for the development of the steep Redwall cliffs is that this limestone layer
1 is more resistant to erosion than the rock layers above and below the cliffs
2 was deposited in a marine environment
3 was uplifted by the granite intrusion
4 is younger than the rock layers above the cliffs

59 The diagram shows a geologic cross section of the rock layers in the vicinity of Niagara Falls in western New York State.

Which statement best explains the irregular shape of the rock face behind the falls?
1 The Lockport dolostone is an evaporite.
2 The Clinton limestone and shale contain many fossils.
3 The Thorold sandstone and the whirlpool sandstone dissolve easily in water.
4 The Rochester and Queenston shale and the Albion sandstone and shale are less resistant to erosion than the other rock layers.

60 The landscape shown below developed in a region with an arid climate.

If the erosion of this plateau had taken place in a much more humid climate, which diagram below best represents how the landscape would appear?

(1)

(2)

(3)

(4)

61 Which cross section best represents the general bedrock structure of New York State's Allegheny Plateau?

(1)   (3)

(2)   (4)

62 The map below shows the location of an ancient sea, which evaporated to form the Silurian-age deposits of rock salt and rock gypsum now found in some New York State bedrock.

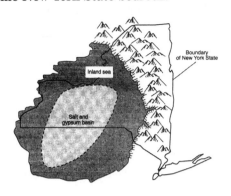

Within which two landscape regions are these large rock salt and rock gypsum deposits found?

1   Hudson Highlands and Taconic Mountains
2   Tug Hill Plateau and Adirondack Mountains
3   Erie-Ontario Lowlands and Allegheny Plateau
4   Catskills and Hudson-Mohawk Lowlands

63 At the present time, glaciers occur mostly in areas of
1   high latitude or high altitude
2   low latitude or low altitude
3   middle latitude and high altitude
4   middle latitude and low altitude

64 Over the past 2 million years, which erosional agent has been most responsible for producing the present landscape surface features of New York State?
1   groundwater
2   wind
3   glaciation
4   human activities

65 What was one of the major effects of the continental glaciers on the landscapes of New York State?
1   They formed numerous sharp mountain peaks and knife-edged ridges.
2   They folded many of the rock layers.
3   They deposited a covering of transported rock material over most of the state.
4   They carved the wide U-shaped valleys into narrow V-shaped valleys.

66 The Adirondack Highlands landscape region was formed primarily by
1   changes in the water levels of the Great Lakes
2   erosion by the Hudson and Mohawk Rivers
3   mountain building and glacial erosion
4   wind erosion in an arid climate

67 Which is the best evidence that more than one glacial advance occurred in a region?
1 ancient forests covered by glacial deposits
2 river valleys buried deeply in glacial deposits
3 scratches in bedrock that is buried by glacial deposits
4 glacial deposits that overlay soils formed from glacial deposits

68 The formation of the Finger Lakes of central New York State and the formation of Long Island are both examples of
1 climatic changes resulting in a modification of the landscape
2 uplifting and leveling forces being in dynamic equilibrium
3 soils differing in composition depending upon the bedrock composition
4 activities of man altering the landscape

69 The diagram represents a landscape and bedrock section of an area of central New York State

clay, sand and gravel

sedimentary rocks

4.0 km.
(Not drawn to scale)

The present surface landscape of this area was produced chiefly by
1 faulting   3 volcanic activity
2 folding   4 glaciation

70 The diagram illustrates the formation of a
1 plunge pool
2 kettle hole
3 sinkhole lake
4 finger lake

ICE

OUTWASH   TILL

71 Wooden stakes were placed on a glacier in a straight line as represented by A–A' in the diagram below. The same stakes were observed later in the positions represented by B–B'.

The pattern of movement of the stakes provides evidence that
1 glacial ice does not move
2 glacial ice is melting faster than it accumulates
3 the glacier is moving faster in the center than on the sides
4 friction is less along the sides of the glacier than in the center

72 Which observation LEAST supports inferences that New York State was covered in the recent past by great sheets of ice?
1 boulders on hilltops
2 increased average annual temperatures
3 stream valleys that have been widened and deepened
4 soils foreign to the bedrock beneath them

73 This section of Long Island shows considerable evidence of

1 Precambrian metamorphism
2 Pleistocene glaciation
3 Triassic intrusions
4 Permian mountain building

74 The graph below shows the average temperature of the Earth during the past 250,000 years and the beginning and end of the most recent glacial and interglacial stages.

According to the graph, the duration of the last glacial stage was from
(1) 250,000 years ago to 240,000 years ago
(2) 240,000 years ago to 120,000 years ago
(3) 120,000 years ago to 10,000 years ago
(4) 10,000 years ago to the present

75 Which force is primarily responsible for the movement of a glacier?
1 ground water
2 running water
3 wind
4 gravity

76 The front of an active glacier is observed to be stationary. Which statement best explains this observation?
1 The ice is not moving at all.
2 The ice is melting as fast as it advances.
3 The ice is advancing faster than it melts.
4 The ice is melting faster than it advances.

77 A glacial deposit would most likely consist of
1 particles in a wide range of sizes
2 particles the size of pebbles and larger
3 sediments in flat, horizontal layers
4 sediments found only in the bottoms of stream valleys

78 Because of glaciation, New York State presently has soils that are best describe as
1 deep and residual
2 rich in gemstone minerals
3 unchanged by glaciation
4 thin and rocky

79 Which landscape region is a flat plain consisting mainly of unsorted clays, gravels, sands, scratched pebbles, boulders, and cobbles?
1 the Adirondacks   3 the Catskills
2 Long Island   4 the Taconics

80 Which event would most likely cause a new ice age in North America?
1 a decrease in the energy produced by the Sun
2 a decrease in the light reflected by the surface of the Earth
3 an increase of carbon dioxide in the Earth's atmosphere
4 an increase in the westward drift of the North American continent

81 Which statement presents the best evidence that a boulder-sized rock is an erratic?
1 The boulder has a rounded shape.
2 The boulder is larger than surrounding rocks.
3 The boulder differs in composition from the underlying bedrock.
4 The boulder is located near potholes.

82 The direction of movement of a glacier is best indicated by the
1 elevation of erratics
2 alignment of grooves in bedrock
3 size of kettle lakes
4 amount of deposited sediments

Base your answers to questions 83 through 85 on the diagrams below. The diagrams represent glacial events in the geologic history of the Yosemite Valley region in California.

83 Which diagram most likely represents the most recent stage of landscape development?
(1) A   (3) C
(2) B   (4) D

84 Which features currently found in this region are the result of glaciation?
1 intrusions of volcanic rock
2 deep U-shaped canyons with steep sides
3 fossils of marine organisms
4 thick soils covering all rock surfaces

85 Which natural resource of economic value would most likely be found in this region?
1 rock salt
2 petroleum
3 natural gas
4 sand and gravel

86 A deposit of rock particles that are scratched and unsorted has most likely been transported and deposited by
1 wind   3 running water
2 glacial ice   4 ocean waves

87 Which statement identifies a result of glaciation that has had a positive effect on the economy of New York State?
1 Large amounts of oil and natural gas were formed.
2 The number of usable water reservoirs was reduced.
3 Many deposits of sand and gravel were formed.
4 Deposits of fertile soil were removed.

88 Another ice age would probably result in a change in
1 sea level
2 Moon phases
3 the speed of the Earth in its orbit
4 the time between high tides

91 Which state would show the smallest percentage of its surface area covered by glacial deposits?
1 Connecticut (CT)
2 Vermont (VT)
3 Pennsylvania (PA)
4 Massachusetts (MA)

92 In which two landscape regions are most of the moraine deposits shown on the map located?
1 Adirondack Mountains and the Catskill Mountains
2 Allegheny Plateau and the Atlantic Coastal Plain
3 Tug Hill Plateau and the Erie-Ontario Lowlands
4 The Atlantic Coastal Plain and the St. Lawrence Lowlands

Base your answers to questions 89 through 92 on the map of New York State and surrounding areas shown below. The short lines indicate the location and direction of streamline features such as drumlins and glacial striations. The moraine deposits and drumlins consist of glacial till.

89 The glacial ice that caused the deposits in the region south of Lake Ontario and north of the Finger Lakes most likely came from which general direction
1 north   3 southwest
2 southeast   4 west

90 According to the *Earth Science Reference Tables*, during which geologic time interval were the glacial deposits in New York State most likely formed?
1 Mesozoic   3 Pleistocene
2 Jurassic   4 Paleocene

Base your answers to questions 93 through 96 on the map below and on your knowledge of Earth science. The map shows the southernmost advance of four major stages of continental glaciation in the central United States. White area represent land once covered by glacial ice. The general direction of ice movement was from north to south.

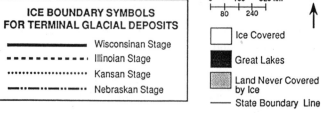

93 The landforms that mark the terminal glacial boundaries are made up of
1 residual soil particles resting on a flat plain
2 rounded grains in a sand dune
3 layered clay particles on a flat plain
4 unsorted gravel in low hills

94 Which state was partly or completely covered by glacial ice during all four stages of ice advance?
1 Iowa
2 Kansas
3 Kentucky
4 Missouri

95 Which map best represents the southernmost advance of the continental ice sheet during the Wisconsinan Stage?

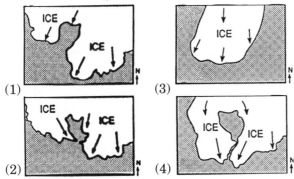

(1)   (3)
(2)   (4)

96 What evidence found on the former ice-covered areas would best show the direction of continental glacial movement?
1 resistant folded metamorphic bedrock
2 high-temperature igneous and volcanic bedrock
3 parallel scratches and grooves in the bedrock
4 bedrock containing fossils of animals that lived in cold water

Base your answers to questions 97 through 100 on the map below and on your knowledge of Earth science. The map shows the inferred position of the continental ice sheet in New York State approximately 12,000 years ago.

97 Which evidence would have been most useful to geologists for locating the edges of the ice sheet shown on the map?
1 flat, thick deposits of impermeable clay
2 piles of unlayered, unsorted sediment
3 folded layers of bedrock
4 formations of rocks with interlocking crystals

98 Which map best represents the inferred position of the ice sheet at the time of glacial deposition on Long Island? [The shaded portion represents the areas covered by glacial ice.]

(1)

(2)

(3)

(4)

99 Which fossil found in sediments in New York State support the inference that these sediments were deposited during the Pleistocene Epoch?
1 eurypterid fossils
2 stromatolite mounds
3 mastodont bones
4 coelophysis footprints

100 The record of glaciation in New York State provides a source of information about
1 changes in bedrock composition
2 changes in the global climate
3 movements of crustal plates
4 plants and animals from the Paleozoic Era

CONSTRUCTED RESPONSE

Base your answers to questions 1 through 6 on the data table below. Samples of three different rock materials, A, B, and C, were placed in three containers of water and shaken vigorously for 20 minutes. At 5-minute intervals, the contents of each container were strained through a sieve. The mass of the materials remaining in the sieve was measured and recorded as shown in the data table below.

Mass of Material Remaining in Sieve

Shaking Time (minutes)	Rock Material A (grams)	Rock Material B (grams)	Rock Material C (grams)
0	25.0	25.0	25.0
5	24.5	20.0	17.5
10	24.0	18.5	12.5
15	23.5	17.0	7.5
20	23.5	12.5	5.0

Directions: Using the information in the data table, construct a line graph on the grid at the right, following the directions below.

1 Plot the data for rock sample A for the 20 minutes of the investigation. Surround each point with a small circle and connect the points.

2 Plot the data for rock sample B for the 20 minutes of the investigation. Surround each point with a small triangle and connect the points.

3 Plot the data for rock sample C for the 20 minutes of the investigation. Surround each point with a small square and connect the points.

4 Using one or more complete sentences, state the most likely reason for the differences in the weathering rate of the three rock materials.

5 Using the directions in parts a through c below, calculate the average rate of change in the mass of rock material C for the 20 minutes of shaking.

  a Write the equation for rate of change in mass.

  b Substitute data into the equation.

  c Calculate the rate of change in mass and label your answer with proper units.

6 Using one or more complete sentences, describe the most likely appearance of the corners and edges of rock material C at the end of the 20 minutes.

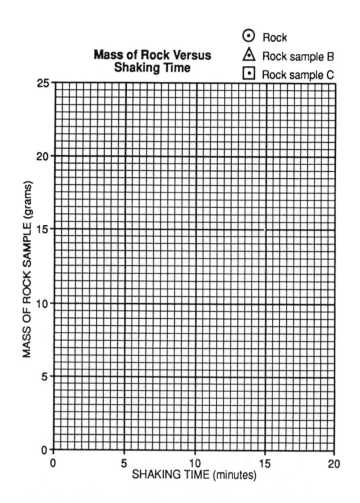

⊙ Rock
△ Rock sample B
⊡ Rock sample C

Mass of Rock Versus Shaking Time

Base your answers to questions 7 through 10 on your knowledge of Earth Science, the *Reference Tables*, and the graph below. The graph was prepared from the results of a study of four different types of cemetery monuments. The graph shows the relationship between the ages of the four monuments and the percentage of each stone which has weathered away.

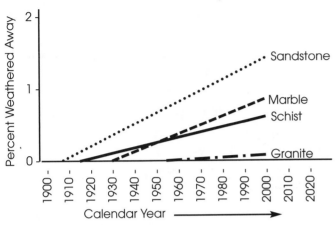

7 Which rock was found to have been exposed to weathering for the greatest number of years?

8 Which rock type in this study was the most resistant to weathering?

9 Predict what total percentage of the schist should have weathered away by the year 2020.

10 Studies have shown that pollutants added to the atmosphere in recent years are accumulating. How are the pollutants likely to affect the rate of weathering of the marble? How will the graph line for marble likely appear in the future?

Base your answers to questions 11 through 13 on your knowledge of Earth science, the *Reference Tables*, and the cross-sectional diagram. The diagram shows a sediment-laden stream entering the ocean. Points *X* and *Y* are in the stream and the ocean is divided into four zones *A, B, C,* and *D*.

11 What type of sediment sorting is shown in the diagram? Explain what causes this type of sorting.

12 In what zone would limestone most likely form?

13 Which zone would contain particles mostly in the range of 0.05 to 0.10 centimeter in diameter?

Base your answers to questions 14 through 17 on your knowledge of Earth science, the *Reference Tables*, and the diagram which represents the geologic cross section and surface features of a portion of the Earth's crust. Locations *A, B, C,* and *D* are reference points of the Earth's surface.

KEY:

- ROADS AND HIGHWAYS
- = HOMES
- = SANDSTONE
- = SHALE

14 In a sentence or two, describe the type of rock structure underlying the regions located west of the town.

15 Index fossils are found in the surface bedrock under the town. Where else are fossils of the same type likely to be found?

16 What type of rock appears to be the most resistant to weathering?

17 Draw a diagram of the stream pattern that would most likely form in the region west of the town. What is the name of this stream pattern?

18 Both of the landscapes shown in the diagrams below are eroded plateaus. In a sentence or two, infer why their surfaces differ in appearance.

Base your answers to questions 19 through 22 on the diagram and the stream data table below.

The diagram represents a stream flowing into a lake. Arrows show the direction of flow. Point *P* is a location in the stream. Line *XY* is a reference line across the stream. Points *X* and *Y* are locations on the banks. The data table gives the depth of water in the stream along line *XY*.

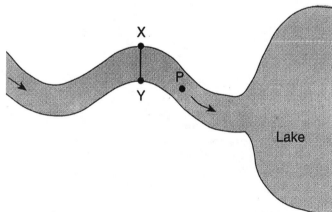

STREAM DATA TABLE

	Location X							Location Y
Distance from X (meters)	0	5	10	15	20	25	30	35
Depth of Water (meters)	0	5.0	5.5	4.5	3.5	2.0	0.5	0

Directions Use the information in the data table to construct a profile of the depth of water. Use the grid provided, following the directions below.

19 On the vertical axis, mark an appropriate scale for the depth of water. Note that the zero (0) at the top of the axis represents the water surface.

20 Plot the data for the depth of water in the stream along line *XY* and connect the points. (Distance is measured from point *X*.)

Example:

21 State why the depth of water near the bank at point *X* is different from the depth of water near the bank at point *Y*.

22 At point *P*, the water velocity is 100 centimeters per second. State the name of the largest sediment that can be transported by the stream at point *P*.

Base your answers to questions 23 through 25 on the information below.

A mountain is a landform with steeply sloping sides whose peak is usually thousands of feet higher than its base. Mountains often contain a great deal of nonsedimentary rock and have distorted rock structures caused by faulting and folding of the crust.

A plateau is a broad, level area at a high elevation. It usually has an undistorted, horizontal rock structure. A plateau may have steep slopes as a result of erosion.

23 State why marine fossils are *not* usually found in the bedrock of the Adirondack Mountains.

24 State the agent of erosion that is most likely responsible for shaping the Catskill Plateau so that it physically resembles a mountainous region.

25 State the approximate age of the surface bedrock of the Catskills.

EARTH'S HISTORY

VOCABULARY

early Earth	igneous intrusion	fossil	Paleozoic Era	radioactive isotope
photosynthesis	igneous extrusion	volcanic ash	Mesozoic Era	carbon-14
relative age	contact metamor-	rock & fossil record	Cenozoic Era	uranium-238
absolute age	phism	index or guide fossil	orogeny	radioactive decay
radioactive dating	faults, folds, & joints	Geologic Time	*principle of uniformi-*	extinct
decay	cracks & veins	eons, eras, periods,	*tarianism*	species
principle of superpo-	unconformity	& epochs	absolute, actual age	organic evolution
sition	correlation	Precambrian Era	half-life	

A. GEOLOGIC EVENTS

The history of the changing Earth is told in the Earth's **geologic events**. The analysis, synthesis, and interpretation of these geologic events is a form of puzzle solving.

EARLY EARTH

Evidence suggests that the atmosphere and oceans of the early Earth began to form with the gases emitted by volcanic eruptions from the Earth's interior. Large quantities of water vapor, carbon dioxide, nitrogen, and other dissolved gases were released by a process called **outgassing**. The vapor was the source of water for both the atmosphere and the oceans.

The early Earth was covered with clouds from which precipitation fell over millions of years cooling the surfaces and forming the oceans. Sedimentary rocks of marine origin dating back approximately 4 billion years provide evidence for the presence of this early ocean.

The mixture of gases that make up the atmosphere today contains about 21% oxygen, but that is not true of the gases erupting from volcanoes. That raises the question, what was the source of the oxygen? Scientists believe that green plants formed in the early waters. The green plants produced their food by **photosynthesis**. This process results in excess oxygen which was released into the atmosphere. As the number of green plants increased, so did the amount of oxygen in the atmosphere.

SEQUENCE OF GEOLOGIC EVENTS

Knowing the sequence of the geologic events that took place during the formation of the Earth's crust makes it possible to develop a **geologic history** of the Earth and to better understand the forces that have and still are changing the Earth's crust.

Relative age is concerned with the sequence of geologic events that have occurred in an area as shown by the appearance of the rock layers. Relative age is not concerned with the actual ages of the rocks. This method uses sedimentary rock layers, igneous extrusions and intrusions, faults, folds, continuity, similarity of rock, fossil evidence, and volcanic time markers as clues to determine the probable order and conditions under which rock layers formed.

The actual age of a rock or fossil is called **absolute age**. The most accurate method of determining the absolute age of geologic events and rock is by techniques such as **radioactive dating**. Every radioactive element decays. A "parent" element emits radiation and particles until it is transformed by **decay** (breakdown) into a stable "daughter" element. Sometimes the "changing" element passes through a series of transformations into other radioactive elements before reaching this stability. Each radioactive element also has its own identifiable pattern and **rate of decay**.

CHRONOLOGY OF LAYERS

The bottom layer in a series of horizontal sedimentary rock layers is the oldest, unless the series has been overturned or has had older rock thrust over it. This concept, called the **principle of superposition**, is used to determine the sequence in which a series of sedimentary layers was formed.

Principle of Superposition with "youngest" on top and "oldest" on the bottom

IGNEOUS INTRUSIONS & EXTRUSIONS

The rock layers through which **igneous intrusions** or **extrusions** cut are older than the intrusions or extrusions themselves, since the rock layers must be formed prior to the intrusion of magma or extrusion of lava.

Contact metamorphism of the rocks, through which the magma has moved, provides an additional clue to their relative age. Contact metamorphism is more recent than the rock layers that were metamorphosed.

KEY
} SEDIMENTARY ROCKS
IGNEOUS ROCK
CONTACT METAMORPHISM

Contact Metamorphism

FAULTS, JOINTS, & FOLDS

Faults (cracks in the rock along which movement has occurred), **joints** (immovable cracks), and **folds** (bends in the rock strata) are younger than the rocks in which they appear. These distortions in rock occur because of changes in temperature and pressure.

INTERNAL CHARACTERISTICS

Fragments that occur within a rock are older than the rocks in which they are found, since they were formed previously from other rocks. However, cracks and **veins** (mineral deposits that have filled a rock crack or permeable zone) are younger than the rocks in which they occur.

Sedimentary rocks are younger than the sediments and the cements that formed them. Another kind of internal characteristic of rock layers is an **unconformity**, which is a zone where rocks of different ages meet. An unconformity is a "gap" in the geologic rock record because of erosion or nondeposition. It is usually seen as a buried erosional surface.

B. RELATIVE AGE

The determination of the relative age of rock in geologic history can be accomplished through the use of correlation techniques. But, it is very important for the observer to distinguish actual evidence from inferences.

Correlation is used to reconstruct the geologic history of a location. It is the process of determining that the rock layers or geologic events in two separate areas are the same. Correlation involves observing the similarity and continuity of rock layers in different locations, comparing fossil evidence and using volcanic time markers.

SIMILARITY OF ROCKS

Rocks can often be tentatively matched on the basis of similarity in **appearance**, **color**, and **composition**. The geologist can use these rock characteristics to help determine if there is a relationship between the rock layers in two different places, such as layers on opposite sides of a valley.

FOSSIL EVIDENCE

The remains or traces of many once-living organisms, found almost exclusively in sedimentary rock, are called **fossils**. These fossils provide clues to the environment in which the organisms once lived. If a geologist finds fossils of a marine organism, evidence is provided that this sedimentary rock was formed in the sea. The geologist may then infer that this region was submerged at some time during geologic history.

Fossil Formation in the Sea generally follows the same **Principle of Superposition** with the oldest fossils in the lower levels and younger above.

VOLCANIC TIME MARKERS

A volcanic eruption is relatively short in duration when compared to the many years required for other constructional forces to build up the Earth's surface. When a volcano erupts, a layer of **volcanic ash** (fine particles of igneous rock ejected during the eruption) is rapidly deposited over a large area.

A layer of volcanic ash occurring between other layers of rock may serve as a time marker. A time marker is found, if a geologist discovers a layer of volcanic ash buried between other layers of the sedimentary rock, and the actual date of the volcanic eruption is known. This time marker will provide very important information in determining the relative age of the rock layers above and below it.

PROBLEMS WITH CORRELATION

The process of "solving the puzzle" of geologic history appears fairly easy according to our discussion of rocks and geologic events and the correlation evidences. However, this is an oversimplification of the processes involved in determining geologic history. It can lead to misconceptions.

The geologist must exercise cautious interpretation to minimize this problem. Very careful study of two similar rock formations may show that the rock formations are actually of different ages. Also, within a single formation, it is possible to find areas of different ages.

C. GEOLOGIC TIME SCALE

THE ROCK RECORD

A close study of the **rock record,** using fossil evidence to develop a geologic time scale and erosional evidence to help fill in any gaps in the fossil record, can lead to an inferred geologic history of an area.

Fossil Evidence. Fossils provide direct (e.g., shells, bones) and indirect evidence (e.g., footprints, burrows) of organisms that had lived on Earth. Events in geologic history can often be placed in order according to relative age by using evidence provided by certain fossils.

The fossils used to correlate rock layers are called **index fossils** or **guide fossils**. Index fossils are used because of their wide-spread horizontal distribution (geographical) in sedimentary rocks and their relatively short period of existence on the Earth (narrow vertical distribution). By comparing these fossils in various locations on the Earth, it is possible to correlate the relative ages of the rock in which they appear.

Scale of Geologic Time. Geologists have subdivided geologic time into units, called **eons** (e.g., Phanerozoic, Proterozoic, Archean), **eras** (e.g., in the Phanerozoic Eon, Cenozoic, Mesozoic, and Paleozoic), **periods** (e.g., in the Mesozoic Era, Cretaceous, Jurassic, and Triassic), and **epochs**, based on the fossil evidence preserved in the rocks. However, most of

the geologic past is devoid of a fossil record (see the *Geologic Time Scale* from the *Reference Tables* on the next page).

A review of the **Geologic Time Scale** suggests the following sequence in the geologic history of Earth.

- The **Precambrian** or **Pre-Paleozoic Era** makes up about 85 percent of the total geologic time of Earth history. There is very little fossil evidence from this era, since the organisms that existed at this time did not lend themselves to making good fossils. They were small, simple, and soft bodied (such as algae and bacteria).

- The **Paleozoic Era** was much shorter, covering about 8 or 9 percent of the geologic history of the Earth. This era, which began the abundant fossil record, progressed from the Age of Invertebrates to the Age of Fishes and ended with the Age of Amphibians. The first vertebrates and the land plants and animals developed during this era. The Periods of the Paleozoic Era began with the Cambrian, passing through the Ordovician, Silurian, Devonian, Carboniferous, and ending with the Permian.

- The **Mesozoic Era** was even shorter, about 3 or 4 percent of the geologic history. This is the era in which the fossils of dinosaurs and the earliest birds and mammals were formed. The Mesozoic Era included the Triassic, Jurassic, and Cretaceous Periods.

- The most recent era, 2 or 3 percent of the geologic time scale, is the **Cenozoic Era,** which includes the fossils of many modern plants and mammals, including the appearance of humans.

Human existence is infinitesimal (0.04% of geologic time) in comparison to the entire geologic time of the Earth (4.6 billion years).

Plate motions and mountain building (**orogeny**) events may also be identified and placed in this time sequence by using the information in the *Earth Science Reference Tables*.

THE EROSIONAL RECORD

Buried erosional surfaces indicate some gaps in the time record of the rock. These gaps represent periods of destruction (erosion) of the geologic record, or nondeposition. It has been suggested that the fossil record would show a complete time scale and history of the Earth, if (1) the principle of superposition held absolutely true, and if (2) no forces of destruction (weathering and erosion) occurred after the origin of life forms. But, it is clear that distructional forces have

GEOLOGIC HISTORY

Eon	Era	Period	Epoch	Life on Earth	NY Rock Record

NY Rock Record legend: ▨ Sediment, ■ Bedrock

Million years ago (Eon scale)

Eon	Era	Period	Epoch (Million years ago)	Life on Earth
PHANEROZOIC	CENOZOIC	QUATERNARY	HOLOCENE — 0 / PLEISTOCENE — 0.01, 1.8	Humans, mastodonts, mammoths
		NEOGENE	PLIOCENE — 5.3 / MIOCENE — 23.0	Large carnivorous mammals / Abundant grazing mammals
		PALEOGENE	OLIGOCENE — 33.9 / EOCENE — 55.8 / PALEOCENE — 65.5	Earliest grasses / Many modern groups of mammals / Mass extinction of dinosaurs, ammonoids, and many land plants
	MESOZOIC	CRETACEOUS	LATE / EARLY	Earliest flowering plants / Diverse bony fishes
		JURASSIC	LATE / MIDDLE / EARLY — 146	Earliest birds / Abundant dinosaurs and ammonoids
		TRIASSIC	LATE / MIDDLE / EARLY — 200, 251	Earliest mammals / Earliest dinosaurs / Mass extinction of many land and marine organisms (including trilobites)
	PALEOZOIC	PERMIAN	LATE / MIDDLE / EARLY — 299	Mammal-like reptiles / Abundant reptiles
		CARBONIFEROUS — PENNSYLVANIAN	LATE / EARLY — 318	Extensive coal-forming forests
		CARBONIFEROUS — MISSISSIPPIAN	LATE / MIDDLE / EARLY — 359	Abundant amphibians / Large and numerous scale trees and seed ferns (vascular plants); earliest reptiles
		DEVONIAN	LATE / MIDDLE / EARLY — 416	Earliest amphibians and plant seeds / Extinction of many marine organisms / Earth's first forests / Earliest ammonoids and sharks / Abundant fish
		SILURIAN	LATE / EARLY — 444	Earliest insects / Earliest land plants and animals / Abundant eurypterids
		ORDOVICIAN	LATE / MIDDLE / EARLY — 488	Invertebrates dominant / Earth's first coral reefs
		CAMBRIAN	LATE / MIDDLE / EARLY — 542	Burgess shale fauna (diverse soft-bodied organisms) / Earliest fishes / Extinction of many primitive marine organisms / Earliest trilobites / Great diversity of life-forms with shelly parts

PRECAMBRIAN — PROTEROZOIC (LATE, MIDDLE, EARLY) / ARCHEAN (LATE, MIDDLE, EARLY)

- First sexually reproducing organisms
- Oceanic oxygen begins to enter the atmosphere
- Oceanic oxygen produced by cyanobacteria combines with iron, forming iron oxide layers on ocean floor
- Earliest stromatolites / Oldest microfossils
- Evidence of biological carbon
- Oldest known rocks
- Estimated time of origin of Earth and solar system

- 580: Ediacaran fauna (first multicellular, soft-bodied marine organisms)
- 1300: Abundant stromatolites

(Index fossils not drawn to scale)

Index fossils (labeled A–N):

- A — Elliptocephala
- B — Cryptolithus
- C — Phacops
- D — Valcouroceras / Hexameroceras
- E — (trilobite)
- F — Centroceras
- G — Manticoceras
- H — Eucalyptocrinus
- I — Ctenocrinus
- J — Tetragraptus
- K — Dicellograptus
- L — Coelophysis
- M — Eurypterus
- N — Stylonurus

OF NEW YORK STATE

Time Distribution of Fossils (including important fossils of New York)	Important Geologic Events in New York	Inferred Positions of Earth's Landmasses

The center of each lettered circle indicates the approximate time of existence of a specific index fossil (e.g. Fossil Ⓐ lived at the end of the Early Cambrian).

Important Geologic Events in New York:

- Advance and retreat of last continental ice
- Sands and clays underlying Long Island and Staten Island deposited on margin of Atlantic Ocean
- Dome-like uplift of Adirondack region begins
- Initial opening of Atlantic Ocean North America and Africa separate
- ⟨ Intrusion of Palisades sill ⟩
- Pangaea begins to break up
- **Alleghenian orogeny** caused by collision of North America and Africa along transform margin, forming Pangaea
- Catskill delta forms
- Erosion of Acadian Mountains
- **Acadian orogeny** caused by collision of North America and Avalon and closing of remaining part of Iapetus Ocean
- Salt and gypsum deposited in evaporite basins
- Erosion of Taconic Mountains; Queenston delta forms
- **Taconian orogeny** caused by closing of western part of Iapetus Ocean and collision between North America and volcanic island arc
- Widespread deposition over most of New York along edge of Iapetus Ocean
- Rifting and initial opening of Iapetus Ocean
- Erosion of Grenville Mountains
- **Grenville orogeny:** metamorphism of bedrock now exposed in the Adirondacks and Hudson Highlands

Inferred Positions of Earth's Landmasses:

- 59 million years ago
- 119 million years ago
- 232 million years ago
- 359 million years ago
- 458 million years ago

Fossil labels (time distribution): NAUTILOIDS, DINOSAURS, MAMMALS, BIRDS, AMMONOIDS, CRINOIDS, VASCULAR PLANTS, CORALS, GASTROPODS, BRACHIOPODS, TRILOBITES, EURYPTERIDS, GRAPTOLITES, PLACODERM FISH

Lettered fossils: O, S, L, C, F, G, I, H, E, B, D, K, J, A, N, Q, R, M, P, V, U, T, X, Z, Y, W

Bottom fossil illustrations:

- Ⓞ Mastodont, Beluga Whale
- Ⓟ Cooksonia
- Ⓠ Aneurophyton, Naples Tree
- Ⓡ Bothriolepis
- Ⓢ Condor
- Ⓣ Lichenaria
- Ⓤ Cystiphyllum
- Ⓥ Pleurodictyum
- Ⓦ Maclurites
- Ⓧ Platyceras
- Ⓨ Eospirifer
- Ⓩ Mucrospirifer

worked in the past and are still changing the Earth's surface, since there is no known location on Earth in which the entire rock record has been preserved.

One of the key principles that geologists use to interpret the Earth's geologic history is the **principle of uniformitarianism**. In general, this principle implies that the geologic processes currently changing the Earth also have changed the Earth in the past. There may have been different rates of change at various times, but the patterns and agents of change remain the same.

THE GEOLOGIC HISTORY OF AN AREA

Using the evidence discovered in the rock record, the geologist can infer the geologic history of an area. The New York State geologic map and the geologic time scale may be used to illustrate the various portions of the rock record that have been preserved in New York State (see the *Earth Science Reference Tables*).

RADIOACTIVE DECAY

The evidences of the rock record discussed in this topic allow the geologist to make relative age estimates in the scale of geologic time and Earth history. To obtain **absolute** or **actual age**, the process of radioactive dating is used.

DECAY RATES

When the spontaneous and natural nuclear breakdown of unstable atoms occurs, particles and energy are released. This constant, predictable process is called **radioactive decay**. By measuring the amount of radioactive isotope, compared to the amount of decay product (more stable form of the element) present in a rock sample, absolute age can be determined. The decay rate is unaffected by external factors, such as pressure and temperature, that would normally affect chemical reactions.

Some, but not all, rocks contain atoms whose nuclei undergo radioactive decay. This decay occurs as a random event and is not influenced by other changes occurring in the rock at the same time.

HALF-LIVES OF RADIOACTIVE SUBSTANCES

The **half-life** of a radioactive substance is the time taken for the activity of decay to reduce the total amount of radioactive substance in a material to half of its original amount. Therefore, by knowing the original content of a radioactive material and comparing it to the present content of the same radioactive material, the age of the material can be determined.

The half-lives of **radioactive isotopes** are different for different substances. Some radioactive isotopes, such as **carbon–14**, have short half-lives and are good for dating recent organic remains (between 1,000 and 50,000 years).

Other radioactive substances, such as uranium–238 which decays to stable Lead–206, have very long half-lives and are good for dating older rock formations (more than 10 million years). Uranium–238 has a half-life of about 4.5 billions years. The Earth itself is estimated to be 4.6 billion years old. Therefore, uranium–238 that formed at the same time the Earth was formed has had time to undergo only one half-life.

DETERMINING AGE BY RADIOACTIVE DECAY

The age of a rock or fossil can be inferred from the relative amounts of the undecayed (radioactive) substance and the decay product. For example, the actual age of a fossil can be inferred by the following method.

Method:
A sample piece of a fossil is taken. The amount of the carbon–14 remaining in that piece is measured at 0.5 grams. An equal sample of an existing organism, shows that the amount of original carbon–14 was 2.0 grams. Since the radioactive decay rate of carbon–14 is the loss of half of the total amount in the sample piece every 5,700 years, the sample was formed 11,400 years ago.

Explanation:
In the first 5,700 years of decay, the 2.0 grams were reduced to 1.0 gram; then, in the second 5,700 years of decay, the 1.0 gram was reduced in half again to 0.5 gram. Since one quarter of the original radioactive substance remained, the fossil had undergone two half-lives.

Radioactive Decay Data		
Radioactive Element	Disintegration	Half-life
Carbon–14	C-14 → N-14	5.7×10^3 years
Potassium–40	K-40 → Ar-40	1.3×10^9 years
Uranium–238	U-238 → Pb-206	4.5×10^9 years
Rubidium–87	Rb-87 → Sr-87	4.9×10^{10} years

D. THE FOSSIL RECORD

Ancient Life. The study of the fossils found in sedimentary rock provides clues to the life that existed on the Earth in past eras and to the environments in which the organisms (e.g., plants, animals) lived (see *NYS Fossils Through Geologic Time* on the next page from the *Earth Science Reference Tables*).

The Variety of Life Forms. The pattern of development of life-forms on Earth is partially preserved in the rocks. Fossils give evidence that a great many kinds of animals and plants have lived in the past on the Earth in a great variety of environmental conditions. Most of these life forms have become **extinct** (do not exist on the Earth today). It is highly probable that, in addition to the fossil types that have been found, there existed an even greater number of life forms that have left no traces (fossils) in the rock.

EVOLUTIONARY DEVELOPMENT

A **species** is defined as organisms that are able to mate and produce offspring capable of continuing the same species. Within a species there are a great number of variations which can be observed, measured, and described.

Theories of **organic evolution** (how change occurs) have suggested that the variations within a species may provide some members of that species with a higher probability of survival. For example, a variation in the color of rabbits living in a snow covered Arctic region, such as white and a brown color difference, provide the white rabbit with a better chance to survive. The white rabbit may be able to better hide in the snow from predators. But, the brown rabbit would be easily seen. As a result, the white rabbit will have a higher probability of producing more offspring.

The similarity among some fossil forms of various time periods suggests a transition that may be a result of evolutionary development. Generally, the older rock formations contain more simple and marine life forms. The younger rock formations have the fossils of more complex land dwelling organisms.

QUESTIONS FOR UNIT 5

1 Volcanic ash layers may serve as excellent time markers in the geologic rock record because most volcanic ash
   1 contains fine-textured particles
   2 contains many minerals
   3 has a very low resistant to weathering
   4 is rapidly deposited over a wide geographic area

2 Unconformities (buried erosional surfaces) are good evidence that
   1 many life-forms have become extinct
   2 the earliest life-forms lived in the sea
   3 part of the geologic rock record is missing
   4 metamorphic rocks have formed from sedimentary rocks

3 Where is metamorphic rock frequently found?
   1 along the boundary between igneous intrusions and sedimentary bedrock
   2 as a thin surface layer covering huge areas of the continents
   3 on mountaintops that have horizontal layers containing marine fossils
   4 within large lava flows

4 What is the relative age of a fault that cuts across many rock layers?
   1 The fault is younger than all the layers it cuts across.
   2 The fault is older than all the layers it cuts across.
   3 The fault is the same age as the top layer it cuts across.
   4 The fault is the same age as the bottom layer it cuts across.

5 Which statement correctly describes an age relationship in the geologic cross section below?

   1 The sandstone is younger than the basalt.
   2 The shale is younger than the basalt.
   3 The limestone is younger than the shale.
   4 The limestone is younger than the basalt.

6 The map shows the relative age of the bedrock in the continental United States.

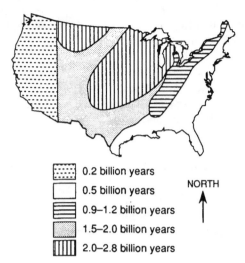

    0.2 billion years
    0.5 billion years
    0.9–1.2 billion years
    1.5–2.0 billion years
    2.0–2.8 billion years

NORTH

The general age of the bedrock is found to be progressively
1 older as an observer moves from the east and west coasts toward the center of the United States
2 younger as an observer moves from the east and west coasts toward the center of the United States
3 older as an observer moves across the United States from the east coast to the west coast
4 younger as an observer moves across the United States from the east coast to the west coast

7 The diagram represents a sample of a sedimentary rock viewed under a microscope.

MINERAL VEIN
CRACK IN ROCK
PEBBLES
MINERAL CEMENT

Which part formed first?
1 the crack
2 the pebbles
3 the mineral vein
4 the mineral cement

8 An igneous intrusion is 50 million years old. What is the most probable age of the rock immediately surrounding the intrusion?
(1) 10 million years
(2) 25 million years
(3) 40 million years
(4) 60 million years

9 The diagrams show geologic cross sections of the same part of the Earth's crust at different times in the geologic past.

Which sequence shows the order in which this part of the crust probably formed?
(1) $A \rightarrow B \rightarrow C \rightarrow D$ (3) $C \rightarrow A \rightarrow D \rightarrow B$
(2) $C \rightarrow D \rightarrow A \rightarrow B$ (4) $A \rightarrow C \rightarrow B \rightarrow D$

10 The diagram below shows a cross section of the Earth's crust. Line XY is a fault.

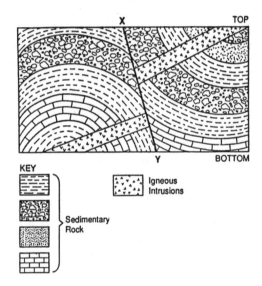

KEY

Sedimentary Rock

Igneous Intrusions

Which sequence of events, from oldest to youngest, has occurred in this outcrop?

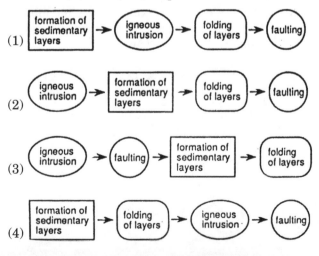

(1) formation of sedimentary layers → igneous intrusion → folding of layers → faulting

(2) igneous intrusion → formation of sedimentary layers → folding of layers → faulting

(3) igneous intrusion → faulting → formation of sedimentary layers → folding of layers

(4) formation of sedimentary layers → folding of layers → igneous intrusion → faulting

11 The diagrams below represent layers of sedimentary rocks from four different locations. Four of the layers are identified as A, B, C, and D. No layers have been overturned.

Which rock layer is youngest?
(1) A   (3) C
(2) B   (4) D

Base your answers to questions 12 and 13 on the geologic cross section diagram.

Key
☐ Sandstone
☰ Shale
▦ Limestone
▨ Conglomerate
▨ Basalt

12 Which geologic event occurred most recently?
1 folding at A
2 the intrusion at B
3 faulting at C
4 the unconformity at D

13 The symbol ⊤⊤⊤⊤⊤⊤ in the diagram most likely represents a
1 metamorphic rock in contact with an igneous rock
2 depression caused by underground erosion
3 convection cell caused by unequal heating
4 large fault from an earthquake or crustal movement

14 The *Geologic Time Scale* has been subdivided into a number of time units called periods based upon
1 fossil evidence
2 rock thickness
3 rock types
4 radioactive dating

Base your answers to questions 15 through 18 on your knowledge of Earth science, the *Earth Science Reference Tables*, and the block diagram below. The diagram represents a geologic cross section in which overturning has not occurred.

KEY:
SEDIMENTARY ROCK ▦
IGNEOUS ROCK ⊠
CONTACT METAMORPHISM ▨

15 Which rock most likely is the oldest?
(1) A   (3) F
(2) B   (4) D

16 When did the folding of rock layer B most likely occur?
1 before the deposition of rock layer A
2 after the deposition of rock layer E
3 after the deposition of rock layer C
4 after the deposition of rock layer D

17 Fossils are *least* likely to be found in which rock?
(1) E   (3) C
(2) F   (4) D

18 What evidence in the rock layers indicates that the formation of igneous rock F occurred after rock layer E was in place?
1 the presence of radioactive minerals in rock F
2 the presence of extrusive igneous rock below rock layer E
3 the unconformity between rock F and rock layer E
4 the zone of contact metamorphism between rock F and rock layer E

19 According to the *Earth Science Reference Tables*, which geologic event is associated with the Grenville Orogeny?
1 the formation of the ancestral Adirondack Mountains
2 the advance and retreat of the last continental ice sheet
3 the separation of South America from Africa
4 the initial opening of the Atlantic Ocean

20 The diagram represents a cross section of a series of rock layers of different geologic ages.

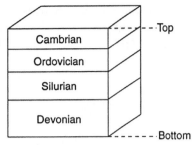

Which statement provides the best explanation for the order of these rock layers?
1 The oldest layer is on the bottom.
2 A buried erosional surface exists between layers.
3 The layers have been overturned.
4 The Permian layer has been totally eroded.

21 According to the *Earth Science Reference Tables*, when did the Jurassic Period end?
(1) 66 million years ago
(2) 144 million years ago
(3) 163 million years ago
(4) 190 million years ago

22 Using the information in the *Reference Tables*, students plan to construct a geologic time line of the Earth's history from its origin to the present time. They will use a scale of 1 meter equals 1 billion years. What should be the total length of the students' time line?
(1) 10.0 m   (3) 3.8 m
(2) 2.5 m   (4) 4.6 m

23 The geologic cross section below shows an unconformity between gneiss and the Cambrium-age Potsdam sandstone in northern New York State.

According to the *Earth Science Reference Tables*, what is the most probable age of the gneiss at this location?
1 Precambrian   3 Ordovician
2 Silurian   4 Cretaceous

Note: Question 24 has only 3 choices.

24 If a sample of a radioactive substance is crushed, the half-life of the substance will
1 decrease
2 increase
3 remain the same

25 Why are radioactive materials useful for measuring geologic time?
1 The disintegration of radioactive materials occurs at a predictable rate.
2 The half-lives of most radioactive materials are less than five minutes.
3 The ratio of decay products to undecayed material remains constant in sedimentary rocks.
4 Measurable samples of radioactive materials are easily collected from most rock types.

26 The decay rates of radioactive substances remain constant when the substances are subjected to different temperature and pressure conditions. The best inference that can be drawn from this statement is that decay rates are
1 independent of external factors
2 independent of the isotope's composition
3 affected by the mass of the isotope
4 affected by pressure, but not by temperature

27 The table at the right gives information about the radioactive decay of carbon–14. [Part of the table has been left blank for student use.] What is the amount of original carbon–14 remaining after 34,200 years?
(1) $1/8$ g
(2) $1/16$ g
(3) $1/32$ g
(4) $1/64$ g

Half-Life	Mass of Original C-14 Remaining (grams)	Number of Years
0	1	0
1	$\frac{1}{2}$	5,700
2	$\frac{1}{4}$	11,400
3	$\frac{1}{8}$	17,100
4		
5		
6		

28 Which radioactive substance shown on the graph below has the longest half-life?

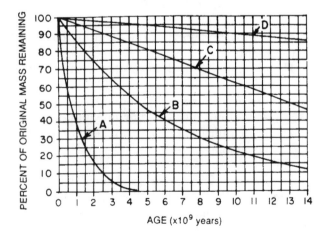

(1) A   (3) C
(2) B   (4) D

29 According to the *Earth Science Reference Tables*, which element is used by Earth scientists for radioactive dating of rocks?
1 cobalt–60   3 potassium–40
2 plutonium–244   4 silicon–28

30 The diagram represents a clock used to time the half-life of a particular radioactive substance. The clock was started at 12:00. The shaded portion on the clock represents the number of hours one-half-life of this radioactive substance took to disintegrate.

Which diagram best represents the clock at the end of the next half-life of this radioactive substance?

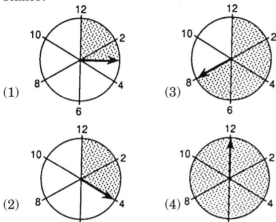

(1)   (3)
(2)   (4)

31 The diagram below represents the radioactive decay of uranium-238.

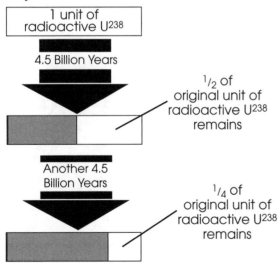

Shaded areas on the diagram represent the amount of
1 undecayed radioactive uranium-238 (U^{238})
2 undecayed radioactive rubidium-87 (Rb^{87})
3 stable carbon-14 (C^{14})
4 stable lead-206 (Pb^{206})

32 A geologist uses carbon–14 to measure the age of some material found in a sedimentary deposit. If the half life of carbon–14 is 5.7×10^3 years and the sample shows that only 1/4 of the original carbon–14 is left, the age of the sample is about
(1) 5,700 years   (3) 17,100 years
(2) 11,400 years   (4) 22,800 years

33 According to the *Reference Tables*, which radioactive element would be most useful for determining the age of clothing that is thought to have been worn 2,000 years ago?
1 carbon–14   3 uranium–238
2 potassium–40   4 rubidium–87

34 In order for an organism to be used as an index fossil, the organism must have been geographically widespread and must have
1 lived on land
2 lived in shallow water
3 been preserved by volcanic ash
4 existed for a geologically short time

35 In the Earth's geologic past there were long warm periods which were much warmer than the present climate. What is the primary evidence that these long warm periods existed?
1 U.S. National Weather Service records
2 polar magnetic directions preserved in the rock record
3 radioactive decay rates
4 plant and animal fossils

36 Why are fossils rarely found in Precambrian rock layers?
1 Few Precambrian rock layers have been discovered.
2 Nearly all fossils from this era have been destroyed by glaciers.
3 Few rock layers were formed during the Precambrian Era.
4 Life that would produce fossils was not abundant during the Precambrian Era.

37 Present-day corals live in warm, tropical ocean water. Which inference is best supported by the discovery of Ordovician-age corals in the surface bedrock of western New York State?
1 Western New York State was covered by a warm, shallow sea during Ordovician time.
2 Ordovician-age corals lived in the forests of western New York State.
3 Ordovician-age corals were transported to western New York State by cold, freshwater streams.
4 Western New York State was covered by a continental ice sheet that created coral fossils of Ordovician time.

38 From the study of fossils, what can be inferred about most species of plants and animals that have lived on the Earth?
1 They are still living today.
2 They are unrelated to modern life forms.
3 They existed during the Cambrian Period.
4 They have become extinct.

39 The geologic columns *A*, *B*, and *C* in the diagrams represent widely spaced outcrops of sedimentary rocks. Symbols are used to indicate fossils found within each rock layer. Each rock layer represents the fossil record of a different geologic period.

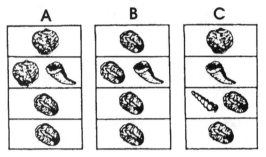

According to the diagrams for all three columns, which would be the best index fossil?

(1)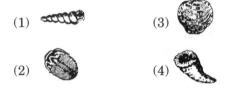

(2)

(3)

(4)

40 The chart below shows index fossils found in rocks of various ages.

BEDROCK AGE	INDEX FOSSIL
MISSISSIPPIAN	SPIRIFER
DEVONIAN	MUCROSPIRIFER
SILURIAN	EOSPIRIFER
ORDOVICIAN	MICHELINOCERAS

According to the *Earth Science Reference Tables*, which fossil could be found in the same rock as fossils of the first corals?
1 *Spirifer*
2 *Mucrospirifer*
3 *Eospirifer*
4 *Michelinoceras*

41 Trilobite fossils from different time periods show small changes in appearance. These observations suggest that the changes may be the result of
1 evolutionary development
2 a variety of geologic processes
3 periods of destruction of the geologic record
4 the gradual disintegration of radioactive substances

Base your answers to questions 42 and 43 on the *Earth Science Reference Tables*, the graph below, and your knowledge of Earth science. The graph shows the development, growth in population, and extinction of the six major groups of trilobites, labeled *A* through *F*.

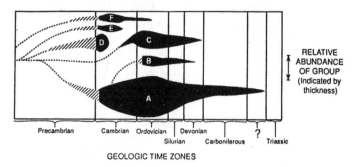

KEY TO SYMBOLS:

◼ Population based on fossil record

▨ Population presumed: fossil evidence rare

⋯⋯ Assumed evolutionary relationship

42 The fossil evidence that forms the basis for this graph was most likely found in
1 lava flows of ancient volcanoes
2 sedimentary rock that formed from ocean sediment
3 granite rock that formed from former sedimentary rocks
4 metamorphic rock that formed from volcanic rocks

43 Which group of trilobites became the most abundant?
(1) *A* (3) *C*
(2) *B* (4) *D*

44 The cartoon at the right represents the time of the last dinosaurs and the earliest mammals.

According to the *Earth Science Reference Tables*, the cartoon could

represent the boundary between which two units of geologic history?

1 Archean and Proterozoic
2 Precambrian and Paleozoic
3 Ordovician and Silurian
4 Mesozoic and Cenozoic

45 The diagram (*Series A*) below and the diagrams (*Series B-D*) represent four series of events over the passage of time.

Which series of events took the least amount of time to complete?

(1) *A*   (3) *C*
(2) *B*   (4) *D*

46 The diagram shows the probable arrangement of some Earth continents during the Mesozoic Era and the present distribution of four fossils.

Which fossil shown in the diagram would be most useful for correlating rocks among all the landmasses shown?

1 *Mesosaurus*   3 *Glossopteris*
2 *Cynognathus*   4 *Lystrosaurus*

47 The diagram shows a possible sequence of evolutionary development of some vertebrates.

Which statement can best be inferred from the diagram?

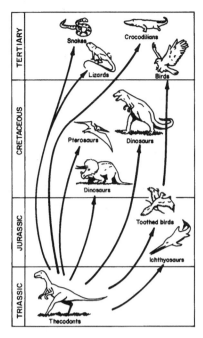

1 The lizard and the bird are both reptiles.
2 The *pterosaurs* and the *ichthyosaurs* became extinct at the same time.
3 The *pterosaurs* evolved into modern birds.
4 The *thecodont* is the ancestor of several different types of animals.

48 The cartoon below is a humorous look at geologic history.

Early Pleistocene mermaids

If Early Pleistocene mermaids had existed, their fossil remains would be the same age as fossils of

1 armored fish   3 trilobites
2 mastodons   4 dinosaurs

CONSTRUCTED RESPONSE

Base your answers to questions 1 through 4 on your knowledge of Earth science, the *Reference Tables*, and the diagrams which represent the bedrock geology of an area outside New York State.

TOP VIEW

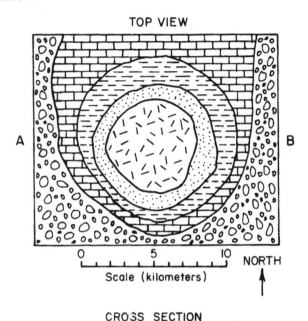

Scale (kilometers)

NORTH

CROSS SECTION
(not drawn to scale)

Key

Triassic granite

Permian conglomerate

Silurian limestone

Ordovician shale

Cambrian sandstone

Sedimentary Rock

1   In which bedrock unit are fossils *least* likely to be found? Why?

2   Which bedrock could be 460 million years old?

3   What kind of fossils might be found in the Silurian limestone? [See *Reference Tables*]

4   Which type of bedrock shown in the diagrams is *not* found in New York State?

Base your answers to questions 5 and 6 on your knowledge of Earth science and the diagram below. The diagram shows a profile view of a bedrock outcropping. None of the layers has been overturned.

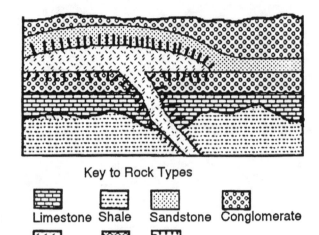

Key to Rock Types

Limestone   Shale   Sandstone   Conglomerate

Granite   Schist   Contact Metamorphism

5   How can one tell that the sandstone is older than the granite below it? Answer in one or more compete sentences.

6   List the names of the rocks in the order of their age from oldest to youngest using the number one for the oldest rock.

1   _____

2   _____

3   _____

4   _____

5   _____

6   _____

Base your answers to questions 7 through 10 on your knowledge of Earth science, the *Reference Tables*, and the chart which illustrates the geologic timespan and the relative abundance of species of ten types of animals and plants.

NUMBER OF DIFFERENT KINDS OF EACH LIFE FORM (Indicated by thickness)

GEOLOGIC TIME

Base your answers to questions 11 through 14 on the diagram below and your knowledge of Earth science. The diagram represents a profile view of a rock outcrop. The layers are labeled *A* through *H*.

Key

Limestone

Shale

Sandstone

Conglomerate

7   Which life form reached a peak three separate times in its existence on Earth?

8   When did the extinction of the dinosaurs occur?

9   Which life form appeared on Earth most recently?

10 Which life form existed for the greatest length of time?

11 State the range of particle sizes of the sediment that formed rock layer *C*.

12 Using one or more complete sentences, briefly describe the geologic process that resulted in the boundary represented by the line *XY*.

13 State two ways in which the composition of rock layer *A* differs from the composition of rock layer *B*.

14 None of the layers has been overturned. Layer *D* is 505 million years old and layer *B* is 438 million year old. State the geologic period during which layer *C* could have formed.

Base your answers to questions 15 and 16 on your knowledge of Earth science, the *Earth Science Reference Tables*, and the diagram which represents a geologic cross section of a volcanic area where overturning of rock layers has not occurred.

VOLCANO

KEY

SANDSTONE   BASALT

LIMESTONE   CINDERS AND ASH

SHALE

GABBRO   CONTACT METAMORPHISM

15 At which location is the oldest rock most likely to be found?

16 In a sentence, explain what most likely happened to rock layers *E*, *F*, *G*, *H*, and *I* where they came in contact with the molten rock that formed *B*.

Base your answers to questions 17 through 19 on the diagram below. The diagram represents the supercontinent Pangaea, which began to break up approximately 220 million years ago.

☐ Continents

N

17 During which geologic period within the Mesozoic Era did the supercontinent Pangaea begin to break apart?

18 State one form of evidence that supports the inference that Pangaea existed.

19 State the compass direction toward which North America has moved since Pangaea began to break apart.

METEOROLOGY & ATMOSPHERIC ENERGY

VOCABULARY

weather	condensation	vapor pressure	pressure "belts"	isotherm field gradient
temperature	monsoon	latent heat	zones of conver-	pressure field gradient
dew point	sea & land breeze	potential energy	gence	weather forecasting
relative humidity	Coriolis E\effect	change of phase	zones of divergence	station model
psychrometer	condensation nuclei	kinetic energy	air mass	synoptic weather
dry bulb thermometer	deposition	melting & freezing	source region (arctic	map
wet bulb thermometer	dew & frost	heat of fusion	A, polar P, tropi-	storm track
air pressure	orographic effect	heat of vaporization	cal T, maritime m,	jet stream
barometer	cumuliform clouds	specific heat	& continental c)	meteorologist
millibars	stratiform clouds	conduction	cyclone (LOW)	thunderstorm
isobars	precipitation	convection	anticyclone (HIGH)	hurricane
wind	evaporation	radiation	front & frontal surface	"eye" of the storm
wind vane	transpiration	cells & currents	warm, cold, occlud-	tornado
anemometer	evapotranspiration	radiational cooling	ed, & stationary	vortex

A. WEATHER

Weather is the short term condition of the atmosphere at any location. It is the result of the interrelationship of temperature, humidity, air pressure, and winds.

TEMPERATURE

Temperature usually varies in a daily cycle. The temperature at Earth's surface is greatly affected by the amount (intensity and duration) of sunlight. Other factors such as different surface materials (land and water), altitude, cloud cover, and movements of air masses contribute to a variety of temperature conditions.

HUMIDITY

The **dew point** temperature is the temperature at which the air is holding the maximum amount of **water vapor**. At this temperature the air is said to be **saturated** with water vapor. The water holding capacity of air is directly related to the temperature of the air so air of different temperatures will have different dew points.

Relative humidity is the percent of saturation of the air. It is the expression of the ratio between the actual amount of water vapor in the atmosphere and the air's capacity at that temperature. When the relative humidity is 50%, the air is holding half of the water vapor it is capable of holding.

The dew point and relative humidity are determined by using an instrument called a **psychrometer**. The psychrometer has two thermometers, a **dry bulb thermometer** and a **wet bulb thermometer** with a wet wick around the bulb (see illustration on next page). When whirled in the air, the wet bulb temperature usually drops because of the evaporation of the water, cooling the bulb of the thermometer. The amount of evaporation depends on the moisture con-

Dewpoint (°C)

Dry-Bulb Tempera-ture (°C)	Difference Between Wet-Bulb and Dry-Bulb Temperatures (C°)															
	0	1	2	3	4	5	6	7	8	9	10	11	12	13	14	15
−20	−20	−33														
−18	−18	−28														
−16	−16	−24														
−14	−14	−21	−36													
−12	−12	−18	−28													
−10	−10	−14	−22													
−8	−8	−12	−18	−29												
−6	−6	−10	−14	−22												
−4	−4	−7	−12	−17	−29											
−2	−2	−5	−8	−13	−20											
0	0	−3	−6	−9	−15	−24										
2	2	−1	−3	−6	−11	−17										
4	4	1	−1	−4	−7	−11	−19									
6	6	4	1	−1	−4	−7	−13	−21								
8	8	6	3	1	−2	−5	−9	−14								
10	10	8	6	4	1	−2	−5	−9	−14	−28						
12	12	10	8	6	4	1	−2	−5	−9	−16						
14	14	12	11	9	6	4	1	−2	−5	−10	−17					
16	16	14	13	11	9	7	4	1	−1	−6	−10	−17				
18	18	16	15	13	11	9	7	4	2	−2	−5	−10	−19			
20	20	19	17	15	14	12	10	7	4	2	−2	−5	−10	−19		
22	22	21	19	17	16	14	12	10	8	5	3	−1	−5	−10	−19	
24	24	23	21	20	18	16	14	12	10	8	6	2	−1	−5	−10	−18
26	26	25	23	22	20	18	17	15	13	11	9	6	3	0	−4	−9
28	28	27	25	24	22	21	19	17	16	14	11	9	7	4	1	−3
30	30	29	27	26	24	23	21	19	18	16	14	12	10	8	5	1

Wet bulb

Dry bulb

Compare the difference between the wet and dry bulb readings. Convert the Fahrenheit (°F) to Celsius (°C) using the Temperature Chart in the *Earth Science Reference Tables,* and use the Dew Point Temperature Chart to determine the Dew Point. Relative Humidity is also determined as above, but with the use of the Relative Humidity Chart.

Relative Humidity (%)

Dry-Bulb Tempera-ture (°C)	Difference Between Wet-Bulb and Dry-Bulb Temperatures (C°)															
	0	1	2	3	4	5	6	7	8	9	10	11	12	13	14	15
−20	100	28														
−18	100	40														
−16	100	48														
−14	100	55	11													
−12	100	61	23													
−10	100	66	33													
−8	100	71	41	13												
−6	100	73	48	20												
−4	100	77	54	32	11											
−2	100	79	58	37	20	1										
0	100	81	63	45	28	11										
2	100	83	67	51	36	20	6									
4	100	85	70	56	42	27	14									
6	100	86	72	59	46	35	22	10								
8	100	87	74	62	51	39	28	17	6							
10	100	88	76	65	54	43	33	24	13	4						
12	100	88	78	67	57	48	38	28	19	10	2					
14	100	89	79	69	60	50	41	33	25	16	8	1				
16	100	90	80	71	62	54	45	37	29	21	14	7	1			
18	100	91	81	72	64	56	48	40	33	26	19	12	6			
20	100	91	82	74	66	58	51	44	36	30	23	17	11	5		
22	100	92	83	75	68	60	53	46	40	33	27	21	15	10	4	
24	100	92	84	76	69	62	55	49	42	36	30	25	20	14	9	4
26	100	92	85	77	70	64	57	51	45	39	34	28	23	18	13	9
28	100	93	86	78	71	65	59	53	47	42	36	31	26	21	17	12
30	100	93	86	79	72	66	61	55	49	44	39	34	29	25	20	16

tent of the air. The lower the moisture content of the air, the more evaporation will occur from the wet bulb, and the lower the wet bulb temperature will be. The bigger the difference between the wet and dry bulb temperatures, the drier the air.

By using the dry bulb temperature and the difference between the wet bulb and dry bulb temperatures (as found of the *Dew point Temperature Chart in the Reference Tables* and on previous page) the dew point may be determined. The same data may be applied to the *Relative Humidity Chart* to determine the relative humidity (in the *Reference Tables* and on this page).

AIR PRESSURE

Air pressure is caused by the weight of the air. Air pressure is measured by a **barometer in inches of mercury** or **millibars**. Standard air pressure, also known as one atmosphere, at sea level is equal to 1013.2 millibars or 29.92 inches of mercury. **Isobars**, lines of equal pressure, are used on a weather map to indicate air pressure variations. On U.S. Weather Bureau maps, the interval between isobars is 4 millibars.

WIND

One major effect of differences in air pressure is the movement of air. The horizontal movement of air is called **wind**. Note: Winds are described in terms of both speed and direction and are named for the direction from which they blow. A north wind blows from the north toward the south and an ocean wind blows from the ocean toward the land.

A **wind vane** is used to indicate the direction the wind is blowing and an **anemometer** with a series of rotating cups measures wind speed. Wind direction is an important weather variable used to predict the weather.

Counterclockwise Rotation of a Hurricane in the Gulf of Mexico (Northern Hemisphere).

B. WEATHER VARIABLES

Warm air has a greater water holding capacity than cool air. Warm air is less dense and has more space between the molecules allowing for a greater capacity to hold water. For every 10°C rise in temperature, the air can hold approximately twice as much water vapor.

As the air temperature changes, so does the dew point and relative humidity. As air is cooled to the temperature at which it becomes saturated (the dew point temperature) the relative humidity approaches 100%. Cooling the air causes it to contract and become more dense, decreasing the space available between the molecules for water vapor.

As the difference between the dew point temperature and the air temperature decreases, there is a greater probability of water vapor condensing and forming precipitation. **Condensation** is the change of phase of water vapor (gas) to liquid water.

Variations in air pressure may be caused by temperature, altitude, or moisture content. A change in temperature brings about a change in pressure. Since warm air is less dense than cool air, warm air has a lower mass per unit volume (weight). Being less dense, warm air exerts less pressure and is lighter. As air cools it contracts increasing its density and so is heavier and exerts more pressure on Earth's surface. Note: Since temperature changes produce pressure variations, pressure changes also produce temperature variations.

Air pressure also decreases with an increase in altitude, because there are fewer gas molecules per unit volume as you go up in the atmosphere. Moist or humid air also exerts less pressure than dry air. This is caused by small, light water vapor molecules replacing the heavier gas molecules.

There is an inverse relationship between air temperature, altitude, and moisture content and the air pressure.

Uneven heating of the Earth's surface causes differences in temperature from one location to another. These temperature variations cause pressure variations which make the wind blow. Winds always move from areas of high pressure to areas of low pressure.

Monsoon means "seasonal wind." These winds bring either very dry or very wet weather, depending upon the season and their direction of flow.

Seasonal differences in temperatures of large land masses, such as Asia cause a disruption in the wind

MONSOONS OF
SOUTH SOUTHEAST ASIA

Sea Breeze

When air over land is warmer than over water, cooler air over water moves over land to replace rising air.

Land Breeze

When air over water is warmer than over land, cooler air over land moves over water to replace rising air.

belts. In the Northern Hemisphere's winter, the huge Asian landmass becomes very cold resulting in the formation of a semipermanent high pressure cell over the land. The warmer oceans surrounding Asia have air with much lower pressure. So in the winter, the descending air over Asia flows outward from the land to the ocean. This is called the winter monsoon. Since the wind is coming from the land, it brings dry weather to places such as India (see map on previous page).

Summer in the Northern Hemisphere brings the opposite temperature and pressure conditions. The Asian landmass heats up and now a semipermanent low pressure cell forms over the landmass. Air streams onto the land from the higher pressure area over the cooler oceans. This is the summer monsoon and since this air is coming from the ocean, it usually brings huge amounts of rain to many places in India. It is often called the wet monsoon.

This monsoonal effect occurs in other places as well, but not to as great an extent. A similar daily effect may be experienced along the immediate coast.

Along the coast on a summer afternoon the land becomes much warmer than the adjacent water surface. The air over the warm land heats, expands, and becomes less dense, forming lower pressure over the land. This results in cooler, denser air moving on to the land from the sea and pushing the warm air over the land upward. This results in a **sea breeze**.

At night, energy radiates more rapidly from the land surface than from the water surface. This results in higher air pressure over the land. As cooler air moves from the land toward the sea, a **land breeze** results.

Winds do not blow in a straight path from high to low pressure because wind direction is also influenced by the rotation of the Earth. In the Northern Hemisphere winds are deflected to their right and in the Southern Hemisphere to their left. This is known as the **Coriolis effect.** Often satellite photographs of cloud patterns show this curvature.

C. CLOUDS - PRECIPITATION

When air is cooled to the dew point and **condensation nuclei** (surfaces) are available, **condensation** will occur in the air. Microscopic particles of dust, salt, or smoke are common condensation nuclei. When the dew point temperature is above freezing, tiny droplets of liquid water form. If the dew point temperature is below freezing, water vapor solidifies directly into solid ice crystals (**deposition**).

The same process occurs at the Earth's surface. **Dew**, often seen in the early morning, is a result of condensation of water vapor from the atmosphere onto the Earth's surface. **Frost**, often seen in the fall and early spring after a cold night, is the result of deposition of water vapor below 0°C.

Orographic Effect

As air mass moves over the mountains, the rising air cools – producing clouds and precipitation on the windward side of the obstruction (mountain).

Cirrus Clouds

Cumulus Clouds

Cumulonimbus Clouds

Stratus Clouds

Wherever air rises, it cools. Rising air results from heating, convection currents, air moving up over a mountain (**orographic effect**) or being forced up at a frontal boundary. When the rising air cools to the dew point, condensation or deposition begins resulting in clouds made of tiny water droplets and/or ice crystals.

Where air is pushed up vertically, tall **cumuliform clouds** (cumulus, cumulonimbus) form. **Stratiform clouds** (cirrus and stratus) layer across the sky where air drifts up at a low angle.

Precipitation does not fall from all clouds because the cloud droplets are so small that the motion of the air keeps them suspended in the air. When condensation droplets and/or ice crystals coalesce (grow together) and become large enough to fall, **precipitation** occurs. As precipitation falls, it acts to clean the atmosphere by bringing down condensation nuclei and other materials suspended in the air.

Conversely, as air descends, it compresses (caused by an increase in pressure), and its temperature rises.

MOISTURE & ENERGY INPUT

Atmospheric moisture content is constantly changing because of evaporation and transpiration. **Evaporation** is the conversion of liquid water to vapor (gas) from the Earth's surface, such as soils, lakes, and streams, but primarily from the oceans. Moisture enters the air by means of evaporation and transpiration.

Transpiration is the loss of water from plants through their leaves. Plants absorb water from the ground through their roots, carry it up through the stems and release the water into the air from their leaves. Combined, these moisture input processes are known as **evapotranspiration**.

D. MOISTURE & ENERGY TRANSFER

CLOUD FORMATION

Most clouds are formed by cooling in rising air. As air rises in the atmosphere, expansion causes cooling as potential energy is released. When the dew point temperature is reached in the rising air, condensation (or deposition) begins to occur forming clouds and perhaps precipitation. Since the condensation process releases heat energy into the air, the cooling rate decreases as the air continues to rise.

Evaporation and Transpiration

Both evaporation and transpiration require the absorption of energy and so constitute an energy input into the atmosphere in the form of more energetic water molecules.

Properties of Water		
Property	in Joules/gram	in Calories/gram
Heat energy gained during melting	334 Joules/gram	80 calories/gram
Heat energy released during freezing	334 Joules/gram	80 calories/gram
Heat energy gained during vaporization	2260 Joules/gram	540 calories/gram
Heat energy gained during condensation	2260 Joules/gram	540 calories/gram
Density at 3.98°C 1,00 gram/milliter		

VAPOR PRESSURE

The rate of evaporation is dependent upon:
- the amount of energy available (temperature)
- the surface area of the water source
- the moisture content of the air (vapor pressure)

The pressure exerted by the water vapor within the atmosphere at a given location is called the **vapor pressure.** Near the surface of water, vapor pressure is greatest, decreasing with altitude above the water's surface.

When there is very little water vapor in the air, evapotranspiration can take place rapidly, but as the amount of vapor pressure increases, the rate of evaporation decreases until the air is saturated and cannot hold any additional moisture.

LATENT HEAT

Water exists in our environment as solid (ice), liquid, and water vapor (gas). **Latent heat** is a form of **potential energy** which is absorbed or released when a change of phase occurs. When heat is transferred within the same phase (solid, liquid, or gas), the temperature of the material is changed.

However, when heat is applied to different states of matter and there is a **change of phase** (such as solid to liquid), the temperature of the material remains the same, since there is no increase in the **kinetic energy** of the molecules. Instead, the heat energy is either **absorbed** (solid to liquid to gas) or **released** (gas to liquid to solid), increasing or decreasing the potential energy of the molecules.

Heat is gained or lost in the phase change. The amount of latent heat is different for various substances and the type of phase change. The amount of heat either gained or lost is equal to the product of the mass of the matter times the latent heat per unit of mass.

Latent Heat in Atmospheric Meterology

Latent heat of condensation (Lc): Refers to the heat gained by the air when water vapor changes into a liquid. Lc=2500 Joules per gram (J/g) of water or 600 calories per gram (cal/g) of water.

Latent heat of fusion (Lf): Refers to the heat lost or gained by the air when liquid water changes to ice or vice versa. Lf=333 Joules per gram (J/g) of water or 80 calories per gram (cal/g) of water.

Latent heat of sublimation (Ls): Refers to the heat lost or gained by the air when ice changes to vapor or vice versa. Ls=2833 Joules per gram (J/g) of water or 680 calories per gram (cal/g) of water.

Latent heat of vaporization (Lv): Refers to the heat lost by the air when liquid water changes into vapor. This is also commonly known as the latent heat of evaporation. Lv= -2500 Joules per gram (J/g) of water or -600 calories per gram (cal/g) of water.

LATENT HEAT OF WATER

Melting occurs when water changes phase from a solid to a liquid. **Freezing** occurs when water changes from a liquid into a solid. The latent heat for these changes is 333 Joules per gram of water and is called the **heat of fusion**. In other words, one gram of ice absorbs (gains) 333 Joules of heat energy when changed to a liquid. When the phase change is reversed, liquid to ice, 333 Joules per gram of heat is released (lost) by the water.

A significantly greater amount of energy is required to change a given mass of liquid water to water vapor than is required to change ice to liquid. Evaporation, requiring the addition of 2500 Joules per gram (J/g) of water (called the **heat of vaporization**) occurs when water in the liquid phase is changed to water vapor (gas).

When **condensation** (vapor to liquid) occurs, latent heat of 2500 Joules per gram (J/g) of water is released. When condensation is taking place in the atmosphere, solar energy that was stored in the process of evaporation is released into the environment. This latent heat is the energy that intensifies and sustains violent storms.

The amount of energy needed to produce an equal temperature change in equal masses of different materials varies with the materials. The amount

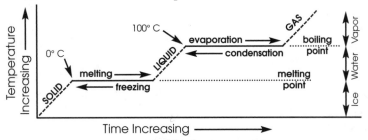

Phase Change Graph for Water

NO PERMISSION HAS BEEN GRANTED BY N&N PUBLISHING COMPANY, INC TO REPRODUCE ANY PART OF THIS BOOK BY ANY MECHANICAL, PHOTOGRAPHIC, OR ELECTRONIC PROCESS.

of heat energy needed to raise the temperature of one gram of a material one degree on the Celsius scale is called **specific heat**. The higher the specific heat a material has, the more energy it takes to heat it and the longer the time it takes for it to cool.

Liquid water has the highest specific heat capacity among all of the naturally occurring materials on Earth: 4.8 Joules/gram/°C (1.0 calories/gram/°C). (See the *Earth Science Reference Tables* for the specific heats.)

ENERGY TRANSFER

Energy may be transferred in three ways: **conduction, convection,** and **radiation**. In matter (solids, liquids, and gases), heat energy may be transferred by either conduction or convection. In space, energy is transferred through electromagnetic wave radiation.

Conduction of thermal (heat) energy occurs as an interaction of matter at the molecular or atomic level. When atoms or molecules collide at an interface, thermal energy is transferred from one atom (or molecule) to another. The efficiency of the energy transfer depends upon the densities of the substances involved. For example, the molecules within a gas are relatively far apart; therefore, the energy transferred is less than within a liquid, where the molecules are relatively close together. Solids have the most compact molecules and have the greatest energy transfer.

Convection is the transfer of thermal energy by the movement of molecules within liquids and gases. The movement is from regions of higher density molecules to lower density molecules. Since warm air is less dense than cool air, the warm air rises as it is displaced by the cool air that settles because of the cool air's greater density.

Specific Heats of Common Materials

MATERIAL	SPECIFIC HEAT (Joules/gram • °C)
Liquid water	4.18
Solid water (ice)	2.11
Water vapor	2.00
Dry air	1.01
Basalt	0.84
Granite	0.79
Iron	0.45
Copper	0.38
Lead	0.13

Conduction in a Pan
Heat energy is transferred (conducted) through the metal spoon from the hot pan to the hand.

For example, heated air rises, because it is displaced by cooler air. As the cool air comes in contact with the heat source, it is warmed and also rises. The warm air moves away from the heat source, then cools and falls, maintaining the cycle. The resulting circulation is referred to as a **convection current** or a **convection cell**.

DENSITY DIFFERENCES

As the moisture content and/or the temperature of the air increases, the density of that volume decreases. Therefore, density increase is expressed as the inverse (opposite) of temperature and moisture increase.

One of the results of density differences and the effect of the gravity field is the formation of convection cells. A **convection cell** is formed when the air circulates by rising in one place and sinking at another. The effect may be observed in the ocean and Earth's mantle as well as the atmosphere.

Convection cells, or currents, occur because cooler, more dense air sinks toward the Earth's surface, pulled by gravity, causing the warmer, less dense air to rise. Variations in insolation and radiation affect the convection in the atmosphere. **Radiational cooling** in the polar regions results in sinking air which begins to move toward the Equator.

E. WINDS & PRESSURE BELTS

There are **pressure "belts"** produced in the atmosphere as a result of convection. Low pressure belts are found at the equator and at the 60° North and South Latitudes. High pressure belts are found at the 30° North and South Latitudes as well as at the Poles.

Planetary Wind Patterns

Convection Cell In a Room
Warm air rises, then cools and falls, maintaining the cycle.

In the low pressure belts, air converges (moves together) and rises; whereas, belts of high pressure are associated with descending air that diverges (moves apart) at the surface. Therefore, regions of low pressure are often called **zones of convergence**, while regions of high pressure are called **zones of divergence**.

Wind is a result of the movement of the air from regions of divergence to regions of convergence. In this way the atmosphere distributes solar energy over the whole Earth. However, the cold, dense, sinking air in the polar regions does not move in a straight path to replace the warm, light air rising in the tropical regions. As the Earth rotates, the wind direction is modified as it flows between the pressure belts. The Coriolis effect deflects the winds to their right in the Northern Hemisphere and their left in the Southern Hemisphere.

The location of the Earth's pressure belts and the affect of the Earth's rotation determines the general position and direction of planetary wind circulation. Factors such as altitude and position relative to mountains and large bodies of water may modify the wind pattern.

source regions. An **arctic** air mass is identified with an **A**, a **polar** with a **P**, and a **tropical** with a **T**. In addition, if the source is over water, it is called **maritime** (**m**). If it forms over land, it is called **continental** (**c**).

Identifying an air mass is easy. If the source of an air mass is a northern land area, such as in Canada, it is identified as continental polar (**cP**) and is described as cold and dry. An air mass formed over the Gulf of Mexico would be identified as an **mT** air mass, being warm and moist.

North American Air Masses

F. AIR MASS CHARACTERISTICS

In the atmosphere, an **air mass** is a large body of air having characteristics, including temperature and moisture, that are fairly uniform at any given level. These air masses are identified on the basis of their **average air pressure, moisture content, winds**, and **temperature**.

AIR MASS SOURCE REGIONS

Air masses have definite characteristics which depend upon their geographic region of origin, called the **source region**. In general, if the origin of an air mass is at high latitude, it is cold. If the source region is at low latitude, it is warm. For example, in the Northern Hemisphere, cool air masses come mainly from the north, and warm air masses come mainly from the south. An air mass formed over water is moist, but if the air mass forms over land, it is dry. As an air mass remains stationary in its source region, it becomes more intense and generally larger.

On a weather map, air masses are identified and described according to their

CYCLONES & ANTICYCLONES

Cyclone (Low Pressure System). In the Northern Hemisphere, air circulates into a low pressure or **cyclone** in a counterclockwise direction. This pattern of air motion in a cyclone may be hundreds of kilometers in diameter. Converging air rises near the center of the low. Cyclones are associated with clouds and precipitation. Decreasing air pressure often brings warm, rainy, or unsettled weather.

Satellite Weather Map

Anticyclone (High Pressure System). In the Northern Hemisphere, the circulation of air in a high pressure air mass or **anticyclone** is clockwise, spiraling outwards at the surface. The descending air in anticyclones is associated with cool and clear weather.

FRONTS

A **front** is the boundary or interface between two air masses on the ground. In the air this boundary is called the **frontal surface**. A front forms between two air masses having differing temperatures. Along the frontal surface, atmospheric conditions are usually unstable, and precipitation is most probable.

NORTHERN HEMISPHERE CYCLONIC WEATHER

A **warm front** forms when the warm air meets and slowly glides up and over the back of cold air. A **cold front** is the result of cold air pushing into a region of warm air. As the fronts are forming, the entire cyclonic storm (low pressure from which the warm and cold fronts extend) generally moves toward the northeast directed by the strong winds high in the troposphere.

Both fronts are associated with clouds and precipitation, because warm air is moving upward, resulting in cooling and condensation.

Warm Front showing warm air rising over cold air and displacing it.

Cold Front showing cold air pushing under warm air and displacing it.

Occluded Front (cold front type) with interface between cool and cold air.

However, at warm fronts stratiform clouds produce steady precipitation, usually of longer duration than cold fronts. The cumuliform clouds associated with the faster moving cold fronts, usually result in brief but heavy precipitation, often accompanied by gusty winds and thunderstorms.

When a cyclone is first developing, it moves rapidly, but as it becomes older, the cyclone slows. Over time, the wedge of warm air tends to narrow, because the cold air moves faster than the warm air, forcing the less dense warm air up. The cold air front eventually overtakes the warm front, resulting in an **occlusion**.

An **occluded front** is the interface between a cool and a cold air mass. When the trailing cold front overtakes the warm front, the two cooler air masses converge and force all of the warm air to rise. Occluded fronts may produce some type of heavy precipitation.

A **stationary front** is produced when the boundary between two air masses of differing characteristics is not moving. The weather of these fronts most closely resembles warm front weather conditions

G. WEATHER FORECASTING

Field values such as temperature and pressure may be shown on weather maps with the use of **isolines**, lines connecting places with the same value. A map may show the temperature field by using **isotherms** or the air pressure field by using **isobars**.

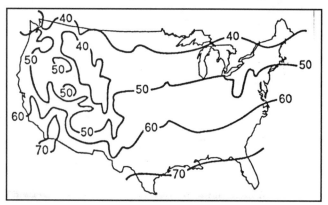

Proximity of the isolines indicates the **gradient** of the field. Where the isolines are close together, the gradient is steep; where the isolines are far apart, the gradient is gentle.

Temperature or pressure gradient may be determined numerically by determining the difference in numerical value between two points and dividing that difference by the distance between the points.

The speed of the wind is directly related to the **pressure field gradient**. The greater the difference between a high and low pressure area and the less distance between the pressure centers, the greater the wind speed. Where the isobars on a weather map are closest together, the wind speed is the greatest.

STATION MODEL

On the daily *United States Weather Bureau Weather Map*, surface data is plotted at many stations using numbers and symbols. The following is a sample station model for a weather map (for further information, see the Weather Map Information section of the *Reference Tables*).

The **weather station model** describes:
- the sky around the weather observation station, including the amount of cloud cover;
- the present weather conditions, including precipitation type and amount;
- the visibility (measured in miles);
- the air temperature and dew point in °F;
- the wind speed and direction; and,
- the barometric pressure (measured in millibars) and the pressure trend.

SYNOPTIC WEATHER MAPS

A **synoptic weather map** offers a "bird's eye view" of the weather. By studying the atmospheric conditions as they exist simultaneously over a broad area (synoptic observations), it is possible to make short term predictions of future weather conditions.

WEATHER FORECASTING

The path that the center of a low or storm travels is called the **storm track**. The rate of movement of a storm can usually be determined and is generally predictable in the continental United States. Tropical air mass-

Using data from weather instruments, weather satellites, and computer analysis has enabled the weather forecaster to make short term forecasts (1-3 days) with good accuracy, 80 to 90 percent of the time. It is far more difficult to make forecasts extending a week or more in advance.

MODERN FORECASTING

Since weather variables are related in a complex way, accurate weather prediction is also complex. The National Weather Service in the United States uses some of the largest computers in the world to analyze the huge amount of data that streams in every hour of the day and night. Ground observations, radar and satellite imagery all contribute to the increasing reliability of the day-to-day weather forecast.

It is, however, unlikely that accurate weather predictions will be made for a week or more in advance, because a small, unexpected disturbance may have world wide unexpected effects on the weather.

H. SEVERE STORMS

The most common of the severe storms is the **thunderstorm**. At any given time it is estimated that approximately 1800 thunderstorms are occurring on the Earth. Thunderstorms form where unstable air laden with water vapor is forced to rise abruptly. As condensation forms clouds, energy is released heating the air and increasing the storm's vertical development.

Lighting, flooding from heavy downpours, and damaging hail are three dangers associated with severe thunderstorms. In the U.S. more people are usually killed each year by lightning than by hurricanes and tornadoes. Seek shelter indoors during these storms avoiding windows and electrical

es most often move northeast, and polar air masses usually move southeast.

In the northern middle latitudes, the prevailing westerly winds blow from west to east and tend to direct the weather patterns. High in the troposphere, there are strong winds capable of slowing down or speeding up a jet airplane as much as 300 kilometers per hour. These wave-like currents with high winds, called the **jet stream**, move toward the east.

Most weather forecasts are based upon movement of air masses. Using data to determine the path and speed of a storm center, forecasters can predict the weather changes ahead of the storm.

Meteorologists use records of past weather data and computer analysis to predict weather conditions as a probability of occurrence. If it rained 4 out of 5 days in a region when the wind was from the east, the pressure was falling, and the relative humidity was rising, when these conditions occur again, the probability of rain would be 80%.

Wind Direction Relationship Between LOW And HIGH Pressure Areas

In the Northern Hemisphere, air currents move out of a HIGH in a clockwise direction and into a LOW in a counterclockwise direction. On a Weather Map, similar symbols are used to represent various fronts.

appliances. Stay in your car if you are traveling. If caught outdoors, avoid high objects like trees which are most likely to be struck.

Thunderstorms are storms of short duration. As soon as immediate lightning danger has passed, quickly move out of low areas subject to flooding.

From June through September, tropical depressions, which may develop into **hurricanes**, form in the low latitudes over warm, tropical water. Energy released by condensation over the warm water surface intensifies these huge rotating storms. With much lower pressure and greater intensity than a middle-latitude cyclone, the hurricane has a central area of calm with descending air currents called the "**eye**." Around the eye there are violent winds (in excess of 119 km/hr) and heavy precipitation.

Hurricanes are the most destructive of the severe storms because of their large size having diameters from 300 to 600 kilometers and paths which may cover a thousand miles. The most severe damage is done by water along low-lying coastal areas. People in these areas need to evacuate. Outdoor objects that are not secured may become missiles of destruction in the strong winds. Early preparation for living several days without electricity, transportation, or fuel is wise.

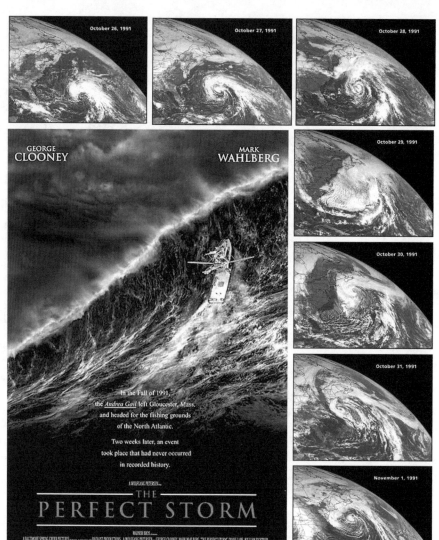

http://perfectstorm.warnerbros.com ©2000 Warner Bros.
satellite images courtesy of NOAA/National Climatic Data Center

Because hurricanes pick up moisture and gain energy when they are over warm water, they die down when their path takes them over land or cool water. The average life span of these destructive storms is nine days.

Data from weather satellites assist the **National Hurricane Center** in Florida and the **National Weather Service** in tracking hurricanes and issuing appropriate warnings.

Severe thunderstorms may spawn the most violent storm, the **tornado**. When warm, moist maritime tropical air collides with cold, dry continental polar air, the conditions are favorable for the development of these storms. Tornadoes are most likely to occur in the late afternoon in spring and early summer when the temperature differences between the air masses is greatest. Most commonly they occur in the Great Plains and Gulf States area.

Their funnel-shaped cloud extends down out of the cumulonimbus cloud of a thunderstorm. The center of the funnel is called the **vortex**. Winds move counterclockwise around the vortex in speeds in excess of 600 km/hr (370 mph). Basements and interior hallways, or small rooms and closets on the lowest floor offer the greatest protection from structural collapse and flying debris. If caught outside, lie flat in the nearest ditch and cover your head and neck.

The "twisters" are fortunately small in size with a maximum diameter approximately 100 meters. These storms travel at 40-60 km/hr as they cause devastating damage in their unpredictable paths which vary from 25-65 kilometers in length. The **National Severe Storm Forecast Center** in Kansas City predicts and tracks tornadoes.

Wet bulb

Dry bulb

QUESTIONS FOR UNIT 6

Base your answers to questions 1 and 2 on the weather instrument shown in the diagram above.

1 What are the equivalent Celsius temperature readings for the Fahrenheit readings shown?
1 wet 21°C, dry 27°C
2 wet 26°C, dry 37°C
3 wet 70°C, dry 80°C
4 wet 158°C, dry 176°C

2 Which weather variables are most easily determined by using this weather instrument?
1 air temperature and windspeed
2 visibility and wind direction
3 relative humidity and dew point
4 air pressure and cloud type

3 A balloon carrying weather instruments is released at the Earth's surface and rises through the troposphere. As the balloon rises, what will the instruments generally indicate? [Refer to the *Earth Science Reference Tables*.]
1 a decrease in both air temperature and air pressure
2 an increase in both air temperature and air pressure
3 an increase in air temperature and a decrease in air pressure
4 a decrease in air temperature and an increase in air pressure

4 Which graph best represents the relationship between air temperature and air density in the atmosphere?

5 The graph shows air temperature for an area near the Earth's surface during a 12-hour period.
Which graph best illustrates the probable change in air pressure during the same time period?

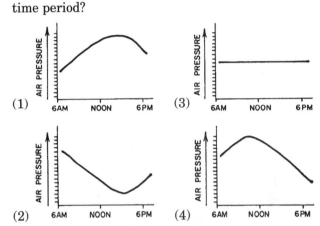

6 Which list shows atmospheric layers in the correct order upward from the Earth's surface?
1 thermosphere, mesosphere, stratosphere, troposphere
2 troposphere, stratosphere, mesosphere, thermosphere
3 stratosphere, mesosphere, troposphere, thermosphere
4 thermosphere, troposphere, mesosphere, stratosphere

7 According to the *Reference Tables*, an air pressure of 29.65 inches of mercury is equal to
(1) 984.0 mb   (3) 1001.0 mb
(2) 999.0 mb   (4) 1004.0 mb

8 Wind moves from regions of
1 high temperature toward regions of low temperature
2 high pressure toward regions of low pressure
3 high precipitation toward regions of low precipitation
4 high humidity toward regions of low humidity

9 The wind speed between two nearby locations is affected most directly by differences in the
1 latitude between the location
2 longitude between the locations
3 air pressure between the locations
4 Coriolis effect between the locations

10 The Coriolis effect is caused by the
   1 rotation of the Earth on its axis
   2 revolution of the Earth around the Sun
   3 movement of the Earth in relation to the Moon
   4 movement of the Earth in relation to the Milky Way

11 The following diagram represents an activity in which an eye dropper was used to place a drop of water on a spinning globe. Instead of flowing due south toward the target point, the drop appeared to follow a curved path and missed the target.

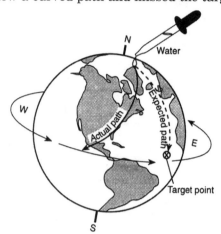

This curved-path phenomenon most directly affects the Earth's
   1 tilt   3 wind belts
   2 Moon phases   4 tectonic plates

12 In the Northern Hemisphere, a wind blowing from the north will be deflected toward the
   1 northwest   3 southwest
   2 northeast   4 southeast

13 The map represents a portion of an air-pressure field at the Earth's surface.

At which position is wind speed lowest?
   (1) A   (3) C
   (2) B   (4) D

Note: Question 14 has only 3 choices.

14 As the amount of moisture in the air increases, the atmospheric pressure will probably
   1 decrease
   2 increase
   3 remains the same

15 The air temperature and the wet bulb temperature were measured and both were found to be 18°C. Two hours later, measurements were taken again and the air temperature was 20°C, while the wet bulb temperature remained at 18°C. The relative humidity of the air during those two hours
   1 decreased
   2 increased
   3 remained the same

16 The two thermometers show the dry-bulb and wet-bulb temperatures of the air. According to the *Reference Tables*, what is the approximate dew point temperature of the air?
   (1) -25° C
   (2) 6° C
   (3) 3° C
   (4) 4° C

17 The graph below shows changes in air temperature and dew point temperature over a 24-hour period at a particular location.

At what time was the relative humidity *lowest*?
   (1) midnight   (3) 10 a.m.
   (2) 6 a.m.   (4) 4 p.m.

18 Which conditions must exist for condensation to occur in the atmosphere?
   1 The air is saturated and a condensation surface is available.
   2 The air temperature is above the dew point and the air pressure is high.
   3 The air is calm and the relative humidity is low.
   4 The relative humidity is low and the air pressure is high.

19 What is the approximate relative humidity if the dry-bulb temperature is 12°C and the wet-bulb temperature is 7°C?
   (1) 28%   (3) 48%
   (2) 35%   (4) 65%

20 In order for clouds to form, cooling air must be
1 saturated and have no condensation nuclei
2 saturated and have condensation nuclei
3 unsaturated and have no condensation nuclei
4 unsaturated and have condensation nuclei

21 Which statement best explains why a cloud is forming as shown in the diagram?

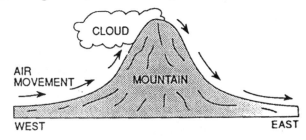

1 Water vapor is condensing.
2 Moisture is evaporating.
3 Cold air rises and compresses.
4 Warm air sinks and expands.

22 Which planetary wind pattern is present in many areas of little rainfall?
1 Winds converge and air sinks.
2 Winds converge and air rises.
3 Winds diverge and air sinks.
4 Winds diverge and air rises.

23 Which source provides the most energy for atmospheric weather changes?
1 radiation from the Sun
2 radioactivity from the Earth's interior
3 heat stored in ocean water
4 heat stored in polar ice caps

24 Which weather conditions are most probable when the moisture content of the air increases, resulting in a lower atmospheric pressure?
1 sunny and fair
2 cold and windy
3 partly cloudy, with skies becoming clear
4 cloudy, with a chance of precipitation

25 Which is a form of precipitation?
1 frost   3 dew
2 snow   4 fog

26 Why is it possible for no rain to be falling from a cloud?
1 The water droplets are too small to fall.
2 The cloud is water vapor.
3 The dew point has not yet been reached in the cloud.
4 There are no condensation nuclei in the cloud.

27 In which atmospheric layer is most water vapor found?
1 troposphere   3 thermosphere
2 stratosphere   4 mesosphere

28 Most moisture enters the atmosphere by processes of
1 convection and conduction
2 condensation and radiation
3 reflection and absorption
4 transpiration and evaporation

29 Equal quantities of water are placed in four uncovered containers with different shapes and left on a table at room temperature. From which container will the water evaporate most rapidly?

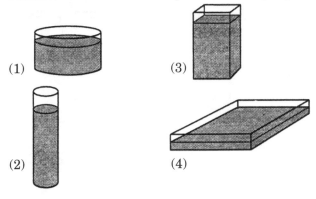

30 At what temperature would ice crystals form from air that has a dew point temperature of -6°C?
(1) 6° C   (3) -2° C
(2) 0° C   (4) -7° C

Base your answers to questions 31 through 33 on the *Reference Tables* and the diagram which represents the water cycle.

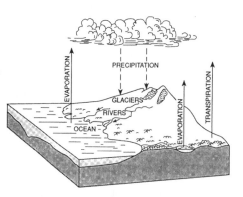

31 By which process does most water vapor enter the atmosphere?
1 evaporation from lakes and rivers
2 evaporation from ocean surfaces
3 evapotranspiration from land areas
4 sublimation from polar ice and snow

32 During which process does water vapor release 2260 Joules per gram of latent heat?
1 condensation   3 transpiration
2 evaporation   4 precipitation

33 Precipitation is most likely occurring at the time represented in the diagram because
1 the air has been warmed because of expansion
2 no condensation nuclei are present in the air
3 the relative humidity of the air is low
4 the water droplets are heavy enough to fall

34 The rate of evaporation from the surface of a lake would be increased by
1 a decrease in wind velocity
2 a decrease in the amount of insolation
3 an increase in the surface area of the lake
4 an increase in the moisture content of the air

35 Each arrow in the diagram represents a process involving a phase change of water

Each process can take place only if
1 mass and volume remain the same
2 heat energy is added or released
3 the number of molecules is increased or decreased
4 the dew point temperature is increased or decreased

36 The change from vapor phase to liquid phase is called
1 evaporation   3 precipitation
2 condensation   4 transpiration

37 Which process results in a release of latent heat energy?
1 melting of ice
2 heating of liquid water
3 condensation of water vapor
4 evaporation of water

38 The diagram shows a container of water that is being heated.

The movement of water shown by the arrows is most likely caused by
1 density differences
2 insolation
3 the Coriolis effect
4 the Earth's rotation

39 On a sunny day at the beach, the dark-colored sand gets hot while the water stays cool because the sand
1 reflects less energy and has a lower specific heat than the water
2 reflects less energy and has a higher specific heat than the water
3 reflects more energy and has a lower specific heat than the water
4 reflects more energy and has a higher specific heat than the water

40 Which cross section best shows the normal movement of the air over Oswego, New York, on a very hot summer afternoon?

41 Wind is part of heat flow by
1 radiation   3 convection
2 conduction   4 reflection

42 Which of the following statements best describes the planetary wind pattern at the equator?
1 Winds converge from higher latitudes.
2 Winds diverge from the equator.
3 Winds sink from higher altitudes.
4 Winds flow as high altitude jet streams.

Base your answers to questions 43 through 47 on the diagram which represents the general circulation of the Earth's atmosphere and the Earth's planetary wind and pressure belts. Points A through F represent locations on the Earth's surface.

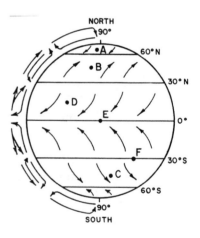

43 The curving path of the surface winds shown in the diagram are caused by the Earth's
1 gravitational field   3 rotation
2 magnetic field   4 revolution

44 Which location might be in New York State?
(1) A   (3) C
(2) B   (4) F

45 Which location is experiencing a southwest planetary wind?
(1) A   (3) C
(2) B   (4) F

46 Which location is near the center of a low-pressure belt where daily rains are common?
(1) E   (3) F
(2) B   (4) D

47 The arrows in the diagram represent energy transfer by which process?
1 conduction   3 convection
2 radiation   4 absorption

48 The air temperature is 10°C. Which dew point temperature would result in the highest probability of precipitation?
(1) 8°C   (3) 0°C
(2) 6°C   (4) -4°C

49 Which letter on the map at the right represents the area closest to the source region of a cT air mass?

(1) A   (3) C
(2) B   (4) D

50 The weather map shows a frontal system that has followed a typical storm track. The air mass located over point X most likely originated over the

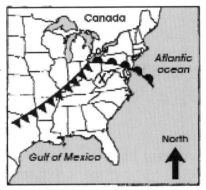

1 northern Atlantic Ocean
2 central part of Canada
3 Gulf of Mexico
4 Pacific Northwest

51 A low-pressure system is shown on the weather map below.

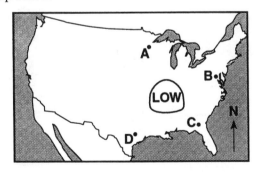

Toward which point will the low-pressure system move if it follows a normal storm track?
(1) A   (3) C
(2) B   (4) D

Base your answers to questions 52 and 53 on the *Reference Tables* and the diagram of the station model.

52 The barometric pressure is
(1) 1013.0 mb   (3) 130.0 mb
(2) 913.0 mb   (4) 10.28 mb

53 The weather forecast for the next six hours at this station most likely would be
1 overcast, hot, unlimited visibility
2 overcast, hot, poor visibility
3 overcast, cold, probable snow
4 sunny, cold, probable rain

54 Which diagram below best represents the air circulation around a Northern Hemisphere low-pressure center?

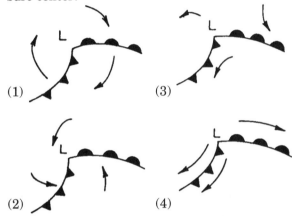

55 Cities A, B, C, and D on the weather map are being affected by a low-pressure system (cyclone).

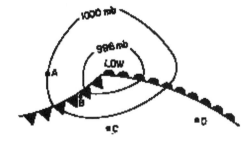

Which city would have the most unstable atmospheric conditions and the greatest chance of precipitation?
(1) A   (3) C
(2) B   (4) D

56 A weather station reporting clear, cold weather with little wind is probably located
1 in the center of a high
2 in the center of a low
3 ahead of a warm front
4 at a cold front

57 Which map best represents the normal air circulation around a high-pressure air mass located over central New York State?

(1) (3)

(2) (4)

58 Which weather station model indicates the greatest probability of precipitation?

60 Why do the clouds begin to form at the elevation of *D*?
1 The air has cooled to the dew point temperature at this elevation.
2 The water droplets are too small to be seen below this elevation.
3 The temperature is 0°C at this elevation.
4 The air below this elevation does not have enough condensation nuclei for clouds to form.

61 What is the dew point temperature at location E when the dry-bulb reading is 18°C and the wet-bulb reading is 11°C?
(1) 1°C   (3) 7°C
(2) −10°C   (4) 4°C

62 Which diagram best shows the probable wind direction for the conditions shown?

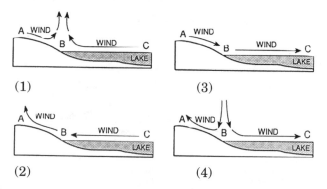

(1) (3)

(2) (4)

Base your answers to questions 59 through 62 on the *Earth Science Reference Tables*, the diagram below, and your knowledge of Earth science. The diagram shows a section of the shore of Lake Ontario. Surface air-pressure readings are shown for three of the locations.

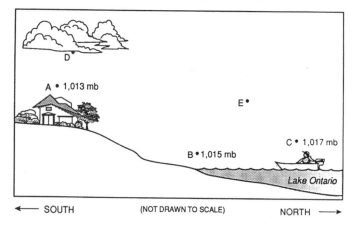

← SOUTH   (NOT DRAWN TO SCALE)   NORTH →

Base your answers to questions 63 through 65 on the *Earth Science Reference Tables*, the map below, and your knowledge of Earth science. The map shows the source regions for various types of air masses affecting the weather of the continental United States. Regions labeled with the same letter produce air masses with similar characteristics. Point *X* represents a location in the central United States.

59 [Refer to the *Earth Science Reference Tables*.] When converted to inches of mercury, the air pressure reading of 1,017 millibars at C is equal to
(1) 33.0 in   (3) 30.03 in
(2) 30.30 in   (4) 30.00 in

63 On a weather map, which symbol would be used to represent an air mass that formed in region B?
(1) mP   (3) cP
(2) mT   (4) cT

64 Which atmospheric conditions will most likely exist when air masses from source regions *B* and *C* meet at point *X*?
1 clearing skies and little wind
2 cloudiness and precipitation
3 decreasing relative humidity and rising temperature
4 appearance of condensation nuclei and constant dew point temperature

65 Which map symbol represents a stationary front that formed when an air mass from source region *B* met an air mass from source region *D*?

(1)

(2)

(3)

(4)

Base your answers to questions 66 through 68 on the *Earth Science Reference Tables*, the information and diagram below, and your knowledge of Earth science.

Mass in grams

Scale

The diagram represents a model that shows how air density is affected by the addition of water vapor to the air. Marbles with different masses, representing nitrogen, oxygen, and carbon dioxide, were used to fill a container to show a certain volume of dry air. The container was placed on a scale to find the mass of this volume of dry air.

A few marbles representing nitrogen (N_2) and oxygen (O_2) were removed and replaced with marbles representing water vapor (H_2O) to show the same volume of air with water vapor present. The relative mass of each gas, as represented by the marbles, is shown in the data table.

DATA TABLE

Molecule Symbol	Gas	Mass
N_2	Nitrogen	28 g
O_2	Oxygen	32 g
CO_2	Carbon Dioxide	44 g
H_2O	Water Vapor	18 g

66 According to the data table, which gas molecule has the *least* mass?
1 nitrogen
2 oxygen
3 carbon dioxide
4 water vapor

67 When a few of the marbles representing nitrogen and oxygen are replaced with marbles representing water vapor, the air model will become
1 lighter and less dense
2 lighter and more dense
3 heavier and less dense
4 heavier and more dense

68 After water vapor molecules enter the Earth's atmosphere, what conditions must occur before they can become liquid?
1 warming temperatures and condensation
2 warming temperatures and evaporation
3 cooling temperatures and condensation
4 cooling temperatures and evaporation

Base your answers to questions 69 through 71 on the *Earth Science Reference Tables*, the weather map below, and your knowledge of Earth science. The map shows part of the southern United States and northern Mexico.

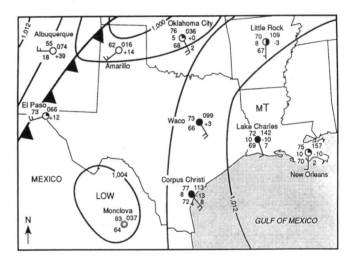

69 At which city is the visibility 8 miles?
1 Little Rock, Arkansas
2 Lake Charles, Louisiana
3 Oklahoma City, Oklahoma
4 New Orleans, Louisiana

70 The isolines on this map connect locations that have the same
1 dew point temperature
2 air temperature
3 barometric pressure
4 relative humidity

71 Which city has the *least* chance of precipitation during the next 3 hours?
1 Oklahoma City, Oklahoma
2 Waco, Texas
3 Lake Charles, Louisiana
4 Albuquerque, New Mexico

72 The following diagram represents a cross section of air masses and frontal surfaces along line *AB*. The dashed lines represent precipitation.

Which weather map best represents this frontal system?

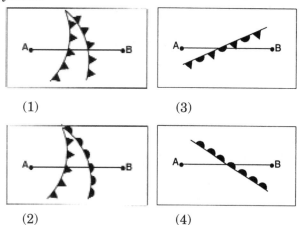

73 Which statement best explains why precipitation occurs at frontal boundaries?
1 Cold fronts move slower than warm fronts.
2 Cold fronts move faster than warm fronts.
3 Warm, moist air sinks when it meets cold, dry air.
4 Warm, moist air rises when it meets cold, dry air.

Base your answers to questions 74 through 76 on the *Earth Science Reference Tables* and the weather map below. The map shows a low-pressure system. Weather data is given for cities *A* through *D*.

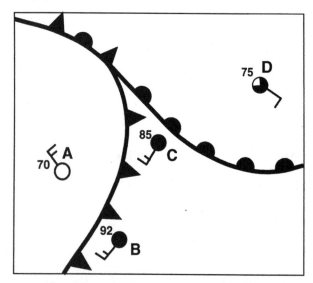

74 Which map correctly shows the locations of the continental polar (cP) and maritime tropical (mT) air masses?

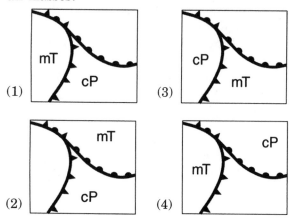

75 Which city is least likely to have precipitation starting in the next few hours?
(1) *A*   (3) *C*
(2) *B*   (4) *D*

76 Which map correctly shows arrows indicating the probable surface wind pattern?

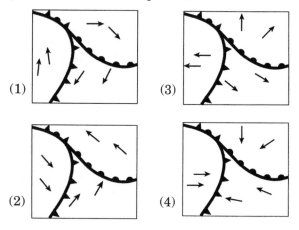

77 An observer reports the following data for a location in New York State:

Air temperature = 35°C
Pressure = 996 mb
Relative humidity = 84%

The weather conditions at this location would best be described as
1 hot and dry   3 cool and dry
2 hot and humid   4 cool and humid

Base your answers to questions 78 through 81 on the *Earth Science Reference Tables*, the diagram below, and your knowledge of Earth science. The diagram represents a satellite image of Hurricane Gilbert in the Gulf of Mexico. Each *X* represents the position of the eye of the storm on the date indicated.

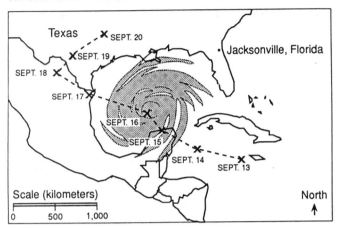

Base your answers to questions 82 through 86 on the *Earth Science Reference Tables*, the weather map above, and your knowledge of Earth science. The weather map shows a hurricane that was located over southern Florida. The isobars show air pressure in inches of mercury. Letters *A* through *D* represent four widely separated locations.

KEY - ⑤ = Hurricane center

78 The surface wind pattern associated with Hurricane Gilbert was
1 counterclockwise and toward the center
2 counterclockwise and away from the center
3 clockwise and toward the center
4 clockwise and away from the center

79 What was the probable source of moisture for this hurricane?
1 carbon dioxide from the atmosphere
2 winds from the coastal deserts
3 transpiration from tropical jungles
4 evaporation from the ocean

80 On September 18, Hurricane Gilbert changed direction. Which statement provides the most probable reason for this change?
1 The air mass was cooled by the land surface.
2 The storm entered the prevailing westerlies wind belt.
3 The amount of precipitation released by the storm changed suddenly.
4 The amount of insolation received by the air mass decreased.

81 The air mass that gave rise to Hurricane Gilbert would be identified as
(1) cP   (3) mT
(2) cT   (4) mP

82 What is the latitude and longitude at the center of the hurricane?
(1) 26° N 81° W   (3) 34° N 81° W
(2) 26° N 89° W   (4) 34° N 89° W

83 At which location were the winds of this hurricane the strongest?
(1) A   (3) C
(2) B   (4) D

84 What was the direction of movement of surface winds associated with this hurricane?
1 counterclockwise and away from the center
2 counterclockwise and toward the center
3 clockwise and away from the center
4 clockwise and toward the center

85 Which station model best represents some of the atmospheric conditions at location *A*?

86 Which map best shows the most likely track of this hurricane?

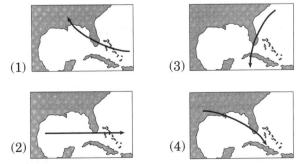

87 Hurricanes accounted for an average of 17 deaths per year from 1972 year 1991. However, the hurricane of 1938 was responsible for at least 600 deaths as it moved across Long Island into New England. What is the best explanation for the decrease in hurricane related deaths in recent years?
1 Hurricanes prior to 1970 were of greater intensity than all recent hurricanes.
2 Recent hurricanes have not struck populated areas.
3 Recent forecasts are more accurate because of the use of satellites.
4 Recent forecasts are more accurate because fewer weather instruments are used.

88 Daily weather forecasts are based primarily on
1 ocean currents   3 phases of the Moon
2 seismic data   4 air-mass movements

89 The most difficult type of weather event to forecast several hours in advance is the development of a
1 thunderstorm along a cold front
2 hurricane in the Atlantic Ocean
3 tornado along a cold front
4 snowstorm along Lake Erie

Note: Question 90 has only 3 choices.

90 As Lake Erie freezes over, the chance of having a lake-effect snowstorm will
1 decrease
2 increase
3 remain the same

91 A map of the United Stated is shown below.

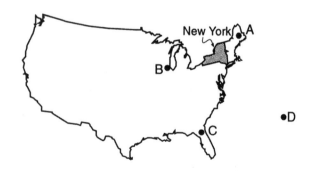

Weather conditions in which location would be of most interest to a person predicting the next day's weather for New York State?
(1) A   (3) C
(2) B   (4) D

CONSTRUCTED RESPONSE

Base your answers to questions 1 through 9 on your knowledge of Earth science, the *Earth Science Reference Tables*, and the diagram which represents a section of a weather map for locations in the central United States. The letters A through I identify reporting weather stations.

1 On the map draw isolines with an interval of 10°F, beginning with the 40°F isoline.

2 Find the station with the lowest barometric pressure. What is the pressure at that station?

3 Place the letter "*L*" just to the north of the station with the lowest pressure.

4 Draw and label a cold front and a warm front on the appropriate places extending out of the Low.

5 Which station has the least amount of cloud cover?

6 Which station has a wind from the southeast at 5 knots?

7 Which station shows the pressure has dropped 2.6 mb in the past three hours?

8 What is the air pressure at station *D*?

9 In order to test the rate of evaporation, equal amounts of water are exposed to the open air outside weather stations *B, E, H,* and *I*. In a sentence explain at which station the water will probably evaporate the fastest.

Base your answers to questions 10 through 15 on your knowledge of Earth science and the satellite photograph of a tropical storm centered in the Gulf of Mexico. An outline of the southeastern United States and the latitude-longitude system have been drawn on the photograph.

Use one or two sentences to answer the following questions.

10 What is the approximate latitude and longitude of the center or eye of the tropical storm on the satellite photograph?

11 What type of air mass would most likely be associated with the storm?

12 Describe the weather conditions at point X at the time this photograph was taken.

13 What will happen to barometric pressure along the coast of Texas as the storm approaches?

14 What is the source of energy for this storm?

15 Describe the general direction of movement of the surface winds associated with this tropical storm.

Base your answers to questions 16 and 17 on the data table below. The data table shows the air temperature and dew point over a 24-hour period for a particular location in New York State.

TIME OF DAY	AIR TEMPERATURE (°C)	DEWPOINT (°C)
12:00 MIDNIGHT	19	12
2:00 a.m.	17	11
4:00 a.m.	14	10
6:00 a.m.	13	12
8:00 a.m.	15	11
10:00 a.m.	17	10
12:00 NOON	18	9
2:00 p.m.	21	7
4:00 p.m.	23	6
6:00 p.m.	21	8
8:00 p.m.	19	10
10:00 p.m.	18	12
12:00 MIDNIGHT	17	13

16 Use the data to construct a graph following the directions below.
   a Mark an appropriate scale on the axis labeled "Temperature."
   b Plot a line graph for air temperature and label the line "Air Temperature."
   c Plot a line graph for dew point and label the line "Dew Point."

17 Based on your graph, state the hour of the day when the relative humidity was *lowest*.

Base your answers to questions 18 and 20 on the *Earth Science Reference Tables*, the diagram below, and your knowledge of Earth science. The diagram represents a weather map of the United States. On the map, station models for selected cities indicate weather conditions and isobars indicate the air pressure pattern. Two fronts, *A* and *B*, have been identified.

18 On the map above, write the words "HIGH" and "LOW" directly on the map to indicate the high and low pressure centers.

19 On the map above, label both front *A* and front *B* with the correct symbol to indicate the type of front and its direction of motion.

20 In one or more complete sentences, write a short weather forecast for the next twenty-four hours at Edville. Include in your forecast any anticipated changes in: temperature and sky conditions.

21 What is the air pressure indicated on the mercury barometer in the diagram at the right?

Base your answers to questions 22 and 23 on the diagram below. The graph shows the air temperature and air pressure recorded over a 30-day period at one location.

22 What were the air temperature and air pressure readings on day 6?

23 In one sentence state what typically happens to the air pressure when the air temperature increases?

Base your answers to questions 24 through 25 on the weather station data shown in the table below.

Air Temperature	21°C
Barometric Pressure	993.1 mb
Wind Direction	From the east
Windspeed	25 knots

24 State the air temperature in degrees Fahrenheit.

25 State the barometric pressure in its proper form, as used on a station model.

26 On the station model below, draw a line with feathers to indicate the wind direction and speed.

N ↑

Base your answers to questions 27 through 29 on the weather maps below. The weather maps show the positions of a tropical storm at 10 a.m. on July 2 and on July 3.

27 State the dew point temperature in Tallahassee on July 2.

28 Windspeed has been omitted from the station models. In one or more sentences, state how an increase in the storm's windspeed from July 2 to July 3 could be inferred from the maps.

29 The storm formed over warm tropical water. State what will most likely happen to the windspeed when the storm moves over land.

Base your answers to questions 30 through 32 on the weather map below. The map represents a weather system located over the central United States. Letters *A*, *B*, *C*, *D*, and *E* locate weather stations on the map.

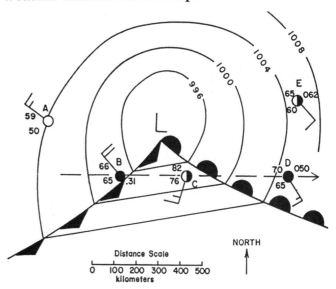

30 What is the air pressure at station *A*?

31 Which station has the highest relative humidity? How can you tell?

32 If the weather system follows the storm track (dashed line) at a speed of 50 kilometers per hour, describe the atmospheric changes which will likely occur at Weather Station *C* in about 6 hours. Consider temperature, wind direction, cloud cover, and probability of precipitation.

Base your answers to questions 33 through 35 on the graph at the right. The graph represents weather data, in inches of mercury, taken during a tropical storm that passed by Orlando, Florida.

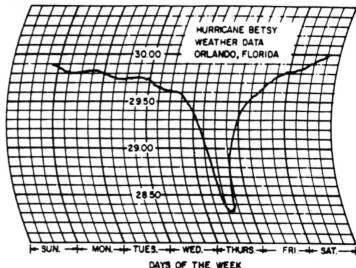

33 Data for which weather variable is shown on the graph?

34 On what day and at what time did the center of Hurricane Betsy reach Orlando, Florida?

35 What kind of airmass would be a source for this storm?

36 State two ways the residents of Orlando might prepare before the hurricane arrives.

WATER CYCLE & CLIMATE

VOCABULARY

water	watershed	angle of insolation	greenhouse effect	evapotranspiration
hydrologic or water cycle	drainage basin	inclination	incident insolation	storage
ground water	stream & streamshed	parallelism	aerosols	usage & recharge
runoff	stream discharge	Earth revolution	reflection & scattering	deficit & drought
porosity & infiltration	surplus water	Earth rotation	potential energy	humid & arid climate
permeability	base flow	summer solstice	terrestrial radiation	marine climate
zone of aeration	solar radiation	equinoxes	greenhouse gases	continental climate
zone of saturation	wavelength	winter solstice	global warming	surface currents
water table	solar electromagnet-ic spectrum	terrestrial radiation	radiative balance	gyres
capillarity	insolation	temperature lag	climate	El Niño & La Niña
		seasonal lag	water budget	orographic effect

A. EARTH'S WATER

There is only one water supply. The water supply of the Earth continually recycles from the atmosphere to the Earth and from the Earth to the atmosphere. This is known as the **hydrologic** or **water cycle**. The water cycle includes the phase changes of water and the movements of water above, on, and below the Earth's surface.

The water cycle is dependent upon the atmosphere to provide water through precipitation to the land and oceans of the Earth. Precipitation amounts vary year to year and from place to place.

This precipitation can:

- infiltrate (sink into) the Earth's surface and become **ground water**;
- runoff from the surface into streams, lakes and the ocean;
- be stored in the form of ice and snow on the Earth's surface; and/or
- be evapotranspired back into the atmosphere from large bodies of water, soil, plants and animals.

The oceans and large lakes act as the temporary storage areas for the majority of water within the water cycle and act as the major stabilizing factor in the Earth's climates.

Water is essential to life, so availability of water is an important key to the habitability of a location.

GROUND WATER POROSITY

How permeable a material is depends on the **porosity**, which is defined as the percentage of open space between the particles. The porosity of loose material is largely dependent upon the particle's shape, how tightly the material is packed, and the degree to which the particles are **sorted**. For example, water will more easily pass through a cylinder full of round beads, than a cylinder full of square blocks of the same size, since there would be more space between the round beads.

Particle Shape Comparison

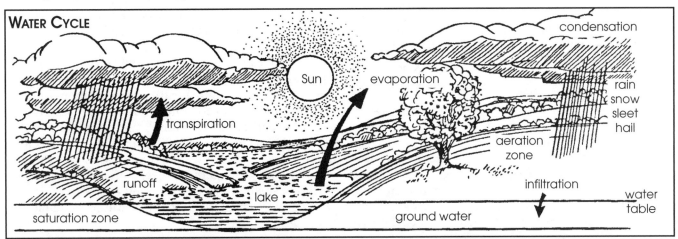

WATER CYCLE

When a test hole is being dug to determine whether or not a septic (waste) field can be placed in a yard, the hole must be dug in "undisturbed" earth, since water will pass through loose soil much faster than the hard packed soil of "undisturbed" ground.

Particle Packing Comparison

Particle Sorting Comparison

When a septic field is made, the fill used must be gravel and pebbles, rather than smaller sized particles, since the larger particles provide bigger pores for better drainage. The gravel and pebbles will pack less with time, allowing the continuous migration of water. The smaller particles, like clay and silt, will pack and become almost impermeable to water flow.

INFILTRATION

The precipitation from the atmosphere can **infiltrate** (sink into), runoff, or evaporate from the Earth's surface.

Before runoff and evapotranspiration, water will usually infiltrate the Earth's surface and become part of the groundwater. In order for water to move into the surface materials of the Earth, these materials must be permeable and unsaturated. Therefore, loose rock materials such as sand and gravel will allow for greater infiltration than the more dense, closely packed particles or the solid rock on the Earth's surface.

PERMEABILITY

A material is said to be permeable if it allows water to pass through the connecting pore spaces in the material.

Permeability Particle Size Comparison

Water that has infiltrated loose material continues downward through the **Zone of Aeration** until the water reaches the **Zone of Saturation**. The top of the zone of saturation is called the **water table**. The depth of the water table is dependent upon the type of earth materials, thickness of those materials, the amount of water infiltrating the ground, and the characteristics of the sur-

rounding materials. For example, the larger the pore spaces between the particles that make up a material, the greater the permeability of that material.

CAPILLARITY

Water can also move upward within a material. This is called **capillarity**. In loose materials, capillarity increases with the decrease in particle size. The finer the loose particle size, the faster and the farther the water can move upward through the material. Along a beach composed of sand, the water will seep up along the shoreline, moving inward from the water line. However, along a rocky beach, the water will not seep very far inward from the water line.

Capillary Action Particle Size Comparison

SURFACE WATER & RUNOFF

When water moves over the surface of the Earth, it is referred to as **runoff**. Surface runoff can occur when rainfall exceeds the permeability rate of the material. For example, a specific sample of soil has a permeability rate of 0.3 liters per hour, but the rate of rainfall is 0.4 liters per hour. The rainfall is greater than the permeability rate by 0.1 liters per hour, which is the amount of runoff from that specific soil sample.

Surface runoff can also occur when the slope of the surface is too steep to allow infiltration to occur. Even though the permeability rate of the slope materials may be greater than the rate of rainfall, the water may not have sufficient "standing" time to allow for the infiltration, before it runs off the surface. Water is less likely to soak into a hill side, than to soak into the soil of a flat valley. Stripping the vegetation from the land surface also allows water to run off slopes more rapidly, thus increasing the amount of water available for flooding.

Electromagnetic Spectrum

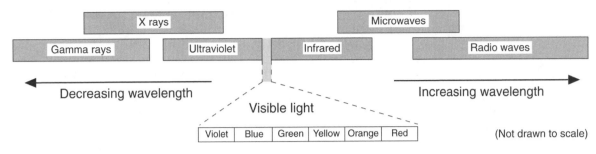

If the saturation level of the soil type has reached the surface, such as after long and heavy rains, the added rainfall will run over the surface. This is often the case in severe lowland flooding associated with hurricanes and large maritime tropical storms. Runoff will also occur when rain falls on a frozen surface. The **capillary water** retained at the points of contact between the soil particles freezes, preventing infiltration of the water which then runs off the surface. Paving and blacktopping land surfaces are human activities that prevent water from infiltrating the ground and increase the amount of water available for runoff.

A stream is only one part of a larger drainage system. The **watershed** or **drainage basin** is made up of the land from which water drains into a stream. The watershed of one stream is separated from another by a drainage divide which is commonly a ridge. Although two streams may be separated by a drainage divide, if the two streams both flow into the same river, they are both part of the larger watershed of the river.

WATER & STREAM DISCHARGE

The rate of streamflow in volume is called **stream discharge** and is measured by determining the amount of water that flows past a specific part of the stream during a specific amount of time. Often the stream discharge is a measurement of the **surplus water** that drains from the area around the stream. However, if there is no surplus water in the area of the stream, then stream discharge may be related to the depletion of groundwater from soil storage. This is the case during dry seasons when streams are being fed by the local water table. This is called **base flow**.

B. EARTH'S ENERGY

The primary source of energy for the Earth's surface systems is **solar radiation** which is responsible for driving the surface systems which change the Earth, such as weather and climate patterns. Solar radiation has its greatest intensity occurring in the visible wavelength (about 50%) of the solar electromagnetic spectrum.

SOLAR ELECTROMAGNETIC SPECTRUM

There are many forms of electromagnetic energy, such as heat and light. They all have the capacity (ability) to do work. Each form is distinguished from the others by its **wavelength** – the distance between the crests (peaks) of successive waves.

The **solar electromagnetic spectrum** is similar to the general electromagnetic spectrum, since the Sun radiates almost every kind of wave energy. The principal solar electromagnetic radiations includes visible light as well as x-rays, ultraviolet rays, and infrared rays.

FACTORS AFFECTING INSOLATION

The primary source of energy for the Surface Systems of Earth is **solar radiation**. Solar radiation has its greatest intensity occurring in the visible wavelength (about 50%) of the solar electromagnetic spectrum. The other forms of insolation include ultraviolet, infrared, x-rays, and other longer and shorter wavelengths.

The term **Insolation** comes from **In**coming **Sol**ar Rad**iation**. It is that portion of the Sun's radiation which is received at the Earth's surface.

INSOLATION

Angle of Insolation. The **intensity of insolation** in any area of the Earth's surface increases as the angle of insolation approaches perpendicular. At an angle of 90° to the Earth's surface, the solar radiation is concentrated in a relatively small area of the sur-

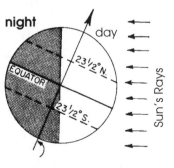

Earth's Axis or Rotation

Angle of Insolation to Earth's Axis

face. Therefore, where the Sun's rays are vertical, the maximum amount of solar energy is received at the surface.

The angle of insolation changes on any particular date with either an increase or decrease in latitude. For example (in the diagram on the previous page), at 23½° North, the Sun's rays are vertical and therefore have maximum intensity. The intensity of insolation per unit area will decrease with increasing latitude towards the North and South Poles, because the insolation received is spread over a greater area.

At the equinoxes, the Sun's rays are perpendicular to the equator (0° latitude), while during the summer and winter solstices, the Sun's rays are perpendicular to the Earth's surface at 23½° North Latitude and 23½° South Latitude, respectively.

In addition to changes in latitude, the angle of insolation varies with the time of day. The intensity of the insolation is the greatest at noon when the Sun is highest in the sky and is least when the Sun is very low in the sky. The greater the angle of insolation, the greater the intensity of insolation.

Relationship of Intensity and Angle of Insolation

Angle Of Insolation Related To Seasons (Arrows indicate the Sun's rays at noon for 42° North latitude.)

DURATION OF INSOLATION

Duration of insolation refers to the number of daylight hours. It is determined by the length of the Sun's path across the sky. For every 15° of arc in the Sun's path, there is one hour of daylight. The longer the Sun's path, the greater the intensity and duration of insolation.

DURATION VARIES WITH LATITUDE & SEASONS

Because of the 23½° tilt of the Earth's axis and the revolution of the Earth around the Sun, the rays of the Sun hit the Earth's surface with varying angles, and the length of the Sun's path across the sky also varies. For every 15° of arc in the Sun's path, the surface receives one hour of insolation. The greater the **angle of insolation** and the longer the duration, the more total energy received.

The seasons are the result of yearly cyclic changes in the duration and intensity of solar radiations or insolation. These cyclic changes result from:

- **Inclination (tilt) of the Earth's axis**, at 23½°, allows the vertical rays of the Sun to fall on different latitudes of the Earth (between the Tropics of Cancer — 23½° North and Capricorn — 23½° South).

- **Parallelism of the Earth's axis**. Since the Earth's axis is always pointing into space in the same direction, the axis of the Earth at any given point in the Earth's orbit around the Sun remains parallel to the axis at any other given point of the orbit.

- **Revolution of the Earth** causes the Sun's perpendicular rays to fall on different Earth latitudes between 23½° North and South Latitude.

- **Rotation of the Earth** causes the alternation of day and night.

In the northern mid-latitudes (42° North), the **maximum insolation** occurs about June 21st (**summer solstice**). The angle of insolation at noon is 71½°, and the duration of insolation is 15 hours.

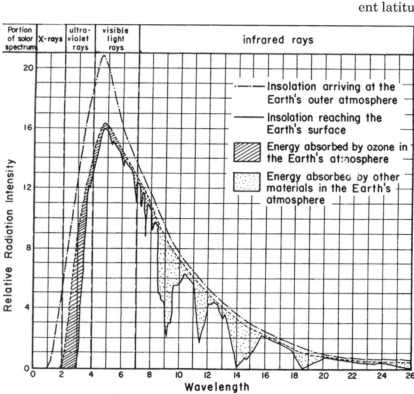

Intensity of Insolation vs. Wavelength Graph

Summer and Winter Solstice (in Northern Hemisphere), Showing
Relative Earth – Sun Positions

Average insolation occurs on or about March 21st and September 23rd (**equinoxes**). The angle of insolation at noon is 48°, and the duration of insolation is 12 hours.

The **minimum insolation** occurs about December 21st (**winter solstice**). The angle of insolation at noon is 24½°, and the duration of insolation is 9 hours.

SUMMER & WINTER SOLSTICE

In the Northern Hemisphere, the Sun's path is the longest on the summer solstice (June 21st). Therefore, New York State has the greatest duration of insolation. The shortest duration of insolation occurs on the winter solstice (December 21st), because the Sun is the lowest in the sky and has the shortest path over New York State.

TEMPERATURE & INSOLATION

The surface temperature of the Earth is directly related to insolation received at the surface.

Incoming solar radiation raises the Earth's surface temperature (heat gain). However, **terrestrial radiation** causes a cooling effect on the Earth's surface (heat loss).

Surface temperature is a result of the relationship between heat gained and lost. Where insolation

Relationship of Average Annual Surface Temperature & Latitude

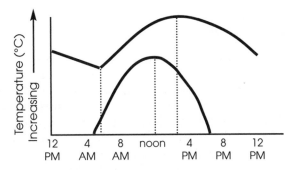

Relationship of Average Daylight Hours and Daily Temperatures

exceeds radiation, the temperature rises. If more heat is lost (radiation) than is gained (insolation), the temperature at the Earth's surface decreases.

DAILY TEMPERATURES

During the day, the **maximum surface temperature** usually occurs sometime *after maximum insolation* – usually during the early afternoon. The minimum surface temperature usually occurs approximately an hour before sunrise, because of the continuous loss of heat during nighttime (radiation). This is called **temperature lag**.

There are other factors which affect the maximum and minimum temperatures, such as cloud cover. Clouds tend to reduce the amount of heat lost caused by surface radiation, but also reduce the amount of insolation reaching the Earth's surface.

YEARLY TEMPERATURES

During the year, the maximum surface temperature most often occurs sometime after the maximum insolation, generally midsummer, following the summer solstice. This is the case because temperatures continue to rise as long as insolation received during the long days exceeds radiation during the shorter nights.

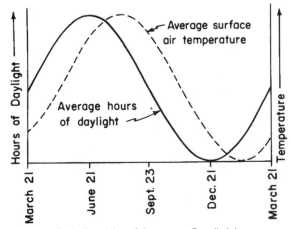

Relationship of Average Daylight Hours & Annual Temperatures (in No. Hemisphere)

The minimum surface temperature usually occurs sometime after the minimum angle of insolation, soon after the winter solstice. This is called **seasonal lag**. Again there are factors (such as weather systems) which affect the yearly maximum and minimum temperatures. As long as radiation during the long nights exceeds insolation received during the shorter days, temperature will continue to decrease.

C. Absorption & Radiation

Since the atmosphere is largely transparent to visible radiation, most of the Sun's visible (light) radiation reaches the Earth's surface. But, because the atmosphere selectively absorbs solar radiation, most of the Sun's ultraviolet radiation is absorbed by the atmosphere's ozone, and much of the infrared radiation is absorbed by the atmosphere's carbon dioxide and water vapor.

To a large extent, the surface of the Earth itself tends to control temperature changes through absorption and radiation. Water surfaces heat more slowly than land surfaces, and water also tends to hold heat longer. Therefore, land surface temperatures change more rapidly and change to a greater degree than water surface temperatures. The resulting temperature differences between land and water masses greatly affect Earth temperatures.

The surface material is one factor that determines how much of the electromagnetic energy will be reflected or absorbed. In the case of light energy, if a surface is rough or dark, it is likely to absorb more energy than if the surface is smooth or light. In the south, houses are built with white or light colored shingles on the roofs to reduce the solar heat absorption. In the north, darker shingles are used, allowing more solar heat absorption during the winter months.

Greenhouse Effect
Solar visible light rays (shorter wavelengths) are absorbed by the Earth and reradiated as infrared or heat (long wavelengths).

Wavelength Absorption & Radiation

A good absorber of energy is also a good radiator. The characteristics of the surface of the material receiving the electromagnetic energy determine the quantity and type of energy absorbed or reflected.

The Earth's surface often absorbs solar electromagnetic energy (generally strong, short wavelengths) and converts the energy to longer wavelengths (having less strength) which are reradiated. For example, solar visible light rays (shorter wavelengths) are absorbed by the Earth and reradiated as infrared or heat (long wavelengths). Gases in the Earth's atmosphere absorb much of the infrared energy. This is referred to as the **greenhouse effect**.

Reflection

Particles in the atmosphere and materials on the surface of the Earth greatly affect the amount of insolation that reaches the Earth's surface and is absorbed. For example, clouds may reflect approximately 25 percent of the incident insolation.

The reflectivity of the Earth also depends upon both the surface and the angle of insolation. The greater the angle of insolation, the greater the absorption, but as the angle of insolation decreases, the reflection becomes greater. A surface of ice and/or snow may reflect almost all of the **incident insolation**.

Scattering

Aerosols (finely dispersed particles, such as water droplets and dust) in the atmosphere cause a **random reflection** or **scattering of insolation**. The amount of insolation reaching the Earth's surface decreases as the amount of random reflection increases.

Scattering Effect of Aerosols In the Atmosphere

For example, a volcanic eruption may put sufficient ash into the air to decrease the amount of insolation reaching the Earth's surface, resulting in a temperature decrease.

Energy Conversion

Not all of the insolation is directly reflected or radiated as heat energy. Instead, some of the insolation is converted into **potential energy** by the evaporation of water and the melting of ice. This energy conversion does not change the surface temperature.

Greenhouse Effect

As previously mentioned, most of the radiant energy from the Sun: 1) passes through the Earth's atmosphere, 2) is absorbed by the atmosphere or Earth's surface, or 3) is reradiated by the Earth's surface back into the atmosphere. Visible light is the most intense energy (from the Sun) to be absorbed by the Earth's surface. After it is absorbed and heats the surface, it is reradiated back into the Earth's atmosphere as infrared energy and is absorbed by water vapor and carbon dioxide. This process, which causes the atmos-

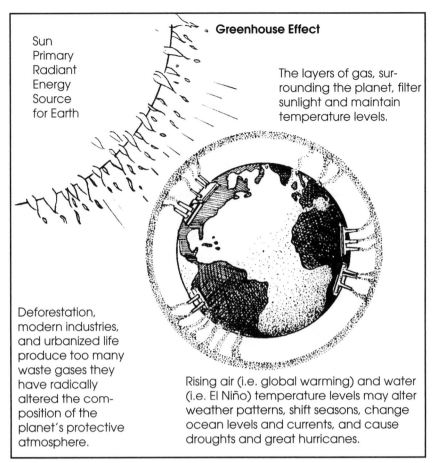

Greenhouse Effect

Sun Primary Radiant Energy Source for Earth

The layers of gas, surrounding the planet, filter sunlight and maintain temperature levels.

Deforestation, modern industries, and urbanized life produce too many waste gases they have radically altered the composition of the planet's protective atmosphere.

Rising air (i.e. global warming) and water (i.e. El Niño) temperature levels may alter weather patterns, shift seasons, change ocean levels and currents, and cause droughts and great hurricanes.

phere to be heated, is known as the greenhouse effect. The warmed atmosphere acts as a "thermal blanket," reducing the loss of energy to space and raising the temperature of the Earth's surface.

The greenhouse effect is the result of the conversion of shortwave energy (insolation, such as visible radiation) to longer wave radiation, infrared, which is prevented from escaping the Earth's atmosphere.

TERRESTRIAL RADIATION

Terrestrial radiation refers to the electromagnetic energy that the Earth gives off to its atmosphere and space. This radiation from the surface is nearly all in the infrared region of the electromagnetic spectrum.

RADIATION

The maximum intensity of outgoing radiation from the Earth's surface, terrestrial radiation, is in the infrared region of the electromagnetic spectrum. As previously discussed, some of this infrared (heat) energy is absorbed by the atmosphere, and the balance of the energy escapes into space. The **greenhouse gases** (i.e., water vapor and carbon dioxide) are the primary absorbers of infrared energy in the Earth's atmosphere. They are responsible for the greenhouse effect. Since carbon dioxide is a good absorber of infrared

energy, scientists today are concerned about **global warming** as a long term effect of increasing amounts of carbon dioxide in the atmosphere.

RADIATIVE BALANCE

The Earth's temperature depends upon the relationship between incoming and outgoing energy. When the average Earth temperature remains stable, the Earth is said to be in **radiative balance**, gaining as much energy as it gives off.

Comparing the radiative balance of the Earth over long and short time periods indicates the following:

• **Long-term Measurements** (thousands of years) of worldwide surface temperatures indicate that the Earth *is not* in radiative balance. At times in the geologic past, the Earth is thought to have been devoid of ice because average temperatures were significantly warmer. Those times, however, have alternated with ice ages which occurred in the middle latitudes. For example, during the Pleistocene Epoch Age, the estimated average temperatures of the Earth varied approximately 5°C to 10°C cooler, resulting in the Ice Age.

• **Annual Measurement** of worldwide surface temperatures indicates that the Earth *is not* in radiative balance. Daily, weekly, monthly, and seasonal temperatures are constantly changing, resulting in variations in the yearly average.

D. CLIMATE

Unlike weather conditions which are short term affects, a **climate** is the average weather conditions over much longer periods of time. Climate is primarily concerned with temperature and moisture conditions.

WATER BUDGET

Local water budget characteristics can be used to distinguish climatic regions. A **water budget** is a system of accounting for moisture income, storage, and outgo for the soil in a specific area. The variables involved in the water budget are precipitation, potential and actual evapotranspiration, storage, usage, deficit, and recharge.

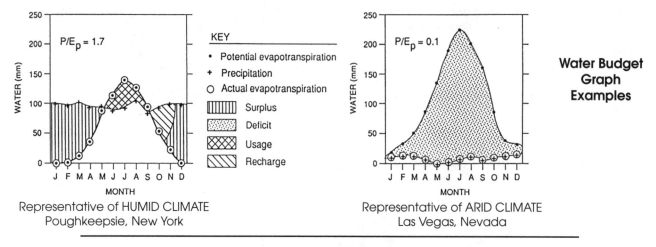

Representative of HUMID CLIMATE
Poughkeepsie, New York

Representative of ARID CLIMATE
Las Vegas, Nevada

The moisture source for the water budget is **precipitation** regardless of the form it takes (i.e. snow, rain, sleet, hail). This moisture is measured in millimeters of water.

Potential evapotranspiration refers to the maximum amount of water that can be evaporated, if the water is available. It is directly proportional to the energy available. Therefore, the greatest potential evapotranspiration occurs in the summer when the temperatures are the highest. The warmer the temperature, the more water can evaporate.

The **actual evapotranspiration** is the amount of water that is really evaporated and/or transpired. It is equal to the potential evapotranspiration if sufficient water is available. The actual can never exceed the potential.

The amount of water stored in the top of the soil (root zone) is called the **storage**. When water evaporates out of the soil the storage decreases. This process is called **usage**. When precipitation infiltrates (sinks into) the soil, the storage increases. This process is called **recharge**.

When the soil moisture is depleted and there is not enough precipitation to meet the potential evapotranspiration there is a **moisture deficit** or **drought**. **Surplus** exists when ground storage is at maximum and there is more precipitation than can be evaporated. This surplus water becomes runoff and contributes water to local streams.

Local water budget characteristics can be used to distinguish climatic regions. **Humid climates** are those in which the total amount of precipitation is greater than the total amount of potential evapotranspiration. The water budget graphs of humid climates show months with surplus water.

Arid climates have significantly more total potential evapotranspiration than precipitation. The water budget graphs of arid climates show months of deficit.

CLIMATE PATTERN FACTORS

The variables which affect climate patterns are latitude, altitude (elevation), and proximity to large bodies of water, ocean currents, mountain barriers, and prevailing winds.

LATITUDE

Latitude is the most important factor in determining climate, especially influencing temperature patterns. Since the duration of insolation at low latitudes is fairly constant, about 12 hours per day, temperature variance is small. Also, at low latitudes, the angle of insolation is always quite high. Therefore, the temperatures remain relatively high. At high latitudes, temperatures vary but remain relatively low because of the generally low angle of insolation. The duration of insolation varies between 0 hours and 24 hours per day causing a great seasonal variation in temperatures.

In general, as the duration of insolation increases, the temperature increases. As latitude increases, average yearly temperature decreases, but the annual temperature range increases.

ELEVATION

The elevation (altitude) influences the temperature and moisture patterns of a region. The effects of elevation are very similar to those of latitude. Lower elevations are generally more stable in temperature and moisture, and higher elevations have more varied conditions. As the altitude or elevation increases, the average yearly temperature decreases, and the precipitation generally increases.

LARGE BODIES OF WATER

Large bodies of water (large lakes and oceans), ocean currents, and prevailing winds modify the latitudinal climate patterns of their shoreline areas. The slow heating and cooling of large bodies of water cause the land masses near them to have modified tempera-

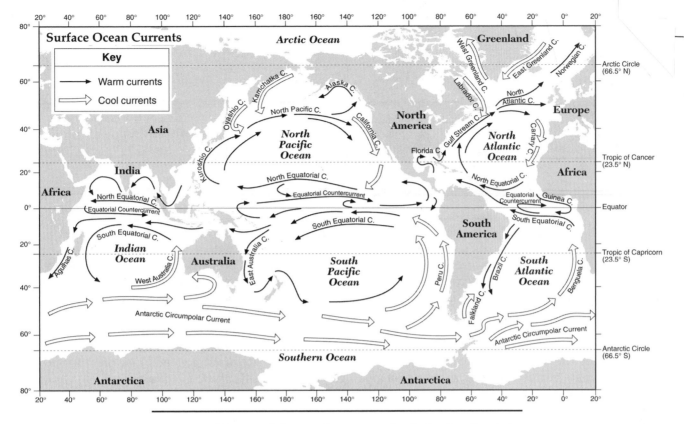

Surface Ocean Currents

Key
→ Warm currents
⇨ Cool currents

tures. For example, the **marine climate** of the northwest coast of the United States is characterized by cooler summers and warmer winters than would normally be expected for that latitude. Areas of marine climate have small temperature ranges.

Inland regions are not directly affected by large bodies of water. They have **continental climates**, that are characterized by large yearly temperature ranges with hot summers and cold winters.

OCEAN CURRENTS

Maps of global winds and ocean currents look similar. This is because the winds blowing over the water surface create a frictional drag on the water resulting in **surface currents**. Currents are like huge "rivers" in the ocean.

The Coriolis Effect, caused by the Earth's rotation, results in surface currents being deflected clockwise in the Northern Hemisphere and counterclockwise in the Southern Hemisphere, circulating in large cells called **gyres**.

Surface currents may be either warm or cold depending upon the temperature of the water through which they are passing and their direction. Warm currents flow away from the Equator and cold currents flow toward the Equator. As the warm water flows away from the Equator, it helps to distribute the solar energy it has absorbed in the low latitudes to the high-

er, cooler latitudes. Land close to warm ocean currents tends to be warmer than would be expected at that latitude. Cold ocean currents have the effect of making nearby land cooler than would normally be expected.

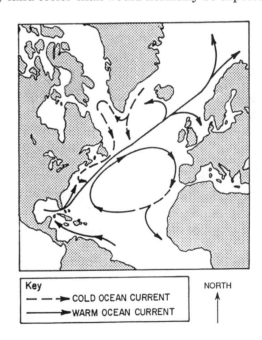

Key
- - → COLD OCEAN CURRENT
── WARM OCEAN CURRENT

NORTH ↑

EL NIÑO

Normally, trade winds blow from east to west and, in the Pacific, toward a low pressure area near Australia. Normally, cool subsurface water full of nutrients moves eastward upwelling off the coast of South America sustaining the sea life with its nutrients.

West

Olympic Mountains

Cascade Mountains

East

Orographic Effect
As air mass moves over the mountains, the rising air cools – producing clouds and precipitation on the windward side of the obstruction (mountain).

High Precip
Quinault

Pacific Ocean

Puget Sound

Seattle
Low Precip

Snoqualimie Pass
High Precip

Yakima

Spokane
Low Precip

Periodically, this flow of ocean water stalls or reverses direction. What results is a warm surface current, **El Niño**, moving nutrients away from coastal fishing banks changing the entire ecosystem. Fish die or disappear, fishermen catch no fish, nor does the other wildlife that depends upon fish for food.

Most meteorologists agree that the sea surface temperatures in the tropics are a major source of weather and climate variability. Several billions of gallons of water evaporate there every hour, picked up into great cumulonimbus clouds. When the vapor condenses forming rain, energy is released into the atmosphere. When an increase in the sea surface temperature induces rainfall, it is "stoking the atmospheric boiler." This speeds up the subtropical jet stream and changes wind patterns worldwide.

El Niños seem to recur every three to five years. Heavy rainfalls with flooding and mudslides along the western coasts of North and South America, severe ice storms in Canada and New England, as well as tornadoes in the southeastern U.S., have all been attributed to El Niño.

The opposite of El Niño is called **La Niña**. When the **trade winds** are very strong, the cold water that upwells along the western coast of South America is pushed westward across the Pacific Ocean. This cold water surface also affects the weather patterns. It is associated with less moisture evaporating into the air and thus less rain falls along the western coasts. The extremes of weather experienced around the world are linked to both El Niño and La Niña changes in ocean currents.

MOUNTAIN (OROGRAPHIC) BARRIERS

The overall effect of mountains on climatic patterns is called the **orographic effect**. Latitudinal climate patterns are modified by mountains that act as barriers to local weather systems by interrupting the normal path of a prevailing wind. The windward side of a mountain is the side facing the prevailing wind. As the wind hits the windward side of a mountain the air is forced upward and cools by expansion until the dew point is reached. Then condensation occurs and cooling slows. These conditions cause the water in the air to condense, forming clouds and precipitation on the windward side of the mountain.

The other side of the mountain, the leeward side (side to which the wind is blowing), will be drier and warmer than the windward side (side exposed to the wind). It is said to be in the rain shadow. As the air rises over the mountain and begins to descend on the leeward side, it warms because of the compression, increasing its ability to hold moisture.

When a mountain is high enough, it can act as a barrier to air masses and prevent warm or cold air from getting past the mountain to the other side. In this case a mountain can be the boundary between two very different climatic areas.

WIND BELTS

The planetary winds and pressure belts affect moisture and temperature patterns. If the prevailing winds first cross a large body of water before coming on land, they will bring moisture to the land. If the prevailing winds cross a large land mass, the effect will be more arid. Prevailing winds from tropical areas, including warm ocean currents, bring warm air. Conversely, winds from polar regions, including cold ocean currents, will bring cool air.

QUESTIONS FOR UNIT 7

1 The diagrams represent two identical containers filled with nonporous uniform particles. The containers represent models of two different sizes of soil particles. Compared to the model containing larger particles, the model containing smaller particles has
1 less permeability and greater porosity
2 greater porosity and greater capillarity
3 less permeability and greater capillarity
4 greater permeability and greater porosity

2 Most infiltration of precipitation will occur when the Earth's soil is
1 unsaturated and impermeable
2 unsaturated and permeable
3 saturated and impermeable
4 saturated and permeable

3 Which type of soil would water infiltrate most slowly?
1 silt   3 fine sand
2 pebbles   4 fine clay

4 In which area will surface runoff most likely be greatest during a heavy rainfall?
1 sandy desert   3 level grassy field
2 wooded forest   4 paved city street

5 Why do many streams continue to flow during long periods when there is no precipitation?
1 Soil moisture storage is recharged by vegetation along the stream.
2 Ground water continues to move into the stream channel.
3 An increase in potential evapotranspiration increases the stream runoff.
4 The porosity beneath the stream channels becomes higher than normal.

6 Electromagnetic energy that reaches the Earth from the Sun is called
1 insolation   3 specific heat
2 conduction   4 terrestrial radiation

7 Short waves of electromagnetic energy are absorbed by the Earth's surface during the day. They are later reradiated into space as
1 visible light rays
2 infrared rays
3 ultraviolet rays
4 x-rays

8 Which form of electromagnetic energy has a wavelength of 0.0001 meter? [Refer to the *Reference Tables*.]
1 ultraviolet
2 infrared
3 FM and TV
4 shortwave and AM radio

9 An object that is a good absorber of electromagnetic energy is also a good
1 reflector of electromagnetic energy
2 refractor of electromagnetic energy
3 radiator of electromagnetic energy
4 convector of electromagnetic energy

10 Which type of surface would most likely be the best reflector of electromagnetic energy?
1 dark-colored and rough
2 dark-colored and smooth
3 light-colored and rough
4 light-colored and smooth

Base your answers to questions 11 and 12 on the diagram which shows part of the electromagnetic spectrum.

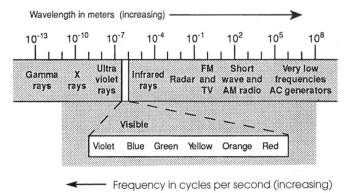

11 Which form of electromagnetic energy shown on the diagram has the lowest frequency and longest wavelength?
1 AM radio   3 red light
2 infrared rays   4 gamma rays

12 Which statement about electromagnetic energy is correct?
1 Violet light has a longer wavelength than red light.
2 Gamma rays have a shorter wavelength than visible light.
3 X-rays have a longer wavelength than infrared waves.
4 Radar waves have a shorter wavelength than ultraviolet rays.

13 The factor that contributes most to the seasonal temperature changes during one year in New York State is the changing
1 speed at which the Earth travels in its orbit around the Sun
2 angle at which the Sun's rays strike the Earth's surface
3 distance between the Earth and the Sun
4 energy given of by the Sun

14 How do clouds affect the temperature at the Earth's surface?
1 Clouds block sunlight during the day and prevent heat from escaping at night.
2 Clouds block sunlight during the day and allow heat to escape at night.
3 Clouds allow sunlight to reach the Earth during the day and prevent heat from escaping at night.
4 Clouds allow sunlight to reach the Earth during the day and allow heat to escape at night.

15 The map shows isolines of average daily insolation received in calories per square centimeter per minute at the Earth's surface.

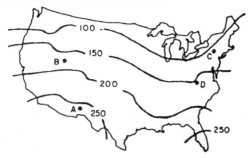

If identical solar collectors are placed at the lettered locations, which collector would receive the least insolation?
(1) A   (3) C
(2) B   (4) D

16 The diagram at the right represents the percentage of total incoming solar radiation that is affected by clouds. What percentage of incoming solar radiation is reflected or absorbed on cloudy days?
(1) 100%
(2) 35% to 80%
(3) 5% to 30%
(4) 0%

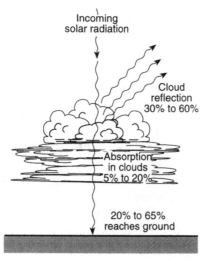

17 The intensity of the insolation that reaches the Earth is affected most by
1 the angle at which the insolation strikes the Earth's surface
2 changes in the length of the Earth's rotational period
3 the temperature of the Earth's surface
4 the distance between the Earth and the Sun

18 In which diagram would the incoming solar radiation reaching Earth's surface heat the ground the most?

19 Which graph best illustrates the relationship between the angle of insolation and the time of day at a location in New York State?

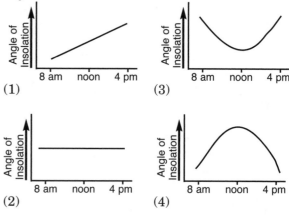

20 Which angle of the Sun above the horizon produces the greatest intensity of sunlight?
(1) 70°   (3) 40°
(2) 60°   (4) 25°

21 The tilt of the Earth on its axis is a cause of Earth's
(1) uniform daylight hours
(2) changing length of day and night
(3) 24-hour day
(4) 365$\frac{1}{2}$-day year

22 Over a period of one year, which location would probably have the greatest average intensity of insolation per unit area? [Assume equal atmospheric transparency at each location.]
1 Tropic of Cancer (23$\frac{1}{2}$°N)
2 New York City (41°N)
3 the Arctic Circle (66$\frac{1}{2}$°N)
4 the North Pole (90°N)

23 Compared to the polar areas, why are equatorial areas of equal size heated much more intensely by the Sun?
1 The Sun's rays are more nearly perpendicular at the Equator than at the poles.
2 The equatorial areas contain more water than the polar areas do.
3 More hours of daylight occur at the Equator than at the poles.
4 The equatorial areas are nearer to the Sun than the polar areas are.

24 What happens to the angle of insolation between solar noon and 6 p.m. in New York State?
1 It decreases steadily.
2 It increases steadily
3 It remains the same.
4 It first increases and then decreases.

25 On which date does the maximum duration of insolation occur in the Northern Hemisphere?
1 March 21   3 September 23
2 June 21   4 December 21

26 The diagram represents a model of the Sun's apparent path across the sky in New York State for selected dates.

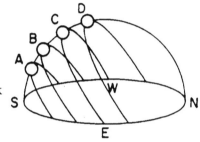

For which path would the duration of insolation be greatest?
(1) A   (3) C
(2) B   (4) D

27 For which date and location will the longest duration of insolation normally occur?
1 June 21, at 60°N.
2 June 21, at 23½°N.
3 December 21, at 60°N.
4 December 21, AT 23½°N.

28 The diagram represents four positions of the Earth as it revolves around the Sun.

At which position is the Earth located on December 21?
(1) A   (3) C
(2) B   (4) D

29 In New York State, which day has the shortest period of daylight?
1 March 21   3 September 21
2 June 21   4 December 21

30 Which diagram shows the position of the Earth relative to the Sun's rays during a winter day in the Northern Hemisphere?

31 To an observer located at the Equator, on which date would the Sun appear to be directly overhead at noon?
1 February 1   3 March 21
2 June 6   4 December 21

32 In New York State, it is observed that the north-facing slopes of mountains usually retain their snow later in the spring than the south-facing slopes. This is caused by the fact that the north slopes of the mountains
1 are protected from the prevailing south winds
2 receive greater rainfall
3 usually are steeper
4 receive less insolation than the south slopes

Note: Question 33 has only 3 choices.

33 The graph shows the average daily temperatures and the duration of insolation for a location in the mid-latitudes of the Northern Hemisphere during a year.

Compared to the date of maximum duration of insolation, the date of maximum surface temperature for this location is
1 earlier in the year
2 later in the year
3 the same day of the year

Base your answers to questions 34 through 36 on your knowledge of Earth science, the *Earth Science Reference Tables*, and the diagram below. The diagram represents a hot-air solar collector consisting of a wooden box frame, an absorber plate, a glass cover, and insulation.

34 The solar collector is placed outside in sunlight, facing south and tilted 40° from the horizontal.

At which position of the Sun would the collector receive the most intense solar radiation?
(1) *A*   (3) *C*
(2) *B*   (4) *D*

35 Which paint should be used on the absorber plate if it is designed to absorb the greatest possible amount of insolation?
1 red paint   3 yellow paint
2 white paint   4 black paint

36 What is the primary function of the glass cover?
1 It reduces the amount of insolation entering the collector.
2 It increases the heat that is lost by convection to the outside air.
3 It allows short wavelengths of radiation to enter, but reduces the amount of long-wavelength radiation that escapes.
4 It allows all wavelengths of radiation to pass through in either direction.

37 Which form of radiation given off by the Earth causes heating of the Earth's atmosphere?
1 infrared   3 visible
2 ultraviolet   4 x-ray

38 Which gases in the atmosphere best absorb infrared radiation?
1 hydrogen and nitrogen
2 hydrogen and carbon dioxide
3 water vapor and carbon dioxide
4 water vapor and nitrogen

39 Which model best represents how a greenhouse remains warm as a result of insolation from the Sun?

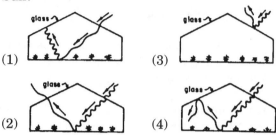

40 What is the primary reason New York State is warmer in July than in February?
1 The Earth is traveling faster in its orbit in February.
2 The altitude of the noon Sun is greater in February.
3 The insolation in New York is greater in July.
4 The Earth is closer to the Sun in July.

Note: Question 41 has only 3 choices.

41 If an object with a constant source of energy is in radiative balance, the temperature of the object will
1 decrease
2 increase
3 remains the same

42 Which type of climate would most likely be found in an area that has a high potential for evaporation of water but a low actual evaporation of water?
1 polar   3 desert
2 rain forest   4 temperate

43 What is the best explanation for the two statements below?

• Some mountains located near the Earth's Equator have snow-covered peaks
• Icecaps exist at the Earth's poles.

1 High elevation and high latitude have a similar effect on climate.
2 Both mountain and polar regions have arid climates.
3 Mountain and polar regions receive more energy from the Sun than other regions do.
4 An increase in snowfall and an increase in temperature have a similar effect on climate.

44 The diagram at the right represents several locations on the surface of the Earth. Each location is at sea level and is surrounded by ocean water.

The average annual air temperature at point P is most likely higher than the average annual air temperature at point

(1) A   (3) C
(2) B   (4) D

45 Compared to a coastal location of the same elevation and latitude, an inland location is likely to have

1 warmer summers and cooler winters
2 warmer summers and warmer winters
3 cooler summers and cooler winters
4 cooler summers and warmer winters

46 Which is a characteristic of water that helps the oceans to moderate the climates of the Earth?

1 Water is a fluid with a high specific heat.
2 Water can exist as a high-density solid.
3 Water can dissolve and transport materials.
4 Water can flow into loose sediments to deposit mineral cements.

47 The diagram below shows the positions of the cities of Seattle and Spokane, Washington. Both cities are located at approximately 48° North latitude, and they are separated by the Cascade Mountains.

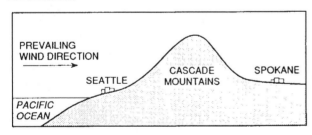

How does the climate of Seattle compare with the climate of Spokane?

1 Seattle – hot and dry
   Spokane – cool and humid
2 Seattle – hot and humid
   Spokane – cool and dry
3 Seattle – cool and humid
   Spokane – hot and dry
4 Seattle – cool and dry
   Spokane – warm and humid

48 The cross section below shows several locations in the State of Washington and the annual precipitation at each location. The arrows represent the prevailing wind direction.

Why do the windward sides of these mountain ranges receive more precipitation than the leeward sides?

1 Sinking air compresses and cools.
2 Sinking air expands and cools.
3 Rising air compresses and cools.
4 Rising air expands and cools.

Base your answers to questions 49 through 52 on your knowledge of Earth science and on the diagram below. The diagram represents an imaginary continent on the Earth surrounded by water. The arrows indicate the direction of the prevailing winds.
Two large mountain regions are also indicated. Points A, B, E, and H are located at sea level; C, D, and F are in the foothills of the mountains; G is high in the mountains.

49 Which graph best represents the average monthly temperatures that would be recorded during one year at location E?

(1)

(3)

(2)

(4)

50 Which physical characteristic would cause location *G* to have a colder yearly climate than any other location?
1 nearness of location *G* to a large ocean
2 location of *G* with respect to the prevailing winds
3 elevation of location *G* above sea level
4 distance of location *G* from the Equator

51 Which location probably has the greatest annual rainfall?
(1) *A*　　(2) *F*　　(3) *C*　　(4) *D*

52 Which location probably has the greatest range in temperature during the year?
(1) *A*　　(2) *B*　　(3) *H*　　(4) *D*

53 The climates of densely populated industrial areas tend to be warmer than similarly located sparsely populated rural areas. From this observation, what can be inferred about the human influence on local climate?
1 Local climates are not affected by increases in population density.
2 The local climate in densely populated areas can be changed by human activities.
3 In densely populated areas, human activities increase the amount of natural pollutants.
4 In sparsely populated areas, human activities have stabilized the rate of energy absorption.

54 Which graph best represents the relationship between average yearly temperature and latitude?

(1)

(3)

(2)

(4)

55 Which conditions describe the ocean current that would be found at position *X* in the diagram? [Use *Reference Tables.*]

1 warm and flowing towards the north
2 warm and flowing towards the south
3 cold and flowing towards the north
4 cold and flowing towards the south

56 What is the primary cause of the major surface currents found in the North Atlantic Ocean?
1 planetary winds
2 mantle plumes beneath ocean plates
3 undersea earthquakes
4 high winds from storms

Base your answers to questions 57 through 59 on your knowledge of Earth science and on the diagram below. Two identical houses, *A* and *B*, were built in a city in New York State. One house was built on the east side of a factory, and the other house was built on the west side of the factory. Both houses originally had white roofs, but the roof on house *B* has been blackened by factory soot falling on it over the years.

57 Which graph best shows the amount of insolation received at house *A* during the daylight insolation hours?

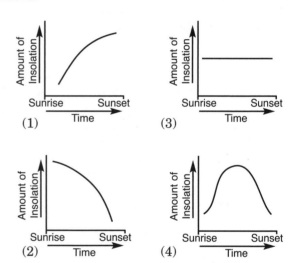

58 On which date would the greatest amount of insolation normally be received at house A?
1 December 21　　3 June 21
2 March 21　　4 September 21

59 Compared to the amount of insolation reflected by the roof of house *A*, the amount of insolation reflected by the roof of house *B* is
1 usually less
2 usually more
3 always the same
4 less in summer and greater in winter

Base your answer to question 60 on the maps below of California. Landscape areas are shown on Map I, and yearly average rainfall in inches is shown on Map II. (Isoline intervals vary.)

Map I
Landscape Areas

Map II
Average Rainfall in Inches

60 Why are rainfall amounts greater in some regions of California than in others?
  1   More evaporation occurs in rainy areas.
  2   Areas closer to the Equator receive more rainfall.
  3   Moist air is cooled as it rises and moves over mountains.
  4   Desert regions produce condensation nuclei for cloud formation.

CONSTRUCTED RESPONSE

Base your answers to questions 1 through 4 on your knowledge of Earth science and the diagram which represents a plastic hemisphere upon which lines have been drawn to show the apparent path of the Sun on four days at a location in New York State. Two of the days are December 21 and June 21. The protractor is placed over the North–South line.

1   What is the solar noon altitude of the Sun for path C–C'?

2   Label the December 21 and June 21 paths on the diagram. How many degrees does the altitude of the Sun change from December 21 to June 21?

3   Which path was recorded on a day that had twelve hours of daylight and twelve hours of darkness? How can you tell?

4   In a sentence or two explain why the apparent path of the Sun changes during the year.

Base your answers to questions 5 through 10 on your knowledge of Earth science, the *Reference Tables* and the diagram and data at the right. The diagram represents a closed glass greenhouse located in New York State. The data table shows the air temperatures inside and outside the greenhouse from 6 a.m. to 6 p.m. on a particular day.

AIR TEMPERATURE

Time	Average Outside Temperature	Average Inside Temperature
6 a.m.	10°C	13°C
8 a.m.	11°C	14°C
10 a.m.	12°C	16°C
12 noon	15°C	20°C
2 p.m.	19°C	25°C
4 p.m.	17°C	24°C
6 p.m.	15°C	23°C

Use one or more complete sentences to answer each of the following questions:

5 Where and when did the highest temperature occur?

6 At what time of day did the greenhouse get maximum intensity of insolation?

7 At what rate, in degrees Celsius/hour, did the temperature rise inside the greenhouse between 8 a.m. and 10 a.m.?

8 What happens to the intensity of insolation received by the greenhouse from February 1 to April 1?

9 Explain why the inside of the greenhouse heats up between 6 a.m. and 2 p.m.

10 Explain how the "greenhouse effect" heats the atmosphere.

_____

Base your answers to questions 11 through 14 on the information below and on your knowledge of Earth science.

The climate of an area is affected by many variables such as elevation, latitude, and distance to a large body of water. The effect of these variables on average surface temperature and temperature range can be represented by graphs on grids that have area labeled as shown below.

Grid I

Grid II

Grid III

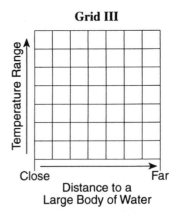

11 On *Grid I*, draw a line to show the relationship between elevation and average surface temperature.

12 On *Grid II*, draw a line to show the relationship between latitude and average surface temperature.

13 On *Grid III*, draw a line to show the relationship between distance to a large body of water and temperature range.

14 The climate of most locations near the Equator is warm and moist.

    a Explain why the climate is warm.

    b Explain why the climate is moist.

Base your answers to questions 15 and 16 on the graph at the right. The graph shows the average water temperature and the dissolved oxygen levels of water in a stream over a 12-month period. The level of dissolved oxygen is measured in parts per million (ppm).

15 State the difference in average water temperature, in degrees Celsius, between January and August.

16 State the relationship between the temperature of the water and the level of dissolved oxygen in the water.

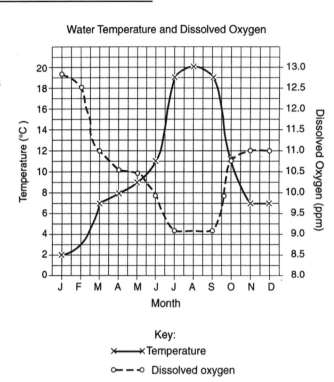

Water Temperature and Dissolved Oxygen

Key:
×———× Temperature
o— — —o Dissolved oxygen

Base your answers to questions 17 through 20 on the graph and your knowledge of Earth science. The graph illustrates the relationship between average air temperature, average soil temperature at a depth of 1 meter, and the duration of insolation for a New York State location.

17 When the highest air temperature occurred what was happening to the duration of insolation?

18 In one or two sentences, explain why maximum air temperature occurred after the time of maximum duration of insolation.

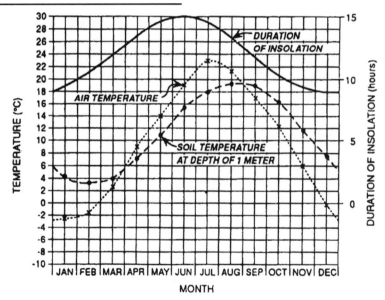

19 What was the average rate of soil temperature change, in C°/month, for the period of time between mid-March and mid-July?

20 The air temperatures at this New York State location are lower in winter than in summer. In a sentence or two, explain why.

Base your answers to questions 21 through 25 on your knowledge of Earth science and the graph which shows the rate of rainfall during a storm and the stream discharge of a nearby stream on July 19.

21 For how many hours did the rainstorm last?

22 What was the maximum rainfall rate? What was the maximum stream discharge?

23 In a sentence or two, explain why the time of maximum stream discharge occurred after the time of maximum rate of rainfall.

24 If the graph shown resulted from a storm in a rural area, predict how the graph might change if the same storm occurred in a nearby urban area.

25 Another rainstorm with the same characteristics as the rainstorm shown on the graph starts at 4 p.m. on July 19. Predict how maximum stream discharge from the second storm would compare with the maximum discharge from the first storm.

ASTRONOMY

VOCABULARY

celestial objects	perpendicular &	*Harmonic Law of*	lunar & solar eclipse	nuclear fusion
arc	direct solar rays	*Planetary Motion*	total solar eclipse	H-R Diagram
Polaris (North Star)	perihelion & aphelion	Astronomical Unit	annular eclipse	sunspots
constellation	local noon	gravitation	solar system	light speed & year
apparent daily	zenith position	kinetic energy	geocentric model	Milky Way Galaxy
motion	equinox	potential energy	heliocentric model	clusters
apparent solar day	Tropic of Cancer	inertia	epicycle	spectroscope
Earth revolution	summer solstice	energy transformation	terrestrial	spectral lines
Earth rotation	Tropic of Capricorn	sidereal month	asteroid belt	Doppler Shift
Foucault pendulum	winter solstice	phases of moon	meteors & fireballs	Edwin Hubble
Coriolis Effect	orbit & focus	synodic, lunar month	comets	Hubble telescope
seasons	eccentricity	spring & neap tides	meteorite	red shift
	orbital velocity	umbra & penumbra	universe	"Big Bang"

A. CELESTIAL OBSERVATIONS

Collectively, the objects observed in the sky during the day or night are called **celestial objects**. These objects include the other planets, our Sun, Moon, the stars, and comets. For the most part, these celestial *objects appear to move daily in a path from east to west* in the sky as observed from the Earth's surface. This apparent motion appears as a part of a circle around the Earth, called an **arc**.

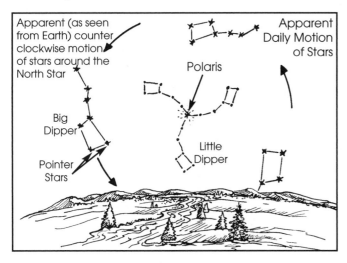

As viewed from Earth, the apparent center of the arcs of the stars or constellations is very near to **Polaris**, the **North Star**. A **constellation** is a group of stars that make an identifiable pattern in the sky. Since Polaris is located above the Earth's axis of rotation, the stars and planets seem to rotate counterclockwise around Polaris at approximately 15° per hour.

Actually, this **apparent daily motion** of the stars, Moon, and planets is because of the Earth's rotation toward the east, at a rate of 15° per hour or 360° in 24 hours.

SOLAR DAY

The **apparent solar day** is the amount of time required for the Earth to rotate from one noon time to the next. It is measured by two successive appearances of the Sun at a given meridian. Because the Earth is revolving as well as rotating, the Earth must actually rotate slightly more than 360° in order to return to noon on successive days.

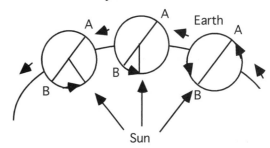

Apparent Solar Day
Earth's rotation and revolution are counterclockwise. As the Earth revolves, the Earth must rotate more than 360° for the Sun's zenith to return to the same Earth longitude.

B. TERRESTRIAL OBSERVATIONS

By observing certain terrestrial evidence, Earth's motions can be determined. There are two main motions of the Earth:

- the Earth's **revolution**, a slightly elliptical orbit around the Sun, and

- the Earth's **rotation**, a spinning about the north – south axis.

MOTION AT THE EARTH'S SURFACE

The Earth rotates once in a 24 hour period, turning 360° or 15° per hour, on its axis. The surface rotational velocity is dependent on the observer's latitude. The closer to the equator – the faster the velocity, and the closer to the poles – the slower the velocity. This apparent speed change can be illustrated with the roller skating game "crack the whip," where skaters are strung out in a long line, turning around one skater in the center. The farther the skater is from the center of the spin, the faster the skater must go to maintain the turning chain.

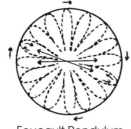

Foucault Pendulum
Back and forth swing is greatly exaggerated.

The rotational velocity at the equator is about 465 m/sec. As the observer moves north or south towards the poles, the speed proportionately decreases (at 20° N or S, 437 m/sec, at 60° N or S, 233 m/sec, and essentially 0 m/sec at the poles).

ROTATIONAL EVIDENCE

The two main evidences of the Earth's rotation are the apparent motion of the **Foucault pendulum** and the **Coriolis effect**.

The Foucault pendulum is a freely swinging pendulum, which, when allowed to swing without interference, appears to change direction in a manner that can be predicted.

The apparent direction change is because of the rotation of the Earth below the pendulum. The actual direction of the pendulum does not change.

All moving materials on the surface of the Earth (fluids in particular) tend to undergo horizontal deflection, known as the Coriolis effect. This pre-

Foucault Pendulum
Pattern is greatly exaggerated.

dictable effect is caused by the Earth rotating. In the Northern Hemisphere currents and projectiles are deflected to their right, whereas in the Southern Hemisphere, they are deflected to their left. This effect accounts for the motions of winds and ocean currents near the surface of the Earth.

The traditional model to explain the Coriolis effect is the spinning platform.

Two persons are standing on a rotating platform (baseball diamond), one at the center and one at the outside edge (perimeter). The platform is rotating counterclockwise. The person at the center throws a ball directly at the other person on the perimeter.

The flight of the ball will be straight, but to the observer the path of the ball will curve behind the person on the edge of the rotating platform. This is because the receiver of the ball has been carried by the moving platform to the right. Had the platform not been moving, the ball would have reached the receiver in a straight line.

Aviators piloting high velocity aircraft over long distances must be familiar with the Coriolis Effect. Any pilot not compensating for Coriolis Effect could find, at the end of a long flight, that his/her airplane had been deflected a significant distance from its scheduled destination.

The Coriolis effect may also be observed during the lift-off of the Space Shuttle. To the observer, the shuttle appears to be tilted as the Earth rotates below it.

APPARENT MOTION OF THE SUN

The Sun appears to move the same as the other celestial objects, in an arc from east to west, sunrise to sunset. For every 15° of arc in the Sun's path, there is one hour of daylight. This apparent path varies with the seasons and with latitude.

Coriolis Effect
A ball being thrown between two persons riding on a rotating platform illustrates Coriolis effect.
A – On a stationary platform, the pitcher throws the baseball to the catcher in an apparent straight line.

B – As the platform rotates counterclockwise, the pitcher throws the baseball in the direction of the catcher, but the turning platform has carried the catcher counterclockwise away from the incoming ball.

C – From above the platform, the baseball appears to have curved to the right as the platform moved counterclockwise to the left, thus demonstrating the Coriolis Effect on the surface of the rotating Earth.

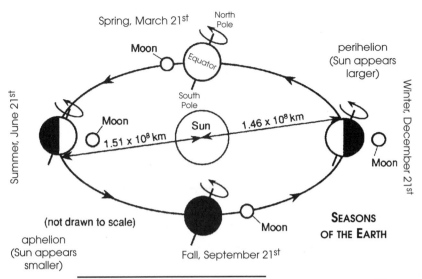

Spring, March 21st

Moon

perihelion (Sun appears larger)

Summer, June 21st

Moon

Sun

1.51 x 10⁸ km

1.46 x 10⁸ km

Winter, December 21st

Moon

(not drawn to scale)

Moon

SEASONS OF THE EARTH

aphelion (Sun appears smaller)

Fall, September 21st

The solar diameter varies in a cyclic pattern during the year, because of the change in the Earth's distance from the Sun. The Sun appears largest at **perihelion** (shortest distance between the Earth and Sun), which occurs during the winter in the Northern Hemisphere (about January 3) and the smallest at **aphelion**, during our (northern hemisphere) summer (approximately July 4).

NOON SUN

Local noon is when the Sun reaches its maximum altitude at the observer's longitude. When the Sun is in the **zenith position** (directly overhead) at the equator (Sun rays are direct or vertical), daylight and dark hours are equal on the Earth. This is known as an **equinox** (generally March 21st and September 23rd).

For the Northern Hemisphere, the first day of summer occurs when the Sun's vertical rays are at 23½° N, over the **Tropic of Cancer**. During the **summer solstice** (usually, June 21st), the Northern Hemisphere has its longest daylight hours.

The **winter solstice** occurs when the Sun's rays are vertical at 23½°S, over the **Tropic of Capricorn** (generally December 21st). At this time, the Northern Hemisphere has its shortest daylight hours. Because the Sun's vertical rays are never seen in the continental United States, an observer in New York State will never see the Sun directly overhead.

SEASONS

The **seasons** on Earth are the direct result of the relative position of the Sun in the sky at different times of the year. Because of the tilt of the Earth's axis (23½° from a perpendicular drawn to the plane of the orbit), the Sun's rays are only perpendicular (directly overhead) at noon, between 23½° North latitude and 23½° South latitude during the year. As the Earth revolves around the Sun the **perpendicular** or **direct rays** of the Sun move between the tropics. This motion causes the points on the horizon of sunrise and sunset to vary during the year.

During summer in the Northern Hemisphere, when the Sun has its highest arc, the Sun rises north of east and sets the same distance north of west. Conversely, during our winter season, the Sun's path is lower, causing shorter daylight hours, and sunrise and sunset occur south of east and south of west, respectively.

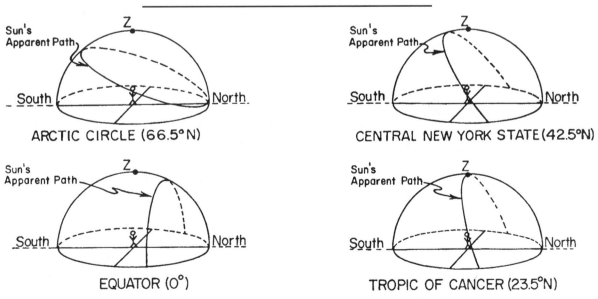

Sun's Apparent Path

Z

South   North

ARCTIC CIRCLE (66.5°N)

Sun's Apparent Path

Z

South   North

CENTRAL NEW YORK STATE (42.5°N)

Sun's Apparent Path

Z

South   North

EQUATOR (0°)

Sun's Apparent Path

Z

South   North

TROPIC OF CANCER (23.5°N)

Apparent Paths of Sun on June 21 as seen by 4 Observers
The zenith (Z) is the point in the sky directly over the observer.

C. GEOMETRY OF ORBITS

A **revolution** is defined as the movement of one body around another body. This motion is also referred to as orbiting. An **orbit** is the path taken by one body as it revolves around the other body. The Earth is orbited by one natural satellite, the moon, and many artificial satellites. Whether satellites are natural or artificial, the same laws of motion apply to their orbits.

A circle has one fixed central point called the **focus**, but an ellipse has two focuses or foci. Ellipses vary in their eccentricity. The **eccentricity** or "out of roundness" of an ellipse may be determine by using the following formula:

$$\text{ECCENTRICITY} = \frac{\text{DISTANCE BETWEEN FOCI}}{\text{LENGTH OF MAJOR AXIS}}$$

The Earth orbits the Sun in a slightly elliptical path with the Sun at one of the foci. The Earth's orbit is so slightly eccentric that, drawn to scale on a piece of paper, it appears to be a circle. It is only careful measurement that shows that the Earth's orbit is elliptical. This small variation in the Earth's yearly distance from the Sun shows why distance from the Sun is ***not*** a cause of seasons on the Earth. The other planets of the solar system also orbit the Sun in much the same manner with orbits of varying eccentricities (see chart in *Reference Tables*).

ORBITAL SPEED

The speed of a satellite is related to the distance from the body around which it orbits. Changes in a planet's **orbital velocity** (time per distance) are based on the following principle:

The areas swept out by an imaginary line connecting the Sun and a planet are equal for equal intervals of time.

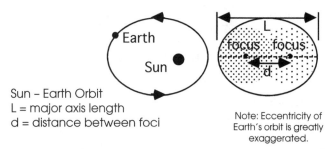

Sun – Earth Orbit
L = major axis length
d = distance between foci

Note: Eccentricity of Earth's orbit is greatly exaggerated.

In an elliptical orbit, the point at which the planet is closest to the Sun is called its perihelion, and the point at which the planet is the farthest from the Sun is its aphelion. A planet's fastest orbital velocity occurs at perihelion, and its slowest orbital velocity occurs at aphelion.

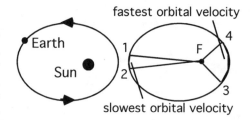

Orbital Velocity Comparison
The Earth orbit time between 1-2 and 3-4 is the same. The areas within 1-2-F and 3-4-F are equal.

Note: Eccentricity of Earth's orbit is greatly exaggerated.

PERIOD OF A PLANET

A planet's **period** is the length of time required for the planet to orbit (revolve) once around the Sun. Therefore, the period of a planet equals one year for that planet.

Johannes Kepler (1571-1630), a German astronomer, was a strong supporter of the heliocentric theory and discoverer of the three **laws of planetary motion** that describe the shape of the orbit, the velocities, and the distances of the planets with respect to the Sun:

1   the planets move in ellipses with the Sun at one focus;

2   the line joining the Sun and a planet sweeps out equal areas in equal intervals of time; and,

3   the square of the time (T^2) of revolution of a planet divided by the cube of its mean distance (R^3) from the Sun gives a number that is the same for all the planets (*Harmonic Law Of Planetary Motion*).

The period of any planet is related to the mean radius of its orbit. The further a planet is from the Sun, the longer its period and time to revolve. This can be illustrated with the use of a formula to explain the relationship.

The square of the planet's period (T^2) is proportional to the cube of its mean distance from the Sun (R^3). In order to determine this relationship for any planet, this formula can be used.

$$T^2 \text{ is proportionally equal to } R^3$$

Where:

T   is expressed in <u>Earth years</u>, and

R   is expressed in <u>Astronomical Units</u>.
(1 Astronomical Unit is the mean distance of the Earth from the Sun – about 150,000,000 kilometers.)

The result should be: **1 = 1**

FORCE & ENERGY TRANSFORMATIONS

Gravitation is the attractive force between any two objects anywhere. The principle that governs the gravitational attraction in the simple celestial model is:

Gravitational force is directly proportional to the product of the masses of the objects and inversely proportional to the distance between their centers squared.

This means the more massive two objects are, the greater the gravitational force between them. The closer two objects are, the greater the gravitational force between them.

Gravity is the force that keeps all satellites, both natural and artificial, moving in their curved orbits.

A cyclic energy transformation between **kinetic energy** (energy of motion) and **potential energy** (stored energy) takes place as the Earth orbits the Sun, resulting in a change in the Earth's speed.

Since the gravitational force acting on the Earth is greatest when the Earth is closest to the Sun, the orbital velocity of the Earth is increased as it moves closer to the Sun in its orbit. As the Earth speeds up, some of the Earth's potential energy is converted to kinetic energy. However, the Earth is not pulled into the Sun, because of inertia. **Inertia** is the tendency of an object in motion to continue in motion in a straight path. It is the balance between gravity and inertia that keeps all satellites in their orbits.

As the Earth moves away from the Sun, its orbital speed will decrease as the Sun's gravitational force opposes the Earth's motion (away from the Sun). The gained kinetic energy is reconverted back into potential energy, causing the **cyclic energy transformation**. In addition to the cyclic energy transformation, the change in the orbital speed of the Earth causes the length of the day to vary slightly.

Note: Eccentricity of Earth's orbit is greatly exaggerated.

INCREASING kinetic energy

orbital velocity increases

Earth

Sun

kinetic energy: HIGHEST

potential energy: LOWEST

orbital velocity decreases

INCREASING potential energy

potential energy: HIGHEST

Earth

kinetic energy: LOWEST

Cyclic Energy Transformation

As the Earth orbits away from the Sun, potential energy increases and kinetic energy decreases. The reverse is true as the Earth moves towards the Sun.

Unlike the apparent motion of stars, the movement of planets through the star field is not uniform. The difference in the uniform motion of the stars and the non-uniform motion of the planets is explained by the orbital velocities of the planets as they move around the Sun.

D. SATELLITE MOTIONS

The **Moon** is the only natural satellite of the Earth, since it revolves around the Earth. (The Earth can be considered a satellite of the Sun for the same reason.) As the Moon revolves around the Earth, it seems to have the same motion characteristics as the other celestial objects. Based on Earth time, one complete revolution of the Moon takes 27$\frac{1}{3}$ days (**sidereal month**).

The angular diameter of the Moon changes as it orbits the Earth. This apparent change in the Moon's diameter is because of the actual orbit of the Moon being slightly elliptical, not circular.

PHASES OF THE MOON

As the Moon revolves it passes through a cyclic series of **phases**. The Sun's light rays are always illuminating one half of the Moon. As the Moon revolves

---

Moon (satellite) Motion Around The Earth

Earth and Moon revolve around their common mass center (**barycenter**). Note that the Moon does not revolve around the Earth's center.

Earth

Moon

around the Earth, the Earth observer sees varying amounts of the illuminated portion of the Moon.

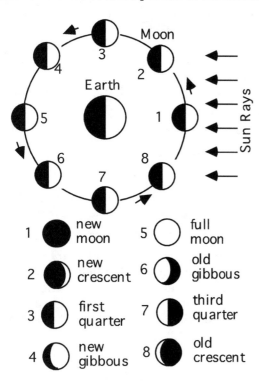

1 ● new moon
2 ● new crescent
3 ◐ first quarter
4 ◑ new gibbous
5 ○ full moon
6 ◐ old gibbous
7 ◑ third quarter
8 ◐ old crescent

The Moon makes a complete phase cycle around the Earth in $27\frac{1}{3}$ days. However, as the Moon revolves around the Earth, the Earth is moving in its orbit around the Sun, constantly changing the relative positions of the Sun, Earth, and Moon.

Therefore, it takes longer (approximately 2 days) for the Moon to complete its full revolution cycle from new Moon to new Moon. The time for this cycle is $29\frac{1}{2}$ days, known as a **synodic** or **lunar month**.

AFFECTS ON EARTH

The thin layer of water covering 71% of the Earth's surface is continually changing in response to the gravitational attraction of the Sun and the Moon. Although the Sun is much more massive than the Moon, the Moon is much closer to the Earth. Thus, its gravitation has a greater impact on the tides. Most coastal locations experience a daily cycle of tides. As the Earth rotates, the tides move around the Earth alternating between high and low tide approximately every six hours.

Tidal range (difference between high and low tide levels) varies during the month. At new and full Moon phases, the Sun's gravitation reinforces that of the Moon's resulting in tides with the greatest range. These tides are called **spring tides.**

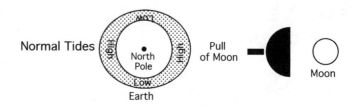

High & Low Tides
Tides are primarily the result of the gravitational attraction between the Earth and the Moon.

Neap tides, those with the smallest tidal range, also occur twice a month but at the first and third quarter phases. At the quarter phases the gravitational attraction of the Sun is pulling at a right angle to that of the Moon.

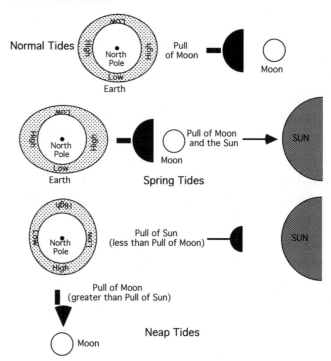

SPRING AND NEAP TIDES

Spring Tides of large range are produced when the gravitational attraction of both the Moon and the Sun is lined on the same axis. Neap Tides of small range are produced when the gravitational attraction of the Sun and the Moon are at right angles (90°) to the Earth.

ECLIPSES

Objects like the Earth and the Moon cast shadows into space. These shadows have a part of total darkness called the **umbra** and a part of partial darkness called the **penumbra**. When the entire Moon passes into the Earth's umbra, a **total lunar eclipse** occurs. This is only possible at full moon phase. Since the plane of the Moon's orbit is inclined approximately 5° to that of the Earth, lunar eclipses do not occur every month (see illustration on next page).

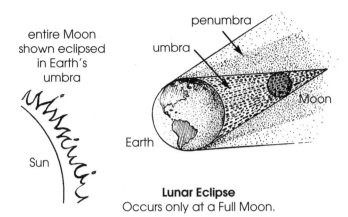

entire Moon
shown eclipsed
in Earth's
umbra

Sun

Lunar Eclipse
Occurs only at a Full Moon.

When the Moon is close enough so that the umbra reaches the Earth's surface, a **total solar eclipse** occurs. This is only possible during the new moon phase. A partial eclipse is seen by areas in the penumbra (see illustration below).

When the Moon is too far from the Earth for its umbra to reach the surface, observers see an **annular eclipse**, a bright ring of solar surface seen behind the dark disk of the moon.

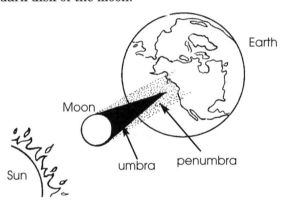

Solar Eclipse
Occurs only at a New Moon. Within the umbra, a total eclipse of the Sun is seen, whereas within the penumbra, only a partial eclipse is seen.

E. SOLAR SYSTEM

The **solar system** is made of the Sun, its eight satellite planets, moons, and other celestial objects revolving around the Sun, most of which have a regular predictable motion. The Sun is estimated to be about 5 billion years old and is expected to last about another 5 billion years. Average in size and temperature, the Sun is several light-years distant from the nearest other star.

Two models have been developed which can be used to explain the apparent motions of celestial objects: the **geocentric model** and the **heliocentric model**.

The **geocentric (Earth-centered) model** was an early attempt to illustrate the motions of the stars, Sun, Moon, and planets as seen from the Earth. It was developed by Aristotle in the 4th century BC and elaborated by Ptolemy in the 2 century AD. The geocentric model shows a stationary Earth as the center with the Sun, Moon, planets, and stars revolving at different speeds in circular orbits. The Moon has the closest orbit to the Earth.

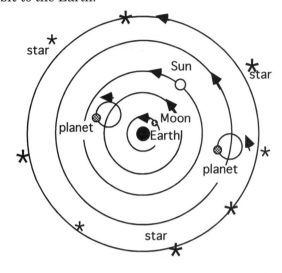

Geocentric Model
Celestial objects revolving about the Earth as depicted by the Geocentric Model which places the Earth as the center.

Although this model does provide an explanation of the daily motions of the Moon, Sun, and stars, it does not easily explain the complex motions of the planets. In order to explain the irregular motions of the planets against the uniform motion of the stars, the geocentric model shows the planets having two orbits. For example, a planet appears to circle the Earth *on* one large orbit (circumference). The center of this orbit is the Earth. However, the planet is actually on a smaller secondary orbit, called an **epicycle**. The center of this smaller orbit moves on the circumference of the larger orbit. Epicycles were an attempt to explain the irregular motions (speed and distance changes) of the planets.

The Sun and stars are seen with the largest circular orbits at great distances from the Earth.

Although the geocentric model cannot explain the terrestrial motions, Coriolis effect, and the apparent change in the path of a Foucault pendulum, it was still believed to be correct for thousands of years, because it seemed so obvious. From the Earth it looks like the Sun, Moon, planets and stars revolve around the Earth.

During the 16th century, Copernicus expounded on a different model for determining planetary motions. Since then, the most commonly accepted model for celestial motions has been the **heliocentric (Sun-centered) model**. It is less complicated than the geocentric model and also explains the terrestrial motions.

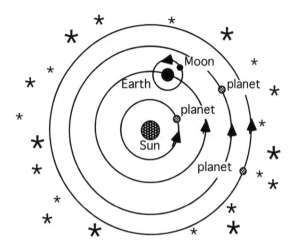

Heliocentric Model
Earth and other celestial objects revolving about the Sun as depicted by the Heliocentric Model which places the Sun as the center.

The Sun, rather than the Earth, is the "stationary" center of the heliocentric model. The Moon orbits the Earth while the rotating Earth revolves around the Sun in an elliptical orbit. The planets also revolve around the Sun in elliptical orbits.

Outside of this solar system, the stars appear stationary because of great distances from the Earth. (Note: All the stars are actually moving.)

The solar system is believed to have formed from a giant rotating, contracting cloud of dust and gas. Most of the material was pulled toward the center forming the Sun. The remaining material orbiting the central mass formed into the planets. The heavier, denser elements forming the planets sank to their centers causing a layered structure.

EARTH & OTHER PLANETS

The eight planets of the solar system revolve around the Sun in orbits of varying eccentricities with the Sun at one of the foci of the orbit. The distance of the planet from the Sun directly affects the characteristics of the planet.

The Earth is the only one of the eight planets in the solar system that has liquid water on its surface, because of the Earth's critical distance from the Sun. This water, along with the atmosphere, helps keep the temperature relatively constant. It is also this water that provided the environment necessary for the beginning, development, and sustenance of life.

Since the average temperatures of the planets decrease as their distances from the Sun increase, and if the Earth were closer to the Sun, then all the water would be in vapor form. A location farther from the Sun would result in all the water being solid ice.

The planets may be classified in different ways. One way is to divide them into those that are Earth-like (**terrestrial**) and those that are Jupiter-like (**Jovian**). Mercury, Venus, Earth, and Mars are terrestrial having rocky cores. Jupiter, Uranus, Saturn, and Neptune are Jovian, gas giants with low densities and thick atmospheres containing hydrogen, helium, methane, and ammonia. The lighter elements surrounding the outer planets have been blown or boiled away by solar radiation.

Pluto , once considered the 9th planet was reclassified in 2006 as a dwarf planet and the largest member a region, the Kuiper belt. Eris and Ceres are also in the new category of dwarf planet according to the International Astronomical Union.

Mercury, the planet closest to the Sun, has many similarities to the Moon. Like the Moon, it has no significant atmosphere. The lack of atmosphere means that incoming meteorites are not destroyed; hence, the

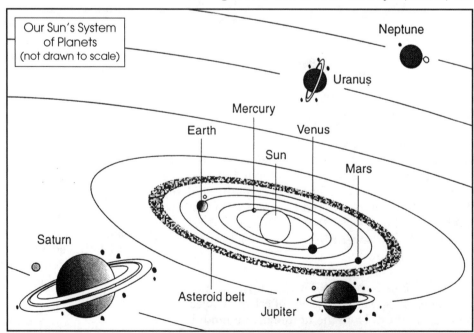

Our Sun's System of Planets (not drawn to scale)

Neptune
Uranus
Mercury
Earth
Venus
Sun
Mars
Saturn
Asteroid belt
Jupiter

Mariner 2 was the world's first successful interplanetary spacecraft. Launched August 27, 1962, on an Atlas-Agena rocket, Mariner 2 passed within about 34,000 kilometers (21,000 miles) of Venus, sending back valuable new information about interplanetary space and the Venusian atmosphere. Mariner 2 recorded the temperature at Venus for the first time, revealing the planet's very hot atmosphere of about 500 degrees Celsius (900 degrees Fahrenheit). NASA Photo

surface of Mercury has impact craters much like the Moon. The tremendous temperature range from the lighted to the dark side of Mercury and lack of chemical weathering is also a result of the absence of an atmosphere.

Venus, similar in size, density, and mass to the Earth, is covered with thick clouds in an atmosphere made mostly of carbon dioxide. The greenhouse effect, resulting from so much carbon dioxide, results in blistering surface temperatures.

An atmosphere containing free oxygen has developed only on the **Earth**. The small percentage of car-

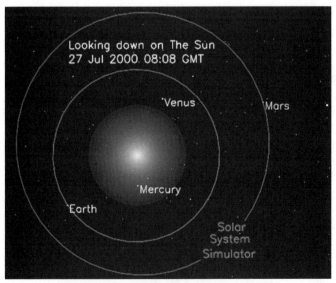

Solar System Simulator. NASA Creation

bon dioxide in Earth's atmosphere helps to heat the atmosphere. However, scientists are concerned that the addition of more of carbon dioxide will increase the greenhouse effect on the Earth causing too much heating (global warming). Like the Moon and Mercury, the surface of the Earth has many craters resulting from the impact of asteroids and meteorites. Unlike the Moon and Mercury which have no atmosphere, weathering, erosion, and deposition have made many of these impact structures less evident than those on the lunar surface.

More than 40 tons of cosmic debris (mostly dust) hit the Earth each day. Occasionally, larger stony or metallic meteorites hit the surface. Many come from the **asteroid belt** between Mars and Jupiter. Ranging in size from a few meters to hundreds of meters, they, like the planets, also revolve around the Sun. As they tumble through space, collisions break off smaller pieces which are bumped out of the belt. As Earth moves through its orbit, some of these pieces are pulled toward Earth by gravity.

Much of the space debris entering Earth's atmosphere is heated by friction with air molecules and vaporized before the debris reaches the surface. Observers may see the streaks of light as **meteors** (shooting stars) streak across the night sky. Occasionally, **fireballs** (bolides) may explode into fiery pieces as they fall toward Earth.

Comets, large masses of frozen gas and pieces of metallic and stony material, (like big dirty snowballs) may also be sources of meteoric material. When their very eccentric orbits bring them closer to the Sun, a tail of gases and particles stream out of their head into space always pointing away from the Sun. These particles left in space may also be pulled toward the Earth.

In July 1994, astronomers saw a comet break up and collide with the surface of Jupiter. Fortunately, for the inner planets like Earth, the gravity of giant Jupiter attracts comets coming from the outer reaches of the solar system toward the Sun.

Regardless of the source, sometimes these stony space travelers are large enough to pass through Earth's atmosphere and impact the surface. Although incidence of impact today is less than early in the Earth's history, it still does occur. One October evening in 1992 a 26 - pound stony **meteorite** crashed through the trunk of a 1980 Chevy Malibu in Peekskill, New York, making a shallow pit beneath the car.

Catastrophic events associated with impact of asteroids making gigantic craters on Earth, are attributed with the periodic mass extinctions of life on the Earth.

Like Venus, the atmosphere of **Mars** is composed primarily of carbon dioxide. Unlike Venus, the Martian atmosphere is very thin so there is little greenhouse effect. Temperatures are significantly colder on the crater marked surface of Mars than those on the Earth.

Although the environments of the other terrestrial planets are hostile to life, exploration, need, and technology may someday enable us to access the resources of these other worlds and perhaps make colonization of these planets possible.

Just as the size of the **universe** is incomprehensible to the human mind, the total number of stars is almost unimaginable in number. The stars vary in size, temperature, and age as they move through their life cycles.

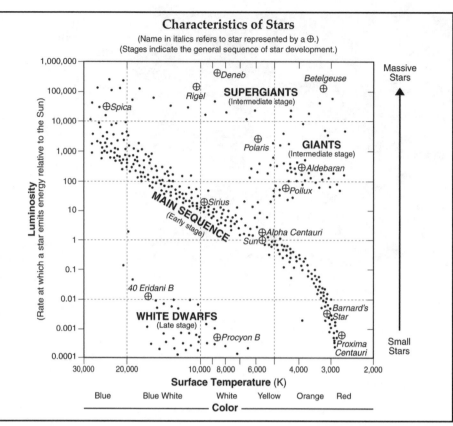

Characteristics of Stars
(Name in italics refers to star represented by a ⊕.)
(Stages indicate the general sequence of star development.)

Gravity causes clouds of dust and gases in space to contract and heat until it becomes hot enough for **nuclear fusion** to begin (several million degrees). In this nuclear reaction process, light elements are fused to form heavier ones. Four hydrogen nuclei are fused together to form one helium nucleus and a small amount of the matter in this process is converted into energy and released. The conversion of a very small amount of hydrogen into helium results in an enormous release of energy.

One way stars are classified is by spectral class. This classification is based upon the physical and chemical characteristics revealed by looking at their light through a spectroscope. By plotting the spectral class (temperature) of stars against their luminosity (brightness), Einar Hertzsprung and Henry Russell each developed a graph called the **H-R Diagram** (see *Luminosity and Temperature of Stars Table* above).

Most known stars, including our Sun, are on the main sequence, a band on the diagram that shows the hottest, brightest stars in the upper left and extends to the cooler, dimmer stars at the lower right. The very luminous giant and super giant stars are to the upper right of the main sequence and the smaller, dimmer dwarf stars are seen toward the lower left.

The H-R Diagram is helpful for showing the changes that occur in a star during its lifetime. Stars, like the Sun, spend most of their life on the main

sequence. When the Sun's core of hydrogen is fused to helium, astronomers believe it will expand and become a red giant star. When its nuclear fuel is used up, it will collapse into a white dwarf star and eventually radiate its remaining energy to end up as a black dwarf.

Stars that are more massive than the Sun may end their lives as supernovae. As their interior implodes, their outer layer explodes out into interstellar space providing clouds of heavy elements from which new stars and planets may later form.

SUNSPOTS

Dark patches visible on the solar surface are called sunspots. They most frequently occur in magnetized pairs or groups. As the Sun rotates they move across the Sun's surface in bands parallel to the solar equator. The size and number of sunspots vary in a cycle of approximately 11 years from one sunspot maximum to the next. Bursts of ionized gases often explode from sunspot areas. Collision of the emitted particles and waves with earth's magnetic field results in the aurora borealis (Northern Lights) and causes disruption in Earth's magnetic field, power surges and interference with radio, television, and radar transmissions. Some scientists think sunspots may have an effect on the Earth's weather and climate, but more research is needed.

F. Earth In The Universe

Outside the solar system, very large units, such as light-years, are necessary to measure the vast distances in space. The **speed of light** is the basis for this measurement (300,000 kilometers per second). Light could travel around the Earth's equator seven times in one second. A **light-year** is the distance light travels in one year, a distance of ten trillion kilometers.

What is the Earth's place in the universe?

It takes light from the Sun, our nearest star, a little more than 8 minutes to reach the Earth. Light reaching your eyes from other stars left those stars long ago. Excluding the Sun, light from the next closest star to Earth left that star over 4 years ago. Since the light that left distant stars long ago is just reaching the Earth, you are looking back in time (often hundreds of years) each time you view the stars.

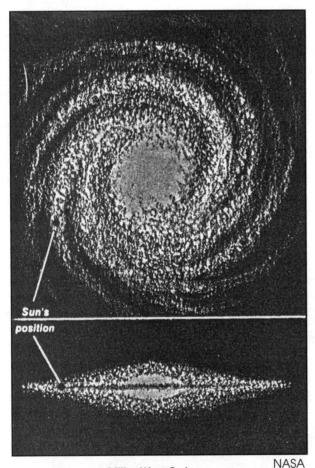

NASA

Milky Way Galaxy
Diameter: 100,000 light years
Thickness: 10,000 light years

Most stars exist in large systems of various shapes (spiral, elliptical, irregular) called galaxies. If you look in toward the center of our galaxy, the sky has a milky-looking appearance. This band of light across the dark night sky is what gives our galaxy its name, the **Milky Way** galaxy.

Only one of billions of other stars in our spiral galaxy, the Sun, a medium-sized star, is not near the center. The Sun orbits the galaxy in one of the outer spiral arms.

Groups of galaxies are called **clusters**. Astronomers estimate the universe to have a radius of 15 billion light-years, containing many clusters of galaxies all having billions of stars.

G. Expanding Universe

When light is passed through a prism, it is separated into its component colors of different wavelengths from red to violet. In this spectrum of colors, red has the longest wavelength and violet the shortest.

The **spectroscope**, which contains a prism, is an important astronomical instrument. By using a spectroscope to study the light from distant stars and galaxies, astronomers obtain information concerning the composition, temperature, and motion of the celestial objects. Each chemical element gives off a characteristic number of wavelengths; therefore, the combination of a star's elements which produce a pattern of **spectral lines** can be used to identify the star, rather like a fingerprint or bar code.

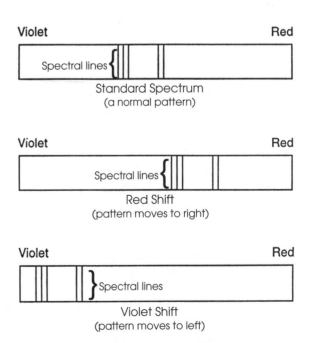

Violet   Red

Spectral lines {

Standard Spectrum
(a normal pattern)

Violet   Red

Spectral lines {

Red Shift
(pattern moves to right)

Violet   Red

} Spectral lines

Violet Shift
(pattern moves to left)

Standard Darkline Spectrum for an Element

Hubble Telescope is pictured in Discovery's cargo bay during the December 1999 servicing mission. NASA Photo

toward the red end of the spectrum, the light source is moving away from the observer; if they shift toward the violet end of the spectrum, the light source is moving toward the observer. The greater the degree in the shift of the lines, the faster the relative motion.

Edwin Hubble, (famed astronomer for whom the **Hubble Space Telescope**, HST was named) while studying the light from distant galaxies, noted a **red shift** in the spectra. He concluded that the galaxies are moving rapidly away from each other. The farther the galaxies are away from the Earth, the greater the red shift in their spectra. This has lead many astronomers to assume the universe is expanding.

Astronomers theorize that approximately 15 billion years ago the universe (entire celestial cosmos) began with a gigantic explosion called the "**Big Bang**." All the material of the universe is assumed to have been in one hot, supermassive, small volume. As this material exploded and expanded, it later condensed into galaxies of dust, gas, and stars that continue to fly apart caused by the explosion. Evidence to support this idea includes cosmic background radiation from this "Big Bang" which can still be detected in space.

The red shift in the light coming from very distant galaxies shows they are rapidly moving away. Will the universe stop expanding in 15 billion years or so and begin to contract back into that small supermassive volume, as some astronomers have suggested? The answer to that question depends upon the total mass of the universe which is a subject still under investigation.

The **Doppler Shift** in spectral lines is an apparent change in wavelength caused by the relative motion of the source of light. If the spectral lines shift

BIG BANG HYPOTHESIS

1st
Ball of
Hydrogen
Explodes

2nd
Cloud of Hydrogen Moves Outwards
Galaxies Formed Through Condensing

3rd
Formed Galaxies Continue
To Move Outward

QUESTIONS FOR UNIT 8

1 A photograph showing circular star trails is evidence that the Earth
   1 rotates on its axis
   2 revolves around the Sun
   3 has a nearly circular orbit
   4 has a nearly spherical shape

2 The diagram below shows an instrument made from a drinking straw, protractor, string, and rock.

This instrument was most likely used to measure the

   1 distance to a star
   2 altitude of a star
   3 mass of the Earth
   4 mass of the suspended weight

3 How would a three-hour time exposure photograph of stars in the northern sky appear if the Earth did not rotate?

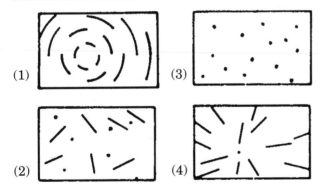

4 In 1851, the French physicist Jean Foucault constructed a large pendulum that always changed its direction of swing at the same rate in a clockwise direction. According to Foucault, this change in direction of swing was caused by the
   1 Moon's rotation on its axis
   2 Moon's revolution around the Earth
   3 Earth's rotation on its axis
   4 Earth's revolution around the Sun

5 The diagram represents a Foucault pendulum in a building in New York State. Points A and A' are fixed points on the floor. As the pendulum swings for six hours, it will

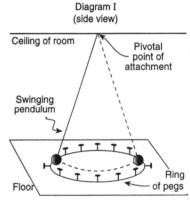

   1 appear to change position because of Earth's rotation
   2 appear to change position because of Earth's revolution
   3 continue to swing between A and A' because of inertia
   4 continue to swing between A and A' because of air pressure

Base your answers to questions 6 and 7 on the diagrams, which represent two views of a swinging Foucault pendulum with a ring of 12 pegs at its base.

6 Diagram II shows two pegs tipped over by the swinging pendulum at the beginning of the demonstration. Which diagram shows the pattern of standing pegs and fallen pegs after several hours?

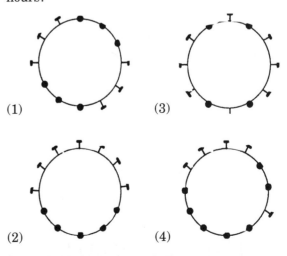

7 The predictable change in the direction of swing of a Foucault pendulum provides evidence that the
1 Sun rotates on its axis
2 Sun revolves around the Earth
3 Earth rotates on its axis
4 Earth revolves around the Sun

8 Major ocean and air currents appear to curve to the right in the Northern Hemisphere because of
1 Earth's rotation
2 Earth's revolution
3 the Sun's rotation
4 the Moon's revolution

Base your answers to questions 9 through 11 on the *Earth Science Reference Tables* and the map below. The map represents a view of the Earth looking down from above the North Pole, showing the Earth's 24 standard time zones. The Sun's rays are striking the Earth from the right. Points *A*, *B*, *C*, and *D* are locations on the Earth's surface.

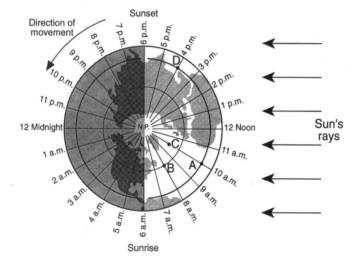

9 At which position would the altitude of the North Star (Polaris) be greatest?
(1) *A*   (3) *C*
(2) *B*   (4) *D*

10 Which date could this diagram represent?
1 January 21   3 June 21
2 March 21   4 August 21

11 Areas within a time zone generally keep the same standard clock time. In degrees of longitude, approximately how wide is one standard time zone?
(1) $7\frac{1}{2}°$ (3) $23\frac{1}{2}°$
(2) 15°   (4) 30°

Base your answers to questions 12 through 16 on the *Earth Science Reference Tables*, the diagram below, and your knowledge of Earth science. The diagram shows the Earth's position in its orbit around the Sun at the beginning of each season. The Moon is shown at various positions as it revolves around the Earth.

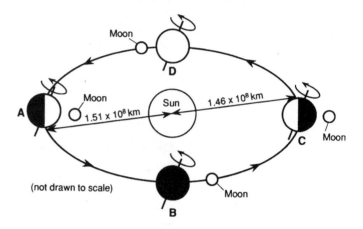

(not drawn to scale)

12 What is most likely represented by the symbol near the Earth's axis at each position?
1 the direction of Earth's rotation
2 the path of the Sun through the sky
3 the changing tilt of Earth's axis
4 convection currents in the atmosphere

13 The Earth's orbit around the Sun is best described as
1 a perfect circle
2 an oblate spheroid
3 a very eccentric ellipse
4 a slightly eccentric ellipse

14 Which position of the Earth represents the beginning of the winter season for New York State?
(1) *A*   (3) *C*
(2) *B*   (4) *D*

15 Which position of the Earth shows the Moon located where its shadow may sometimes reach the Earth?
(1) *A*   (3) *C*
(2) *B*   (4) *D*

16 As the Earth moves from position *B* to position *C*, what change will occur in the gravitational attraction between the Earth and the Sun?
1 It will decrease, only.
2 It will increase, only.
3 It will decrease, then increase.
4 It will remain the same.

Base your answers to questions 17 through 21 on the diagram below and your knowledge of Earth science. The diagram represents a plastic hemisphere upon which lines have been drawn to show the apparent paths of the Sun on four days at one location in the Northern Hemisphere. Two paths are dated. The protractor is placed over the north-south line. X represents the position of a vertical post.

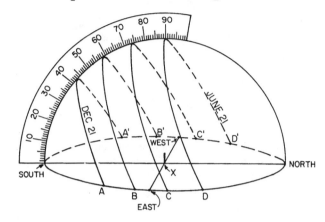

17 For which path is the altitude of the noon Sun 74°?
(1) A-A'   (3) C-C'
(2) B-B'   (4) D-D'

18 How many degrees does the altitude of the Sun change from December 21 to June 21?
(1) 43°   (3) 66½°
(2) 47°   (4) 74°

19 Which path of the Sun would result in the longest shadow of the vertical post at solar noon?
(1) A-A'   (3) C-C'
(2) B-B'   (4) D-D'

20 Which statement best explains the apparent daily motion of the Sun?
1   The Earth's orbit is an ellipse.
2   The Earth's shape is an oblate spheroid.
3   The Earth is closest to the Sun in winter.
4   The Earth rotates on its axis.

21 What is the latitude of this location?
(1) 0°   (3) 66½° N
(2) 23½° N   (4) 90° N

22 When observed from sunrise to sunset in New York State, the length of the shadow cast by a vertical pole will
1   decrease, only
2   increase, only
3   first decrease, then increase
4   first increase, then decrease

23 Why do the locations of sunrise and sunset vary in a cyclical pattern throughout the year?
1   The Earth rotates on a tilted axis while revolving around the Sun.
2   The Sun rotates on a tilted axis while revolving around the Earth.
3   The Earth's orbit around the Sun is an ellipse.
4   The Sun's orbit around the Earth is an ellipse.

24 The diagram below represents the elliptical orbit of the Earth around the Sun.

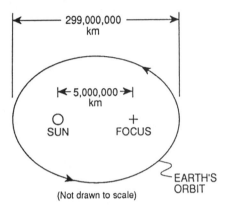

(Not drawn to scale)

According to the distances shown in the diagram and the *Earth Science Reference Tables*, which equation should be used to find the eccentricity of the Earth's orbit?

1   $\text{eccentricity} = \dfrac{299{,}000{,}000 \text{ km}}{5{,}000{,}000 \text{ km}}$

2   $\text{eccentricity} = \dfrac{5{,}000{,}000 \text{ km}}{299{,}000{,}000 \text{ km}}$

3   $\text{eccentricity} = 299{,}000{,}000 \text{ km} - 5{,}000{,}000 \text{ km}$

4   $\text{eccentricity} = \dfrac{5{,}000{,}000 \text{ km}}{299{,}000{,}000 \text{ km} - 5{,}000{,}000 \text{ km}}$

25 According to the *Reference Tables*, what is the approximate eccentricity of the ellipse shown below?

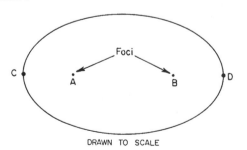

DRAWN TO SCALE

(1) 0.50   (3) 0.25
(2) 2.0   (4) 4.0

Base your answers to questions 26 through 29 on the diagrams below and your knowledge of Earth science. The diagrams represent four locations on the Earth's surface at the same time on March 21. Lines have been drawn to represent the apparent path of the Sun across the sky. The present position of the Sun, the position of Polaris, and the zenith (Z) are shown for an observer at each location.

Location A

Location C

Location B

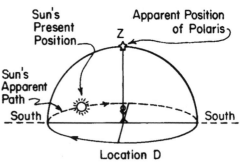

Location D

26 To an observer at location *A*, the Sun will appear to move from
1   east to west at 15° per hour
2   west to east at 15° per hour
3   east to west at 1° per hour
4   west to east at 1° per hour

27 The Sun's apparent path through the sky on this day is a direct result of the
1   Sun's rotation
2   Earth's rotation
3   Sun's revolution around the Earth
4   Earth's revolution around the Sun

28 What is the latitude of the observer at location *D*?
(1) 90° N
(2) 66½° N
(3) 23½° N
(4) 0°

29 What time of day is shown by the Sun's Present position at location *A*?
1   morning
2   noon
3   afternoon
4   midnight

Base your answers to questions 30 through 31 on the diagram below and your knowledge of Earth science.

30 The diagram represents the Earth's orbital path around the Sun. The Earth takes the same amount of time to move from *A* to *B* as from *C* to *D*.

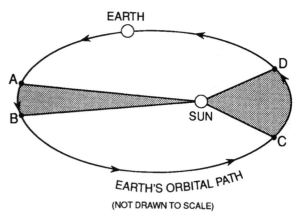

Which values are equal within the system?
1   The shaded sections of the diagram are equal in area.
2   The distance from the Sun to the Earth is the same at point *A* and at point *D*.
3   The orbital velocity of the Earth at point *A* equals its orbital velocity at point *C*.
4   The gravitational force between the Earth and the Sun at point *B* is the same as the gravitational force at point *D*.

31 Planet *A* has a greater mean distance from the Sun than planet *B*. On the basis of this fact, which further comparison can be correctly made between the two planets?
1 Planet *A* is larger.
2 Planet *A*'s revolution period is longer.
3 Planet *A*'s speed of rotation is greater.
4 Planet *A*'s day is longer.

Questions 32 and 33 refer to the diagram which shows the Earth's orbit and the partial orbit of a comet on the same plane around the Sun.

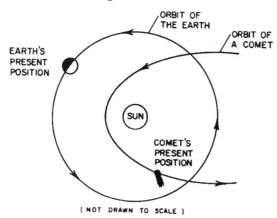

32 Which observation is true for an observer at the Earth's Equator at midnight on a clear night for the positions shown in the diagram?
1 The comet is directly overhead.
2 The comet is rising.
3 The comet is setting.
4 The comet is *not* visible.

Note: Question 33 has only 3 choices.

33 Compared with the Earth's orbit, the comet's orbit has
1 less eccentricity
2 more eccentricity
3 the same eccentricity

Base your answers to questions 34 and 35 on the diagram at the right, which represents the path of a planet in an elliptical orbit around a star. Points *A*, *B*, *C*, and *D* indicate four orbital positions of the planet.

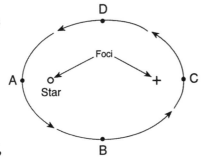

34 The eccentricity of the planet's orbit is approximately
(1) 0.18   (3) 1.55
(2) 0.65   (4) 5.64

35 Which graph best represents the gravitational attraction between the star and the planet?

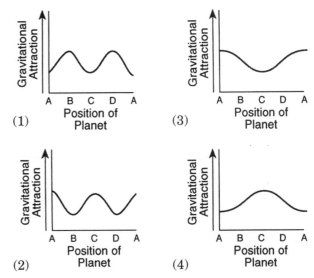

36 The phases of the Moon are caused by the
1 Earth's revolution around the Sun
2 Moon's revolution around the Earth
3 Moon's varying distance from the Earth
4 Sun's varying distance from the Moon

37 The diagram shows the relative position of the Earth, Moon, and Sun for a one-month period.

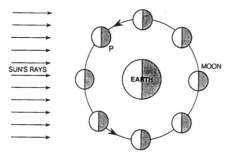

Which diagram best represents the appearance of the Moon at position *P* when viewed from the Earth?

38 The new-moon phase occurs when the Moon is positioned between the Earth and the Sun. However, these positions do not always cause an eclipse (blocking) of the Sun because the
1 Moon's orbit is tilted relative to the Earth's orbit
2 new-moon phase is visible only at night
3 night side of the Moon faces toward the Earth
4 apparent diameter of the Moon is greatest during the new-moon phase

39 The diagram shows four different positions (*W*, *X*, *Y*, and *Z*) of the Moon in its orbit around the Earth.

In which position will the full moon phase be seen from the Earth?
(1) *W*   (3) *Y*
(2) *X*   (4) *Z*

40 A student drew the phase of the Moon observed from one location on the Earth on each of the dates shown below.

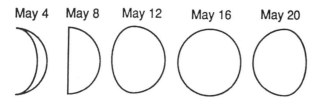

Which diagram best shows the Moon's phase on May 24?

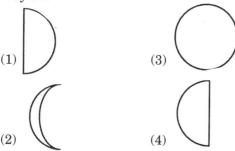

41 The graph below shows the changes in height of ocean water tides over the course of 2 days at one Earth location.

Which statement concerning these changes is best supported by the graph?
1   The changes are cyclic and occur at predictable time intervals.
2   The changes are cyclic and occur at the same time every day.
3   The changes are noncyclic and occur at sunrise and sunset.
4   The changes are noncyclic and may occur at any time.

42 The average time interval between one high tide and the next high tide is approximately
(1) 24 hours
(2) 12 hours
(3) 3 hours
(4) 6 hours

43 The high tides which occur at both the New Moon and the Full Moon are called
1   flood tides
2   neap tides
3   spring tides
4   ebb tides

44 The bedrock of the flat areas on the Moon is mostly basalt. This fine-grained igneous rock was most likely formed by the
1   cementing and compacting of sediments
2   changes caused by heat and pressure on preexisting rocks
3   slow cooling of magma deep under the surface
4   rapid cooling of molten rock in lava flows

45 When the Moon is completely covered within the Earth's umbra, which occurs?
1   a lunar eclipse
2   a solar eclipse
3   an annular eclipse
4   no eclipse

46 In which type of model are the Sun, other stars, and the Moon in orbit around the Earth?
1   heliocentric model
2   tetrahedral model
3   concentric model
4   geocentric model

47 Which diagram best represents a heliocentric model of a portion of the solar system?
[Key: *E* = Earth, *P* = Planet, *S* = Sun. Diagrams are not drawn to scale.]

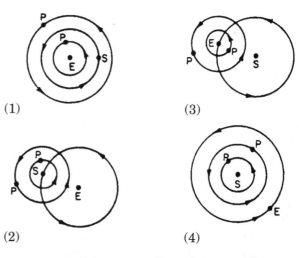

48 Which graph best illustrates the average tempera- tures of the planets in the solar system?

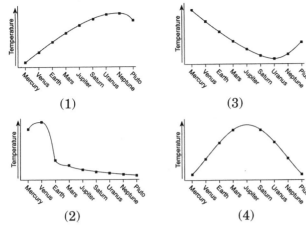

(1)   (3)

(2)   (4)

49 According to current data, the Earth is apparently the only planet in our solar system that has
1   an orbiting moon
2   an axis of rotation
3   atmospheric gases
4   liquid water on its surface

Base your answers to questions 50 and 51 on the graphs below. The graphs show the composition of the atmospheres of Venus, Earth, Mars, and Jupiter.

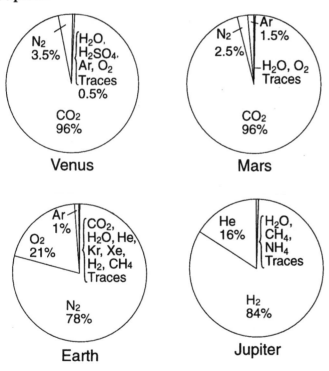

Venus

Mars

Earth

Jupiter

50 Which gas is present in the atmospheres of Venus, Earth, and Mars but is not present in the atmos- phere of Jupiter?
1   argon (Ar)   3   hydrogen (H_2)
2   methane (CH_4)   4   water vapor (H_2O)

51 Which planet has an atmosphere composed pri- marily of CO_2 and a period of rotation greater than its period of revolution?
1   Venus   3   Earth
2   Mercury   4   Mars

52 Compared to Jupiter and Saturn, Venus, and Mars have greater
1   periods of revolution
2   orbital velocities
3   mean distances from the Sun
4   equatorial diameters

53 According to the *Earth Science Reference Tables*, three planets known as gas giants because of their large size and low density are
1   Venus, Neptune, and Jupiter
2   Jupiter, Saturn, and Venus
3   Jupiter, Saturn, and Uranus
4   Venus, Uranus, and Jupiter

54 Which planet has vast amounts of liquid water at its surface?
1   Venus   3   Jupiter
2   Mars   4   Earth

55 In what way are the planets Mars, Mercury, and Earth similar?
1   They have the same period of revolution.
2   They are perfect spheres.
3   They exert the same gravitational force on each other.
4   They have elliptical orbits with the Sun at one focus.

56 Why are impact structures (craters) more common on the surface of Mars than on the surfaces of Venus, Earth, and Jupiter?
1   Mars has the greatest surface area and receives more impacts.
2   The tiny moons of Mars are breaking into pieces and showering its surface with rock fragments.
3   Mars has a strong magnetic field that attracts iron-containing rock fragments from space.
4   The thin atmosphere of Mars offers little pro- tection against falling rock fragments from space.

57 Impact craters are more obvious on the Moon and Mercury than on Earth because
1   meteorites have not struck Earth
2   weathering processes on Earth have removed most craters
3   Earth is younger than Mercury of the Moon
4   all meteorites burn up in Earth's atmosphere

Base your answers to questions 58 through 62 on the diagram of the solar system below, the *Earth Science Reference Tables*, **and your knowledge of Earth science.**

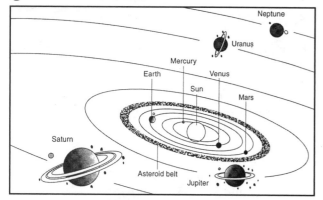

58 Which kind of model of the solar system is represented by the diagram?
1 heliocentric model   3 sidereal model
2 geocentric model   4 lunar model

59 If the Earth's distance from the Sun were doubled, the gravitational attraction between the Sun and Earth would be
1 one-ninth as great
2 nine times as great
3 one-fourth as great
4 four times as great

60 Which of the following planets does *not* have a satellite ?
1 Saturn   3 Jupiter
2 Earth   4 Mercury

61 According to *Kepler's Harmonic Law of Planetary Motion*, the farther a planet is located from the Sun, the
1 shorter its period of rotation
2 shorter its period of revolution
3 longer its period of rotation
4 longer its period of revolution

62 On which planet would a measuring instrument placed at the planet's equator record the longest time from sunrise to sunset?
1 Mercury   3 Earth
2 Venus   4 Mars

63 The surface of Venus is much hotter than would be expected, considering its distance from the Sun. Which statement best explains this condition?
1 Venus has many active volcanoes.
2 Venus has a slow rate of rotation.
3 The clouds of Venus are highly reflective.
4 The atmosphere of Venus contains a high percentage of carbon dioxide.

64 The greatest difference in seasons would occur on a planet that has
1 a circular orbit
2 a slightly elliptical orbit
3 its axis of rotation perpendicular to the plane of its orbit around the Sun
4 its axis of rotation inclined 45° to the plane of its orbit around the Sun

65 Rock samples brought back from the Moon show absolutely no evidence of chemical weathering. This is most likely because of
1 the lack of an atmosphere on the Moon
2 extremely low surface temperatures on the Moon
3 lack of biological activity on the Moon
4 large quantities of water in the lunar "seas"

Base your answers to questions 66 and 67 on the diagram below which shows four planets orbiting the Sun.

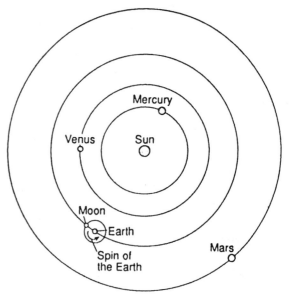

(not drawn to scale)

66 Which object will be visible from the Earth in the eastern sky after midnight?
1 the Moon   3 Mercury
2 Mars   4 Venus

67 Which planet's day is longer than its year?
1 Mercury   3 Mars
2 Venus   4 Jupiter

68 A belt of asteroids is located an average distance of 503 million kilometers from the Sun. Between which two planets is this belt located?
1 Mars and Jupiter
2 Mars and Earth
3 Jupiter and Saturn
4 Saturn and Uranus

69 Compared to the distances between the planets of our solar system, the distances between stars are usually
1   much less
2   much greater
3   about the same

70 Earth and our solar system are
1   older than the universe
2   younger than the universe
3   the same age as the universe

71 The diagram below represents part of the night sky including the constellation Leo. The black circles represent stars. The open circles represent the changing positions of one celestial object over a period of a few weeks.

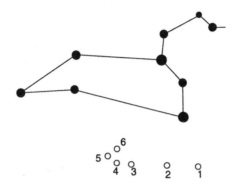

The celestial object represented by the open circles most likely is
1   a galaxy   3   Earth's Moon
2   a planet   4   another star

72 Which diagram best represents how Venus and the Moon would appear in the sky at sunset to an observer in New York State? [Diagrams are not drawn to scale.]

(1)

(3)

(2)

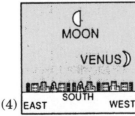
(4)

73 The presence of which atmospheric gas causes the high temperature of Venus?
1   nitrogen (N_2)   3   hydrogen (H_2)
2   oxygen (O_2)   4   carbon dioxide (CO_2)

74 Which planet's orbital shape would be most similar to Jupiter's orbital shape?
1   Mercury   3   Earth
2   Venus   4   Uranus

75 A comparison of the age of the Earth obtained from radioactive dating and the age of the universe based on Galactic Doppler shifts suggest that
1   the Earth is about the same age as the universe
2   the Earth is immeasurably older than the universe
3   the Earth was formed after the universe began
4   the two dating methods contradict one another

76 Billions of stars in the same region of the universe are called
1   solar systems   3   constellations
2   asteroid belts   4   galaxies

77 An example of a galaxy is
1   Ursa Major
2   the Milky Way
3   the Solar System
4   Polaris

78 Which statement best describes how galaxies generally move?
1   Galaxies move toward one another.
2   Galaxies move away from one another.
3   Galaxies move randomly.
4   Galaxies do not move.

79 The symbols below represent the Milky Way galaxy, the solar system, the Sun, and the universe.

◯ = Milky Way Galaxy

⬭ = Solar System

• = Sun

▢ = Universe

Which arrangement of symbols is most accurate?

(1)

(3)

(2)

(4)

80 The diagram below represents the Milky Way galaxy.

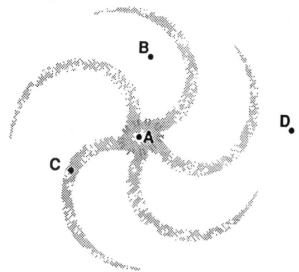

Which letter best represents the location of the Earth's solar system?

(1) A   (3) C
(2) B   (4) D

Base your answer to question 81 on the diagram below, the *Earth Science Reference Tables*, and your knowledge of Earth science. The diagram below shows reference lines on a standard spectrum and a spectrum from a distance galaxy moving away from Earth.

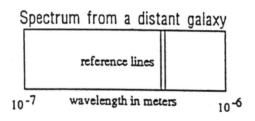

81 If the spectral lines produced by the light from a distant galaxy are
   1   shifted toward the violet, the galaxy is moving away from us
   2   shifted toward the violet, the galaxy is stationary
   3   are shifted toward the red, the galaxy is moving away from us
   4   shifted toward the red, the galaxy is moving towards us

82 The diagram below represents a standard dark-line spectrum for an element.

The spectral lines of this element are observed in light from a distant galaxy. Which diagram represents these spectral lines?

83 In which group are the parts listed from oldest to youngest?
   1   universe, Milky Way, solar system
   2   solar system, Milky Way, universe
   3   Milky Way, solar system, universe
   4   universe, solar system, Milky Way

84 Background radiation detected in space is believed to be evidence that
   1   the Universe began with a primeval explosion
   2   the Universe is contracting
   3   all matter in the Universe is stationary
   4   galaxies are evenly spaced throughout the Universe

CONSTRUCTED RESPONSE

Base your answers to questions 1 through 5 on your knowledge of Earth science, the *Reference Tables*, and the diagram below. The diagram represents four planets A, B, C, and D, traveling in elliptical orbits around a star. The center of the star and letter *f* represent the foci for the orbit of planet A. Points 1 through 4 are locations of the orbit of planet A.

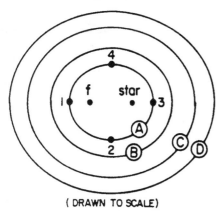

(DRAWN TO SCALE)

Base your answers to questions 6 through 8 on the diagrams below. Diagram I represents the Moon orbiting the Earth as viewed from space above the North Pole. The Moon is shown at 8 different positions in orbit. Diagram II represents phases of the Moon as seen from the Earth when the Moon is at position 2 and position 4.

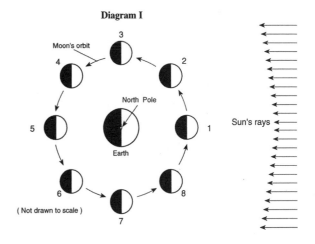

Diagram I

Diagram II

Phase of the Moon as seen from the Earth

1 List the order of the planets from the shortest period of revolution to the longest.

2 If planets A, B, C, and D have the same mass and are located at the positions shown in the diagram, explain in a sentence which planet has the greatest gravitational attraction to the star and why.

3 Write the equation for determining the eccentricity of an ellipse.

4 Using the metric ruler in the *Reference Tables* and the equation for eccentricity, determine the eccentricity of planet A's orbit.

5 At which numbered position on the orbit of Planet A will Planet A have the greatest orbital velocity? Why?

6 Shade the circle provided to illustrate the Moon's phase as seen from the Earth when the Moon is at position 7.

7 State the two positions of the Moon at which an eclipse could occur.

8 State the approximate length of time required for one complete revolution of the Moon around the Earth.

DIAGRAM I   DIAGRAM II

The satellite was at position 1 precisely at midnight on the first day. It arrived at position 2 the next midnight, 3 the next, and so on.

Table 1

Planet	Eccentricity of Orbit
Mercury	0.206
Venus	0.0007
Earth	0.017
Mars	0.093
Jupiter	0.048
Saturn	0.056
Uranus	0.047
Neptune	0.008

Base your answers to questions 9 through 12 on your knowledge of Earth science, the *Reference Tables*, and the diagrams and table above. Diagram I represents the orbit of an Earth satellite, and Diagram II shows how to construct an elliptical orbit using two pins and a loop of string. Table I shows the eccentricities of the orbits of the planets in the solar system.

9   Determine the eccentricity of the satellite's orbit.

10   The Earth satellite takes 24 hours to move between each numbered position on the orbit. In one sentence tell how area *A* (between positions 1 and 2) compares to area *B* (between positions 8 and 9)?

11   In one sentence, explain how moving the pins closer together in Diagram II would effect the eccentricity of the ellipse being constructed.

12   According to Table I, which planet's orbit would most closely resemble a circle?

Base your answers to questions 13 through 15 on the diagram below and on your knowledge of Earth science. The diagram represents the apparent path of the Sun on the dates indicated for an observer in New York State. The diagram also shows the angle of Polaris above the horizon.

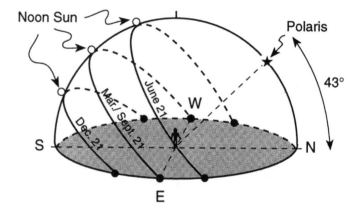

13   State the latitude of the location represented by the diagram to the *nearest degree*. Include the latitude direction in your answer.

14   On the diagram, label the zenith.

15   On the diagram, draw the apparent path of the Sun on May 21. Mark the position of sunrise on May 21 and label it *Sunrise*.

Base your answers to questions 16 through 19 on your knowledge of Earth science and the *Earth Science Reference Table* at the right which represents the Luminosity and Temperature of Stars.

Characteristics of Stars
(Name in italics refers to star represented by a ⊕.)
(Stages indicate the general sequence of star development.)

16 In which group are the stars most varied in both size and luminosity?

17 The Sun is more luminous than any stars in what group?

18 State one way in which the Sun and Polaris are similar and one way in which they are different.

19 Barnard's Star and Betelgeuse are both red stars. Why is Betelgeuse much more luminous?

VOCABULARY

environmental equilibrium	PCBs & oil spills	disease-causing microörganisms	greenhouse gases	agriculture
environmental pollution	water pollution	aerobic bacteria	global cooling	conservation of natural resources
natural pollution	acid rain	anaerobic bacteria	ozone depletion	reuse & recylce
purge	pH (acidity & alkalinity scale)	*Clean Water Acts*	ultraviolet radiation	pollution controls
toxins	organic wastes	*Wetland Acts*	biocide	environmental protection laws
heat, sewage, & chemicals	inorganic wastes	air pollution	pesticide	research & education
	thermal wastes	hydrocarbons	herbicide	
	radioactive wastes	global warming	population growth	
			toxic waste dumps	

A. INTERRELATIONSHIPS

The Earth consists of a great variety of interrelated organisms and systems. Modern technology has given humans the capability to influence the **environmental equilibrium** rapidly and on a large scale. The influence on these organisms and systems may be constructive such as positive conservation or it may be negative and destructive.

A change in one part of the environment may cause a dramatic effect on other parts of the environment. For example, the building of dams, roadways, and communities have destroyed millions of acres of forest and natural wetlands.

On the other hand, technology has enabled humans to preserve many of nature's wonders. For example, major erosion of the American side of Niagara Falls during the first part of this century endangered the very survival of the falls. By changing the direction and flow of the water and by building unseen reinforcement in the cliffs, human engineering has been able to insure the continuance of the American Falls.

How can we describe the interdependence of Earth's living and nonliving systems?

Environmental pollutants are the result of both natural environmental disruptions and the technological oversights of humans (such as activities of individuals and industrial processes). The eruption of Mt. Saint Helens in the state of Washington, was an example of **natural pollution**. It produced millions of tons of ash and destroyed thousands of acres of plant and animal life. In addition, the airborne particles (such as dust) from the eruptions caused climatic and weather changes all across North America, affecting farm crops and air quality. Another example of a common natural pollutant is pollen.

People appear to have done much more damage than natural pollutants have done to the environmental equilibrium. This has been through the excessive addition of pollutants to the environment. Pollutants include such diverse materials as solids, liquids, gases, biologic organisms, and forms of energy such as heat, sound, and nuclear radiation and wastes.

B. ENVIRONMENTAL POLLUTION

Environmental pollution has reached serious levels in recent years, caused by human neglect of the environmental equilibrium. The environment is considered polluted when the concentration of any substance or form of energy reaches a proportion that adversely affects humans, plants, and/or animals or the environment on which all living things depend.

Both natural processes and human pollution tend to vary with seasons, days of the week, and times of days. In nature, rivers tend to **purge** (churn up from the bottom) accumulated wastes during the late summer or early fall. This is a "cleaning" process for the rivers, but leads to increased surface pollution, disruption of wildlife, and damaging river banks and water supplies. During weekdays and high traffic times, humans add more air pollutants to the atmosphere, producing smog and industrial **toxins** (poisonous waste chemicals).

> *What pollutants affect the Earth's water?*

Water pollution is one of the most serious injuries to the landscape, since the Earth requires the purifying capabilities of water to clean and recycle many of Earth's natural resources. Major water pollutants include **heat** (caused by utility companies, industrial plants, and nuclear power facilities), **sewage** (as the overflow of improper waste management systems, home, industrial, and farm wastes), and **chemicals** such as phosphates (from fertilizers and detergents), heavy metals (such as mercury from several industrial processes), **PCBs** (wastes from manufacturing), and **oil spills** (from industrial accidents, well drilling rigs, and fuel tanker cleaning).

Although technological advances have improved our quality of life in many ways, technological oversights have also brought about unplanned negative consequences.

SOURCES OF WATER POLLUTANTS

Pollutants are added to the hydrosphere through the activities of individuals, communities, and industrial processes. There is heightened public awareness of the harmful effects of pollution on the health, safely, and well being of humans, animals, plants, and the environment in general. To a large degree, the awareness is because of the recent discoveries of severely polluted streams, lakes, and ground water across all of North America, including the United States, Canada, and Mexico. For example, two generations of increased health problems in the Love Canal area of western New York State led to the discovery of the landfill toxic-waste dumps.

For many years, industry has had the problem of what to do with the harmful wastes produced during the manufacturing of commercial products. Due to the ignorance of the effects produced by many of these toxic wastes and the economics of dumping these wastes, pollutants have been buried in the ground

without the concern for, or knowledge of, ground water systems.

Over the years, these poisons have seeped into ground water supplies and spread to surrounding areas, contaminating the water sources for communities even miles away from the actual dump sites. Cleaning up these dumps has proven to be, at the least, very difficult and in many cases impossible.

Two decades ago, the lakes of the Adirondack region were known as some of the best fishing areas in New York State. However, many of the lakes (those over 2000 feet in elevation) now have little or no fish and plant life, caused by the pollution of the lakes by **acid rain**.

> *What has killed some of the Adirondack lakes?*

The wastes from industrial smoke and exhaust emissions (mostly sulfur dioxide and nitrogen oxide) pollute the air to such a great extent that precipitation has become acid. This acid rain falls into the lakes and surrounding water sheds, lowering the pH (acidity and alkalinity scale) of the water to such a degree as to make it impossible for animals and plants to survive. Aluminum concentrations toxic to fish are also released by ionized hydrogen exchange, as water percolates through the soil. Attempts to neutralize the lake water have met with only a limited success in small bodies of water. Acid rain may be one of the most serious pollution problems over the next few decades.

Other sources polluting the hydrosphere include, sewage waste from cities, towns, and communities, polluting lakes, streams, and rivers, such as the Hudson River, heated water waste from nuclear power plants and the ground water pollution around the industrial plants in the central and southern areas of New York State.

Polluted Clouds

Airborne Pollutants

Acid Rain

L. Michigan

Canada

L. Ontario

Adirondacks

Detroit

L. Erie

Chicago

United States

Acid Rain
The detrimental effects of acid rain know no boundaries. Airborne pollutants are transported by weather systems across international borders.

TYPES OF POLLUTANTS

Hydrospheric pollutants include dissolved and suspended materials such as organic and inorganic wastes, thermal energy effluent from industrial processes, radioactive substances, and the abnormal concentration of various organisms.

- **Organic wastes** include the sewage wastes from communities that contaminate lakes, rivers, and ground water supplies. The biggest danger from organic wastes is the spread of disease in wells and community drinking water supplies.

- **Inorganic wastes** include metal and plastic wastes, pesticide and herbicide often associated with landfills and community dumps, farming, and industry. Heavy metals, such as lead, mercury, and cadmium cause poisoning, health problems, cancer, and deformities in plants, animals, and humans.

- **Thermal wastes** often come from the cooling water of power plants and industrial complexes. The greatest effect of the heated water is the destruction of aquatic life caused by oxygen depletion in the warm water.

- **Radioactive wastes** come from a variety of sources, such as manufacturing, research, and nuclear power plants. Since many radioactive wastes remain dangerous for very long periods of times (sometimes millions of years), the major problem is how to keep them safe and

store the radioactive wastes until they decay to harmless materials. The storage problem has led to other related nuclear material problems, such as safe transportation to storage areas and security in keeping the potentially dangerous materials out of the hands of terrorists.

- **Harmful organisms**, such as disease-causing microörganisms, tend to breed in toxic waste dumps and polluted ground water. Some microorganisms cause cancer, other serious diseases, and many other health problems.

The release of heated water from industrial and nuclear power plants and the increased activity of **aerobic bacteria** causes a loss of dissolved oxygen from the water. This form of pollution leads to an increase in the concentration of **anaerobic bacteria**, whose waste products are toxic. Biologic pollutants disrupt the normal living and nonliving cycles in the environment.

If the heated effluent pollutes the breeding grounds of fish, the fish may become extinct or move to other waters, thus destroying fishing and recreational water areas. This form of pollution can be observed in several areas of the Hudson River estuary.

CONCENTRATION OF POLLUTANTS

Most often the most severe pollution areas are in the vicinity of population centers. The highest concentrations of pollutants found in the Hudson River are generally located near cities, such as New York City, Poughkeepsie, and Albany. Generally, the same is true around lakes. Ground water pollution tends to be directly proportional to the size of the communities or industrial population. The larger the population, the greater the pollution problem.

INCREASING ATMOSPHERIC CARBON DIOXIDE

Carbon dioxide concentrations in the atmosphere were recorded using a non-dispersive infrared gas analyzer at the Mauna Loa Observatory, Hawaii.

Source: *NOAA*

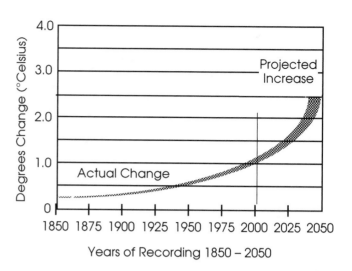

PROJECTIONS OF GLOBAL WARMING

The graph represents a compilation and averaging of several computer models, which using historical trends, predict that global warming will increase drastically in the coming 21st century.

Source: *United Nations*

LONG RANGE EFFECTS

Left uncontrolled and unchecked, the increase of the hydrospheric pollution could eventually cause the water sources of the Earth to become unfit for human use. Community groups, industry, and government have determined that this should not happen. Beginning with the *Clean Water Act of 1972*, the U.S. has spent billions of dollars to clean up the nation's water supply. In 1980, the United States Congress formed a "Superfund" for the clean up of toxic waste dumps. New York State passed its own *Clean Water Act*, the *Freshwater and Saltwater Wetland Acts*, and the environmental quality regulations to protect the waters of New York State and the rights of citizen groups to know the impact on the environment of industrial and public projects.

AIR POLLUTION

The atmosphere around us makes the Earth unique. All life is dependent directly or indirectly on a source of clean, unpolluted air. Although there are natural air pollutants such as volcanic ash, pollen and dust, the most abundant and harmful pollutants are those that result from human activities.

Two current concerns related to **air pollution** are global warming and ozone depletion.

Air pollution comes from cars, mass transportation vehicles, homes, industrial plants, and natural catastrophic events, such as forest fires and volcanic eruptions (e.g., Mt. St. Helens).

The major air pollutants include carbon monoxide (from burning), hydrocarbons (from fossil fuel burning cars, utilities, manufacturing), and particulates (dust, ash, smog). Acid Rain has now become a very serious result of air pollution. It develops from nitrogen oxides and sulfur dioxide, from industrial wastes and motor vehicles, combining with water droplets in the atmosphere.

One of the most serious problems with various air pollutants, including acid rain, is that weather fronts cause the pollutants to be carried to other landscape regions polluting the water and soil. The effects produced are not just localized.

GLOBAL WARMING

There is an unusually powerful consensus among climatologists that the main influence on global climate over the next centuries will be a warming driven by the accumulation of heat-trapping gases. The consequences are threatening enough so that many scientists, citizens, and even political leaders are urging immediate action to halt activities that contribute to the warming trend.

At one time, carbon dioxide (CO_2) was considered as 0.03% of the atmosphere. This figure has changed considerably since the Industrial Revolution began. The burning of wood and wood products, but especially fossil fuels, has contributed huge quantities of carbon dioxide to the Earth's atmosphere.

Humans, animals, the processing of oil and petroleum products, as well as naturally occurring processes such as fermentation and decay add methane gas (CH_4) to the air. Other **greenhouse gases** sent into the air by human activities are chlorofluorocarbons (CFCs) and nitrogen oxides (NO_x). Collectively, although these gases in the troposphere allow solar radiation to reach the Earth's surface and be absorbed, they tend to absorb the reradiated heat from the earth's surface and cause the troposphere to warm.

GREENHOUSE GASES			
Gas	Source	Greenhouse Gases	Life Span
CO_2	burning fossil fuels, wood, oil, coal, plant, animal respiration	540 %	500 years
CH_4	cattle, termites, biomass, decay, reice paddies, mining	15-20 %	7-10 years
N_2O	burning fossil fuels, wood, coal, oil	18 %	140-190 years
CFCs	refrigeration, air conditioning, aerosols, foams, solvents	10 %	65-110 years
O_3 & other trace gases	Cars, power plant emissions, solvents	5 %	hours to days (in stratosphere)

A major concern today is the Earth's average temperature. An international body of scientists, the United Nations Intergovernmental Panel of Climate Change (IPCC) predicts that the gases collecting in the air could raise the average global temperature by about 1.8°F by 2025. By the end of the century, the average temperature could be 10°F warmer than today's.

Although global warming would allow agriculture in some areas presently too cold, and would increase the number of ice free ports in higher latitudes, the negative effects could be devastating. Sea level would rise because the seawater would expand as the water heated; and ice on mountains and in polar regions would melt contributing enormous amounts of water to the sea. Some of the negative results would be:

- drowning of coastal port cities,
- saltwater contamination of coastal freshwater rivers and ground water (drinking water) aquifers,
- damage or destruction of the ecology of coastal wetland, salt marshes, swamps, and bayous,
- changes in precipitation patterns and amounts
- an increase in number and intensity of hurricanes,
- drought conditions in areas presently used to grow grain, and
- serious loss of plant and animal life.

People are becoming aware that their actions can have global, as well as local consequences. Both nations and individuals are recognizing that human activities are threatening to alter climate and are willing to take steps that would decrease the amounts of greenhouse gases released into the atmosphere. The production of cleaner burning fuels, more efficient vehicular engines and stopping deforestation are but three changes that will help.

GLOBAL COOLING

Periods of global cooling have also occurred in the geologic past, such as the well known Ice Ages. These periods have been the result of nature rather than human activities. Events such as extensive volcanic activity and impact of meteorites cause great amounts of material to be thrown into the air and swept around the world in the atmosphere. These particles prevent solar energy from reaching the Earth's surface, thus the temperature drops. Changes in inclination of the Earth's axis and eruptions on the sun, such as sunspot, may cause climatic changes on Earth. A mysterious lack of sunspot activity during the 17th and 18th centuries coincided with an overall temperature drop in Europe which became known as the "Little Ice Age."

The continuing growth of the ozone hole over Antarctica is evident in these plots of the October mean ozone concentration for 1979-1990. The brighter ("whiter") areas indicate the higher concentrations of ozone; whereas, the grays indicate lower concentrations.

Source: *NOAA – Nimbus 7 Satellite Photos*

OZONE DEPLETION

Ozone appears to be a substance that will "kill or cure." Close to Earth's surface it is a pollutant which can kill or cause serious harm. Forty-eight kilometers up in the stratosphere, ozone is essential for life to exist on Earth.

Atmospheric ozone (O_3) is the natural consequence of the interaction of sunlight and molecular oxygen. Small amounts of ozone in the troposphere are normal. However, in high concentration at ground level, ozone is a pollutant that negatively affects human lungs and plant growth.

Ozone has been intensely studied because, in the stratosphere, it acts as a filter for biologically harmful radiation that would otherwise reach the Earth's surface. Eighty to ninety percent of atmospheric ozone is normally found in this layer. Here it absorbs much of the UV (ultraviolet) radiation from the sun. At this distance and in this concentration, O_3 is needed to protect the life existing on the Earth's surface.

In the mid 1980s, atmospheric research indicated a serious thinning of the ozone shield. Various types of chlorofluorocarbons (CFCs) are considered major culprits responsible for ozone depletion. Without the protective shield of the ozone, excessive amounts of UV radiation can affect DNA, life's genetic material resulting in mutations and death. Excessive UV radiation causes skin cancer and cataracts and reduced the effectiveness of the immune system making humans more prone to diseases.

Since the first signs of ozone depletion were discovered measures have been taken to curtail further deterioration. Research has found some alternatives to CFCs and laws have made careful CFC disposal and recycling measures mandatory.

C. NEGATIVE AFFECTS BY HUMANS

Both intentional and unintentional technological oversights have brought about unplanned consequences that have destroyed or reduced the quality of life in many landscape regions. In some cases, technological advances have produced waste products which humans do not know how to dispose of safely. In other cases, industrial wastes are disposed of carelessly and/or criminally.

Biocides, including pesticides and herbicides, have been used without complete knowledge of the possible harmful effects to the landscape. The environmental impact of various biocides has temporarily and in some cases permanently, contaminated the atmosphere, ground and surface water supplies, and the soil.

Disposal problems for the many toxic and even relatively harmless wastes of people's affluent life-style have become more and more serious in recent years. The discovery of hundreds of toxic waste dumps, such as the Love Canal in western New York State, have caused people and government to become concerned. Major disposal wastes often go into landfills and, when improperly disposed of, some wastes leak out of the dumps and into the ground water where they are transported to many different landscape regions.

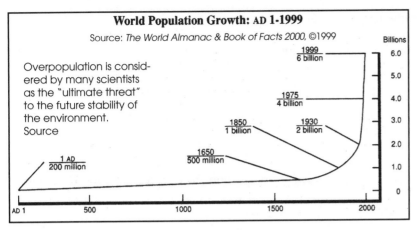

World Population Growth: AD 1-1999

Source: *The World Almanac & Book of Facts 2000,* ©1999

Overpopulation is considered by many scientists as the "ultimate threat" to the future stability of the environment.
Source

1 AD / 200 million
1650 / 500 million
1850 / 1 billion
1930 / 2 billion
1975 / 4 billion
1999 / 6 billion

Population control methods have been developed to balance the rate of population growth with the environment's capabilities for food production and shelter. Most modern countries have developed laws, produced guidelines for family planning, and provided education for their populations. However, many "third world" and "developing" countries still have not been able to solve their increasing population growth rates.

The conservation of natural resources, such as reforestation efforts and cover-cropping techniques, have helped to reclaim lost ecosystems. Water conservation practices have led to the use of land that was previously unusable for agricultural needs. States, including New York State, have passed laws requiring the recycling of cans and bottles, and encouraging the conservation of materials such as paper, plastics, and fuels for energy. In addition to the obvious advantages for the environment, conservation measures have a great economic affect on individuals, employment, industry, and government.

Pollution controls put on industrial plants, public utilities, and automobiles have produced marked improvements in air and water quality. The use of unleaded gasoline in vehicles and special filters on industrial smoke stacks have reduced the incidence of smog and poor air quality alerts in cities, causing a decrease in respiratory problems for many Americans. Many towns and cities have made improvements in sewage disposal through the development and use of new sanitation techniques.

Environmental protection laws have been passed by state, local, and federal governments which regulate and guide the use of public lands and natural habitats. New York State designed a law (SEQR, *NYS Environmental Quality Review Act*) which provides citizens with the opportunity to review and comment on the environmental impact of any proposed development, that may have a significant effect upon the landscape. Several state governments, including New York State, have passed freshwater and saltwater wetlands acts. These laws are designed to regulate and protect the large or unique wetland landscapes from development which would destroy them. These laws apply to both private and public owners and developers. These laws have helped to protect many species and maintain valuable landscapes for the future.

Some of the disposal wastes are solid (such as cans, bottles, plastics, discarded appliances, and cars), chemical (from chemical pesticides, industrial wastes and excesses, breakdown products from "thought to be" harmless wastes), and nuclear (radioactive particles, some remaining dangerous for millions of years).

The human population growth has risen rapidly over the years, in part because of the ability to control diseases and modify environments to produce greater amounts of food and provide adequate shelter. It is forecasted that the total world population by the year 2050 will exceed the nine and a quarter billion mark.

Humans have been able to adjust the environment in ways that have made relatively uninhabitable land, habitable. However, this continued, unchecked growth in population (at an exponential rate) has far exceeded the food and shelter–producing capacities of many world ecosystems.

Agricultural lands, water sources, grazing grasslands for livestock, and forests have been so badly misused as to have resulted in the starvation and extinction of total populations of plants and animals.

High population density areas are most affected because of the concentration of the landscape pollution or the misuse of the landscape.

D. POSITIVE AFFECTS BY HUMANS

Positive affects of human activities on the environment have come through an increased awareness of various ecological and landscape interactions. Humans have begun to intervene in the widespread destruction, through the efforts of individuals, community groups, and conservation clubs. There are attempts to clean up toxic waste dumps, reclaim wasted lands, and prevent continued disruption of the environment.

How can we live in balance with our natural environment?

The future may be better if people and technological advances continue to keep the survival of our environment as a primary consideration, when making decisions that affect the landscape. Careful planning, conservation, and education are necessary to insure a high standard of living for the future and protect the environment. As resources dwindle, alternatives must be found to meet our needs.

Research on complex issues such as global warming and ozone depletion is needed in order to understand and work to reduce the adverse effects of these problems.

Education must also be provided to instill:
• an awareness of the interdependence of all parts of the environment,
• a real concern for future generations, and
• a personal sense of responsibility and commitment for the survival of the environment.

QUESTIONS FOR UNIT 9

1 When the amounts of biologic organisms, sound, and radiation added to the environment reach a level that harms people, these factors are referred to as environmental
  1 interfaces
  2 pollutants
  3 phase changes
  4 equilibrium exchanges

2 Which is the least probable source of atmospheric pollution in heavily populated cities?
  1 human activities
  2 industrial plants
  3 natural processes
  4 automobile traffic

3 Pollution has become a serious problem chiefly because
  1 modern man's input of pollutants exceeds the rate at which nature can remove pollutants
  2 recent changes in landforms have disturbed the rate at which nature can remove pollutants
  3 there has been a gradual decrease in the amount of energy available for removal of pollutants
  4 there have been recent increases in natural environmental pollutants

4 The graph at the right shows the amount of ground water pollution at four different cities: A, B, C, and D. Ground water pollution

tends to vary directly with population density. In which order would these cities most likely be listed if ranked by population density *from highest* population *to lowest* population?

(1) *A, B, C, D*   (3) *C, D, A, B*
(2) *B, A, D, C*   (4) *D, C, B, A*

5 Which graph best illustrates the relationship between lake water pollution and human population density near the lake?

(1)

(2)

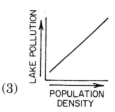

(3)

(4)

6 Air pollution from industrial processes may be most effectively reduced by
  1 growing more green plants to absorb the pollutants
  2 adding anti-irritants to the air
  3 removing waste materials before they enter the atmosphere
  4 precipitating the pollutants by heating the air

7 Some scientists believe that high-flying airplanes and the discharge of fluorocarbons from coolants and making foam products are affecting the atmosphere. Which characteristic of the atmosphere do they believe is affected?
  1 composition of the ozone layer of the stratosphere
  2 wind velocity of the tropopause
  3 location of continental polar highs
  4 air movement in the doldrums

8 The map below illustrates the distribution of acid rain over the United States on a particular day. The isolines represent acidity measured in pH units.

pH SCALE

0 1 2 3 4 5 6 7 8 9 10 11 12 13 14

STRONGER ACID   NEUTRAL   STRONGER BASE
                  WATER

According to the pH scale shown below the map, which region of the United States has the greatest acid rain problem?

1   northeast   3   southeast
2   northwest   4   southwest

Base your answers to questions 9 through 13 on your knowledge of Earth science and the air pollution field map shown below. The isolines represent the concentration of pollutants measured in particles / cm³.

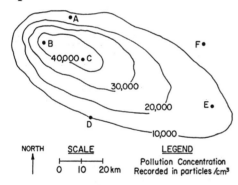

9 The major source of air pollution is most likely at
(1) A   (3) E
(2) B   (4) D

10 The winds responsible for this air pollution pattern are most likely blowing from the
1   northeast   3   southeast
2   northwest   4   southwest

11 The most rapid increase in air pollution would be encountered when traveling between points
(1) A and B   (3) C and D
(2) A and F   (4) D and E

12 The air pollution field illustrated on the map is located in a heavily populated area. Which is the *least* probable source of the pollution?
1   human activities   3   automobile traffic
2   industrial plants   4   natural processes

13 Which graph best represents the relationship between the pollution concentration and distance from point B toward point E?

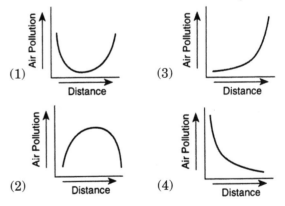

14 Which graph best represents the most common relationship between the amount of air pollution and the distance from an industrial city?

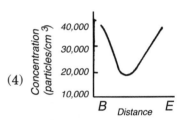

15 According to the diagram at the right, at which location would the water probably be most polluted?

(1) A
(2) B
(3) C
(4) D

Base your answers to questions 16 through 19 on your knowledge of Earth science and on the map below which represents an area of New York State during April.

16 Which environmental region has probably been altered least by the activities of humans?
1 suburbia　　　　3 farmland
2 sanitary landfill　4 forest preserve

17 Which graph best represents the probable number of bacteria (anaerobic) along line A-B in the river?

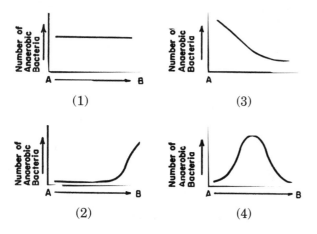

18 The people of this area defeated legislation that would have allowed the sale of a large section of the public owned forest preserve for the purpose of a second industrial park. They also passed a bond issue providing funds for an additional sewage treatment plant for the city. These actions are an indication that a majority of the voters
1 are opposed to higher taxes for any reason
2 feel technology can solve all the problems of the environment
3 are aware of the delicate balance in nature
4 feel that nature can take care of itself

19 Which diagram best illustrates the probable air pollution field of this area at an elevation of 100 meters on a windless spring afternoon?

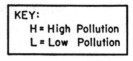

KEY:
H = High Pollution
L = Low Pollution

Base your answers to questions 20 through 24 on your knowledge of Earth science and on the diagram below which shows air, water, and noise pollution in a densely populated industrial area.

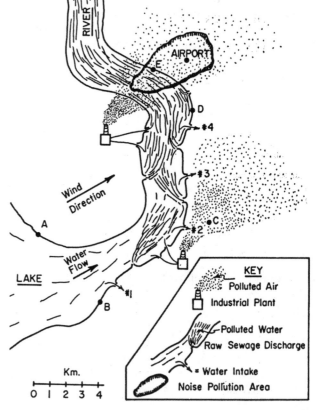

20 Air pollution would probably be greatest at which location?
(1) A　　　　(3) C
(2) B　　　　(4) D

21 Water pollution would probably be greatest at which location?
(1) A　　　　(3) C
(2) B　　　　(4) D

22 Noise pollution would be greatest at which location?
(1) *E*   (3) *C*
(2) *B*   (4) *D*

23 Which location is subjected to the greatest number of pollution factors?
(1) *A*   (3) *E*
(2) *B*   (4) *D*

24 If the water intakes supplied drinking water to the area, which intake would most likely require the most extensive purification procedures?
(1) *#1*   (3) *#3*
(2) *#2*   (4) *#4*

Base your answers to questions 25 and 26 on your knowledge of Earth science and on the graph below showing measurements of air pollutants as recorded in a city during a two-day period.

25 What is a probable cause for the increase in pollutants at 8 a.m. and 5 p.m. on the two days?
1 change in insolation
2 occurrence of precipitation
3 high wind velocity
4 heavy automobile traffic

26 On the basis of the trends indicated by the graph, at what time on Thursday, July 12, will the greatest amount of pollutants probably be observed?
(1) 12 noon   (3) 3 a.m.
(2) 5 p.m.   (4) 8 a.m.

Base your answers to questions 27 through 31 on your knowledge of Earth science, the *Reference Tables*, and the diagrams and map in the next column. The graphs in diagram I show the sources of nitrogen and sulfur dioxide emissions in the U.S. Diagram II gives information about the acidity of Adirondack lakes. The map shows regions of the U.S. affected by acid rain.

DIAGRAM I

DIAGRAM II

REGIONS OF THE UNITED STATES SENSITIVE TO ACID RAIN

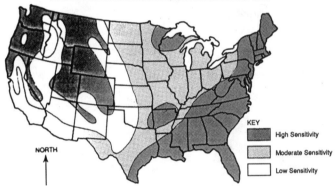

27 Which pH level of lake water would not support any fish life?
(1) 7.0   (3) 5.0
(2) 6.0   (4) 4.0

28 Which graph best shows the acidity (pH) of Adirondack lakes since 1930?

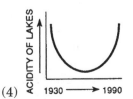

29 The primary cause of acid rain is the
1 weathering and erosion of limestone rocks
2 decay of plant and animal organisms
3 burning of fossil fuels by humans
4 destruction of the ozone layer

30 Acid rain can best be reduced by
1 increasing the use of high-sulfur coal
2 controlling pollutants at the source
3 reducing the cost of petroleum
4 eliminating all use of nuclear energy

31 In addition to its effects on living organisms, acid rain may cause changes in the landscape by
1 decreasing chemical weathering caused by an increase in destruction of vegetation
2 decreasing physical weathering caused by less frost action
3 increasing the breakdown of rock material caused by an increase in chemical weathering
4 increasing physical weathering of rock material caused by an increase in the circulation of ground water

32 The shaded areas of the map below indicate concentrations of pollutants along the coastlines of North America.

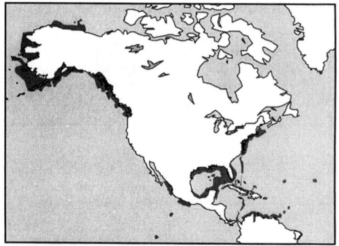

Polluting material may have been carried to the Alaska area by the
1 California Current
2 North Pacific Current
3 Florida Current
4 Labrador Current

33 At which location is ocean water most likely to be clean and unpolluted?
1 near the west coast of North America
2 near the east coast of South America
3 in the mid-Pacific
4 around Australia

CONSTRUCTED RESPONSE

Base your answers to questions 1 and 2 on the table below which provides information about several different gases and their relationship to the greenhouse effect.

Name of Gas	Symbol	Concentration in Troposphere (parts per billion)	Relative Greenhouse Effect per Kilogram of Gas (in equal concentrations)	Decay Time (years)
Carbon dioxide	CO_2	353,000	1	120
Methane	CH_4	1,700	70	10
Ozone	O_3	10-50	1,800	0.1
Chlorofluorocarbon	CFC-11	0.28	4,000	6.5
	CFC-12	0.48	6,000	120

1 In one or more complete sentences, state *one* reason that a scientist would recommend restricting the emission of chlorofluorocarbon CFC-12 into the atmosphere, based on the information in the table.

2 Which of the actions below would contribute more to the greenhouse effect? State a reason for your answer.

a releasing 1 kilogram of methane directly into the atmosphere

or

b burning 1 kilogram of methane, resulting in the release of about 3 kilograms of carbon dioxide into the atmosphere

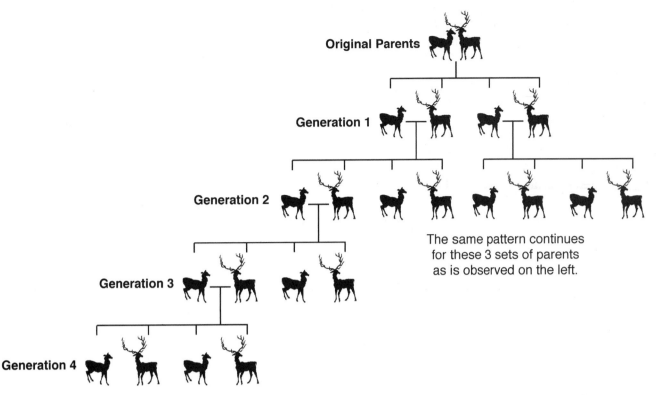

Original Parents

Generation 1

Generation 2

The same pattern continues
for these 3 sets of parents
as is observed on the left.

Generation 3

Generation 4

Base your answers to questions 3 and 4 on the diagram above, the following information and your knowledge of Earth science.

3   On an imaginary island with much plant-life and no predators, a doe and buck parent four fawns – two males (bucks) and two females (doe). The four offspring pair off into two new sets of parents, each having four offspring themselves. This population pattern continues through ten generations. Assuming no loss of life or infertility in the deer population, what is the total number of fawns (the 10th generation) that will be born to the entire group of 9th generation parents?

4   In one or more complete sentences, describe at least two kinds of stress that this population growth could place on the island's environment.

[Information for question 5: Like the deer population in the previous questions, the human population of the Earth also grows exponentially. Although it took two and a half million years for the Earth's human population to reach 5.4 billion, it will only take 40 years to double this number.]

5   List three ways this human population growth will impact the environment of the Earth in the future. Be specific. Identify each impact as a "negative human effect" or a "positive human effect."

Base your answer to question 6 on the newspaper article below and your knowledge of Earth science.

Legislation Protects Ozone

The governor of New York signed environmental legislation that restricted the use of ozone-depleting chemicals employed in refrigeration systems, air-conditioners, and fire extinguishers.

The law restricts, and in some cases bans, the sale of chlorofluorocarbons and halons. Both have been found to contribute to the destruction of the Earth's ozone layer, which protects the Earth from dangerous ultraviolet rays of the Sun.

6   Using one or more complete sentences, state one reason that ultraviolet rays are dangerous.

7   How does the effect of ozone in the troposphere differ from the effect of ozone in the stratosphere?

8   How does UV radiation affect living tissue?

9   Over 70 countries signed a U.N. Agreement which called for a total phaseout of CFC production by the year 2000. Some less developed countries refused to sign at first saying it was not their responsibility to clean up the mess industrial countries had created. Do you agree with their position? Why or why not?

10 Assume the year is 2060 and global warming has raised the temperature considerably.

    State two ways the people living along the northeast coast of the U.S. have been affected.

11 Name 2 air pollutants and tell how each one might affect the climate.

12 Name a natural pollutant in the environment over which people have no control and tell what effect it may have.

13 Name a pollutant resulting from human activities and tell what effect it may have. Suggest one way people might lessen the impact of this pollutant.

Reference Tables for Physical Setting/EARTH SCIENCE

Radioactive Decay Data

RADIOACTIVE ISOTOPE	DISINTEGRATION	HALF-LIFE (years)
Carbon-14	$^{14}C \rightarrow \,^{14}N$	5.7×10^3
Potassium-40	$^{40}K \nearrow \,^{40}Ar \searrow \,^{40}Ca$	1.3×10^9
Uranium-238	$^{238}U \rightarrow \,^{206}Pb$	4.5×10^9
Rubidium-87	$^{87}Rb \rightarrow \,^{87}Sr$	4.9×10^{10}

Equations

$$\text{Eccentricity} = \frac{\text{distance between foci}}{\text{length of major axis}}$$

$$\text{Gradient} = \frac{\text{change in field value}}{\text{distance}}$$

$$\text{Rate of change} = \frac{\text{change in value}}{\text{time}}$$

$$\text{Density} = \frac{\text{mass}}{\text{volume}}$$

Specific Heats of Common Materials

MATERIAL	SPECIFIC HEAT (Joules/gram • °C)
Liquid water	4.18
Solid water (ice)	2.11
Water vapor	2.00
Dry air	1.01
Basalt	0.84
Granite	0.79
Iron	0.45
Copper	0.38
Lead	0.13

Properties of Water

Heat energy gained during melting . . . . 334 J/g

Heat energy released during freezing . . . . 334 J/g

Heat energy gained during vaporization . . . . . 2260 J/g

Heat energy released during condensation . . . 2260 J/g

Density at 3.98°C . . . . 1.0 g/mL

Average Chemical Composition of Earth's Crust, Hydrosphere, and Troposphere

ELEMENT (symbol)	CRUST		HYDROSPHERE	TROPOSPHERE
	Percent by mass	Percent by volume	Percent by volume	Percent by volume
Oxygen (O)	46.10	94.04	33.0	21.0
Silicon (Si)	28.20	0.88		
Aluminum (Al)	8.23	0.48		
Iron (Fe)	5.63	0.49		
Calcium (Ca)	4.15	1.18		
Sodium (Na)	2.36	1.11		
Magnesium (Mg)	2.33	0.33		
Potassium (K)	2.09	1.42		
Nitrogen (N)				78.0
Hydrogen (H)			66.0	
Other	0.91	0.07	1.0	1.0

2011 EDITION

This edition of the Earth Science Reference Tables should be used in the classroom beginning in the 2011–12 school year. The first examination for which these tables will be used is the January 2012 Regents Examination in Physical Setting/Earth Science.

Eurypterus remipes

New York State Fossil

Generalized Landscape Regions of New York State

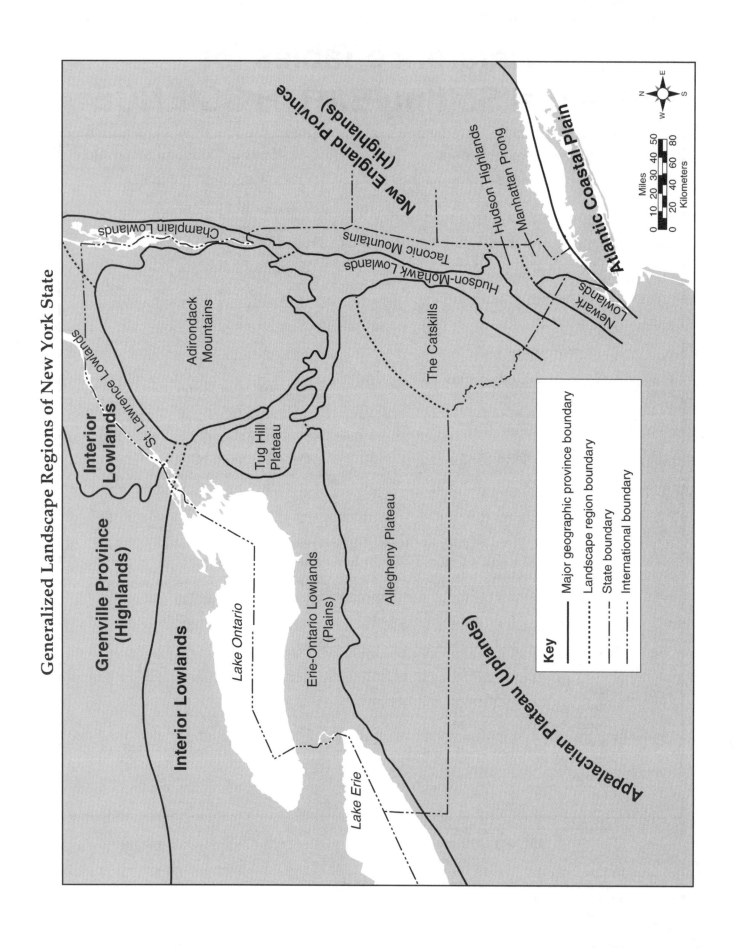

New England Province (Highlands)

Champlain Lowlands

Hudson Highlands

Manhattan Prong

Taconic Mountains

Hudson-Mohawk Lowlands

Newark Lowlands

Atlantic Coastal Plain

Adirondack Mountains

The Catskills

St. Lawrence Lowlands

Interior Lowlands

Interior Lowlands

Grenville Province (Highlands)

Tug Hill Plateau

Lake Ontario

Erie-Ontario Lowlands (Plains)

Allegheny Plateau

Lake Erie

Appalachian Plateau (Uplands)

Miles
0 10 20 30 40 50
Kilometers
0 20 40 60 80

Key

— Major geographic province boundary

········· Landscape region boundary

—··— State boundary

—·—·— International boundary

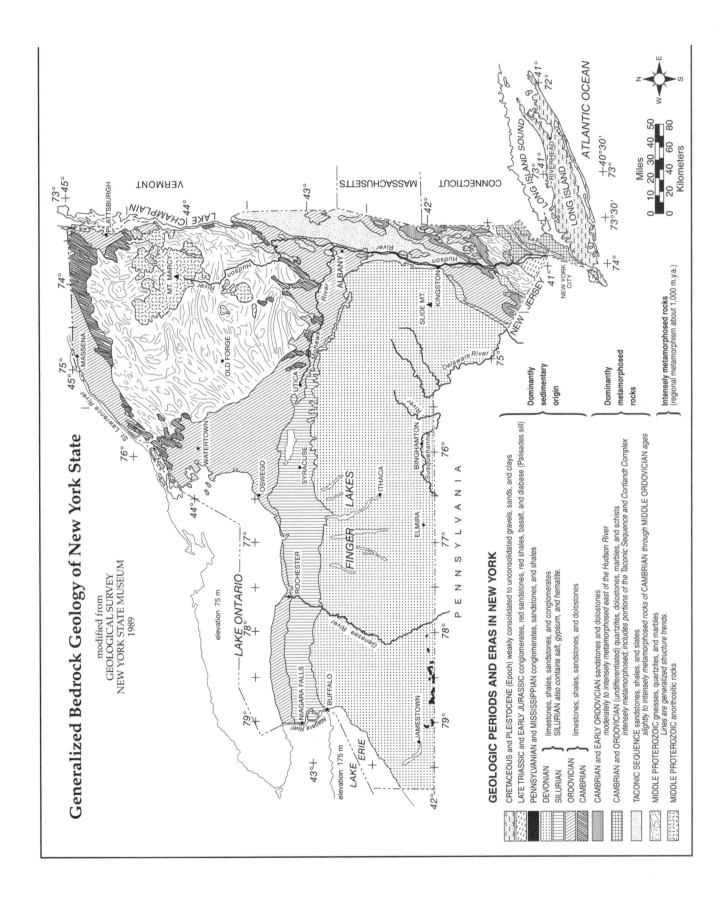

Generalized Bedrock Geology of New York State

modified from
GEOLOGICAL SURVEY
NEW YORK STATE MUSEUM
1989

GEOLOGIC PERIODS AND ERAS IN NEW YORK

CRETACEOUS and PLEISTOCENE (Epoch) weakly consolidated to unconsolidated gravels, sands, and clays

LATE TRIASSIC and EARLY JURASSIC conglomerates, red sandstones, red shales, basalt, and diabase (Palisades sill)

PENNSYLVANIAN and MISSISSIPPIAN conglomerates, sandstones, and shales

DEVONIAN   limestones, shales, sandstones, and conglomerates

SILURIAN   *also contains salt, gypsum, and hematite.*

ORDOVICIAN   limestones, shales, sandstones, and dolostones

CAMBRIAN

CAMBRIAN and EARLY ORDOVICIAN sandstones and dolostones
moderately to intensely metamorphosed east of the Hudson River

CAMBRIAN and ORDOVICIAN (undifferentiated) quartzites, dolostones, marbles, and schists
intensely metamorphosed; includes portions of the Taconic Sequence and Cortlandt Complex

TACONIC SEQUENCE sandstones, shales, and slates
slightly to intensely metamorphosed rocks of CAMBRIAN through MIDDLE ORDOVICIAN ages

MIDDLE PROTEROZOIC gneisses, quartzites, and marbles
Lines are generalized structure trends.

MIDDLE PROTEROZOIC anorthositic rocks

Dominantly
sedimentary
origin

Dominantly
metamorphosed
rocks

Intensely metamorphosed rocks
(regional metamorphism about 1,000 m.y.a.)

Surface Ocean Currents

Key
→ Warm currents
⇨ Cool currents

NOTE: Not all surface ocean currents are shown.

Tectonic Plates

Key

Relative motion at plate boundary

Transform plate boundary (transform fault)

Divergent plate boundary (usually broken by transform faults along mid-ocean ridges)

Convergent plate boundary (subduction zone)

overriding plate

subducting plate

Complex or uncertain plate boundary

Mantle hot spot

NOTE: Not all mantle hot spots, plates, and boundaries are shown.

Rock Cycle in Earth's Crust

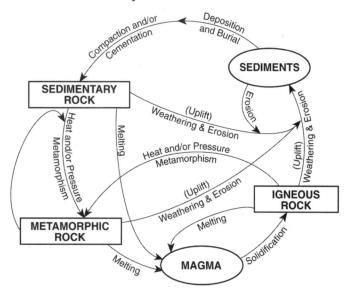

Relationship of Transported Particle Size to Water Velocity

This generalized graph shows the water velocity needed to maintain, but not start, movement. Variations occur due to differences in particle density and shape.

Scheme for Igneous Rock Identification

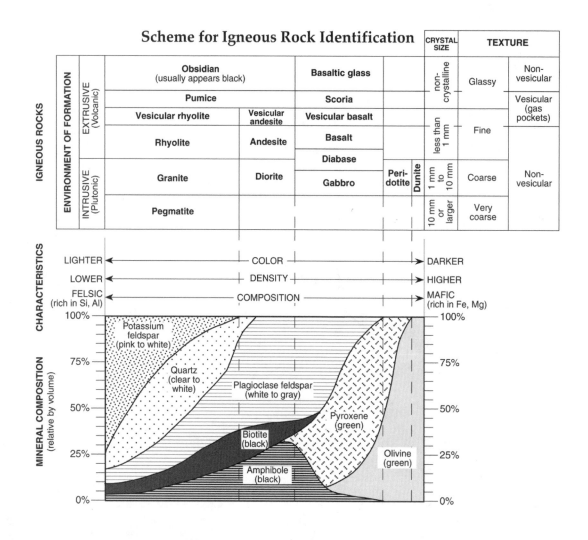

Scheme for Sedimentary Rock Identification

INORGANIC LAND-DERIVED SEDIMENTARY ROCKS					
TEXTURE	GRAIN SIZE	COMPOSITION	COMMENTS	ROCK NAME	MAP SYMBOL
Clastic (fragmental)	Pebbles, cobbles, and/or boulders embedded in sand, silt, and/or clay	Mostly quartz, feldspar, and clay minerals; may contain fragments of other rocks and minerals	Rounded fragments	Conglomerate	
			Angular fragments	Breccia	
	Sand (0.006 to 0.2 cm)		Fine to coarse	Sandstone	
	Silt (0.0004 to 0.006 cm)		Very fine grain	Siltstone	
	Clay (less than 0.0004 cm)		Compact; may split easily	Shale	

CHEMICALLY AND/OR ORGANICALLY FORMED SEDIMENTARY ROCKS					
TEXTURE	GRAIN SIZE	COMPOSITION	COMMENTS	ROCK NAME	MAP SYMBOL
Crystalline	Fine to coarse crystals	Halite	Crystals from chemical precipitates and evaporites	Rock salt	
		Gypsum		Rock gypsum	
		Dolomite		Dolostone	
Crystalline or bioclastic	Microscopic to very coarse	Calcite	Precipitates of biologic origin or cemented shell fragments	Limestone	
Bioclastic		Carbon	Compacted plant remains	Bituminous coal	

Scheme for Metamorphic Rock Identification

TEXTURE		GRAIN SIZE	COMPOSITION	TYPE OF METAMORPHISM	COMMENTS	ROCK NAME	MAP SYMBOL
FOLIATED	MINERAL ALIGNMENT	Fine	MICA QUARTZ FELDSPAR AMPHIBOLE GARNET PYROXENE	Regional (Heat and pressure increases)	Low-grade metamorphism of shale	Slate	
		Fine to medium			Foliation surfaces shiny from microscopic mica crystals	Phyllite	
					Platy mica crystals visible from metamorphism of clay or feldspars	Schist	
	BANDING	Medium to coarse			High-grade metamorphism; mineral types segregated into bands	Gneiss	
NONFOLIATED		Fine	Carbon	Regional	Metamorphism of bituminous coal	Anthracite coal	
		Fine	Various minerals	Contact (heat)	Various rocks changed by heat from nearby magma/lava	Hornfels	
		Fine to coarse	Quartz	Regional or contact	Metamorphism of quartz sandstone	Quartzite	
			Calcite and/or dolomite		Metamorphism of limestone or dolostone	Marble	
		Coarse	Various minerals		Pebbles may be distorted or stretched	Metaconglomerate	

Eon	Era	Period	Epoch	Life on Earth	NY Rock Record

Million years ago (left scale): 0, 500, 1000, 2000, 3000, 4000, 4600

Million years ago (Epoch scale)

NY Rock Record: ▨ Sediment ■ Bedrock

Era	Period	Epoch	Million years ago	Life on Earth
CENOZOIC	QUATERNARY	HOLOCENE	0 / 0.01	
		PLEISTOCENE	1.8	Humans, mastodonts, mammoths
	NEOGENE	PLIOCENE	5.3	Large carnivorous mammals
		MIOCENE	23.0	Abundant grazing mammals
	PALEOGENE	OLIGOCENE	33.9	Earliest grasses
		EOCENE	55.8	Many modern groups of mammals
		PALEOCENE	65.5	Mass extinction of dinosaurs, ammonoids, and many land plants
MESOZOIC	CRETACEOUS	LATE		
		EARLY	146	Earliest flowering plants / Diverse bony fishes
	JURASSIC	LATE		Earliest birds
		MIDDLE		Abundant dinosaurs and ammonoids
		EARLY	200	
	TRIASSIC	LATE		Earliest mammals
		MIDDLE		Earliest dinosaurs
		EARLY	251	Mass extinction of many land and marine organisms (including trilobites)
PALEOZOIC	PERMIAN	LATE		
		MIDDLE		Mammal-like reptiles
		EARLY	299	Abundant reptiles
	CARBONIF-EROUS (PENNSYLVANIAN)	LATE		
		EARLY	318	Extensive coal-forming forests
	CARBONIF-EROUS (MISSISSIPPIAN)	LATE		Abundant amphibians
		MIDDLE		Large and numerous scale trees and seed ferns (vascular plants); earliest reptiles
		EARLY	359	
	DEVONIAN	LATE		Earliest amphibians and plant seeds / Extinction of many marine organisms
		MIDDLE		Earth's first forests / Earliest ammonoids and sharks
		EARLY	416	Abundant fish
	SILURIAN	LATE		Earliest insects / Earliest land plants and animals
		EARLY	444	Abundant eurypterids
	ORDOVICIAN	LATE		
		MIDDLE		Invertebrates dominant / Earth's first coral reefs
		EARLY	488	
	CAMBRIAN	LATE		Burgess shale fauna (diverse soft-bodied organisms)
		MIDDLE		Earliest fishes / Extinction of many primitive marine organisms / Earliest trilobites
		EARLY	542	Great diversity of life-forms with shelly parts
			580	Ediacaran fauna (first multicellular, soft-bodied marine organisms)
			1300	Abundant stromatolites

Eon column: PHANEROZOIC; PROTEROZOIC; ARCHEAN; PRECAMBRIAN

Era/division column (Precambrian): LATE / MIDDLE / EARLY (Proterozoic); LATE / MIDDLE / EARLY (Archean)

Precambrian events:
- First sexually reproducing organisms
- Oceanic oxygen begins to enter the atmosphere
- Oceanic oxygen produced by cyanobacteria combines with iron, forming iron oxide layers on ocean floor
- Earliest stromatolites / Oldest microfossils
- Evidence of biological carbon
- Oldest known rocks
- Estimated time of origin of Earth and solar system

(Index fossils not drawn to scale)

A — Elliptocephala
B — Cryptolithus
C — Phacops
D — Valcouroceras
E — Hexameroceras
F — Centroceras
G — Manticoceras
H — Eucalyptocrinus
I — Ctenocrinus
J — Tetragraptus
K — Dicellograptus
L — Coelophysis
M — Eurypterus
N — Stylonurus

Time Distribution of Fossils
(including important fossils of New York)

The center of each lettered circle indicates the approximate time of existence of a specific index fossil (e.g. Fossil Ⓐ lived at the end of the Early Cambrian).

NAUTILOIDS, DINOSAURS, MAMMALS, BIRDS, AMMONOIDS, CRINOIDS, VASCULAR PLANTS, CORALS, GASTROPODS, BRACHIOPODS, TRILOBITES, EURYPTERIDS, GRAPTOLITES, PLACODERM FISH

Ⓞ Ⓢ Ⓛ Ⓒ Ⓕ Ⓖ Ⓝ Ⓠ Ⓡ Ⓧ Ⓩ Ⓘ Ⓗ Ⓜ Ⓟ Ⓥ Ⓨ Ⓔ Ⓤ Ⓚ Ⓣ Ⓦ Ⓑ Ⓓ Ⓙ Ⓐ

Important Geologic Events in New York

Advance and retreat of last continental ice

Sands and clays underlying Long Island and Staten Island deposited on margin of Atlantic Ocean

Dome-like uplift of Adirondack region begins

Initial opening of Atlantic Ocean
North America and Africa separate
⟨ Intrusion of Palisades sill ⟩
Pangaea begins to break up

Alleghenian orogeny caused by collision of North America and Africa along transform margin, forming Pangaea

Catskill delta forms
Erosion of Acadian Mountains
Acadian orogeny caused by collision of North America and Avalon and closing of remaining part of Iapetus Ocean

Salt and gypsum deposited in evaporite basins

Erosion of Taconic Mountains; Queenston delta forms
Taconian orogeny caused by closing of western part of Iapetus Ocean and collision between North America and volcanic island arc

Widespread deposition over most of New York along edge of Iapetus Ocean

Rifting and initial opening of Iapetus Ocean

Erosion of Grenville Mountains

Grenville orogeny: metamorphism of bedrock now exposed in the Adirondacks and Hudson Highlands

Inferred Positions of Earth's Landmasses

59 million years ago

119 million years ago

232 million years ago

359 million years ago

458 million years ago

Ⓞ Mastodont / Beluga Whale
Ⓟ Cooksonia / Aneurophyton
Ⓠ Naples Tree
Ⓡ Bothriolepis
Ⓢ Condor / Lichenaria
Ⓣ
Ⓤ Cystiphyllum / Pleurodictyum
Ⓥ
Ⓦ Maclurites
Ⓧ Platyceras
Ⓨ Eospirifer
Ⓩ Mucrospirifer

Inferred Properties of Earth's Interior

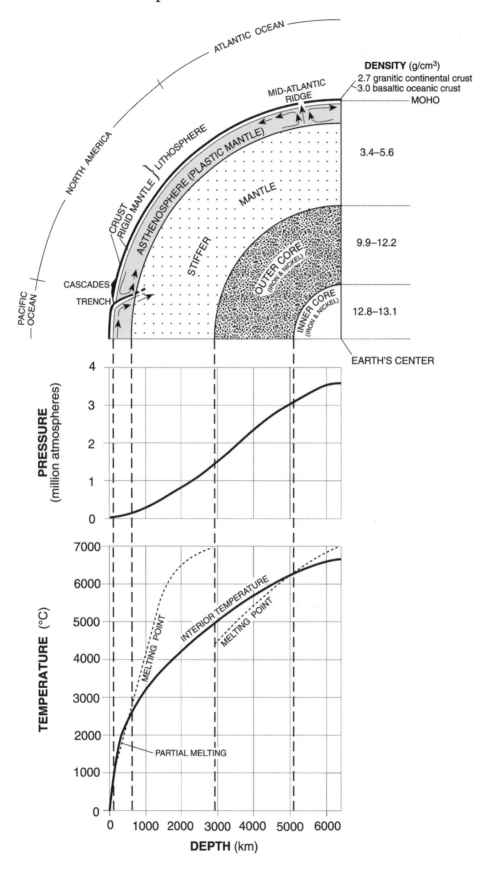

Earthquake P-Wave and S-Wave Travel Time

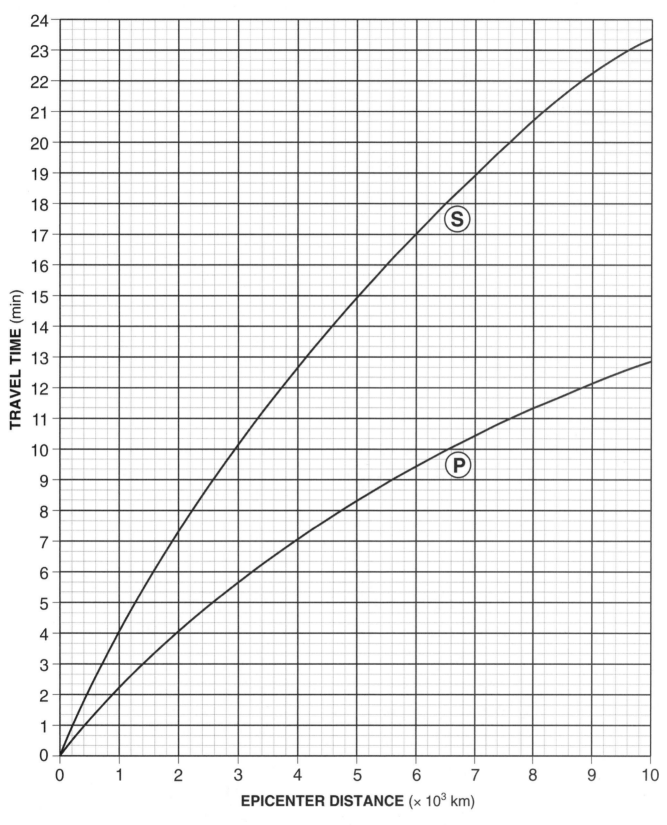

TRAVEL TIME (min)

EPICENTER DISTANCE (× 10³ km)

Dewpoint (°C)

Dry-Bulb Temperature (°C)	Difference Between Wet-Bulb and Dry-Bulb Temperatures (C°)															
	0	1	2	3	4	5	6	7	8	9	10	11	12	13	14	15
−20	−20	−33														
−18	−18	−28														
−16	−16	−24														
−14	−14	−21	−36													
−12	−12	−18	−28													
−10	−10	−14	−22													
−8	−8	−12	−18	−29												
−6	−6	−10	−14	−22												
−4	−4	−7	−12	−17	−29											
−2	−2	−5	−8	−13	−20											
0	0	−3	−6	−9	−15	−24										
2	2	−1	−3	−6	−11	−17										
4	4	1	−1	−4	−7	−11	−19									
6	6	4	1	−1	−4	−7	−13	−21								
8	8	6	3	1	−2	−5	−9	−14								
10	10	8	6	4	1	−2	−5	−9	−14	−28						
12	12	10	8	6	4	1	−2	−5	−9	−16						
14	14	12	11	9	6	4	1	−2	−5	−10	−17					
16	16	14	13	11	9	7	4	1	−1	−6	−10	−17				
18	18	16	15	13	11	9	7	4	2	−2	−5	−10	−19			
20	20	19	17	15	14	12	10	7	4	2	−2	−5	−10	−19		
22	22	21	19	17	16	14	12	10	8	5	3	−1	−5	−10	−19	
24	24	23	21	20	18	16	14	12	10	8	6	2	−1	−5	−10	−18
26	26	25	23	22	20	18	17	15	13	11	9	6	3	0	−4	−9
28	28	27	25	24	22	21	19	17	16	14	11	9	7	4	1	−3
30	30	29	27	26	24	23	21	19	18	16	14	12	10	8	5	1

Relative Humidity (%)

Dry-Bulb Temperature (°C)	Difference Between Wet-Bulb and Dry-Bulb Temperatures (C°)															
	0	1	2	3	4	5	6	7	8	9	10	11	12	13	14	15
−20	100	28														
−18	100	40														
−16	100	48														
−14	100	55	11													
−12	100	61	23													
−10	100	66	33													
−8	100	71	41	13												
−6	100	73	48	20												
−4	100	77	54	32	11											
−2	100	79	58	37	20	1										
0	100	81	63	45	28	11										
2	100	83	67	51	36	20	6									
4	100	85	70	56	42	27	14									
6	100	86	72	59	46	35	22	10								
8	100	87	74	62	51	39	28	17	6							
10	100	88	76	65	54	43	33	24	13	4						
12	100	88	78	67	57	48	38	28	19	10	2					
14	100	89	79	69	60	50	41	33	25	16	8	1				
16	100	90	80	71	62	54	45	37	29	21	14	7	1			
18	100	91	81	72	64	56	48	40	33	26	19	12	6			
20	100	91	82	74	66	58	51	44	36	30	23	17	11	5		
22	100	92	83	75	68	60	53	46	40	33	27	21	15	10	4	
24	100	92	84	76	69	62	55	49	42	36	30	25	20	14	9	4
26	100	92	85	77	70	64	57	51	45	39	34	28	23	18	13	9
28	100	93	86	78	71	65	59	53	47	42	36	31	26	21	17	12
30	100	93	86	79	72	66	61	55	49	44	39	34	29	25	20	16

Temperature

Fahrenheit (°F) / **Celsius (°C)** / **Kelvin (K)**

Water boils

Room temperature

Water freezes

Pressure

millibars (mb) / inches (in of Hg*)

One atmosphere

*Hg = mercury

Key to Weather Map Symbols

Station Model

```
  28        196
 1/2 *      +19/
  27        .25
```

Station Model Explanation

Present weather

Amount of cloud cover (approximately 75% covered)

Temperature (°F) **28**

196 Barometric pressure (1019.6 mb)

Visibility (mi) **1/2** ✱

+19/ Barometric trend (a steady 1.9-mb rise in past 3 hours)

Dewpoint (°F) **27**

.25 Precipitation (0.25 inches in past 6 hours)

Wind speed

Wind direction (from the southwest)

whole feather = 10 knots
half feather = 5 knots
total = 15 knots

(1 knot = 1.15 mi/h)

Present Weather

Drizzle Rain Smog Hail Thunder-storms Rain showers

Snow Sleet Freezing rain Fog Haze Snow showers

Air Masses

cA   continental arctic
cP   continental polar
cT   continental tropical
mT   maritime tropical
mP   maritime polar

Fronts

Cold
Warm
Stationary
Occluded

Hurricane

Tornado

Selected Properties of Earth's Atmosphere

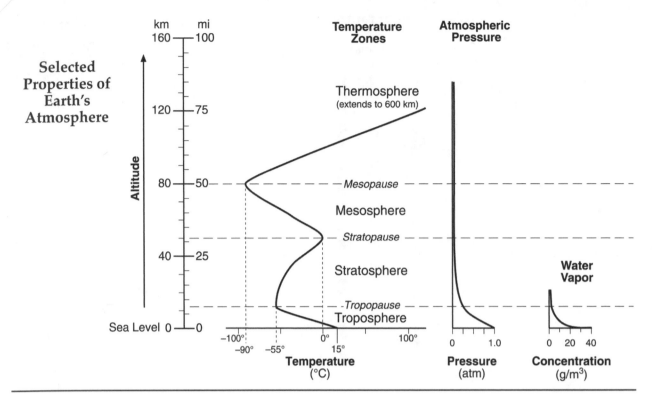

Temperature Zones

Thermosphere (extends to 600 km)

Mesopause

Mesosphere

Stratopause

Stratosphere

Tropopause

Troposphere

Atmospheric Pressure

Water Vapor

Altitude

km / mi
- 160 / 100
- 120 / 75
- 80 / 50
- 40 / 25
- Sea Level 0 / 0

Temperature (°C): −100° −90° −55° 0° 15° 100°

Pressure (atm): 0 ... 1.0

Concentration (g/m³): 0 20 40

Planetary Wind and Moisture Belts in the Troposphere

The drawing on the right shows the locations of the belts near the time of an equinox. The locations shift somewhat with the changing latitude of the Sun's vertical ray. In the Northern Hemisphere, the belts shift northward in the summer and southward in the winter.

(Not drawn to scale)

Tropopause
Polar front jet stream
Polar front
Subtropical jet streams
Polar front jet stream

DRY
N.E.
WET — 60° N
S.W. Winds
DRY — 30° N
N.E. Winds
WET — 0°
S.E. Winds
DRY — 30° S
N.W. Winds
WET — 60° S
S.E.
DRY

Electromagnetic Spectrum

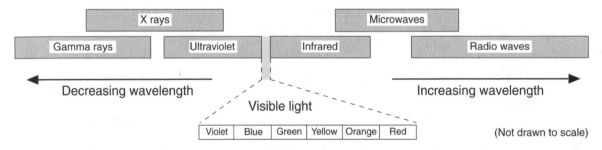

X rays
Microwaves
Gamma rays
Ultraviolet
Infrared
Radio waves

◄ Decreasing wavelength

Increasing wavelength ►

Visible light

| Violet | Blue | Green | Yellow | Orange | Red |

(Not drawn to scale)

Properties of Common Minerals

LUSTER	HARD-NESS	CLEAVAGE	FRACTURE	COMMON COLORS	DISTINGUISHING CHARACTERISTICS	USE(S)	COMPOSITION*	MINERAL NAME
Metallic luster	1–2	✔		silver to gray	black streak, greasy feel	pencil lead, lubricants	C	Graphite
Metallic luster	2.5	✔		metallic silver	gray-black streak, cubic cleavage, density = 7.6 g/cm³	ore of lead, batteries	PbS	Galena
Metallic luster	5.5–6.5		✔	black to silver	black streak, magnetic	ore of iron, steel	Fe_3O_4	Magnetite
Metallic luster	6.5		✔	brassy yellow	green-black streak, (fool's gold)	ore of sulfur	FeS_2	Pyrite
Either	5.5–6.5 or 1		✔	metallic silver or earthy red	red-brown streak	ore of iron, jewelry	Fe_2O_3	Hematite
Nonmetallic luster	1	✔		white to green	greasy feel	ceramics, paper	$Mg_3Si_4O_{10}(OH)_2$	Talc
Nonmetallic luster	2		✔	yellow to amber	white-yellow streak	sulfuric acid	S	Sulfur
Nonmetallic luster	2	✔		white to pink or gray	easily scratched by fingernail	plaster of paris, drywall	$CaSO_4 \cdot 2H_2O$	Selenite gypsum
Nonmetallic luster	2–2.5	✔		colorless to yellow	flexible in thin sheets	paint, roofing	$KAl_3Si_3O_{10}(OH)_2$	Muscovite mica
Nonmetallic luster	2.5	✔		colorless to white	cubic cleavage, salty taste	food additive, melts ice	$NaCl$	Halite
Nonmetallic luster	2.5–3	✔		black to dark brown	flexible in thin sheets	construction materials	$K(Mg,Fe)_3$ $AlSi_3O_{10}(OH)_2$	Biotite mica
Nonmetallic luster	3	✔		colorless or variable	bubbles with acid, rhombohedral cleavage	cement, lime	$CaCO_3$	Calcite
Nonmetallic luster	3.5	✔		colorless or variable	bubbles with acid when powdered	building stones	$CaMg(CO_3)_2$	Dolomite
Nonmetallic luster	4	✔		colorless or variable	cleaves in 4 directions	hydrofluoric acid	CaF_2	Fluorite
Nonmetallic luster	5–6	✔		black to dark green	cleaves in 2 directions at 90°	mineral collections, jewelry	$(Ca,Na)(Mg,Fe,Al)$ $(Si,Al)_2O_6$	Pyroxene (commonly augite)
Nonmetallic luster	5.5	✔		black to dark green	cleaves at 56° and 124°	mineral collections, jewelry	$CaNa(Mg,Fe)_4 (Al,Fe,Ti)_3$ $Si_6O_{22}(O,OH)_2$	Amphibole (commonly hornblende)
Nonmetallic luster	6	✔		white to pink	cleaves in 2 directions at 90°	ceramics, glass	$KAlSi_3O_8$	Potassium feldspar (commonly orthoclase)
Nonmetallic luster	6	✔		white to gray	cleaves in 2 directions, striations visible	ceramics, glass	$(Na,Ca)AlSi_3O_8$	Plagioclase feldspar
Nonmetallic luster	6.5		✔	green to gray or brown	commonly light green and granular	furnace bricks, jewelry	$(Fe,Mg)_2SiO_4$	Olivine
Nonmetallic luster	7		✔	colorless or variable	glassy luster, may form hexagonal crystals	glass, jewelry, electronics	SiO_2	Quartz
Nonmetallic luster	6.5–7.5		✔	dark red to green	often seen as red glassy grains in NYS metamorphic rocks	jewelry (NYS gem), abrasives	$Fe_3Al_2Si_3O_{12}$	Garnet

*Chemical symbols:

Al = aluminum	Cl = chlorine	H = hydrogen	Na = sodium	S = sulfur
C = carbon	F = fluorine	K = potassium	O = oxygen	Si = silicon
Ca = calcium	Fe = iron	Mg = magnesium	Pb = lead	Ti = titanium

✔ = dominant form of breakage

Properties of Common Minerals

LUSTER	HARD-NESS	CLEAVAGE	FRACTURE	COMMON COLORS	DISTINGUISHING CHARACTERISTICS	USE(S)	COMPOSITION*	MINERAL NAME
Metallic luster	1–2	✔		silver to gray	black streak, greasy feel	pencil lead, lubricants	C	Graphite
	2.5	✔		metallic silver	gray-black streak, cubic cleavage, density = 7.6 g/cm³	ore of lead, batteries	PbS	Galena
	5.5–6.5		✔	black to silver	black streak, magnetic	ore of iron, steel	Fe_3O_4	Magnetite
	6.5		✔	brassy yellow	green-black streak, (fool's gold)	ore of sulfur	FeS_2	Pyrite
Either	5.5 – 6.5 or 1		✔	metallic silver or earthy red	red-brown streak	ore of iron, jewelry	Fe_2O_3	Hematite
Nonmetallic luster	1	✔		white to green	greasy feel	ceramics, paper	$Mg_3Si_4O_{10}(OH)_2$	Talc
	2		✔	yellow to amber	white-yellow streak	sulfuric acid	S	Sulfur
	2	✔		white to pink or gray	easily scratched by fingernail	plaster of paris, drywall	$CaSO_4\cdot2H_2O$	Selenite gypsum
	2–2.5	✔		colorless to yellow	flexible in thin sheets	paint, roofing	$KAl_3Si_3O_{10}(OH)_2$	Muscovite mica
	2.5	✔		colorless to white	cubic cleavage, salty taste	food additive, melts ice	$NaCl$	Halite
	2.5–3	✔		black to dark brown	flexible in thin sheets	construction materials	$K(Mg,Fe)_3$ $AlSi_3O_{10}(OH)_2$	Biotite mica
	3	✔		colorless or variable	bubbles with acid, rhombohedral cleavage	cement, lime	$CaCO_3$	Calcite
	3.5	✔		colorless or variable	bubbles with acid when powdered	building stones	$CaMg(CO_3)_2$	Dolomite
	4	✔		colorless or variable	cleaves in 4 directions	hydrofluoric acid	CaF_2	Fluorite
	5–6	✔		black to dark green	cleaves in 2 directions at 90°	mineral collections, jewelry	$(Ca,Na)(Mg,Fe,Al)$ $(Si,Al)_2O_6$	Pyroxene (commonly augite)
	5.5	✔		black to dark green	cleaves at 56° and 124°	mineral collections, jewelry	$CaNa(Mg,Fe)_4(Al,Fe,Ti)_3$ $Si_6O_{22}(O,OH)_2$	Amphibole (commonly hornblende)
	6	✔		white to pink	cleaves in 2 directions at 90°	ceramics, glass	$KAlSi_3O_8$	Potassium feldspar (commonly orthoclase)
	6	✔		white to gray	cleaves in 2 directions, striations visible	ceramics, glass	$(Na,Ca)AlSi_3O_8$	Plagioclase feldspar
	6.5		✔	green to gray or brown	commonly light green and granular	furnace bricks, jewelry	$(Fe,Mg)_2SiO_4$	Olivine
	7		✔	colorless or variable	glassy luster, may form hexagonal crystals	glass, jewelry, electronics	SiO_2	Quartz
	6.5–7.5		✔	dark red to green	often seen as red glassy grains in NYS metamorphic rocks	jewelry (NYS gem), abrasives	$Fe_3Al_2Si_3O_{12}$	Garnet

*Chemical symbols:

Al = aluminum	Cl = chlorine	H = hydrogen	Na = sodium	S = sulfur
C = carbon	F = fluorine	K = potassium	O = oxygen	Si = silicon
Ca = calcium	Fe = iron	Mg = magnesium	Pb = lead	Ti = titanium

✔ = dominant form of breakage

Beach (71) – shoreline region of deposited particles; may contain sand, gravel, pebble, cobble and/or boulders.

Bedrock (77) – solid rock underneath soil or exposed rock at Earth's surface.

Bedrock, Generalized Geology in NYS (201) – *Reference Table*.

Bench Mark (48) – ground marker indicating the exact elevation of that location above sea level.

"Big Bang" (170) – theory that the universe began with a gigantic explosion.

Biocide (190) – substance harmful to plants and animals.

Biological Pollutant (187) – biologic organisms in concentrations that are harmful.

Breaker (71) – when the crest of a wave falls over onto the shore.

Calorie (118) – heat quantity unit; amount of energy required to raise the temperature of 1 gram of water through 1°C.; a large calorie (kilocalorie) is 1000 calories.

Capillarity (140) – upward movement of water against the force of gravity in a narrow space, such as a tube, plant vessel, or fine sand particles.

Capillary Water (141) – water that is found in the small spaces between fine grains of rock, sand, clay, or soil.

Carbon-14 Dating (101) – process for determining the absolute age of a fossil or other material containing the element Carbon-14 (a radioactive isotope of Carbon-12 with a half-life of 5,600 years).

Carbonate (32) a group made up of one or more metals combined with a carbon and three oxygen atoms (CO_3).

Carbonation (67) – the process of carbonic acid reaction with other materials.

Celestial Object (159) – "heavenly bodies," any object observed in the area above the Earth's atmosphere, including the Sun, Moon, stars, comets, planets, etc.

Celsius Scale (211) – a temperature scale that registers the freezing point of water as 0° and the boiling point as 100° under normal atmospheric pressure.

Cementation (34) – process in some sedimentary rocks, in which various sized sediments are cemented (glued) together by the action of precipitated minerals, resembles man-made concrete.

Cenozoic Era (99, 100) – most recent Earth history era representing 2 or 3% of the geologic time scale including modern plants, animals, and humans.

Center of Accumulation (75) – large area or center of accumulation for snow and ice of a continental glacier.

Centimeter Scale (199) – *Reference Table*.

Centrifugal Effect (20) – produced by Earth's rotation, tends to maintain movement away from the center or axis of the Earth.

Change of Phase (118) – see phase change.

Chemical Composition of Earth's Crust, Hydrosphere, and Troposphere (199) – *Reference Table*.

Chemical Pollutants (186) – toxic materials such as phosphates and heavy metals that reach harmful levels in the environment.

Chemical Properties (31) – used for identification of minerals.

Chemical Sedimentary Rock (35) – sedimentary rock formed from dissolved mineral material which settles or precipitates out of water.

Chemical Weathering (67) – process that alters the chemical characteristics of rocks and minerals, such as oxidation and hydration.

Circumference of Earth (19) – formula; see Earth Dimensions.

Cirque (75) – bowl-shaped depression gouged out of the side of a mountain by a glacier.

Cirrus Clouds (117) – high-altitude cloud composed of narrow bands or patches of thin, generally white, fleecy parts.

Classification System (7) – organized data, based on observable properties.

Clastic (35) – see fragmented sedimentary rocks.

Clean Air Act (188) – 1970, standards for clean air.

Clean Water Act (188) – 1972, waste discharge regs.

Cleavage (32) – the tendency of a mineral to break along one or more smooth planes or surfaces.

Climate (68, 74, 145-148) – discounting local weather changes, the average or normal weather of a particular large Earth area.

Cloud (116, 117) – type of aerosol in the atmosphere composed of suspended small water droplets and/or ice crystals.

Cluster (169) – a group of galaxies.

Cold Front (121) – the interface, leading edge, of an air mass which has cooler temperatures than the preceding warmer air mass, usually associated with moisture and precipitation.

Colloid (34, 72) – small particles, from 10^{-4} to 10^{-6} millimeters across, which tend to remain in solution for long periods of time.

Color (31) – property used for the identification of minerals.

Comet (167) – celestial body, observed only in that part of its orbit that is relatively close to the Sun, having a head consisting of a solid nucleus surrounded by a nebulous coma up to 2.4 million kilometers (1.5 million miles) in diameter and an elongated, curved vapor tail arising from the coma when sufficiently close to the Sun.

Competent Rocks (77) – resistant to weathering and erosion.

Compression (34) – process involved in the production of some sedimentary and metamorphic rocks, in which the weight of deposited sediments, water, and/or Earth movements presses underlying sediments together.

Compressional Wave (Primary, *P-wave*) (48) – seismic wave (action is like the expansion and contraction of a spring) which travels at a speed of thousands of kilometers per hour, through solids, liquids, or gases.

Conclusion (7) – see inferences.

Condensation (115, 116, 118, 139) – change in state from vapor (gas) to liquid, the loss of water vapor from warmer air onto a cooler surface, such as the condensation (fog) on an ice water glass.

Condensation Surface, or Nucleus (116) – solid surface onto which water vapor may condense to form liquid droplets, in the formation of clouds – water condenses on dust or other particles, in the formation of early morning dew – water condenses on any solid and cooler surface.

Conduction (119) – transfer of energy, usually heat, by contact from one atom to another atom within a liquid, gas, or solid.

Conglomerates (34) – rock consisting of unsorted pebbles and gravel embedded in cement.

Conservation (37) – controlled use and systematic protection of natural resources, such as forests, soil, and water systems.

Conservation of Natural Resources (191) – controlled use and systematic protection of natural resources, such as forests, soil, and water systems.

Constellation (159) – a group of stars that make up a recognizable pattern in the sky.

Constructional Forces (74) – see Uplifting (forces).

Contact Metamorphism (35, 36, 98) – the process of rock changing due to contact with hot magma or lava.

Continental Climate (147) – average weather of a land mass, little affected by large bodies of water, characterized by extremes in temperature.

Continental Crust (50, 51) – thick, low density upper part of the lithosphere that makes up the blocks (land mass) of a continent.

Continental Drift (51) – theory, backed by continual evidences, that continents (Earth plates) are now, as well as in the past, shifting positions.

Continental Glacier (75) – a massive ice sheet covering a large area such as the Antarctic ice sheet.

Continental Margin (53) – the area along the edge of the continents made of the continental shelf, continental slope and continental rise.

Continental Polar Air Mass (120) – cP, usually a cold air mass originating in the land polar regions, such as in the northern most regions of Canada.

Continental Tropical Air Mass (120) – cT, warm air mass originating over warm land regions.

Contour Interval (23) – the difference in elevation between two consecutive contour lines.

Contour Line (23) – type of isoline on a topographic (contour) map, represents equal elevation points.

Contour Map (23, 24) – a topographic map, used as a model indicating elevations of the Earth's surface with the use of contour lines and symbols.

Convection (119) – transfer of energy, due to differences in substances' densities, in gases and liquids.

Convection Cell (current) (54, 119) – circulatory motion in which heat energy is transferred from one place to another, due to density differences.

Convergence (119) – interfacing of air masses at the Earth's surface, in upper regions of the troposphere, making "air streams" or vertical currents.

Convergent Plate Boundary (53) – boundary between two colliding plates.

Coordinate System (21) – system or group of defined lines (may be imaginary lines) used for the determination or location of point(s) on a surface (such as graph, Longitude and Latitude).

Coriolis Effect (116, 120, 160, 165) – observed path of an object (or fluid) at the surface of the Earth undergoing a predictable horizontal deflection; rightward deflection in the northern hemisphere and leftward in the southern hemisphere.

Correlation (99) – match up of rock ages and geologic events.

Crest (71) – the top of a wave.

Crossbedding (73) – layers or beds of sediment deposited at different angles.

Cross Section (24) – view by cutting through an object, usually at right angles to an axis.

Crust (36, 47, 50) – layer of granite or basalt rock forming the outer part of the Earth's lithosphere.

Crustal Plates (48) – large pieces of the lithosphere that move in relation to each other.

Crystal (32) – Earth material having a repeating pattern of characteristic shapes, due to a material's internal atomic structure, such as a cube (halite) and a tetrahedron (silicate).

Crystalline Structure (32) – definite atomic pattern within a mineral (see Crystal).

Crystallization (33, 37) – formation of solid crystals into a rock, such as igneous rock, when the crystals separate from a magma solution.

Cumulus Clouds (117, 119) – dense, white, fluffy, flat-based cloud with a multiple rounded top and a well-defined outline, usually formed by the ascent of thermally unstable air masses.

Cumuliform Clouds (117) – having the shape of cumulus clouds; see Cumulus Clouds.

Cumulonimbus Clouds (117) – extremely dense, vertically developed cumulus with a relatively hazy outline and a glaciated top extending to great heights, usually producing heavy rains, thunderstorms, or hailstorms.

Currents (147) – movement or flow of "rivers" of water in a direction; see the specific type: warm, cold.

Cycles (11) – usually an orderly manner in which events in time and space repeat.

Cyclic Change (10, 11) – a predictable change that occurs in a repeating pattern.

Cyclic Energy Transformation (163) – alternating changes of energy from kinetic to potential and potential to kinetic; as seen in the Earth's changes of energy and orbital speed around the Sun.

Cyclone (120) – also called LOW; low pressure air mass with counterclockwise winds in the northern hemisphere, including violent weather, such as tornadoes and hurricanes.

Daily Motion (159) – apparent motion in an arc path across the Earth's sky from east to west during each 24 hour period.

Daily Temperatures (143) – see Temperature and Insolation.

Decay, Radioactive (97) – transformation or break down into a stable "daughter" element.

Deficit (146) – local condition when the actual evapotranspiration is not equal to the potential evapotranspiration, due to insufficient precipitation and water soil storage; see Drought.

Degree Metamorphism (36) – different metamorphic rocks formed from the same parent rock due to different pressure and temperature environments.

Dendritic Drainage (78) – random pattern of streams associated with plains and plateaus

Density (8, 9, 32, 72) – formula; mass of a material divided by the material's volume.

Density Variables (32) – characteristics such as temperature and pressure that causes changes in density and phase changes.

Deposition (116) – the process of water vapor changing directly into ice crystals.

Deposition (72) – settling out of solution of sediments and minerals in an erosional system.

Destructional Forces (74) – see Leveling Forces.

Dew (116) – condensation occurring on Earth's surface.

Dew Point Temperature (113) – temperature at which water vapor present in the air saturates air and begins to condense; dew forms.

Dew Point Temperatures (113, 210) – *Reference Table*.

Deviation (9) – difference between one number in a set and the mean of the set.

Diastrophism (74) – process of deformation by which the major features of the Earth's crust, including continents, mountains, ocean beds, folds, and faults, are formed.

Dimensional Quantities (8) – time, length, or mass.

Direct (Vertical) Rays (161) – rays of solar energy hitting the surface of the Earth at an angle of 90°, also called perpendicular rays.

Direct Relationship (10) – when both variables change in the same direction; see graphing.

Displaced Fossils (47) – example: marine fossils found in layers of sedimentary rock in mountains.

Displaced Sediments (34, 69) – rock and mineral particles that are removed from their source and transported by water/wind to another place.

Displaced Strata (47, 48) – see displaced sediments.

Distorted Structure (35, 36) – resulting rock formations caused by Earth forces, such as heat and pressure, which bend, break, and fold rock layers.

Divergence (120) – following air mass convergence, ascending or descending, the spreading apart of air currents.

Divergent Plate Boundary (53) – boundary between two plates that are moving apart.

Doppler Shift (170) – apparent change in wavelength of light caused by relative motion of the source.

Drainage Basin (141) – area drained by a river system.

Drainage Patterns (78) – dendritic (random drainage over bedrock), trellised (parallel folds and faults), and radial (volcanic cones, young domes).

Drought (146) – a prolonged period of deficit weather conditions.

Drumlin (76) – glacial hill shaped like back of a spoon.

Dry-bulb Thermometer (113, 114) – see Psychrometer.

Duration of Insolation (142) – length of time that the Sun's rays are received at a particular location on the Earth's surface; varies with latitude and season; Earth surface temperature is directly proportional to the duration of insolation.

Dwarf Planet (166) – celestial body within the Solar System that: orbits the Sun but is not a satellite, has self-gravity to assume a near-spherical shape, but cannot clear its orbital neighborhood.

Dynamic Equilibrium (12, 70) – a balance between two opposing processes going on at the same rate in a system, such as erosion and deposition and evaporation and condensation; refers to a landscape as well.

Earth (164-169) – third planet from the Sun, having a sidereal period of revolution about the Sun of 365.26 days at a mean distance of approximately 149 million kilometers (92.96 million miles), an axial rotation period of 23 hours 56.07 minutes, an average radius of 6,374 kilometers (3,959 miles).

Earth Axis (19) – see Axis.

Earth Dimensions (19) – includes the Earth's circumference, radius, diameter, volume, and surface area.

Earth Energy (141) – primary source is solar radiation which drives the Earth's surface systems.

Earth's Interior, Inferred Properties of (51, 208) – *Reference Table*.

Earth Positions (21) see Coordinate System.

Earth Shape (19) – oblate spheroid with greater diameter at the equator than through the poles.

Earth Spheres (20) – atmosphere, hydrosphere, lithosphere.

Earthquake (48) – sudden trembling or shaking of the ground, usually caused by a shifting of rock layers along a fault or fissure under the Earth's surface.

Earthquake *P-wave* and *S-wave* Travel Time (49, 209) – *Reference Table*.

Eccentricity of Ellipse (162) – formula; degree of the "out of roundness" of the ellipse, as determined by the distance between the two foci divided by the length of the major axis of the ellipse.

Eclipse (164) – shadows on Earth caused by the position of the Sun or Moon.

El Niño (147) – warming of the ocean surface off the western coast of South America that occurs every 4 to 12 years when upwelling of cold, nutrient-rich water does not occur. It causes plankton and fish to die and affects weather over much of the Pacific Ocean, South, Central, and North America.

Electromagnetic Energy (141) – any energy radiated in transverse wave form, such as radio, sound, light, X-rays, etc.

Electromagnetic Spectrum (141) – wide range of wavelengths from lower frequencies such as radio waves short wave, AM , FM, TV, and radar to mid frequencies such as infrared rays, visible light, and ultraviolet, to high frequencies such as x-rays and gamma rays.

Electromagnetic Spectrum (141, 212) – *Reference Table*.

Element (31) substance composed of atoms having an identical number of protons in each nucleus; cannot be reduced to simpler substances by normal chemical means.

Ellipse (162) – flattened circular path, having two foci (fixed radii); typical of the orbits of most all celestial objects and the Earth.

Energy (11) – ability to do work; forms: kinetic and potential.

Energy Flow (11) – energy moving from one place in the environment to another.

Environment (74, 185) – the climatic and ecologic surroundings in which we live.

Environmental Equilibrium, or Balance (185) – general stable and balanced state of the environment, changeable easily on a small scale.

Environmental Protection Laws (191) – government legislation to help preserve the environment and prevent or clean-up pollution and toxic wastes.

Eon (99) – longest division of geologic time, containing two or more eras.

Epicenter (48, 49) – point on Earth's surface that is directly above the focus of an earthquake.

Epicycle (165) – smaller secondary orbit off a main orbit.

Epoch (99) – unit of geologic time that is a division of a period.

Equations and Proportions (199) – *Reference Table*.

Equator, Earth's (21, 161) – center circumference of Earth, equally dividing Northern and Southern Hemispheres, 0° latitude.

Equilibrium, State of (12) – the tendency to remain unchanged.

Equinox (142, 143, 161) – time at which the Sun's rays are directly perpendicular to the Earth's equator; equal day and night on the Earth; usually March 21st and September 23rd.

Era (99) – longest division of geologic time, made up of one or more periods.

Erosion (35, 69, 99) – altering of the Earth's surface by the removing of rock, soil, and mineral pieces from one location to another by the action of water (liquid or solid) or wind.

Erosional-Depositional System (69-72) – the system involving the opposing processes of erosion and deposition, involving energy relationships and dynamic equilibrium.

Erratic (75) – large boulder left by a glacier.

Error (8, 9) – difference between the actual and observed measurements.

Escarpment (787) – steep slope separating two gently sloping surfaces.

Esker (76) – long, narrow ridge of coarse gravel deposited by a stream flowing in or under a decaying glacial ice sheet.

Evaporation (34, 117, 139) – change of phase from liquid to vapor (gas) occurring at the surface of that liquid.

Evaporite (34) – form of sedimentary rock, caused by the precipitation of minerals from evaporating water, such as limestone, dolostone, gypsum, and salt.

Evapotranspiration (117) – combination of both processes evaporation and transpiration.

Event (10) – the occurrence of a change in the environment.

Extinct (102) – no longer existing or living: an extinct species; no longer burning or active: an extinct volcano.

Extrusion (33, 36, 98) – mass of hardened lava at the Earth's surface, a type of igneous rock formation.

Extrusive Igneous Rock (33) – igneous rock that forms by the hardening of magma (hot liquid rock beneath the Earth's surface) after reaching the surface of the Earth.

Eye of the Storm (124) – the central area of calm in a hurricane.

Fault Strata (47, 78, 98) – crack in the crust of the Earth along which rocks have moved.

Felsic (34) – Light-colored igneous rocks that are high in feldspar and quartz.

Fetch (71) – expanse of open water over which the wind blows.

Field (22) – region of space which contains a measurable quantity at every point.

Field Values (23, 122) – information shown on weather maps, such as temperature and pressure.

Finger Lake (76) – long narrow lake formed when glacial sediment dams up a river valley.

Fireball (167) – also called bolide; meteoric fireball, appearing to be as bright or brighter than the brightest planets.

Flood (140) – overflowing of water onto land that is normally dry.

Focus (earthquake) (48) – point of origin of an earthquake.

Focus (geometric definition) (162) (plural is foci) – fixed point from which a radius of 360° is a circle or sphere; two fixed points (foci) are required to produce an ellipse or oblate spheroid.

Folded Strata (47, 78, 98) – bend in the rock strata produced during the mountain-building process.

Foliation (35) – alignment of mineral flakes or bands in metamorphic rocks.

Fossil (35, 37, 98, 99, 101) – remains or traces of a once-living organism in sedimentary rock.

Fossil fuel (37, 188) – fuels such as coal, oil, and natural gas which formed from organic matter in the ancient past.

Foucault Pendulum (160, 165) – freely swinging pendulum, which when allowed to swing without interference appears to change direction in a predictable manner due to the Earth's rotation.

Fracture (32) – the way a mineral breaks if it does not have cleavage.

Fragmental Sedimentary Rock (35) – rocks formed by the compaction and cementation of sediments.

Freezing (118) – pass from the liquid to the solid state by loss of heat, as in water to ice.

Friction (71) – force found at the contact of two surfaces that offers resistance to motion, often producing heat or another form of energy.

Front (121) – the interface between two different air masses, such as the point of contact between warm and cold air masses.

Frost (116) – deposit of minute ice crystals formed when water vapor condenses at a temperature below freezing.

Galaxy (169) – a huge system of billions of stars.

Geocentric Model (165) – early attempt to explain the motions of celestial objects using the Earth as the stationary center for the orbiting celestial objects.

Geographic Poles (20, 21, 142, 143, 160, 161) – actual axis points on the Earth, north and south, on which the Earth rotates.

Geologic History of NYS (206-207) – *Reference Table*.

Geologic Time Scale (99, 100) – geological periods, a scale of time that serves as a reference for correlating various events in the history of the Earth, divided into three main groups: eras, periods, and epochs, based on the study of rock history.

Geometry of a Sphere, Principle of (19) – as a sphere is rotated, the angle of a fixed point outside of the sphere as compared to the surface of that sphere, is equal to the angle of the sphere's rotation.

Geometry of orbits (162) – mathematics of the properties, measurement, and relationships of points, lines, angles, and surfaces in the relationships of celestial bodies (orbits).

Glacier (71, 75) – huge mass of ice slowly flowing over a land mass, formed from compacted snow in an area where snow accumulation exceeds melting and sublimation.

Glacial Features (75) – see individual features.

Glacial Ice (75) – usually glacial snow that has accumulated, compacted, and recrystallized.

Glacial Till (75) – unsorted sediment pushed, carried, or dragged by a glacier.

Glacial Valley (76) – rounded, often a river valley with characteristic U-shape.

Global Cooling (189) – brought about Earth's Ice Ages.

Global Positioning System, or GPS (22) – modern navigation system capable of 3-D, precise latitude, longitude, and altitude with use of satellites.

Global Warming (145, 188) – the theory that the atmosphere of the Earth is becoming warmer caused primarily by increasing amounts of carbon dioxide and other greenhouse gases in the air.

Globe (19) – body with the shape of a sphere, especially a representation of the Earth in the form of a hollow ball.

Graded Bedding (72) – layering of sediment in a fashion where heavier and/or larger particles are on the bottom and lighter and/or smaller particles are on top, in decreasing size.

Gradient (23, 122) – formula; expression of the degree of change of a field quantity from place to place; may also be referred to as an average slope.

Grams (8) – metric unit of mass equal to one thousandth (10^{-3}) of a kilogram.

Graphing (10, 11) – types of graphs illustrated.

Gravitation, Law of (20, 163) – gravitational force is proportional to the square of the distance between the two centers of attracted objects.

Gravitational Force, or Gravity (20, 163) – attraction between any two objects in the universe.

Gravity (20, 22, 69, 70, 163) – natural phenomenon of attraction between massive bodies.

Greenhouse Effect (144, 145) – process which increases the atmospheric temperature of the Earth, due to the transmission of short wave radiation through the atmosphere, absorption and conversion to long wave radiation at the Earth's surface.

Greenhouse Gases (145, 189) – gases associated with the greenhouse effect including CO_2, CH_4, N_2O, CFCs, and other trace elements and compounds.

Greenwich Mean Time (22) – also Universal Time (UT); international reference time at Greenwich, England; the Prime Meridian with a longitude of 0° (neither East nor West).

Grid (21) – coordinate or graphing structure.

Ground Moraine (76) – unsorted glacial sediment covering the ground surface deposited directly by glacial ice.

Groin (71) – wall built along a coastline to slow down or prevent the transport of sand away from that coastline area.

Ground Water (139) – water that is found under the Earth's surface as the result of infiltration and storage.

Gyre (147) – large, circular pattern of surface currents found in the ocean.

Hachure Marks (24) – short lines used on maps to shade or to indicate slopes and their degree and direction.

Half-life (101) – time taken for half of a radioactive material to decay to its stable decay product; time for half of the atoms present to disintegrate.

Hardness (31) – the resistance of a mineral to being scratched.

Harmonic Law of Planetary Motion (162) – by Kepler states that a planet's period is the length of time required for the planet to orbit (revolve) once around the Sun.

Headland (71) – an area of high land jutting out into the ocean.

Heat of Fusion (118) – amount of latent heat involved in melting or freezing.

Heat of Vaporization (118) – amount of latent heat involved in evaporation or condensation.

Heliocentric Model (165, 166) – a modern attempt to explain the motions of celestial objects using the Sun as the stationary center for the orbiting celestial objects and fixed star positions.

Herbicide (187, 190) – chemical substance used to destroy or inhibit the growth of plants, especially weeds.

HIGH (120, 123) – high pressure air mass, clockwise rotation in the northern hemisphere, more dense than a LOW; see Anticyclone.

High Noon (161) – 12:00 (noon) point in time when the Sun is at its highest altitude (zenith) on the observer's meridian.

Horizontal Displacement (48) – sideways shift of the Earth's surface along a transform fault or crack in the crust; see Faulting.

Horizontal Layers (35) – sediments deposited through settling.

Horizontal Sorting (72) – sorting of sediments in a stream by decreasing velocity, larger particles first laid down, followed by smaller and smaller particles down stream.

Horn (75) – a pyramid-shaped mountain formed by glaciers; named after Matterhorn in Switzerland.

Hot Spots (54) – high heat flows on Earth's surface.

H-R Diagram (168) – graph developed by Einar Hertzsprung and Henry Russell useful in comparing luminosity and temperature of the stars.

Hubble, Edwin (170) – American astronomer who discovered (1929) that the velocities of nebulae increase with distance.

Hubble Space Telescope, or HST (170) – launched in 1990, American satellite-based telescope for deep space study.

Humidity (113) – dampness, especially of the air.

Humid Climate (75, 146) – an area where the precipitation is greater than the potential evaporation for the majority of months in a year.

Hurricane (124) – tropical cyclone with winds in excess of 119 km/hr [75mph].

Hydration (118) – the chemical reaction of water with other materials.

Hydrologic Cycle (139) – See Water Cycle

Hydrosphere (21) – thin layer of water which covers a majority [71%] of the Earth's surface.

Hypothesis (7) – tentative explanation that accounts for a set of facts and can be tested by further investigation.

Ice Age, the Great (75) – most recent glacial period, which occurred during the Pleistocene epoch.

Igneous Rock (33, 53) – rock formed by the solidification and crystallization of magma or lava (hot molten rock).

Igneous Rock Identification (33, 204) – Reference Table.

Incident Insolation (144) – point and time of solar radiation hitting the Earth's surface; see Angle of Insolation and Insolation.

Inclination (tilt) of Earth Axis (142) – see Earth's axis.

Incompetent Rocks (77) – poor resistant to weathering and erosion.

Index Contour Line (23, 24) – usually every 5th line on a contour map which is printed darker and interrupted to give elevation.

Index Fossil (99) – fossil that is characteristic of a certain geologic time, sometimes referred to as a guide fossil.

Inertia (163) – the tendency of an object in motion to remain in motion in a straight path unless acted upon by an outside force.

Inferences (7) – interpretations (conclusions) based on observations.

Infiltration (140) – seeping and absorption of water into ground storage.

Infrared Rays (141, 212) – range of invisible radiation wavelengths from about 750 nanometers, just longer than red in the visible spectrum, to 1 millimeter, on the border of the microwave region.

Inner Core (50) – iron/nickel solid inner sphere (zone) of the Earth's interior.

Inorganic pollution (187) – wastes that are not from organic life or the products of organic life.

Insolation (141, 143) – incoming solar radiation; Sun's energy that transmits through Earth's atmosphere and reaches Earth's surface.

Instruments (7) – tools used by the observer to improve on detail or extend the ability to obtain information and measurements.

Intensity of Insolation (142) – rate (amount and duration) of solar radiation reaching the Earth's surface.

Intensity Scale (49) – see Modified Mercalli Scale.

Interface (11) – boundary between materials at which a change in environmental equilibrium occurs involving a loss or gain in energy states.

Interglacial Period (76) – the time between periods of glaciation.

International Dateline (22) – imaginary line through the Pacific Ocean roughly corresponding to 180° longitude, to the east of which, by international agreement, the calendar date is one day earlier than to the west.

Interpretation (7) – see Inferences.

Interrelationships (185) – the mutual dependence between the Earth's living and nonliving systems.

Intrusion (33, 36, 98) – rock mass formed from liquid rock (magma) cooling below the Earth's surface, igneous rock.

Intrusive Igneous Rock (33) – igneous rock formed below the Earth's surface by the hardening of magma (hot liquid rock).

Inverse Relationship (10, 115) – when one variable increases as the other variable decreases; see Graphing.

Island Arc (53) – where two ocean plates converge, a chain of islands form along a trench.

Isobar (23, 114, 122) – type of isoline on a weather map used to indicate equal air pressure points.

Isoline (23, 122) – line representing equal values on a map or model (such as contours, isotherms, isobars) of field characteristics in two dimensions.

Isostasy (74) – condition of equilibrium in the Earth's crust in which masses of greatest density are lower than those of lesser density.

Isotherm (23, 122) – type of isoline on a weather map used to indicate equal temperature points.

Isotope (101) – a variety of an element that has the same atomic number, but a different atomic mass, due to a difference in the number of neutrons present in the nucleus, used for correlation studies when radioactive.

Iso-surface (23) – model representing field characteristics in 3 dimensions.

Jet Stream (123) – wavelike currents with high winds at upper levels which tend to control storm tracks.

Jetty (71) – rock barriers build on both sides of a harbor entrance to prevent the deposition of sediment from clogging the entrance.

Joint (78, 98) – crack in a rock mass or rock where unlike a fault, no vertical or horizontal displacement has occurred.

Jovian Planets (166) – Jupiter-like planets; large gaseous giant planets; includes Jupiter, Uranus, Saturn, and Neptune.

Kame (76) – cone-shaped hill formed at the ice front of a glacier.

Kepler's Harmonic Law (162) – explanation of planetary motion; relates a planet's period to its distance from the Sun.

Kettle Hole (76)– depression in glacial sediment formed when a large block of buried ice melts.

Kettle Lake (76) – kettle hole filled with water.

Kinetic Energy (118, 163) – energy of action, motion or at work.

Kuiper Belt (166) – region of the Solar System beyond the planets, consists of small bodies composed largely of methane, ammonia, and water ices.

La Niña (147) – generally, the opposite of El Niño, having cold water origins.

Land Breeze (116) – local wind blowing from the land toward the sea when the air pressure over the land is greater than the air pressure over the sea.

Landfill (186) – method of solid waste disposal in which refuse is buried between layers of dirt so as to fill in or reclaim low-lying ground.

Landscape (73) – topography of the land, including the characteristics of the Earth's surface.

Landscape Regions, NYS (200) – *Reference Table*.

Landscape Regions, US (73) – Reference Map.

Landslide (71) – downward sliding of a mass of earth and rock both under the ocean or on relatively dry hillsides or mountainsides.

Latent Heat (118) – formula; energy released or absorbed during a phase change, such as a liquid to a gas, but with no temperature change involved.

Latitude (19, 21, 22, 142, 146) – distance north or south of the equator measured in degrees (parallels) from 0° at the equator, to 90° at the geographic poles.

Lava (33) – magma that reaches the Earth's surface.

Length (8) – distance between the ends or sections of an object; usually measured in meters, centimeters, of millimeters.

Leveling Forces (Destructional) (74) – forces of weathering, erosion, transportation, deposition, and subsidence.

Light-year (169) – a unit of measurement equal to the distance light travels in one year; ten trillion kilometers.

Lithosphere (21, 31, 47, 51) – continuous outer solid rock shell of the Earth.

Local Water Budget (146) – system of accounting for an area's water yearly supply.

L-Waves (48) – long period waves (Rayleigh and Love waves) that travel along the Earth's surface.

Longitude (21, 22) – distance east or west of the Prime Meridian measured in degrees from 0° at the Prime Meridian (runs through Greenwich, England – Greenwich Mean Time) to 180° east or west (in the Pacific Ocean – International Date Line).

Longshore Current (71) – current moving sediment parallel to the coastline.

LOW (120, 123) – low pressure air mass, counterclockwise rotation in the northern hemisphere, less dense than a HIGH; see Cyclone.

Luminosity (168) – emitting self-generated light.

Luminosity of Stars (168, 213) – *Reference Table.*

Lunar Eclipse (164) – when the Moon passes into the shadow of the Earth.

Lunar Month (164) – average time between successive new or full moons, 29 days 12 hours 44 minutes.

Luster (32) – the appearance of light reflected from a mineral's surface.

Mafic (34) – dark-colored igneous rocks high in iron and magnesium.

Magma (33, 51) – molten rock material beneath the Earth's surface.

Magnetic Polarity (53) – see Mid-Oceanic Ridge and change due to ocean ridge movement.

Magnetism (22) – force exerted by a magnetic field.

Magnitude Scale (49) – see Richter Scale.

Major Axis (162) – the longest diameter of an ellipse.

Mantle (50) – layer of the Earth between the crust and the core.

Mantle Convection Cells (54) – the movement of heat and matter caused by differences in density within the Earth's mantle.

Map Legend (24) – explanatory table or list of the symbols appearing on a map or chart.

Map Scale (24) – the ratio between the distance on a map and the distance on the Earth's surface.

Marine Climate (147) – long term weather characteristics of an area near water bodies, such as large oceans characterized by small seasonal temperature ranges and abundant precipitation.

Maritime Polar Air Mass (120) – mP – a cool, moist air mass originating over a cold water surface.

Maritime Tropical Air Mass (120) – mT – usually a warm air mass originating over tropical waters, such as the Caribbean region.

Mars (166, 168) – fourth planet from the Sun, having a sidereal period of revolution about the Sun of 687 days at a mean distance of 227.8 million kilometers (141.6 million miles) and a mean diameter of approximately 6,726 kilometers (4,180 miles).

Mass (8) – amount (quantity) of matter which an object contains.

Meander (70) – curving pattern of a river due to erosion and deposition.

Measurement (8) – use of time, length, or mass as a basic dimensional quantity (numerical).

Melting (118) – changing from a solid to a liquid state by application of heat or pressure or both.

Meridians (21) – grid "lines" (imaginary great circles) running between the North Pole and the South Pole; used to measure longitude.

Mesosphere (21) – portion of the atmosphere from about 30 to 80 kilometers (20 to 50 miles) above the Earth's surface, characterized by temperatures that decrease from 10°C to -90°C (50°F to -130°F) with increasing altitude.

Mesozoic Era (99, 100) – third era of geologic time, includes Triassic Period, Jurassic Period, and Cretaceous Period; characterized by the development of flying reptiles, birds, and flowering plants and the appearance and extinction of dinosaurs.

Metamorphic Rock (35) – rocks formed by the effect of heat pressure and/or chemical action on other rocks, a recrystallization of pre-existing rocks.

Metamorphic Rock Identification (36, 205) – *Reference Table.*

Meteor (167) – bright trail or streak that appears in the sky when a meteoroid is heated to incandescence by friction with the Earth's atmosphere.

Meteorite (167) – stony or metallic mass of matter that has fallen to Earth's surface from outer space.

Meteorologist (123) – studies, reports, and forecasts weather conditions, as on television.

Meters (8) – international standard unit of length, approximately equivalent to 39.37 inches.

Metric System (8) – decimal system of units based on the meter as a unit length, the kilogram as a unit mass, and the second as a unit time.

Mid-Ocean Ridge (53) – mountain ridge in mid-ocean, such as the Mid-Atlantic Ridge, which extends for about 64,000 kilometers roughly parallel to continental margins.

Milky Way Galaxy (169) – a spiral assembly of stars; home to the Sun and solar system.

Millibar (114) – unit used to measure air pressure.

Millimeters (8) – unit of length equal to one thousandth (10^{-3}) of a meter

Mineral (31) – inorganic (nonliving) crystalline, solid substance with a definite chemical (atomic) shape and composition.

Model (22, 23) – description or representation of an idea or concept which helps to illustrate actions or information (for example, models can be used to illustrate the Earth's shape and size).

Modified Mercalli Scale (49) – earthquake intensity scale based upon damage.

Moho (50) – shortened form of Mohorovicic discontinuity which is the crust-mantle boundary.

Mohs' Scale (31) – list of ten minerals from softest (#1) to hardest (#10) used to determine relative hardness of other minerals.

Moisture (117) water in any form in the atmosphere and other places.

Moisture Capacity (146) – amount of water that can be held by an air mass, cold air generally hold less water than warm air; amount of moisture that can be held by soil, see Absolute Humidity.

Moisture Deficit (146) – see Drought.

Monomineralic Rock (31, 34) – rock composed of just one mineral type.

Monsoon (115) – wind system, most often with heavy rains that influences large climatic regions and reverses direction seasonally.

Moon (163) – Earth's natural satellite.

Moraines (76) – features made of glacial till.

Mountain (73, 148) – elevated landscape with distorted rock structure.

National Hurricane Center (124) – in Florida, tracks hurricanes and issues appropriate warnings.

National Severe Storm Forecast Center (124) – in Kansas City predicts and tracks tornadoes.

National Weather Service (123, 124) – uses satellites to track weather systems and issue appropriate warnings.

Natural Pollutants (185) – materials produced by nature having a negative effect on people, plants, animals, or property; i.e. pollen or volcanic ash.

Neap Tide (164) – tides of the smallest tidal range occurring at the quarter phases of the Moon.

Nonrenewable Resources (37) – resources that are used much faster and in greater amounts than they can form.

Noon (161) – point in time when the Sun is directly on observer's meridian.

North Pole (19, 22) – 90° north latitude.

North Star (19, 159) – see Polaris.

Nuclear fusion (168) – when the high energy of atomic nuclei cause light elements come together to form heavier ones.

Nuclear Waste (187) – long-term harmful by-products of nuclear reactions.

Oblate Spheroid (19, 20) – slightly flattened sphere; shape of the Earth, flattened at the geographic poles and bulging at the equator.

Observation (7) – use of senses in measuring and collecting data concerning environment.

Occluded Front (121) – interface formed when a cold front overtakes a warm front.

Ocean (70) – entire body of salt water that covers more than 70 percent of the Earth's surface.

Ocean Currents (147) – see the specific current.

Ocean Currents, Surface (202) – *Reference Table*.

Ocean Trenches (51, 53) – deep, sharp valleys under the ocean associated with colliding plates.

Oceanic Crust (51) – thinner, more dense part of the Earth's crust composed of basaltic material.

Ocean-Floor Spreading (51) – theory supported by past and present evidence that the ocean floor is moving outwards from the mid-ocean ridge.

Orbit (162) – path of a celestial object, satellite, and/or Earth about a center, usually an ellipse.

Orbital Velocity (Speed) (162) – the speed of an object at any given time in its orbit; usually changing due to distances from its gravitational center.

Organic Evolution (103) – theory of change, an explanation of how new species develop by punctuated (rapid) or gradual (slow) changes.

Organic Sedimentary Rock (35) – rock formed from the remains of plant and/or animal material.

Organic Sediments (35) – sediments formed from skeletal remains and shells of microscopic marine organisms.

Organic Substance (35) – material containing the element Carbon, usually associated with living or once living things.

Organic Wastes (187) – produced from either organic life or the products of organic life.

Orogeny (99, 100) – mountain building processes.

Orographic Effect (116, 117, 148) – effect that mountains have on weather and climate; blockage of precipitation from the leeward side of mountains.

Outgassing (97) – removing embedded gas [i.e., water vapor, carbon dioxide, nitrogen] from [a solid], as by heating or reducing the pressure.

Outer Core (50) – liquid Earth zone between the inner core of the Earth and the mantle, like the inner core composed of iron and nickel.

Outwash Plain (76) – horizontal layers of sorted glacial material deposited in front of the glacier by the meltwaters of the glacier.

Oxidation (67) – the chemical reaction of oxygen with other materials.

Oxide (32) – binary compound of an element or a radical with oxygen (O_2).

Ozone (190) – a form of oxygen containing three atoms in the molecule (O_3).

Ozone Depletion (190) – loss of ozone from the Earth's Stratosphere.

P-waves (48) – see Primary Wave.

Paleozoic Era (99, 100) – geologic time that includes the Cambrian, Ordovician, Silurian, Devonian, Mississippian, Pennsylvanian, and Permian periods and is characterized by the appearance of marine invertebrates, primitive fishes, land plants, and primitive reptiles.

Parallelism of the Axis (142) – the Earth's axis at any place in its orbit is parallel to the axis in any other place in the Earth's orbit.

Parallels (21) – grid lines on a map or globe; another term used to determine latitude.

Parent Rock (35) – the original rock from which a metamorphic rock forms.

Particle Size (Transported) to Water Velocity Relationship (70, 140, 204) – *Reference Table*.

Penumbra (164) – partial shadow cast by the Earth, Moon, or Sun during an eclipse.

Percent Error (8) – mathematical expression of a calculated error in percent (%).

Perihelion (161, 162) – point on the Earth's orbit when it is closest to the Sun; a distance of 147 million kilometers, usually occurring January 1st.

Period (99) – unit of geological time, longer than an epoch and shorter than an era.

Period of Revolution (162) – amount of time an object takes to make one complete orbit around its center, in the case of the Earth, 365+ days to orbit the Sun.

Permeability (140) – rate at which moisture passes through a material.

Permeability Rate (140) – speed at which water pass through a porous material; see Permeability and Porosity.

Perpendicular Insolation (161) – vertical rays of the Sun; 90° radiation at Earth's surface.

Pesticides (187, 190) – chemical used to kill pests, especially insects.

Phase Change (118) – change of a material through states of solid, liquid, and gas.

Phases (States) of Matter (9, 118) – solid, liquid, and gas.

Phases of the Moon (163) – changes in the amount of the illuminated surface of the Moon as seen from the Earth, cyclic over a 29½ day period.

Physical Constants (199) – *Reference Table*.

Physical Properties (31) – used for identification of minerals.

Physical Weathering (67) – the process that alters the physical characteristics of rocks/minerals, generally leading to breaking into smaller pieces.

Photosynthesis (97) – process in green plants and certain other organisms by which carbohydrates are synthesized from carbon dioxide and water using light as an energy source.

Plain (73) – low elevation landscape, gentle slopes and relatively stable, often composed of horizontal layers of sedimentary rocks.

Planets (166-167) – (8 planets in Solar System) Mercury, Venus, Earth, Mars, Jupiter, Uranus, Saturn, and Neptune; (exception is 134340 Pluto, in 2006, recognized as a dwarf planet).

Planetary Motions (165, 166) – the non uniform movement of planets.

Planetary Period (162, 165) – the time it takes a planet to make one revolution around the Sun.

Planetary Wind and Moisture Belts in the Troposphere (212) – *Reference Table*.

Planetary Wind Belts (148) – zones on the Earth where winds generally blow in one direction only, such as the prevailing southwest winds of the U.S.

Plate Tectonic Theory (51) – idea that there are six large crustal plates, and many smaller ones, moving on the surface of Earth in a way that can be calculated and predicted.

Plate Boundaries (53, 54) – areas adjoining pieces of the Earth's lithosphere.

Plates (47, 51) – solid pieces of the Earth's lithosphere.

Plateau (73) – high elevation landscape, relatively stable with little or no distortion of the rock layers.

Pleistocene Epoch (76) – time beginning two or three million years ago and ending about 10,000 years ago; called the Great Ice Age.

Pointer Stars (159) – outer two stars of Big Dipper which align with Polaris, the end star of the Little Dipper.

Polaris (19, 159) – North Star, used in navigation since it is almost directly over the north geographic pole of the Earth.

Pollutants (185-187) – solids, liquids, gases, biological organisms, forms of energy such as heat, sound and nuclear radiation (see Pollution).

Pollution (185-187, 191) – when the concentration of any substance or form of energy reaches a proportion that adversely affects man, his property, or the plant and animal life.

Pollution of Water (186-187) – examples: PCBs, oil spills.

Polymineralic Rock (31) – rock composed of more than one (several) mineral types.

Population Density (191) – areas affected by landscape pollution and the misuse of the landscape due to concentrated population.

Population Growth in Humans (191) – exponential increase in Earth's human population.

Porosity (139) – percent of open space in a volume of a certain material.

Potential Energy (118, 144, 163) – stored energy or energy at rest as the result of its state or position.

Potential Evapotranspiration (146) – estimated amount of water loss that can occur due to heat energy available.

Precambrian Era (99, 100) – oldest and largest division of geologic time, preceding the Cambrian Period, often subdivided into the Archeozoic and Proterozoic eras, and characterized by the appearance of primitive forms of life.

Precipitation (rock formation definition) (34) – type of sedimentation (deposition) involved in the production of evaporites, in which dissolved solids come out of solution.

Precipitation (weather definition) (117, 146) – generally from clouds, the falling of water as liquid (rain) or solid (ice, hail, and snow).

Prediction (12) – the use of natural evidence to predetermine the scope and direction of a future environmental change.

Predominant Agent (70) – main or primary agent (cause affect) of a specific action, such as in weathering and erosion on Earth the main agent is running water.

Pressure (8) – combination of gravitational force compared to surface area.

Pressure Belt (119) – band of high or low pressure in the atmosphere caused by regions of rising or settling air.

Pressure Gradient (122) – degree of difference over a specified distance of high and low pressures, the greater the pressure gradient difference, the greater the wind speeds.

Pressure Scale (211) – *Reference Table*.

Primary Wave, or *P-wave* (48) – compressional wave generated by an earthquake which travels through solids, liquids, and gases.

Prime Meridian (21, 22) – 0° longitude on the Earth, passing through Greenwich, England.

Principle of Geometry of a Sphere (19) – as a sphere is rotated, the angle of a fixed point outside of the sphere as compared to the surface of that sphere, is equal to the angle of the sphere's rotation.

Principle of Superposition (97) – idea that the oldest bed in a sequence of horizontal sedimentary rock layers is the one on the bottom.

Principle of Uniformitarianism (100, 101) – all geologic phenomena may be explained as the result of existing forces having operated uniformly from the origin of the Earth to the present time.

Probability of Occurrence (122) – chance that a specific event will occur, often used in the prediction of weather systems.

Profile (24) – vertical section of soil or rock showing the sequence of the various layers.

Properties of Earth's Atmosphere (212) – *Reference Tables*.

Psychrometer (114) – instrument consisting of a dry bulb and wet bulb thermometer used to determine the dew point temperature and the relative humidity.

Purge (186) – in bodies of water, materials churn up from the bottom.

Quiet Medium (72) – still water, ice, or air in which settling occurs, generally in a graded bedding, a process which is more complex than in a moving medium.

Radial Drainage (78) – streams radiate out like the spokes of a wheel from a central high elevation such as on a volcano.

Radiation (119, 144) – object's electromagnetic wave transmission.

Radiational Cooling (119) – decrease in temperature at the Earth's surface caused by energy radiating out into space.

Radiative Balance (145) – average energy levels on the Earth remain constant due to the Earth giving off as much energy as it receives; stable Earth temperature; gaining as much energy as the Earth gives off.

Radioactive Dating (97) – process of determining the age of rock by measuring the half-life of radioactive materials in the rock.

Radioactive Isotope (101) – materials that decay from more unstable forms into more stable forms; see Half-life.

Radioactive Waste (187) – see Nuclear Waste.

Radioactivity (Decay) (97, 101) – secondary source of energy for the Earth; spontaneous and natural nuclear breakdown from unstable to stable atomic forms, energy is released, the process has a constant and predictable rate, not affected by environmental changes.

Random Reflection (144) – reflection of insolation due to aerosols in the atmosphere; dust and water droplets increase the amount of random reflection, causing a decrease in the amount of insolation reaching the Earth's surface; see Scattering.

Rate of Decay (97, 101) see Half-life, Radioactive Dating.

Recharge (146) – replacement of water by infiltration into the soil storage area.

Recrystallization (35) – formation of new crystalline materials by the enlargement of preexisting crystals by the action of thermal metamorphism.

Recycle (37) – extract and reuse (useful substances found in waste)

Red Shift (170) – spectral lines move toward the red end of the spectrum from a celestial object moving away from the Earth; see Doppler Shift.

Reflection (144) – change in electromagnetic wave direction due to the non penetration of a wave into a surface; a smooth surface will reflect a wave at the same angle at which it strikes the surface.

Refraction (50) – change in direction when an electromagnetic wave goes from one material to another material with a different density.

Regional Metamorphism (36) – recrystallization of rocks over a large area caused by extreme pressure associated with mountain building.

Relative Age (Date) (97, 98) – dates in the Earth's history determined with reference to other events helpful in determining relationships in a time line.

Relative Humidity (113) – ratio of the mass of water vapor per unit volume of the air to the mass of water vapor per unit volume of saturated air at the same temperature.

Relative Humidity (114, 210) – *Reference Table*.

Residual Sediment (69) – sediment that remains at the site of weathering.

Resource Conservation (37) – see Conservation of Natural Resources.

Reversal of Magnetic Polarity (53) – reference to changing polarity as observed in rocks because of the Earth's magnetic poles reversing.

Revolution (142, 159, 162) – orbiting of one body around another body.

Richter Scale (49) – earthquake magnitude scale based upon energy released.

Rock (31-33) – relatively hard, naturally formed mineral or petrified matter; stone.

Rock Cycle (36, 37) – model to explain the changes in rocks and the formation of sedimentary and nonsedimentary rocks, igneous and metamorphic rocks.

Rock Cycle in Earth's Crust (36, 204) – *Reference Table*.

Rock Formation (31) – body or mass of rock with similar features and characteristics.

Rock Forming Minerals (31) – minerals, mostly silicates, that form 90% of the Earth's crust.

Rock Properties (37) – characteristics of various rocks.

Rock Resistance (77) – characteristic of rock types to resist the forces of change, including weathering and erosion.

Rotation (142, 159) – spinning of an object about its own axis.

Runoff (139, 140) – water that does not infiltrate the soil storage area and flows over the land surface to lakes, streams, and oceans.

S-wave (49, 50) – see Shear Wave and Secondary Wave.

Satellite (163) – any object which is held by another object's force of gravitation, around which it revolves (orbits); the Moon is the Earth's satellite; a man-made object which orbits the Earth.

Saturation Point (113) – point at which the air is completely filled with water vapor to the air's maximum capacity, after which water will condense.

Scattering (144) – wave movement in different directions due to reflection.

Sea Breeze (116) – local wind blowing from the sea toward the land when the air pressure is higher over the sea than over the land.

Sea-floor Spreading (53) – the process by which ocean plates move apart allowing new ocean crust to form between them.

Seasonal Lag (143) – the maximum surface temperature occurs after the time of maximum insolation and the minimum surface temperature occurs after the time of minimum insolation.

Seasons (142, 143, 161) – divisions of the year caused by climatic changes, angle of insolation, Earth tilt; generally, spring, summer, fall, and winter.

Secondary Wave, or *S-wave* (48) – transverse earthquake waves which only travel through solids and travel more slowly than *P-waves*.

Sediment (34, 67, 72) – rock particles that are produced and/or transported by erosion and weathering.

Sediment Laden Flow (72) – movement of an erosional transport agent containing some forms of sediment, such as a glacier, turbidity current.

Sedimentary Rock (34, 77) – rock formed from compaction and cementation of sediment.

Sedimentary Rock Identification (34, 205) – *Reference Table*.

Sedimentation (72) – settling out of solution of sediments, including minerals, in an erosional system; deposition; see Deposition.

Seismic Wave (48) – wave that radiates from the point of origin of an earthquake, moving in all directions through solid rock.

Seismograph (48) – very delicate instrument that detects and records passing earthquake waves.

Sensory Perception (7) use of senses of sight, hearing, touch, smell, taste.

SEQR (191) – New york State Environmental Quality Review Acts requiring an environmental impact study before approval is given for projects.

Settling Rate (71, 72) – time required for a certain sediment to settle out of water or air.

Sewage (186) – liquid and solid waste produced through human activities, carried off in sewers or drains.

Shadow Zone (50) – a band from 102° to 143° away from an earthquake in which neither *P-waves* nor *S-waves* are recorded on seismographs.

Shear Wave (Secondary, *S-wave*) (48) – wave that causes individual rock particles to vibrate at right angles to the direction that the wave is traveling; cannot pass through liquids.

Sidereal Month (163) – one complete revolution of the Moon around the Earth – $27\frac{1}{3}$ days.

Silicates (31, 32) – minerals containing silicon-oxygen tetrahedra.

Silicon-Oxygen Tetrahedron (32) – structural model of a silicate mineral.

Sink (11) – portion of an energy system with lower energy concentrations, into which energy usually flows.

Snowfield (75) – area where snow accumulates and recrystallizes into the ice that feeds glaciers.

Soil (68) – top layer of the Earth's surface, consisting of rock and mineral particles mixed with organic matter.

Soil Association (69) – unit of soil classification, including the characteristics of the soil, composition, porosity, permeability, structure, and the ability to support life.

Soil Conservation (69) – using the soil in ways to preserve and protect it.

Soil Formation (68) – production of soil, particles of rocks and minerals, and organic matter.

Soil Layers (69) – also horizons; layers of soil produced as a result of the weathering processes and biologic activity; examples: horizontal topsoil, horizontal subsoil.

Soil Storage (140, 146) – amount of water held below Earth's surface in the soil.

Solar Eclipse (165) – eclipse that occurs when the Moon's umbra reaches the Earth's surface.

Solar Electromagnetic Spectrum (141, 143) – full range of wavelengths emitted from the Sun with the maximum intensity occurring in the visible region.

Solar Energy (141) – any energy forms radiated from the Sun.

Solar Radiation (141, 144) – energy from the Sun.

Solar System (165, 166) – orbiting system of the eight planets (including Earth), and moons with the Sun as the center of revolution.

Solidification (33, 37) – see Crystallization.

Solstice (142) – times when the Sun's rays are perpendicular (at zenith) to the $23\frac{1}{2}$° north latitude (about June 21st), summer solstice and $23\frac{1}{2}$° south latitude (about December 21st), winter solstice.

Solution (71) – dissolved minerals carried in water.

Solvent (71) – substance in which another substance is dissolved, forming a solution; substance, usually a liquid, capable of dissolving another substance.

Solvent, Universal (71) – water.

Sorted and Unsorted Particles (139) – selection of various materials, based on size, the more similar the particle sizes, the greater the sorting, the greater the difference in the particle sizes, the less the sorting.

Sorting of Sediments (72) – manner in which materials in suspension settle out of a transport medium in a definite pattern.

Source (11) – portion of an energy system with the highest energy concentrations, from which energy usually flows.

Source Region (120) – place on the Earth where an air mass forms.

South Pole (22) – 90° South latitude.

Species (103) – most specific part of the classification system, or two organisms of the same species are able to mate and produce fertile offspring.

Specific Gravity (32) – the ratio of the weight of a mineral to the weight of an equal volume of water.

Specific Heat (118, 119) – amount of heat needed to raise the temperature of 1 gram of any substance 1°C, measured in calories/gram °C or Joules/gram/°C; specific heat of water is 1 calories/gram °C (4.8 Joules/gram/°C); most other substances have lower specific heats.

Spectral Lines (169) – lines corresponding to various wavelengths seen in an elements spectrum.

Spectroscope (169) – astronomical instrument used to study the light from celestial objects.

Spectrum (169) – see Electromagnetic Spectrum.

Speed of Light (169) – 300,000 kilometers per second.

Spring Tides (164) – tides of maximum tidal range occurring at New and Full Moon phases.

Station Model (122) – on a weather map, describes weather conditions at a reporting station.

Station Model, Weather Maps (122, 211) – *Reference Table*.

Stationary Front (122) – interface of two air masses that do not move.

Storage of Water (146) – amount of water stored in the top of the soil, the root zone.

Storm Track (122) – path taken by the center of a storm or low pressure system.

Strata (47) – layers of rock material, usually sedimentary rock.

Stratiform Clouds (117) – see Stratus Clouds.

Stratosphere (21) – region of the atmosphere above the troposphere and below the mesosphere.

Stratus Clouds (117) – low-altitude cloud formation consisting of a horizontal layer of gray clouds.

Streak (32) – the color of the powder of a mineral.

Stream Bed (70) – interface of the water and bottom of a stream, including the rock particles and bottom materials.

Stream Discharge (141) – measurement of amount of water passing a certain point in a stream in a certain amount of time; rate of flow in volume.

Stream Drainage Pattern (78) – pattern that forms due to the way water drains across the land in a stream or river system.

Stream Velocity (70) – graphs comparing with discharge, slope, and particle size carried.

Striations (75) – scratches in rock caused by glaciers dragging rocks over the surface.

Subduction Zones (52) – form from the collision of plates with the denser ocean plate diving down (subducting) into the mantle.

Sublimation (118) – phase change from a solid to a gas without a liquid phase, as in the sublimation of ice to water vapor without melting to a liquid form.

Subsidence (55) – act of sinking or settling of the Earth's surface.

Summer Solstice (142, 161) – in Northern Hemisphere occurs about June 21, when the Sun is in the zenith at the Tropic of Cancer.

Sun (165, 168) – star, center of solar system.

Sunspot (168) – relatively cool dark spot appearing periodically in groups on the surface of the Sun that are associated with strong magnetic fields.

Sun's Path (159) – see Apparent Motions.

Superposition, Principle of (97) – "youngest" rock layers appear on top of "oldest" rock layers.

Surf (71) – foaming water formed by breaking waves.

Surface Ocean Currents 147, (202) – *Reference Tables*.

Surplus Water (141, 146) – surface water that neither evaporates nor infiltrates, but is runoff.

Suspension (71) – particles transported in all levels of water in a stream held up by the motion of the stream.

Swash (71) – the water that surges forward onto the beach from the breaking waves.

Synodic Month (164) – see Lunar Month.

Synoptic Weather Map (122) – broad "bird's eye view" of the weather.

Technology (185, 186, 191) – application of modern science, especially to industrial or commercial objectives.

Technological Oversights (185) – types; human errors involving the environment.

Temperature (113, 143) – specific degree of hotness or coldness as indicated on or referred to a standard scale; see Celsius.

Terminal Moraine (76) – large ridge of glacial till marking the farthest advance of glacial ice.

Terrestrial (Earth-like) Planets (166) – having rocky cores; includes Mercury, Venus, Earth, and Mars.

Terrestrial Radiation (143, 145) – outgoing Earth radiation.

Tetrahedral Unit (32) – as seen in the bonds between oxygen and silicon; the basic building block of the silicates.

Texture (33) – appearance and feel of a surface; used in rock identification.

Thermal Metamorphism (35) – see contact metamorphism by heat.

Thermosphere (21) – outermost shell of the atmosphere, between the mesosphere and outer space, where temperatures increase steadily with altitude.

Thunderstorm (123) – transient, sometimes violent storm of thunder and lightning, often accompanied by rain and sometimes hail.

Tidal Range (164) – difference between high and low tide water levels.

Tidal Wave (50, 71) – see Tsunami.

Tides (164) – periodic variation in the surface level of the oceans and of bays, gulfs, inlets, and estuaries, caused by gravitational attraction of the Moon and Sun.

Till (75, 76) – unsorted glacial sediment.

Tilting (47) – Earth movement resulting in a change in the position of rock layers.

Time (8) – number, as of years, days, or minutes, representing such an interval separating two points on this continuum; a duration.

Time Marker (98, 99) – a known substance or a known geological event that helps in identifying a surrounding geological event.

Topographic Map (24) – see Contour Map.

Tornado (124) – small, violent storm with a characteristic funnel-shaped cloud.

Toxic Waste Dump (186) – location of disposal of environmentally harmful materials.

Toxins (186) – poisonous substance, especially a protein, that is produced by living cells or organisms and is capable of causing disease when introduced into the body tissues but is often also capable of inducing neutralizing antibodies or antitoxins.

Trade Winds (148) – prevailing tropical winds, blowing northeasterly in the Northern Hemisphere and southeasterly in the Southern Hemisphere.

Transform Plate Boundary (53, 54) – boundary between plates that are grinding past each other.

Transition Zones (36) – boundary between rock types.

Transpiration (117) – process which adds water to the atmosphere by transpiring, especially through the stomata of plant tissue or the pores of the skin.

Transported Sediments (69) – erosional product moved from the source of weathering to a different location.

Transporting Agents (34, 69) – actions that affect erosion and move sediments from one place to another.

Transporting Systems (70) – all agents involved in erosion and movement; e.g. erosion, the transporting agent, energy, and the material moved.

Trellis Drainage (78) – drainage pattern with parallel mainstreams and right-angled tributaries found in regions with parallel folds or faults.

Tropic of Cancer (161) – 23$\frac{1}{2}$° North latitude.

Tropic of Capricorn (161) – 23$\frac{1}{2}$° South latitude.

Tropopause (20) – boundary between the troposphere and the stratosphere varying in altitude from approximately 8 kilometers at the poles to approximately 18 kilometers at the equator.

Trough (71) – bottom part of a wave.

Tsunami (50, 71) – seismic sea wave commonly referred to as a tidal wave although it is not caused by tides.

U-shaped Valley (75) – round bottomed valleys carved as a result of glaciers.

Ultraviolet Rays (144, 190) – range of invisible radiation wavelengths from about 4 nanometers, on the border of the x-ray region, to about 380 nanometers, just beyond the violet in the visible spectrum.

Umbra (165) – completely dark portion of the shadow cast by the Earth, Moon, or the Sun during an eclipse.

Unconformity (98) – surface of erosion between rock layers of different ages indicating that deposition was not continuous.

Universal Time (22) – UT, see Greenwich Mean Time.

Universe (168-170) – all matter and energy, including Earth, the galaxies and all therein, and the contents of intergalactic space, regarded as a whole.

Uplifting (47, 74) – vertical displacement of the Earth's surface; faulting.

Vapor Pressure (118) – pressure exerted by water within the atmosphere.

Variable (10) – factors involved in change.

Vein (98) – mineral deposits that have filled a rock crack or permeable zone; regularly shaped and lengthy occurrence of an ore; a lode.

Venus (166, 167) – second planet from the Sun, having an average radius of 6,052 kilometers (3,760 miles), a mass 0.815 times that of Earth, and a sidereal period of revolution about the Sun of 224.7 days at a mean distance of approximately 108.1 million kilometers (67.2 million miles).

Vertical Displacement (48) – faulting in which a portion of the Earth's surface is either uplifted or subsides.

Vertical Sorting (72) – graded bedding; layering of sediment so that the largest, densest particles are on the bottom of the layer and the smallest, least dense particles are on the top.

Vesicles (33) – small cavity formed in volcanic rock by entrapment of a gas bubble during solidification.

Violet Shift (170) – on a darkline spectrum for an element, the pattern moves to the left indicating that the light source is moving toward the Earth; see Doppler Shift.

Visible Light (141) – wavelengths of the electromagnetic spectrum perceptible to the eye.

Volcanic Time Markers (98) – layers of ash from a volcano used in dating geological events.

Volcano (50) – opening in the Earth's crust through which molten lava, ash, and gases are ejected.

Volume (8) – amount of space occupied by a three-dimensional object or region of space, expressed in cubic units.

Vortex (124) – the center of a tornadoes funnel-shaped cloud.

Warm Front (121) – the interface, leading edge, of an air mass which has warmer temperatures than the preceding cooler air mass.

Wastes (187) – types of, including organic, inorganic, thermal and radioactive.

Water (9, 70) – hydrogen and oxygen (H_2O); universal solvent.

Water Budget (145) – system of accounting for an area's water yearly supply.

Water Cycle (139) – also, hydrologic cycle; Earth system in which water is continually moving from the atmosphere to the Earth and from the Earth to the atmosphere.

Water Pollution (186) – types.

Water Shed (141) – land from which water drains into a stream.

Water Table (140) – within the ground surface of the Earth, top of the zone of saturation.

Water Vapor (113) – gaseous state of water in air.

Wave (48) – movement in a cyclic pattern, evidenced in energy transfer, such as ocean or seismic waves

Wave Height (71) – vertical distance between the crest and trough of a wave.

Wave Refraction (71) – the bending of a line of waves as it approaches the shore.

Wave Velocity (70) – in water, speed of motion of an ocean wave.

Wavelength (71, 141, 144) – distance between two successive wave crests.

Weather (113) – state of the atmosphere at a given time and place, with respect to variables such as temperature, moisture, wind velocity, and barometric pressure.

Weather Forecasting (122, 123)

Weather Map Information (122, 123)

Weather Map Symbols (122)

Weathering (35, 67, 68) – physical and chemical processes that change the surface of the Earth.

Wegener, Alfred (51, 53) – see Continental Drift.

Weight (8) – unit measure of gravitational force.

Wet-bulb Thermometer (113, 114) – see Psychrometer.

Wind (71, 73, 114, 115, 119, 148) – movement of air caused by Earth systems.

Wind Vane (114) – weather instrument used to determine the direction of the wind.

Winter Solstice (142, 161) – occurs about December 21, when the Sun is over theTtropic of Capricorn.

X-ray (141) – relatively high-energy photon with wavelength in the approximate range from 0.01 to 10 nanometers.

Yearly Temperatures (143) – Earth's annual surface temperature due to insolation.

Zenith (161) – point on the celestial sphere that is directly above the observer.

Zone of Aeration (139, 140) – portion of ground through which water passes until the water reaches the zone of saturation.

Zone of Convergence (120) – region of low pressure.

Zone of Divergence (120) – region of high pressure.

Zone of Saturation (140) – portion of ground with an upper boundary called the water table.

PART A
Answer all questions in this part.

Directions (1-35): For *each* statement or question, select the word or expression that, of those given, best completes the statement or answers the question. Some questions may require the use of the *2010 Edition Earth Science Reference Tables*.

1 Why do the planets in our solar system have a layered internal structure?
(1) All planets cooled rapidly after they formed.
(2) The Sun exerts a gravitational force on the planets.
(3) Each planet is composed of materials of different densities.
(4) Cosmic dust settled in layers on the planets' surfaces.

2 The diagram at the right shows a large pendulum in motion over an 8-hour period.

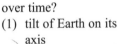

What is the main reason the pendulum appears to change its direction of swing over time?
(1) tilt of Earth on its axis
(2) rotation of Earth on its axis
(3) revolution of Earth in its orbit
(4) speed of Earth in its orbit

3 On which day of the year does the Sun reach the greatest altitude at solar noon in New York City?
(1) June 21   (3) August 21
(2) July 21   (4) September 21

4 Cosmic background radiation provides direct evidence for the origin of
(1) the universe   (3) Earth's ozone layer
(2) our solar system   (4) Earth's earliest atmosphere

5 Planetary winds and ocean currents are deflected to the right in the Northern Hemisphere and to the left in the Southern Hemisphere due to
(1) seasonal changes   (3) the Doppler effect
(2) plate tectonics   (4) the Coriolis effect

6 What is the approximate altitude of Polaris at Syracuse, New York?
(1) 43°   (3) 76°
(2) 47°   (4) 90°

7 Most rocks that form from fragmental rock particles are classified as
(1) extrusive igneous   (3) clastic sedimentary
(2) intrusive igneous   (4) chemical sedimentary

8 Which group of organisms has the shortest record of life on Earth?
(1) eurypterids   (3) birds
(2) graptolites   (4) placoderm fish

9 What is inferred to be the main source of the free oxygen that first entered Earth's atmosphere?
(1) meteorite impacts releasing oxygen
(2) oxygen-producing organisms
(3) melting of glacial ice into hydrogen and oxygen
(4) radioactive decay of rocks containing oxygen

10 The drill-core samples at the right were taken from two locations 1000 kilometers apart. Rock layers 1 through 8 have been labeled. Some index fossils are shown in the layers.

Drill Core 1   Drill Core 2

Which numbered layers most likely formed at the same time?
(1) 1 and 6   (3) 3 and 5
(2) 2 and 8   (4) 4 and 7

11 A tree in New York State casts a shadow as shown in the diagram at the right. What time of day and season are represented by the diagram?

(1) early morning in winter
(2) early morning in summer
(3) late afternoon in winter
(4) late afternoon in summer

12 Near which two latitudes are most of Earth's major deserts located?
(1) 0° and 90° N   (3) 30° N and 30° S
(2) 30° S and 60° S   (4) 60° S and 60° N

13 How much of an 800-gram sample of potassium-40 will remain after 3.9×10^9 years of radioactive decay?
(1) 50 grams   (3) 200 grams
(2) 100 grams   (4) 400 grams

14 Thin layers of volcanic ash act as excellent time markers in the correlation of bedrock because volcanic ash
(1) is easily eroded and lasts only a short time on Earth's surface
(2) stays in the atmosphere for millions of years
(3) is deposited over millions of years
(4) falls to Earth over a large area in a short period of time

15 Evidence indicates that 251 million years ago a mass extinction of many life-forms occurred on Earth. Which form of life became extinct at this time?
(1) trilobites   (3) mammoths
(2) dinosaurs   (4) eurypterids

16 What is the dewpoint when the air temperature is 26°C and the relative humidity is 77%?
(1) 3°C   (2) 20°C   (3) 22°C   (4) 23°C

17 On the map at the right, dark-gray areas represent regions of lake-effect snow on a December day.

Which New York State location appears to be experiencing a lake-effect snow-storm?

(1) New York City   (3) Plattsburgh
(2) Utica   (4) Watertown

18 The cross section at the right shows the general bedrock structure of an area containing three different

A   B   C

2 km

(Not drawn to scale)

landscape regions, A, B, and C. Which list correctly identifies the type of landscapes represented by letters A, B, and C?
(1) A = plain, B = plateau, C = mountain
(2) A = mountain, B = plateau, C = plain
(3) A = mountain, B = plain, C = plateau
(4) A = plateau, B = plain, C = mountain

19 In New York State, the surface bedrock of the Catskills consists mainly of
(1) weakly consolidated gravels and sands
(2) quartzites, dolostones, marbles, and schists
(3) conglomerates, red sandstones, basalt, and diabase
(4) limestones, shales, sandstones, and conglomerates

20 The topographic map at the right shows a stream crossing several contour lines and passing through points X and Y. Elevations are measured in feet. What is the approximate gradient between point X and point Y?

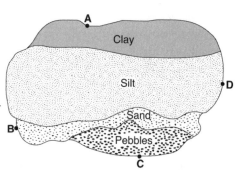

(1) 10 ft/mi   (3) 40 ft/mi
(2) 20 ft/mi   (4) 80 ft/mi

21 The map at the right shows an overhead view of sediments that have accumulated at the bottom of a lake. Points A through D represent locations on the shoreline of the lake. A river most likely flows into the lake nearest to location

(1) A   (3) C
(2) B   (4) D

22 An increase in which gas in Earth's atmosphere will most significantly increase global temperatures?
(1) methane   (3) nitrogen
(2) oxygen   (4) hydrogen

23 The topographic map at the right shows two hills located in upstate New York.

Which agent of erosion is most responsible for the shape of these hills?
(1) wind
(2) gravity
(3) waves
(4) glaciers

24 During an El Niño event, surface water temperatures increase along the west coast of South America. Which weather changes are likely to occur in this region?
(1) decreased air temperature and decreased precipitation
(2) decreased air temperature and increased precipitation
(3) increased air temperature and increased precipitation
(4) increased air temperature and decreased precipitation

25 The diagram at the right shows air movement over a mountain.

Compared to the climate on the windward side of the mountain, the climate on the leeward side of the mountain is
(1) drier and warmer   (3) more humid and warmer
(2) drier and cooler   (4) more humid and cooler

26 Which factor has the greatest influence on the number of daylight hours that a particular Earth surface location receives?
(1) longitude   (3) diameter of Earth
(2) latitude   (4) distance from the Sun

27 Energy is transferred from *Barnard's Star* to Earth mainly by
(1) red shifts   (3) conduction
(2) density currents   (4) electromagnetic waves

28 A stream's velocity decreases from 100 cm/s to 5 cm/s. Which size sediment particles will still be transported by the stream?
(1) pebbles, sand, silt, and clay
(2) sand, silt, and clay, only
(3) silt and clay, only
(4) clay, only

29 Which diagram most accurately represents the relative diameters of Earth and Mercury?

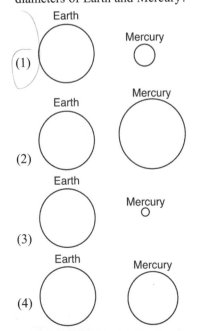

30 Which diagram represents the tilt of Earth's axis relative to the Sun's rays on December 15?

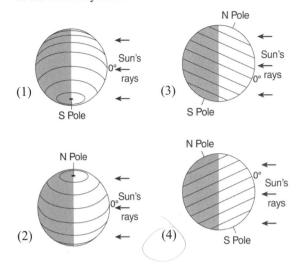

31 The cross section below shows four rock units, A, B, C, and D.

Which rock unit is youngest in age?
(1) A   (2) B   (3) C   (4) D

32 The incomplete flowchart below shows some of the changes that occur in warm air as it rises to form a cloud.

Which statement should be placed in the empty box to accurately complete the flowchart?
(1) The air warms as it expands.
(2) The air cools until it reaches the dewpoint.
(3) The air's relative humidity decreases to zero.
(4) The air enters the thermosphere.

33 The highest surface wind speeds occur when there is a
(1) 4-millibar air-pressure difference between two nearby locations
(2) 4-millibar air-pressure difference between two distant locations
(3) 20-millibar air-pressure difference between two nearby locations
(4) 20-millibar air-pressure difference between two distant locations

34 The block diagram at the right shows a portion of Earth's crust.

Which stream drainage pattern is most likely present on this crustal surface?

(1)   (2)   (3)   (4)

35 The contour map at the right shows elevations recorded in meters. Line *AB* is a reference line on the map.

Which graph best represents the profile from point *A* to point *B*?

(1)

(2)

(3)

(4)

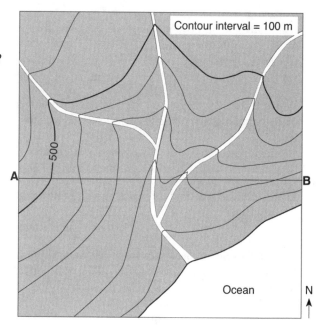

Part B–1
Answer all questions in this part.

Directions (36–50): For *each* statement or question, write the *number* of the word or expression that, of those given, best completes the statement or answers the question. Some questions may require the use of the *Earth Science Reference Tables*.

Base your answers to questions 36 through 40 on the diagram at the right, which represents zones of Earth's interior, identified by letters *A* through *E*. The scale shows depths below Earth's surface, measured in kilometers.

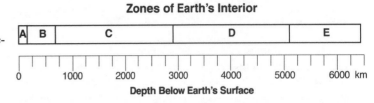

Zones of Earth's Interior

Depth Below Earth's Surface

36 The Moho is a boundary located in zone
   (1) *A*   (2) *B*   (3) *E*   (4) *D*

37 What is the approximate thickness of zone *C*?
   (1) 650 km   (2) 1600 km   (3) 2250 km   (4) 2900 km

38 Which zone is characterized by partially melted rock and large-scale convection currents?
   (1) zone *A*   (2) zone *B*   (3) zone *C*   (4) zone *E*

39 Which zone of Earth's interior has a density closest to the densities of the other terrestrial planets?
   (1) zone *A*   (2) zone *E*   (3) zone *C*   (4) zone *D*

40 *S*-waves produced by an earthquake are transmitted through zones
   (1) *A* and *B*, but not zones *C*, *D*, and *E*   (3) *C*, *D*, and *E*, but not zones *A* and *B*
   (2) *A*, *B*, and *C*, but not zones *D* and *E*   (4) *D* and *E*, but not zones *A*, *B*, and *C*

Base your answers to questions 41 through 43 on the data table at the right, which lists some properties of four minerals that are used as ores of zinc (Zn).

Mineral Property	Mineral			
	Smithsonite	**Sphalerite**	**Willemite**	**Zincite**
Composition	$ZnCO_3$	ZnS	Zn_2SiO_4	ZnO
Hardness	4–4.5	3.5–4	5.5	4
Density (g/cm³)	4.4	4.0	4.0	5.6
Color	white, gray, green, blue, yellow	brown, yellow, red, green, black	white, yellow, green, reddish brown, black	deep red to orange yellow
Streak	white	white to yellow to brown	white	orange yellow

41 A mineral with a hardness of 5 would scratch
   (1) all four zinc minerals in the table
   (2) zincite, but not sphalerite, smithsonite, or willemite
   (3) zincite and sphalerite, but not smithsonite or willemite
   (4) zincite, sphalerite, and smithsonite, but not willemite

42 A sample of sphalerite has a mass of 176.0 grams. What is the volume of the sample?
   (1) 22.7 cm³   (2) 31.4 cm³   (3) 40.0 cm³   (4) 44.0 cm³

43 Which mineral belongs in the same mineral group as quartz and olivine?
   (1) zincite   (2) willemite   (3) sphalerite   (4) smithsonite

---

Base your answers to questions 44 through 46 on the map at the right, which shows a portion of the continent of North America and outlines the Mississippi River watershed. Points *A*, *B*, *C*, *D*, and *E* represent locations on Earth's surface.

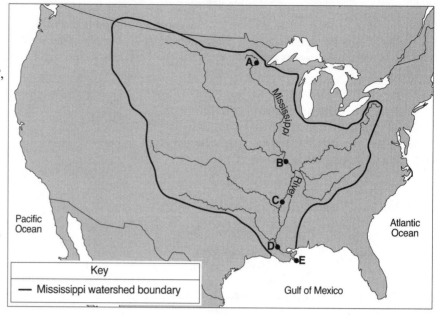

44 At which location would the Mississippi River's discharge most likely be the greatest?
(1) *A*   (3) *C*
(2) *B*   (4) *D*

45 Sediments deposited by the river at location *B* are best described as
(1) sorted and layered
(2) sorted and not layered
(3) unsorted and layered
(4) unsorted and not layered

46 Which landform is produced at location *E* where the Mississippi River enters the Gulf of Mexico?
(1) a delta   (2) a drumlin   (3) an escarpment   (4) an outwash plain

---

Base your answers to questions 47 through 50 on the calendar at the right, which shows the month of July of a recent year. The dates of major Moon phases, as seen in New York State, are shown.

July

Sunday	Monday	Tuesday	Wednesday	Thursday	Friday	Saturday
1	2	3	4	5	6	7
8	9	10	11	12	13	14
15	16	17	18	19	20	21
22	23	24	25	26	27	28
29	30	31				

Key
- New Moon
- First-quarter Moon
- Full Moon
- Last-quarter Moon

47 The diagram below represents the phase of the Moon observed from New York State one night during the month of July.

On which date was this phase of the Moon visible from New York State?
(1) July 4   (2) July 11   (3) July 19   (4) July 26

48 On which date will the next first-quarter Moon phase occur?
(1) August 6   (2) August 10   (3) August 16   (4) August 22

49 Eclipses do *not* occur every month because the Moon's
(1) rate of rotation is 15° each hour
(2) orbit is inclined to Earth's orbit
(3) period of revolution is 27.3 days
(4) period of rotation and period of revolution are the same

50 Why does the Moon's gravity have a greater effect on Earth's ocean tides than the Sun's gravity?
(1) The Sun is composed mostly of gases.   (3) The Moon has a greater mass.
(2) The Sun's gravity influences more planets.   (4) The Moon is much closer to Earth.

Answer all questions in this part.

Directions (51–65): Record your answers in the spaces provided. Some questions may require the use of the 2010 Edition of the *Earth Science Reference Tables*.

Base your answers to questions 51 and 52 on the block diagram and information below. The diagram is of the Niagara Falls region as viewed from the north.

The Niagara River began to flow over the Niagara Escarpment about 12,000 years ago when the last Pleistocene ice sheet melted and retreated north from the Niagara Escarpment. Since that time, Niagara Falls has eroded upriver, leaving a deep, steepsided valley that is 11,000 meters long. The top bedrock layer of the escarpment is the Lockport dolostone which lies above the Rochester shale. The shale is more easily weathered than the dolostone. This causes the dolostone to be undercut. As a result, the dolostone breaks off in large blocks that tumble to the base of Niagara Falls.

51 In which New York State landscape region is Niagara Falls located? [1]

Erie-Ontario Lowlands

52 Toward which compass direction is the location of Niagara Falls likely to move in the future? [1]

Toward the _West Southwest_

Base your answers to questions 53 through 55 on the diagram at the right, which represents Earth's water cycle. The arrows represent some water cycle processes. Letter *A* indicates a surface location on Earth.

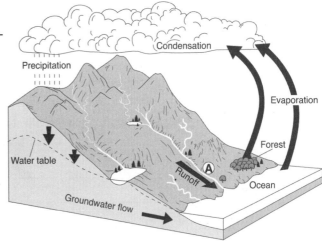

53 Other than evaporation, which water cycle process transfers large amounts of water vapor into the atmosphere from the forest? [1]

transpiration

54 Describe *one* surface condition change at location *A* that would *decrease* the rate of runoff. [1]

55 How many joules (**J**) of heat energy are released by each gram of water vapor that condenses to form cloud droplets? [1]

2260 **J**

Base your answers to questions 56 through 59 on the graphs and map below. The map shows a view of Earth from above the North Pole. Points on the map indicate the positions of Reykjavik, Iceland, and Yakutsk, Russia. The graphs show average monthly air temperature (line graphs) and amount of precipitation (bar graphs) for both locations.

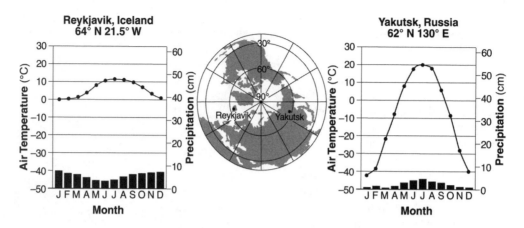

56 Write the two-letter weather map symbol for an air mass that originates over Yakutsk. [1]

cP

57 Explain why Reykjavik has cooler summers and warmer winters than Yakutsk. [1]

It has a maritime airmass, meaning more balanced weather

58 Describe *one* way the yearly precipitation in Yakutsk differs from that in Reykjavik. [1]

There's a lot more of it in May, June and July

59 Identify *one* warm and *one* cool ocean current that affect the climate of Iceland. [1]

Warm: Norwegian   Cold: East Greenland

Base your answers to questions 60 through 65 on the star chart at the right, which shows the locations of several constellations visible in the night sky. These constellations appear to move counterclockwise around the star in the center of the chart. Straight lines are at 15-degree intervals. *Merak* and *Dubhe* are two stars in the Big Dipper.

(Not drawn to scale)

60 Identify the star located in the center of this star chart. [1]

Polaris

61 How many degrees would the star directly below the "ss" in Cassiopeia appear to move in 3 hours? [1]

45 °

62 Which Earth motion causes the apparent daily movement of these constellations? [1]

Rotation

63 Complete the table below by identifying the classification of the star *Dubhe*. The classification for the star *Merak* has been provided as an example. [1]

Star	Luminosity	Temperature (K)	Classification
Merak	50	10,000	main sequence
Dubhe	230	4,800	

64 The stars *Merak* and *Dubhe* are located within the same galaxy as our Sun. Identify the galaxy in which these stars are located. [1]

Milky Way

65 On the chart of the night sky below, place an **X** to indicate the location of the Big Dipper at the same time of night 6 months later. [1]

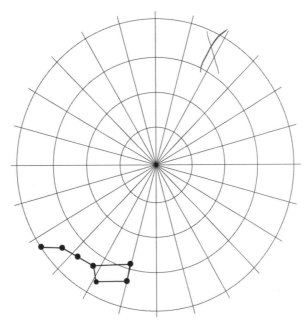

Answer all questions in this part.

Directions (66–85): Record your answers in the spaces provided. Some questions may require the use of the *Earth Science Reference Tables*.

Base your answers to questions 66 through 68 on the table at the right, which shows information about five large objects in the Kuiper Belt. The Kuiper Belt is located approximately 30 to 1000 astronomical units (AU) from the Sun. An astronomical unit is the average distance between Earth and the Sun, 149.6 million kilometers.

Kuiper Belt Data

| Kuiper Belt Objects | Orbit Characteristics | | | Approximate Equatorial Diameter (km) |
	Closest Distance to the Sun (AU)	Farthest Distance from the Sun (AU)	Eccentricity	
Varuna	40.47	45.13	0.053	900
Eris	37.77	97.56	0.442	2400
Quaoar	41.92	45.28	0.039	1260
Sedna	76.15	975.05	0.855	1500
Ixion	30.04	49.36	0.243	1065

66 The diagram at the right shows the orbits of some of the planets in our solar system. The approximate average distances from the Sun, in astronomical units, are indicated. On the diagram, place an **X** to show the closest distance of Ixion to the Sun. [1]

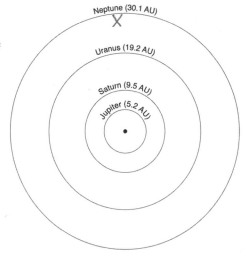

67 On the graph at the right, construct a bar graph of the equatorial diameter of each of the Kuiper Belt objects listed in the table. The diameter of Earth's Moon has been graphed for comparison. [1]

68 Identify the Kuiper Belt object with the longest period of revolution and state the evidence that supports that conclusion. [1]

Object: _Sedna_

Evidence: _It's the furthest from the sun, therefore it takes the longest to revolve_

69 On the weather station model at the right, using the proper format, record the *four* weather conditions shown below. [1]

Dewpoint: 48°F
Air pressure: 998.3 mb
Wind: from the southeast
Wind speed: 10 knots

Base your answers to questions 70 through 74 on the two maps below. Map 1 shows air temperatures in the United States and Mexico, recorded in °F, at the points shown on the map. Map 2 shows the location of a low-pressure system at the time these air temperatures were measured. An occluded front extends from the center of the low-pressure system (**L**) to point *A*. Lines *AB* and *AC* are two other frontal boundaries. Two air masses are shown. The storm system later moved toward New York State and produced an ice storm.

70 On map 1 at the right, draw the 32°F isotherm. [1]

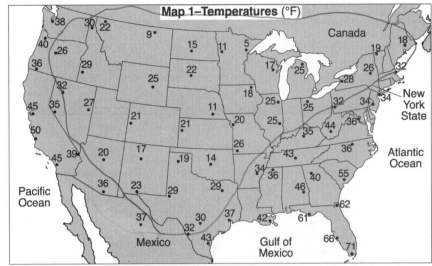

71 On map 2 at the right, draw weather front symbols on the correct sides of both line *AB* and line *AC* to show the most probable type and direction of movement of each front. [1]

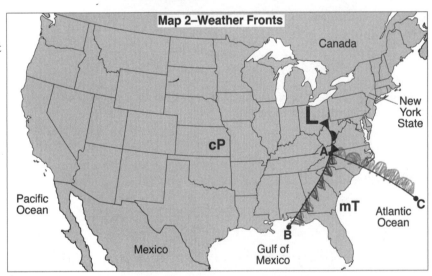

72 Describe the general surface wind pattern associated with the low-pressure system shown on map 2. [1]

Counter-clockwise & toward

73 Explain what caused the center of this low-pressure system to move toward New York State. [1]

The wacky wind belt/Jet stream

74 State *one* action New York State residents should have taken to prepare for the approaching ice storm. [1]

Lock doors, get blankets, hot chocolate

Base your answers to questions 75 through 79 on the block diagram below, which shows rock units that have not been overturned. Point *A* is located in the zone of contact metamorphism. A New York State index fossil is shown in one of the rock units.

(Not drawn to scale)

Key
+ + + Rhyolite
⊔⊔⊔⊔ Contact metamorphism

75 State the evidence shown by the block diagram that supports the inference that the fault is older than the rhyolite. [1]

The fault doesn't go through the Rhyolite

76 Identify the geologic time period when the index fossil shown in the block diagram was a living organism. [1]

Devonian **Period**

77 Identify the crystal size of the minerals in rhyolite and explain what this size indicates about the rate of cooling of the magma from which it formed. [1]

Crystal size: _Less than 1mm_

Explanation: _The faster a rock cools, the smaller the crystals_

78 Identify the metamorphic rock that most likely formed at point *A*. [1]

Quartzite

79 Describe *one* piece of evidence that would indicate that the valley shown on the surface of the block diagram had been eroded and deepened by a glacier. [1]

Its U-shaped

Base your answers to questions 80 through 85 on the passage below and map at the right. The map shows the volcanic island, Krakatau, before and after the 1883 eruption.

Volcanic Island of Krakatau

Part of Krakatau Island destroyed in 1883

Krakatau Island today

Krakatau

On August 27, 1883, one of the largest volcanic eruptions ever recorded in history occurred. Krakatau, a volcanic island nearly 800 meters in height, located at 6° S 105.5° E, exploded. Two-thirds of the island was destroyed by the blast. Blocks of pumice produced by the eruption were found floating in the ocean for months afterward.

Tsunamis produced by the eruption reached heights of 40 meters as they came ashore on nearby islands. These destructive waves traveled 6360 kilometers in just 12 hours. Over 36,000 people died and 165 coastal villages were destroyed.

Volcanic ash was blasted into the atmosphere to heights between 36 and 48 kilometers. Global temperatures cooled as the ash traveled on air currents around the world.

80 The diagram at the right shows where Krakatau formed, then exploded. Draw *one* arrow on each lithospheric plate to show the relative direction that both plates are moving to produce this type of volcano. [1]

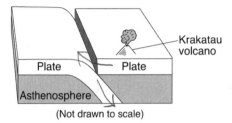

Krakatau volcano

Plate   Plate

Asthenosphere

(Not drawn to scale)

81 The diagram at the right represents an average size person standing next to a tall building. Draw a horizontal line across the building to show the maximum height of the tsunami waves produced by the 1883 eruption of Krakatau. [1]

82 Determine the rate the tsunamis traveled across the ocean. Label your answer with the correct units. [1]

$$\frac{6360}{12} = 530$$

Rate = _____ 530 k/h _____

Scale: 1 centimeter = 5 meters

83 Identify the layer of the atmosphere into which the highest volcanic ash was blasted from the Krakatau eruption. [1]

_____ Stratosphere _____

84 Explain how the volcanic ash from the Krakatau eruption caused global temperatures to decrease. [1]

The ash blocked out sunlight

85 Describe the texture and density of pumice that allowed the blocks of pumice to float on the ocean. [1]

Texture: _____ Vesicular _____

Density: _____ Not much; less than 1.0 _____

STOP

PART A

Answer all questions in this part.

Directions (1-35): For *each* statement or question, select the word or expression that, of those given, best completes the statement or answers the question. Some questions may require the use of the *2010 Edition Earth Science Reference Tables.*

1 The diagram at the right shows the orbital paths of Earth, Mars, Jupiter, and a comet named Wild 2. What is the approximate distance between the Sun and Wild 2 when this comet is closest to the Sun?
(1) 150 million kilometers
(2) 228 million kilometers
(3) 778 million kilometers
(4) 820 million kilometers

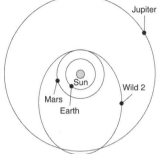
(Not drawn to scale)

2 The Sun revolves around the center of
(1) *Polaris*
(2) *Aldebaran*
(3) Earth
(4) the Milky Way Galaxy

3 Which motion is responsible for the regular seasonal changes of the constellations visible in the night sky?
(1) The stars orbit Earth.
(2) The stars orbit the Sun.
(3) The Moon orbits Earth.
(4) Earth orbits the Sun.

4 What evidence suggests that a mass extinction of the dinosaurs occurred at the end of the Cretaceous Period?
(1) an absence of dinosaur fossils in Paleocene bedrock
(2) drawings of dinosaurs made by humans in caves during the Paleocene Epoch
(3) an abundance of dinosaur fossils in Early Cretaceous bedrock
(4) evolution of dinosaurs during the Late Cretaceous Epoch

5 Compared to Jovian planets, terrestrial planets have
(1) larger masses
(2) larger equatorial diameters
(3) shorter periods of revolution
(4) shorter periods of rotation

6 The motion of a Foucault pendulum provides evidence that Earth
(1) varies in distance from the Sun
(2) is tilted on its axis
(3) spins on its axis
(4) travels around the Sun

7 In the Northern Hemisphere, planetary winds deflect to the
(1) right, due to the Coriolis effect
(2) right, due to the Doppler effect
(3) left, due to the Coriolis effect
(4) left, due to the Doppler effect

8 Which air mass is associated with low relative humidity and high air temperature?
(1) maritime polar   (3) continental polar
(2) maritime tropical   (4) continental tropical

9 The arrows in the block diagram at the right show the movement of water after it has fallen as precipitation. Which arrow indicates the process of transpiration?
(1) 1
(2) 2
(3) 3
(4) 4

10 What are the dewpoint and wind direction shown on the station model at the right?
(1) 72°F and wind from the northeast
(2) 72°F and wind from the southeast
(3) 74°F and wind from the northwest
(4) 74°F and wind from the southwest

11 Most of the air in the lower troposphere at the equatorial low-pressure belt is
(1) warm, moist, and rising
(2) warm, dry, and rising
(3) cool, moist, and sinking
(4) cool, dry, and sinking

12 The diagram at the right shows dry-bulb and wet-bulb temperature readings for a parcel of air. What is the dewpoint of the air?
(1) 27°C
(2) 10°C
(3) 3°C
(4) –5°C

Dry-bulb temperature   Wet-bulb temperature

13 Which atmospheric temperature zone is located between 8 and 32 miles above Earth's surface and contains an abundance of ozone?
(1) troposphere
(2) stratosphere
(3) mesosphere
(4) thermosphere

14 Which natural event temporarily slows or reverses surface ocean currents in the equatorial region of the Pacific Ocean, causing a disruption of normal weather patterns?
(1) monsoons   (3) El Niño
(2) volcanic eruptions (4) deforestation

15 Which form of electromagnetic energy has the longest wavelength?
(1) ultraviolet rays
(2) visible light
(3) gamma rays
(4) radio waves

16 The table below shows the average January air temperature from 1901 to 2006 in two different cities in New York State.

Data Table

City	Average January Air Temperature (°F)
Albany	21.4
New York City	29.7

The most likely cause of this air temperature difference is that New York City is located
(1) in a different prevailing wind belt
(2) at a higher latitude
(3) near a large body of water
(4) at a higher elevation

17 Which igneous rock has a vesicular texture and a felsic composition?
(1) pumice
(2) basalt
(3) granite
(4) scoria

18 Which radioactive element is used to determine the absolute age of late Pleistocene animal remains?
(1) rubidium-87
(2) uranium-238
(3) potassium-40
(4) carbon-14

19 Which mineral precipitates from oceans and forms rock salt?
(1) quartz
(2) fluorite
(3) halite
(4) olivine

20 Which river in New York State flows for several miles over surface bedrock that is more than 542 million years old?
(1) Mohawk
(2) Susquehanna
(3) Genesee
(4) Hudson

21 Which sediment is most easily picked up and transported by the wind?
(1) cobbles
(2) pebbles
(3) sand
(4) silt

22 The presence of coal in Antarctica indicates that
(1) forests can grow on continental glaciers
(2) coal can form in cold climates
(3) Antarctica's climate was once warmer
(4) Antarctica currently has areas of tropical climate

23 Organisms that later became good index fossils lived over a
(1) wide geographic area and existed for a long geologic time
(2) wide geographic area and existed for a short geologic time
(3) limited geographic area and existed for a long geologic time
(4) limited geographic area and existed for a short geologic time

24 The cross section of Earth at the right shows a *P*-wave moving away from an earthquake epicenter to seismic station *A*. No *S*-waves arrive directly at seismic station *A* because

(1) some parts of the core are liquid
(2) *S*-waves travel too slowly
(3) the distance to seismic station *A* is too great
(4) seismic station *A* is located on glacial ice

25 Which graph best represents the textures of granite, pegmatite, and rhyolite?

(1)   (3)

(3)   (4)

26 Which type of surface bedrock is commonly found in New York State between Elmira and Ithaca?
(1) granite
(2) quartzite
(3) shale
(4) marble

27 New York's Tug Hill landscape region is classified as a plateau because this region has a
(1) high elevation with distorted bedrock
(2) high elevation with nearly horizontal layers of bedrock
(3) low elevation with distorted bedrock
(4) low elevation with nearly horizontal layers of bedrock

28 Which two locations are found in the same major geographic landscape province?
(1) Albany and Old Forge
(2) Elmira and Riverhead
(3) Jamestown and Slide Mountain
(4) Massena and Mount Marcy

29 Which mineral is most frequently found in both granitic continental crust and basaltic oceanic crust?
(1) olivine
(2) potassium feldspar
(3) plagioclase feldspar
(4) quartz

30 The map at the right shows a meandering stream as it enters a lake. The arrow shows the direction of stream flow. Points *A* through *D* represent locations on the surface of the stream. The greatest stream velocities are found closest to points

(1) *A* and *B*
(2) *B* and *C*
(3) *C* and *D*
(4) *D* and *A*

31 The diagram below shows Earth and the Moon in four locations during their orbits. Arrows *A* through *D* represent different motions of Earth, the Moon, and the Sun.

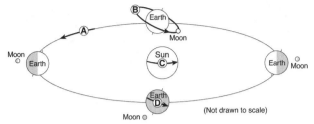

(Not drawn to scale)

Which arrow represents a rate of movement of approximately 1° per day?
(1) *A*   (3) *C*
(2) *B*   (4) *D*

32 The diagram below shows columns *A*, *B*, *C*, and *D* that contain different sediments. Equal volumes of water were poured through each column.

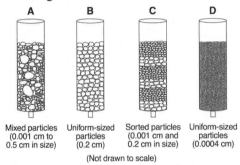

Mixed particles (0.001 cm to 0.5 cm in size) Uniform-sized particles (0.2 cm) Sorted particles (0.001 cm and 0.2 cm in size) Uniform-sized particles (0.0004 cm)

(Not drawn to scale)

Which column of sediment retained the most water?
(1) *A*   (3) *C*
(2) *B*   (4) *D*

33 The weather map at the right shows a portion of the United States. Line *AB* represents a frontal boundary between two air masses. The two large arrows indicate the direction that a cP air mass is moving.

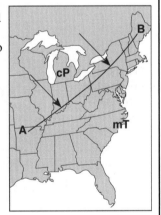

Which symbol correctly represents the frontal boundary at line *AB*?

34 Which cross section below best shows the locations of high air pressure and low air pressure near a beach on a hot, sunny, summer afternoon?

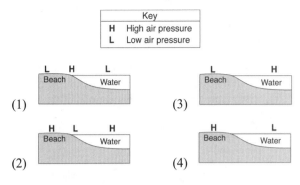

35 The diagram below shows the flow of air over a mountain, from location *A* to *B* to *C*.

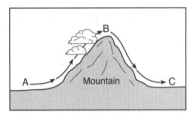

Which graph best shows how the air temperature and probability of precipitation change during this air movement?

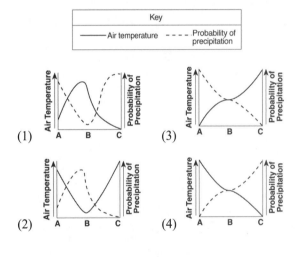

Part B–1
Answer all questions in this part.

Directions (36–50): For each statement or question, write the *number* of the word or expression that, of those given, best completes the statement or answers the question. Some questions may require the use of the *2010 Edition Reference Tables for Physical Setting/Earth Science.*

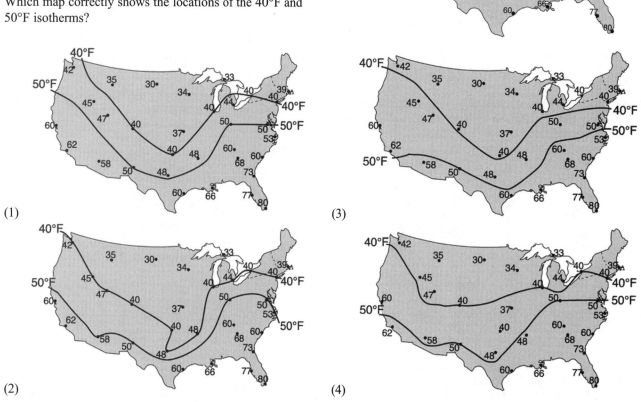

36 The weather map at the right shows the air temperatures recorded at the same time at cities across the United States. Which map correctly shows the locations of the 40°F and 50°F isotherms?

(1)

(2)

(3)

(4)

Base your answers to questions 37 through 39 on the map at the right and the passage below. The map shows the extent of summer ice-melt zones on Greenland in 1992 and 2002. The summer melt zone is an area where summer heat turns snow and ice around the edges of the ice sheet into slush and ponds of meltwater. Three coastal locations are shown on the map.

Arctic Meltdown

Scientists are concerned because average arctic temperatures are rising. The Greenland Ice Sheet, the dominant area of continental ice in the arctic region, broke all previous records for melting in 2002.

In 2004, the total amount of ice resting on top of the continental crust in the arctic region was estimated to be about 3,100,000 cubic kilometers. If all this ice were to melt, the ocean levels would rise approximately 8.5 meters. A reduction in ice-covered areas exposes more land surfaces. This increases absorption of insolation and accelerates arctic warming. Scientists continue to collect data to define the role of greenhouse gases in the warming of the arctic region.

Key		
Summer melt zone 1992	Land	
Unmelted ice sheet	Additional summer melt zone 2002	

37 Two of the greenhouse gases that may be responsible for the increased ice melting in Greenland are
(1) nitrogen and oxygen
(2) oxygen and silicon
(3) hydrogen and helium
(4) carbon dioxide and methane

38 What is the approximate latitude and longitude of Godthab, Greenland?
(1) 51.5° N 64° W
(2) 70.5° N 22° W
(3) 64° N 51.5° W
(4) 22° N 70.5° W

39 A decrease in areas covered in snow and ice leads to an increase in the absorption of insolation because exposed land surfaces are
(1) rougher and darker
(2) rougher and lighter
(3) smoother and darker
(4) smoother and lighter

Base your answers to questions 40 through 42 on the map at the right, which shows coral reef distribution and diversity (number of different coral types) around the world. Isolines on the map represent the number of different types of coral. Coral reefs are found mostly in shallow tropical waters and do not grow when ocean temperatures fall below 18°C. The 18°C barrier ( ) represents the outer boundaries within which coral reefs normally grow. Points *X* and *Y* are locations on the map.

40 Which index fossil is an ancestor of the organisms whose distribution is shown on the map?

(1)

(2)

(3)

(4)

41 Which factor most likely determines why a greater number of coral types are found farther south along the east coast of southern Africa than along the west coast?
(1) angle of the Sun's rays
(2) temperature of the ocean currents
(3) distance from the equator
(4) seasonal air temperature range

42 Which graph shows the number of coral types found along the 165° east longitude line between point *X* and point *Y*?

(1)   (2)   (3)   (4)

Base your answers to questions 43 and 44 on the map and the modified Mercalli scale shown at the right. The map shows the intensities of the earthquake that occurred slightly southwest of New Madrid, Missouri, on December 16, 1811. The epicenter of this earthquake is represented by ✳. The Roman numerals on the map show zones of earthquake intensities determined by using the modified Mercalli scale.

Earthquake Intensity with Modified Mercalli Scale

Modified Mercalli Intensity Scale

I:	Not felt except under unusual conditions
II:	Felt by only a few persons Suspended objects might swing
III:	Quite noticeable indoors
IV:	Dishes and windows rattle
V:	Felt by nearly everyone Some dishes and windows break
VI:	Furniture moves Some plaster falls
VII:	Everybody runs outdoors Some chimneys break
VIII:	Chimneys, smokestacks, and walls fall Heavy furniture is overturned
IX:	Buildings shift off foundations Ground cracks
X:	Most ordinary structures are destroyed Landslides are common
XI:	Few structures remain standing Bridges are destroyed Broad cracks form in the ground
XII:	Damage is total Objects are thrown upward into the air

43 Which location would most probably have issued the report: "Many structures shifted off foundations"?
   (1) New Madrid   (3) Pittsburgh
   (2) Syracuse   (4) Nashville

44 The intensity numbers shown on the map were determined by
   (1) the arrival time of the first *P*-wave recorded at each city
   (2) the recorded time difference in the arrival of the first *P*-wave and *S*-wave at each city
   (3) observations made at different locations during and after the earthquake
   (4) observations made only at the earthquake epicenter

Base your answers to questions 45 and 46 on the map at the right, which shows the tectonic plate boundaries near the East African Rift. Arrows show relative tectonic plate movement.

A region of Africa is crosshatched ( ).

East African Rift Region

Key	
▲	Volcano
——	Plate boundaries
▬ ▬	East African Rift

45 What appears to be happening to the crosshatched region of eastern Africa?
   (1) A folded mountain range is forming as this region collides with the rest of Africa.
   (2) Several volcanic mountains are forming as the rest of Africa subducts under this region.
   (3) This region is moving eastward relative to the rest of Africa.
   (4) This region is moving northward relative to the rest of Africa.

46 Which diagram best represents the polarity of the magnetic field preserved in the ocean-floor bedrock found on both sides of the Mid-Indian Ridge?

Key
Reversed polarity
Normal polarity

(1)

(2)

(3)

(4)

Base your answers to questions 47 through 50 on the diagram at the right, which shows positions of the Moon in its orbit and phases of the Moon as viewed from New York State.

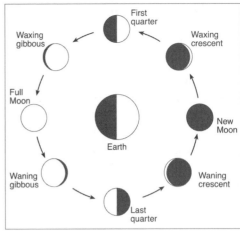

(Not drawn to scale)

47 Approximately how many days occur between the Moon's first-quarter phase and the Moon's last-quarter phase?
(1) 7 d   (3) 29.5 d
(2) 15 d   (4) 365.26 d

48 During which Moon phase might a solar eclipse be viewed on Earth?
(1) new Moon   (3) full Moon
(2) first quarter   (4) last quarter

49 What is the eccentricity of the Moon's orbit?
(1) 0.017   (3) 0.386
(2) 0.055   (4) 0.723

50 Which statement best explains why the same side of the Moon is viewed from Earth as the Moon goes through its phases?
(1) The Moon does not rotate as it revolves around Earth.
(2) The Moon's period of rotation equals Earth's period of rotation.
(3) The Moon's period of rotation equals Earth's period of revolution around the Sun.
(4) The Moon's period of rotation equals the Moon's period of revolution around Earth.

Part B–2
Answer all questions in this part.

Directions (51–65): Record your answers in the spaces provided. Some questions may require the use of the 2010 Edition Reference Tables for Physical Setting/Earth Science.

Base your answers to questions 51 through 55 on the topographic map shown below. Letters *A*, *B*, *C*, and *D* represent locations on Earth's surface. The ⚠ symbol marks the highest elevation on Patty Hill. Elevations are shown in feet.

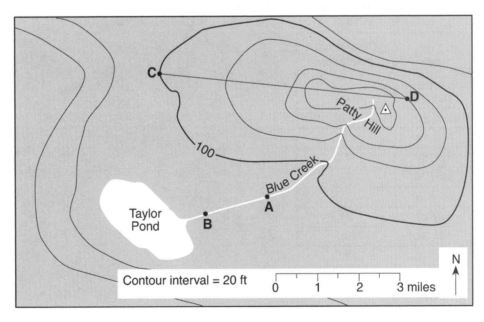

51 What is a possible elevation at the ⚠ symbol at the top of Patty Hill? [1]

_____ **ft**

52 Indicate, using a compass direction, the steepest side of Patty Hill. [1]

_____

53 Explain how the shape of the contour lines crossing Blue Creek shows the direction that the creek is flowing. [1]

_____

_____

54 A student placed a floating wooden block in Blue Creek at location *A*. Fifteen minutes later, the floating block arrived at location *B*. What was the creek's rate of flow from *A* to *B*? Express your answer to the nearest tenth. [1]

_____ **mi/min**

55 On the grid below, construct a profile of the land surface along line *CD*. Plot the elevation of each contour line that crosses line *CD*. Connect the plots with a line to complete the profile. [1]

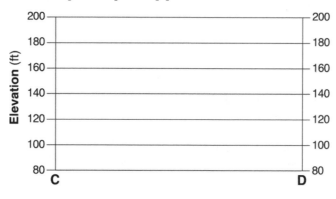

Base your answers to questions 56 through 60 on the table and map below. The table shows the duration of insolation, in hours, at Barrow, Alaska, on the twentieth day of each month during 2008. The map shows the location of Barrow at 71° N 156.5° W.

Duration of Insolation at Barrow, Alaska

Date	Duration of Insolation (h)
Jan 20	0
Feb 20	7.8
Mar 20	12.5
Apr 20	17.6
May 20	24
June 20	24
July 20	24
Aug 20	16.7
Sept 20	12.6
Oct 20	7.8
Nov 20	0
Dec 20	0

Barrow, Alaska

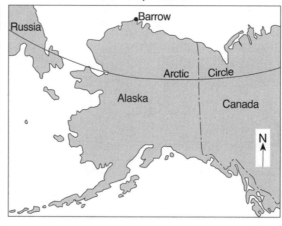

56 On the grid below, construct a line graph by plotting the data for the duration of insolation at Barrow for *each* date shown on the data table. Connect the plots with a line. [1]

57 Explain why Barrow receives 0 hours of insolation on December 20. [1]

_____

_____

58 State the altitude of *Polaris* as seen from Barrow. [1]

_____ °

59 Explain why Barrow is in a different time zone than New York City. [1]

_____

_____

60 On what date was the noontime Sun highest in the sky at Barrow? [1]

_____

_____

Base your answers to questions 61 through 63 on the cross section below, which shows water flowing out of a well drilled through tilted sedimentary bedrock. Point *A* represents a location on Earth's surface.

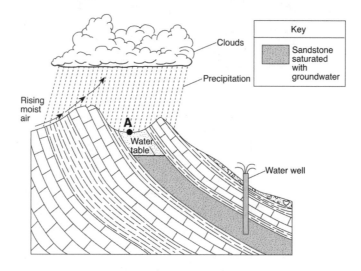

61 Describe *one* characteristic of the sandstone layer that allowed part of this layer to become saturated with groundwater. [1]

_____

62 Identify *one* process that causes the clouds to form in the rising moist air. [1]

_____

63 Explain why point *A* would be a poor location for a garbage dump or landfill. [1]

_____

_____

_____

Base your answers to questions 64 and 65 on the diagram below, which shows the locations of high and low tides on Earth at a particular time.

(Not drawn to scale)

64 Identify the force that causes ocean tides on Earth. [1]

_____

65 Approximately how many hours will pass between high tide and the following low tide? [1]

_____ **h**

_____

Answer all questions in this part.

Directions (66–85): Record your answers in the spaces provided. Some questions may require the use of the *2010 Edition Reference Tables for Physical Setting/Earth Science.*

Base your answers to questions 66 through 68 on the passage below.

Carbon

Carbon may be the most important element on our planet because it is the chemical building block of all living things. The element carbon is formed in dying stars and scattered when the stars explode. Our solar system formed from such star remnants. Pure carbon comes in several forms, which include the minerals graphite and diamond (hardness = 10), and the fossil fuels bituminous coal and anthracite coal. Almost all diamonds are mined from igneous rocks that originate at an approximate depth of 150 kilometers under immense pressure. Most graphite is formed through the metamorphism of organic material in rocks closer to Earth's surface.

66 Identify *two* uses for the mineral graphite. [1]

(1) _____

(2) _____

67 Explain why graphite and diamond have different properties. [1]

_____

_____

68 Complete the table below to show the properties of the minerals diamond and graphite. [1]

Property	Diamond	Graphite
color	variable	
luster	nonmetallic	
hardness		

Base your answers to questions 69 through 72 on the geologic cross section of bedrock in your answer booklet. Letters *A* through *G* identify rock units and line *XY* represents a fault. The rocks have not been overturned.

69 On the cross section below, draw a dark line (⌣) to indicate the most likely location of an unconformity. [1]

70 What evidence indicates that the folded bedrock is older than fault line *XY*? [1]

_____

_____

71 Identify *one* metamorphic rock that would likely form in layer *G* along igneous intrusion *A*. [1]

_____

72 *Maclurites* fossils are found in rock unit *F*. During which geologic time period were the sediments that formed rock unit *F* deposited? [1]

_____ **Period**

_____

Base your answers to questions 73 through 77 on the table below, which lists some information about *Barnard's Star*.

Barnard's Star

Distance from Sun	• 6.0 light-years* • currently moving toward the Sun (and Earth) and will get as close as 3.8 light-years in approximately 11,000 years
Characteristics of Barnard's Star	• less than 17 percent of the Sun's mass • approximately 20 percent of the Sun's diameter • age thought to be between 11 and 12 billion years old and may last another 40 billion years • no planets observed orbiting Barnard's Star

* A light-year is the distance light travels in one year.

73 The diagram below shows four spectral lines produced by glowing hydrogen gas in a laboratory and four spectral lines produced by hydrogen gas as seen in the light from *Barnard's Star*.

Laboratory spectral lines

Blue   Red

Barnard's Star spectral lines

Blue   Red

Explain why the positions of the spectral lines of *Barnard's Star* are all shifted toward the blue end of the spectrum. [1]

_____

_____

74 The distance from point *A* to point *S* on the line below represents the equatorial diameter of the Sun. On this line, place a point labeled *B* at the correct scale distance from point   to represent the equatorial diameter of *Barnard's Star*. [1]

A   S

1 centimeter = 100,000 kilometers

75 Compared to the surface temperature and luminosity of the Sun, describe the relative surface temperature and the relative luminosity of *Barnard's Star*. [1]

Relative surface temperature: _____

_____

Relative luminosity: _____

_____

76 List *Barnard's Star*, the Sun, and the universe in order by age from oldest to youngest. [1]

Oldest   (1) _____

          (2) _____

Youngest (3) _____

77 If a planet with the same mass as Earth were discovered orbiting *Barnard's Star* at the same distance that Earth is orbiting the Sun, why would there be less gravitational attraction between this new planet and *Barnard's Star* than there is between Earth and the Sun? [1]

_____

_____

_____

Base your answers to questions 78 through 82 on the weather graphs below, which show data recorded at Syracuse, New York, as a winter storm moved across the region between December 1 and December 4, 2007. Graph 1 shows air temperatures and dewpoints. Graph 2 shows barometric pressures.

78 State the relationship between the air temperature and the barometric pressure in Syracuse on December 2. [1]

_____

_____

79 On which date and at what time did the relative humidity reach 100% in Syracuse? [1]

Date: _____

Time: _____

80 On the station model below, record the barometric pressure for Syracuse at 4 p.m. on December 2. [1]

81 A radar image of this storm is shown below. The darkest regions on the radar image show areas of precipitation. Letter *L* marks the location of the center of the low-pressure system. Draw an arrow on the radar image to show the most probable path this winter storm followed. Begin the arrow at letter *L*. [1]

Radar Image

82 Complete the table below by identifying *one* instrument used to determine barometric pressure and *one* weather variable determined by using a psychrometer. [1]

Weather Variable	Instrument Used
barometric pressure	
	psychrometer

Base your answers to questions 83 through 85 on the cross section below, which represents a glacier moving down a mountain valley. The water from the melting glacier is flowing into a lake. Letter *A* represents a location on the bottom of the lake.

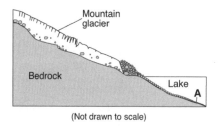

(Not drawn to scale)

83 Describe the most likely shape of a cross section of the glacial valley as viewed from the lake. [1]

84 After the glacier melts, what evidence might be found on the surface of the bedrock indicating that the glacier had passed over the surface? [1]

85 Sediments found at location *A* range in diameter from 0.0004 to 0.006 centimeter. What name is given to this size sediment? [1]

PART A

Answer all questions in this part.

Directions (1-35): For *each* statement or question, select the word or expression that, of those given, best completes the statement or answers the question. Some questions may require the use of the *2011 Edition Reference Tables for Physical Setting/Earth Science.*

1 Which planet's day (period of rotation) is longer than its year (period of revolution)?
(1) Mercury (3) Jupiter
(2) Venus (4) Saturn

2 Which event is cyclic and predictable?
(1) a volcano erupting above a subducting tectonic plate
(2) an earthquake occurring at the San Andreas Fault
(3) Jupiter's apparent movement across the night sky
(4) an asteroid striking Earth's surface

3 A high tide occurred at 6:00 a.m. at a beach on Long Island. The next high tide at this same beach would occur at approximately
(1) 12:15 p.m. on the same day
(2) 6:30 p.m. on the same day
(3) 12:45 p.m. on the following day
(4) 7:00 a.m. on the following day

4 The best evidence that Earth rotates on its axis is the changing
(1) phases of the Moon
(2) altitude of the noontime Sun from day to day
(3) apparent path of a Foucault pendulum
(4) velocity of Earth in its orbit

5 The curving of the planetary winds to the right in the Northern Hemisphere is evidence of
(1) the Coriolis effect
(2) high- and low-pressure belts
(3) Earth's revolution
(4) the tilt of Earth's axis

6 Which star is cooler and less luminous than the Sun?
(1) *Proxima Centauri* (3) *Rigel*
(2) *Pollux* (4) *40 Eridani B*

7 Seasonal changes on Earth are primarily caused by the
(1) parallelism of the Sun's axis as the Sun revolves around Earth
(2) changes in distance between Earth and the Sun
(3) elliptical shape of Earth's orbit around the Sun
(4) tilt of Earth's axis as Earth revolves around the Sun

8 A ship is at a location of 40° S 77° W. Which type of surface ocean current and tectonic plate boundary are located beneath this ship?
(1) warm ocean current and a transform boundary
(2) warm ocean current and a convergent boundary
(3) cool ocean current and a transform boundary
(4) cool ocean current and a convergent boundary

9 What best explains why, in early spring, ice remains longer on Lake Erie than on the surrounding land areas when the air temperature is above freezing?
(1) Water has a higher specific heat than land.
(2) Energy is needed for water to evaporate.
(3) Cool winds from the surrounding land cool the ice on the lake.
(4) Air temperature does not affect water temperature.

10 What controls the direction of movement of most surface ocean currents?
(1) density differences at various ocean depths
(2) varying salt content in the ocean
(3) prevailing winds
(4) seismic activity

11 Due to radioactive decay, an igneous rock sample now contains one-fourth of the amount of potassium-40 that it originally contained. The age, in years, of this rock sample is approximately
(1) 0.7×10^9 y (3) 2.6×10^9 y
(2) 1.3×10^9 y (4) 5.2×10^9 y

12 Which geologic event occured in New York State at about the same time as the extinction of dinosaurs and ammonoids?
(1) formation of the Queenston Delta
(2) deposition of the sands and clays underlying Long Island
(3) initial opening of the Atlantic Ocean
(4) advance and retreat of the last continental ice sheet

13 The geologic cross section below shows bedrock layers *A* through *D*. Line *XY* is a fault. The fault most likely occurred after
(1) all bedrock layers were formed
(2) layer *C* formed, but before layer *D* formed
(3) layer *A* formed, but before layer *B* formed
(4) layer *B* formed, but before layer *C* formed

14 The Gulf Stream and North Atlantic Current modify the climate of northwestern Europe by making the climate
(1) warmer and drier
(2) warmer and more humid
(3) cooler and drier
(4) cooler and more humid

15 What is the approximate density of a mineral with a mass of 262.2 grams that displaces 46 cubic centimeters of water?
(1) 1.8 g/cm³
(2) 5.7 g/cm³
(3) 6.1 g/cm³
(4) 12.2 g/cm³

16 Obsidian's glassy texture indicates that it formed
(1) slowly, deep below Earth's surface
(2) slowly, on Earth's surface
(3) quickly, deep below Earth's surface
(4) quickly, on Earth's surface

17 What is the color and type of rock that forms oceanic crust at mid-ocean ridges?
(1) light colored and igneous
(2) light colored and sedimentary
(3) dark colored and igneous
(4) dark colored and sedimentary

18 A plane traveling in a straight line from Watertown to Utica would fly over which landscape region?
(1) Tug Hill Plateau
(2) Adirondack Mountains
(3) St. Lawrence Lowlands
(4) Champlain Lowlands

19 Which graph best represents the correct relationship between the discharge of a river and the particle size that can be transported by that river?

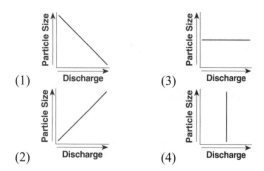

(1) (2) (3) (4)

20 The diagram at the right shows the relative positions of Earth and Mars in their orbits on a particular date during the winter of 2007. Which diagram correctly shows the locations of Earth and Mars on the same date during the winter of 2008?

(Not drawn to scale)

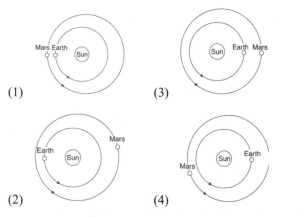

(1) (3) (2) (4)

21 A cross section of a weather front is shown at the right. Which symbol would be used to represent this front on a weather map?

(1) (2) (3) (4)

22 According to the Big Bang theory, which graph best represents the relationship between time and the size of the universe from the beginning of the universe to the present?

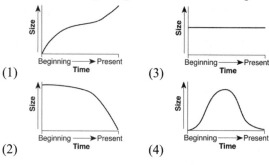

(1) (3) (2) (4)

23 Which map at the right shows the most likely storm track for a hurricane ( ) in the Atlantic Ocean?

(1)

(2)

(3)

(4)

24 The weather map below shows isobars labeled in millibars. Points *A*, *B*, *C*, and *D* are locations on Earth's surface.

Which location was probably experiencing the highest wind speed?

(1) *A*   (3) *C*
(2) *B*   (4) *D*

25 The map below shows two seasonal positions of the polar front jet stream over North America.

Which statement best explains why the position of the polar front jet stream varies with the seasons?
(1) Rising air compresses and cools in winter.
(2) Water heats and cools more rapidly than land in winter.
(3) Prevailing winds reverse direction in summer.
(4) The vertical rays of the Sun shift north of the equator in summer.

26 The cross section below shows two cities, *A* and *B*, at different elevations.

Compared to the yearly temperature and precipitation at city *B*, city *A* most likely has
(1) lower temperatures and less precipitation
(2) lower temperatures and more precipitation
(3) higher temperatures and less precipitation
(4) higher temperatures and more precipitation

27 The graph at the right shows changes in carbon dioxide concentrations in Earth's atmosphere over a 140-year period. Carbon dioxide concentrations are shown in parts per million (ppm).

This significant change in CO_2 concentration is most likely caused by

(1) decreased cloud cover, and is predicted to decrease average global temperatures
(2) decreased volcanic activity, and is predicted to increase average global temperatures
(3) increased use of fossil fuels, and is predicted to increase average global temperatures
(4) increased El Niño activity, and is predicted to decrease average global temperatures

28 The solar system object in the photograph below is 56 kilometers long. The object in the photograph is most likely

(1) an asteroid   (3) Earth's Moon
(2) Neptune   (4) Mercury

29 Which graph best shows the range of density in each of Earth's layers?

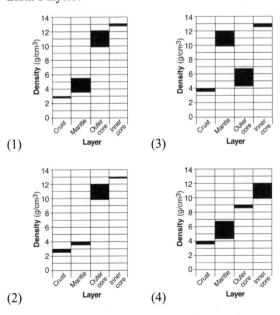

30 Which world map shows the locations where most earthquakes and volcanoes occur on Earth?

(1)

(3)

(2)

(4)

31 Which graph shows the general relationship between soil particle size and the capillarity of the soil?

(1)

(2)

(3)

(4)

32 The diagram at the right is a portion of a geologic timeline. Letters *A* through *D* represent the time intervals between the labeled events, as estimated by scientists. Fossil evidence indicates that the earliest birds developed during which time interval?

(1) *A*   (3) *C*
(2) *B*   (4) *D*

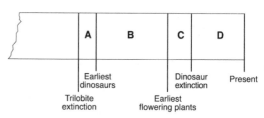

(Not drawn to scale)

33 The block diagram at the right shows a volcano. Which map shows the stream drainage pattern that most likely formed on the surface of this volcano?

(1)

(2)

(3)

(4)

34 A cross section of Niagara Falls is shown at the right. Which two rock units appear to be most resistant to weathering and erosion?
(1) Lockport dolostone and Whirlpool sandstone
(2) Rochester shale and Albion sandstone and shale
(3) Clinton limestone and shale and Queenston shale
(4) Thorold sandstone and Queenston shale

35 Which index fossil has been found in Ordovician-age bedrock?

 (1)   (2)   (3)   (4)

Part B–1
Answer all questions in this part.

Directions (36–50): For each statement or question, write the number of the word or expression that, of those given, best completes the statement or answers the question. Some questions may require the use of the 2011 Edition Reference Tables for Physical Setting/Earth Science.

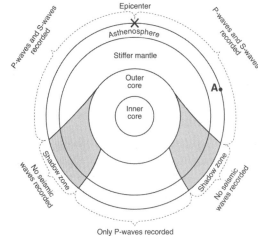

Base your answers to questions 36 and 37 on the cross section at the right, which shows the type of seismic waves recorded at various locations after an earthquake has occurred. Point *A* is a location on Earth's surface and *X* is the epicenter of the earthquake.

36 Point A is located 7600 kilometers from the epicenter of this earthquake. How many minutes did it take the first *S*-wave to reach point *A*?
(1) 9 min   (3) 16 min
(2) 11 min   (4) 20 min

37 How many kilometers did the seismic waves travel from the earthquake directly to the outside of the outer core?
(1 800 km   (3) 2900 km
(2) 1400 km   (4) 6400 km

Base your answers to questions 38 through 41 on the diagram at the right. The diagram represents the inferred stages in the formation of our solar system. Stage 1 shows a contracting gas cloud. The remaining stages show the gas cloud flattening into a spinning disk as planets formed around our Sun.

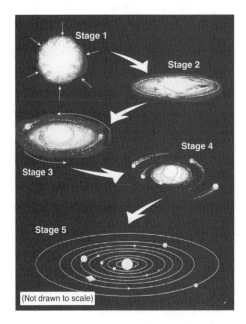

38 Which force was mostly responsible for the contraction of the gas cloud?
(1) friction   (3) magnetism
(2) gravity   (4) inertia

39 Which process was occurring during some of these stages that resulted in the formation of heavier elements from lighter elements?
(1) conduction   (3) radioactive decay
(2) radiation   (4) nuclear fusion

40 Approximately how long ago did stage 4 end and stage 5 begin?
(1) 1 billion years   (3) 20 billion years
(2) 5 billion years   (4) 100 billion years

41 Compared to the terrestrial planets, the Jovian planets in stage 5 have
(1) larger diameters   (3) shorter periods of revolution
(2) higher densities   (4) longer periods of rotation

Base your answers to questions 42 through 45 on the weather map below. The map shows isobars and seven weather station models. Four of the weather stations are identified by letters *A*, *B*, *C*, and *D*.

42 Which New York State weather station had clear skies?
(1) Albany   (3) New York City
(2) Buffalo   (4) Syracuse

43 Which weather station had the highest relative humidity?
(1) *A*   (3) *C*
(2) *B*   (4) *D*

44 What was the probable air pressure, in millibars, at station D?
(1) 1015.0 mb   (3) 1021.0 mb
(2) 1017.0 mb   (4) 1036.0 mb

45 Which weather information shown at station *B* was measured with an anemometer and weather vane?

(1) 34   (2)   (3)   (4) 138

Base your answers to questions 46 through 48 on the diagram below, which shows the edge of a continental glacier that is receding. *R* indicates elongated hills. The ridge of sediments from *X* to *Y* represents a landscape feature.

46 The elongated hills labeled *R* are most useful in determining the
(1) age of the glacier
(2) direction the glacier has moved
(3) thickness of the glacier
(4) rate at which the glacier is melting

47 Which feature will most likely form when the partially buried ice block melts?
(1) drumlin   (2) moraine   (3) kettle lake   (4) finger lake

48 The ridge of sediments from *X* to *Y* can best be described as
(1) sorted and deposited by ice   (3) unsorted and deposited by ice
(2) sorted and deposited by meltwater   (4) unsorted and deposited by meltwater

---

Base your answers to questions 49 and 50 on the time-exposure photograph shown at the right. The photograph was taken by aiming a camera at a portion of the night sky above a New York State location and leaving the camera's shutter open for a period of time to record star trails.

49 Which celestial object is shown in the photograph near the center of the star trails?
(1) the Sun   (3) *Sirius*
(2) the Moon   (4) *Polaris*

50 During the time exposure of the photograph, the stars appear to have moved through an arc of 120°. How many hours did this time exposure take?
(1) 5 h   (2) 8 h   (3) 12 h   (4) 15 h

Part B–2
Answer all questions in this part.

Directions (51–65): Record your answers in the spaces provided. Some questions may require the use of the 2011 Edition Reference Tables for Physical Setting/Earth Science.

Base your answers to questions 51 through 54 on the diagram at the right, which shows the Moon at position 1 in its orbit around Earth. Numbers 2 through 8 represent other positions in the Moon's orbit.

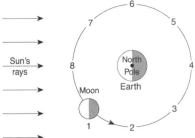

51 On the diagram at the right, shade the portion of the Moon that is in darkness as viewed from New York State when the Moon is at position 1. [1]

52 A solar eclipse could occur when the Moon is located at which numbered position? [1]

Position number: _____

53 How many days does it take the Moon to go from one full-Moon phase to the next full-Moon phase when viewed from Earth? [1]

_____ **d**

54 Identify *one* numbered orbital position where the gravitational attraction of the Moon and the Sun cause Earth to experience the highest high tides. [1]

Position number: _____

_____

Base your answers to questions 55 and 56 on the data table at the right, which shows the air temperature, in degrees Fahrenheit, and air pressure, in inches of mercury (Hg), recorded at a weather station in New York State from 11 a.m. to 7 p.m. on a day in September.

Time	Air Temperature (°F)	Air Pressure (in of Hg)
11 a.m.	77	29.81
12 noon	81	29.79
1 p.m.	84	29.77
2 p.m.	88	29.75
3 p.m.	87	29.74
4 p.m.	86	29.73
5 p.m.	85	29.73
6 p.m.	82	29.74
7 p.m.	79	29.76

55 On the grid below, construct a line graph by plotting the data for the air temperature for *each* time from 11 a.m. to 7 p.m. Connect the plots with a line. The data for air pressure have been plotted. [1]

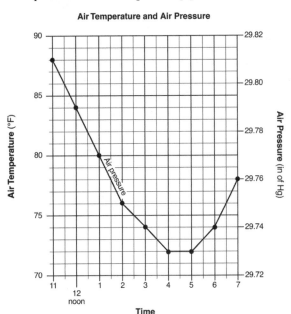

56 State the relationship between air temperature and air pressure from 11 a.m. to 2 p.m. [1]

_____

_____

_____

Base your responses to questions 57 through 59 on the passage below.

Frozen Mammoth

A wooly mammoth was found in 1999 buried in the frozen soil of the Siberian tundra. Carbon-14 dating indicated that it had died about 20,000 years ago. Many fossils represent only the partial remains of organisms. However, a complete mammoth with bones, skin, hair, and internal organs intact represented a unique opportunity for scientists to investigate the lifestyle of this animal and the environment in which it lived.

57 Identify *both* the period and epoch of geologic time during which the wooly mammoth lived. [1]

_____ **Period**

58 Identify *one* New York State index fossil of an organism that lived during the same time as the wooly mammoth. [1]

_____ **Epoch**

59 The low permeability of the tundra soil helped to preserve the mammoth. Explain why the tundra soil has a low permeability. [1]

_____

_____

_____

Base your answers to questions 60 through 62 on the passage and map of a portion of the East African Rift system shown below. Point *X* represents a location on Earth's surface within a rift valley on the Ethiopian Dome.

The Great Rift Valley

Rifting of Earth's crust in eastern Africa began during the Neogene Period as the Ethiopian and Kenyan Domes formed. These two huge domes were created as Earth's mantle pushed up the overlying crust. As the crust was forced upward, the resulting tension cracked the crust, resulting in the eruption of volcanoes and the formation of large rifts. The crust continued to pull apart, forming rift valleys. These valleys have become deeper and are currently becoming filled with sediments, igneous rock, and water.

60 How many million years ago did the Ethiopian and Kenyan Domes form? [1]

_____ **million years ago**

61 On the cross section below, draw *two* curved arrows, one on each side of the dashed line, to show the direction of movement of the convection currents within the asthenosphere that caused the formation of the dome and the rift valley near location *X*. [1]

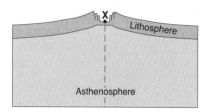

62 Which *two* lithospheric plates are separated by a mid-ocean ridge in the northeastern portion of the Ethiopian Dome? [1]

_____ **Plate** and _____ **Plate**

_____

Base your answers to questions 63 through 65 on the experiment description and diagram below.

A student was interested in how the angle of insolation affects absorption of radiation. The student took three black metal plates, each containing a built-in thermometer, and placed them at the same distance from three identical lamps. The plates were tilted so that the light from the lamps created three different angles of incidence with the center of the plates, as shown in the diagram. The starting temperatures of the plates were recorded. The lamps were turned on for 10 minutes. Then the final temperatures were recorded.

Angles of Incidence

63 Explain why the metal plate at a 90° angle of incidence had a final temperature higher than the other two plates. [1]

_____

_____

64 How would the final temperatures of the three metal plates be different if the experiment was repeated using white metal plates? Explain why the white plates would have these final temperatures. [1]

Final Temperatures: _____

Explanation: _____

_____

65 The metal plate at a 90° angle of incidence represents a location on Earth at solar noon on March 21. What is the latitude of this location? [1]

_____

_____

Part C
Answer all questions in this part.

Directions (66–85): Record your answers in the spaces provided. Some questions may require the use of the *2011 Edition Reference Tables for Physical Setting/Earth Science.*

Base your answers to questions 66 through 69 on the map in your answer booklet, which shows elevations in feet at various points. The southern part of the map has contour lines representing elevations at 20-foot intervals. Lines *AB* and *CD* are reference lines on the map.

66 On the map at the right, draw contour lines for the 780-ft, 760-ft, and 740-ft elevations. Extend your contour lines to the edges of the map. [1]

67 On the grid below right, construct a topographic profile along line *AB* by plotting the elevation of each contour line that crosses line *AB*. Connect the plots with a line to complete the profile. [1]

68 Calculate the gradient along line *CD* and label your answer with the correct units. [1]

Gradient: _____

69 Explain how the contour lines indicate the direction of flow of Otter Creek. [1]

_____

_____

_____

Base your answers to questions 70 and 71 on the diagram below, which shows some processes in the water cycle

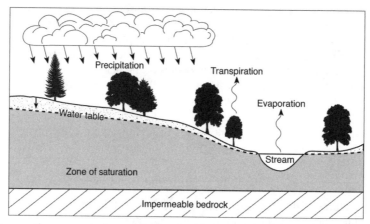

70 State the relationship between the amount of precipitation in this area and the height of the water table above the impermeable bedrock. [1]

_____

_____

71 Describe *one* change that would cause more water to evaporate from this stream. [1]

_____

_____

Base your answers to questions 72 through 75 on the diagram at the right, which shows several different landscape features. Points *X* and Y indicate locations on the streambank.

72 Explain why the upper valley in the mountains is U-shaped and the lower valley is V-shaped. [1]

   U-shaped: _____

   V-shaped: _____

73 Identify which point, *X* or *Y*, has more stream erosion and explain why the amounts of erosion are different. [1]

   Point: _____

   Explanation: _____

   _____

   _____

74 Explain why the stream meanders on the floodplain, but *not* in the mountains. [1]

_____

_____

75 The beach consists of particles with diameters from 0.01 cm to 0.1 cm. Identify the sedimentary rock that will form when burial and cementation of these sediments occur. [1]

   _____

   _____

Base your answers to questions 76 through 78 on the cross section below showing the underlying bedrock of New York and New Jersey along the Hudson River.

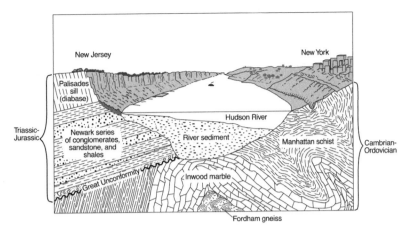

76 Identify the oldest bedrock shown in the diagram. [1]

_____

77 Describe *one* piece of evidence shown in the cross section that indicates that the Inwood marble was formed by regional metamorphism. [1]

_____

_____

78 Identify *two* processes that led directly to the development of the Great Unconformity beneath the Newark series. [1]

(1) _____

(2) _____

_____

Base your answers to questions 79 through 81 on the information below.

A student on a field trip in New York State collected a sample of metamorphic bedrock containing bands of coarse-grained crystals of plagioclase feldspar, pyroxene, quartz, and mica.

79 List *two* of the chemical elements found in plagioclase feldspar. [1]

(1) _____

(2) _____

80 Describe *two* physical properties of pyroxene. [1]

(1) _____

(2) _____

81 Identify the metamorphic rock found by the student. [1]

_____

_____

Base your answers to questions 82 through 84 on the diagram of the Sun, Earth, and the constellation Sagittarius shown below. Positions *A* through *D* show Earth in its orbit around the Sun on the first day of each season. Sagittarius is represented in its position in space relative to Earth's orbit.

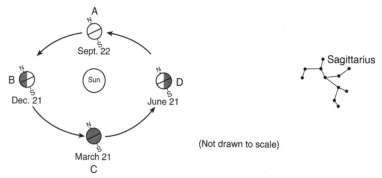

(Not drawn to scale)

82　At which lettered position does Sagittarius appear highest in the sky at midnight to observers near Earth's equator? [1]

Lettered position: _____

83　How many hours of daylight will an observer in New York State experience when Earth is at position C? [1]

_____ **h**

84　The diagram at the right shows the yearly range of altitudes of the noontime Sun as seen by an observer in New York State. Write the letters for each of the four Earth positions, *A*, *B*, *C*, and *D*, in the Sun circles on this diagram to identify when the observer will see the Sun at these noontime altitudes in New York State. More than one letter may be written in a circle. [1]

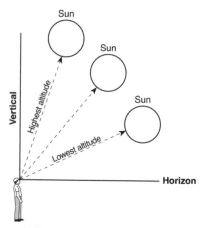

85　The graph below shows the depth and temperature conditions in Earth's interior under which carbon becomes either the mineral graphite or the mineral diamond.

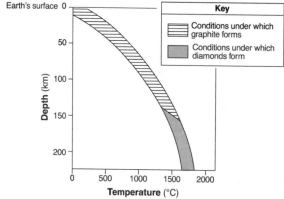

Compared to the depth and temperature conditions under which graphite forms, describe the difference in the relative depth and relative temperature conditions under which most diamonds form. [1]

Lettered position: _____

Relative Temperature: _____

_____

PART A
Answer all questions in this part.

Directions (1-35): For *each* statement or question, select the word or expression that, of those given, best completes the statement or answers the question. Some questions may require the use of the *2011 Edition Reference Tables for Physical Setting/Earth Science*.

1 A Foucault pendulum appears to change its direction of swing because Earth
(1) is tilted on its axis
(2) is spinning on its axis
(3) has a curved surface
(4) has a density of 5.5 g/cm³

2 The modern heliocentric model of planetary motion states that the planets travel around
(1) the Sun in slightly elliptical orbits
(2) the Sun in circular orbits
(3) Earth in slightly elliptical orbits
(4) Earth in circular orbits

3 To an observer on Earth, the Sun appears brighter than the star *Rigel* because the Sun is
(1) hotter than *Rigel*
(2) more luminous than *Rigel*
(3) closer than *Rigel*
(4) larger than *Rigel*

4 The cross section below represents four locations on a mountain. The arrow indicates the prevailing wind direction.

Which location has the warmest and most arid climate?
(1) *A*   (3) *C*
(2) *B*   (4) *D*

5 The map at the right shows an eastern portion of North America. Points *A* and *B* represent locations on the eastern shoreline.

Which factor is primarily responsible for location *A* having a lower average yearly temperature than location *B*?
(1) nearness to a large body of water
(2) elevation
(3) latitude
(4) prevailing winds

6 El Cuy is a South American city located at 40° south latitude. The first day of winter at this location occurs on June 21. During which month would the coldest day of the year most likely occur at this location?
(1) May   (3) November
(2) July   (4) January

7 The map at the right shows a typical position and average velocity of the polar front jet stream during two different seasons.

For the eastern United States, the change of the polar front jet stream from this summer position to this winter position causes
(1) warmer temperatures farther north and causes storms to move more slowly
(2) warmer temperatures farther north and causes storms to move more rapidly
(3) cooler temperatures farther south and causes storms to move more slowly
(4) cooler temperatures farther south and causes storms to move more rapidly

8 Which soil characteristic allows greater amounts of water retention?
(1) large-size particles   (3) high-density particles
(2) small-size particles   (4) low-density particles

9 A paved blacktop parking lot was built on what was once a soil-covered field. This area will now experience increased runoff when rain occurs because the paved parking lot has
(1) less capillarity   (3) greater infiltration
(2) less permeability   (4) greater porosity

10 Which processes of the water cycle return water vapor directly to the atmosphere?
(1) evaporation and transpiration
(2) infiltration and capillarity
(3) freezing and precipitation
(4) water retention and runoff

11 Evidence supports the idea that increases in carbon dioxide and methane in Earth's atmosphere are major contributors to global warming. This is based primarily on the fact that carbon dioxide and methane are excellent absorbers of
(1) gamma rays   (3) visible light
(2) microwaves   (4) infrared radiation

12 The bedrock of the Adirondack Mountains was formed mainly by the
(1) cementation of clastic sediments and precipitates from seawater
(2) compaction and recrystallization of volcanic material
(3) regional metamorphism of sedimentary and igneous rocks
(4) contact metamorphism of unconsolidated gravels

13 Which element, found in both biotite mica and muscovite mica, makes up the greatest percent by volume of Earth's crust?
(1) nitrogen   (3) potassium
(2) oxygen   (4) silicon

14 The inferred temperature and pressure of Earth's interior at a depth of 3,000 kilometers are approximately
(1) 1000°C and 0.5 million atmospheres
(2) 1000°C and 1.0 million atmospheres
(3) 5000°C and 1.5 million atmospheres
(4) 5000°C and 3.0 million atmospheres

15 Which agent of erosion most likely formed the drumlins and finger lakes in New York State?
(1) running water   (3) wave action
(2) moving ice   (4) mass movement

16 The longest portion of the Genesee River in New York State flows through which landscape region?
(1) Erie-Ontario Lowlands
(2) Tug Hill Plateau
(3) Allegheny Plateau
(4) St. Lawrence Lowlands

17 A model of Earth's internal structure is shown at the right. Analysis of which type of data led to the development of this model?
(1) seismic waves
(2) depth of Earth's oceans
(3) electromagnetic radiation
(4) isobar gradients

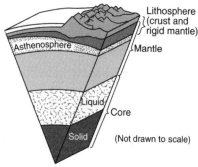

18 What caused the interior of Earth to separate into layers?
(1) a decrease in the rate of rotation of Earth
(2) the gravitational pull on materials of varying densities
(3) variations in heating by the Sun due to Earth's tilt
(4) collisions with meteors and comets

19 Which plate tectonic events occurred as the Iapetus Ocean closed?
(1) Taconian orogeny and Grenville orogeny
(2) Taconian orogeny and Acadian orogeny
(3) Alleghenian orogeny and Acadian orogeny
(4) Alleghenian orogeny and Grenville orogeny

20 Which mineral will scratch fluorite, galena, and pyroxene?
(1) graphite   (3) olivine
(2) calcite   (4) dolomite

21 Which radioactive isotope is most often used when determining the age of fossil bones found in sediments deposited during the Holocene Epoch?
(1) carbon-14   (3) uranium-238
(2) potassium-40   (4) rubidium-87

22 The photograph at the right shows index fossil shells found in bedrock in New York State. These index fossil shells were most likely found in the surface bedrock of which landscape region?
(1) Adirondack Mountains   (3) St. Lawrence Lowlands
(2) the Catskills   (4) Tug Hill Plateau

Base your answers to questions 23 and 24 on the weather map below, which represents a low-pressure system over New York State. The L on the map represents the center of the low-pressure system. Two fronts extend from the center of the low, and are labeled front 1 and front 2. Cloud cover has been omitted from the station models.

23 The arrows on which map best represent the surface wind pattern around this low-pressure center?

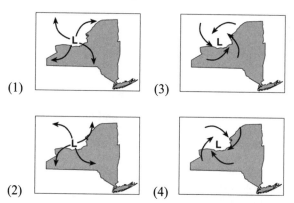

24 Which map best represents the type of fronts and direction of movement of these fronts in relation to the low-pressure center?

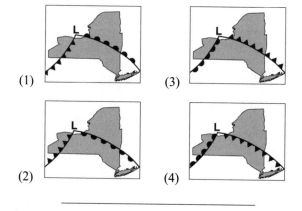

25 A timeline from the origin of Earth until the present is shown below.

Origin of Earth   Present

At which letter on the timeline did the Ediacaran fauna exist?

(1) A   (3) C
(2) B   (4) D

26 The diagram below represents three identical beakers filled to the same level with spherical beads.

If the packing of the beads within each beaker is the same, which graph best represents the porosity within each beaker?

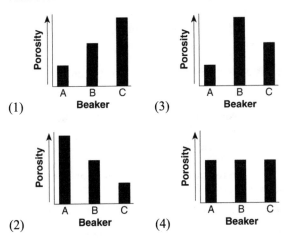

(1)   (3)

(2)   (4)

27 Which diagram correctly represents the curving of Earth's ocean currents and prevailing winds due to the Coriolis effect?

Key

➜ = Ocean currents
⇨ = Prevailing winds

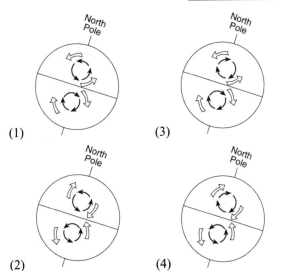

(1)   (3)

(2)   (4)

28 A topographic map and an *incorrectly* constructed profile from point *A* to point *H* on the map are shown below.

Topographic Map

Incorrect Profile

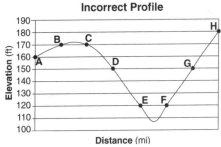

What mistake was made in the construction of this profile?

(1) using a contour interval of 10 feet
(2) plotting points *A* through *H* the same distance apart horizontally
(3) drawing a curved line instead of a straight line from point *B* to point *C*
(4) increasing the elevation from point *F* to point *H*

Base your answers to questions 29 and 30 on the map of the night sky at the right, which represents the apparent locations of some of the constellations that are visible to an observer at approximately 40° N latitude at 9 p.m. in April. The point directly above the observer is labeled zenith.

29 Which map best illustrates the apparent path of Virgo during the next 4 hours?

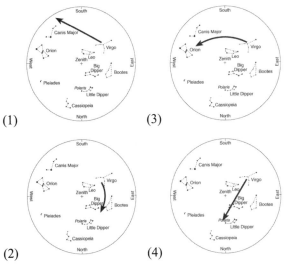

(1)   (3)

(2)   (4)

30 Which motion causes the constellation Leo to no longer be visible to an observer at 40° N in October?

(1) spin of the constellation on its axis
(2) revolution of the constellation around the Sun
(3) spin of Earth on its axis
(4) revolution of Earth around the Sun

31 An earthquake occurs at 12:02 p.m. A seismic station records the first *S*-wave at 12:19 p.m. Which set of data shows the approximate arrival time of the first *P*-wave and the distance to the epicenter?
(1) 12:11:25 p.m. and 4000 km
(3) 12:19:40 p.m. and 4000 km
(2) 12:11:25 p.m. and 6000 km
(4) 12:19:40 p.m. and 6000 km

32 The cross section below right represents a portion of Earth's crust. Letters *A* through *D* are locations within the rock units. At which location is quartzite most likely found?
(1) *A*
(2) *B*
(3) *C*
(4) *D*

Key	
	Igneous intrusion
	Contact metamorphism

33 The diagram at the right represents a total solar eclipse as seen from Earth. Which diagram correctly represents the relative positions of the Sun (*S*), Earth (*E*), and the Moon (*M*) in space during a total solar eclipse? [The diagrams are not drawn to scale.]

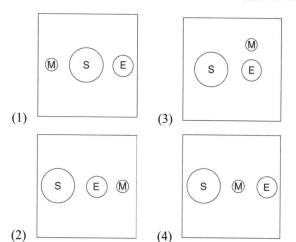

(1)

(2)

(3)

(4)

Base your answers to questions 34 and 35 on the diagram and data table below. The diagram shows the equipment used to determine the factors affecting the rate of erosion in a stream.

Data Table

Rain Gutter Slope	Water Velocity	Erosion Time (s)	
		Fine Sand	Coarse Sand
5°	slow	20	60
	fast	15	40
10°	slow	15	40
	fast	10	30
20°	slow	10	30
	fast	5	15

The data table shows the time it took a 10-gram sample of quartz sand to move 100 centimeters down the rain gutter under various conditions.

34 In this experiment, the water velocity could be increased by
(1) decreasing the slope of the rain gutter
(2) increasing the amount of water from the faucet
(3) lowering the flexible hose
(4) widening the rain gutter

35 What is the relationship between the water velocity and the rate of erosion?
(1) If the water velocity decreases, the rate of erosion increases.
(2) If the water velocity increases, the rate of erosion increases.
(3) If the water velocity remains constant, the rate of erosion decreases.
(4) If the water velocity remains constant, the rate of erosion increases.

Directions (36–50): For *each* statement or question, write the *number* of the word or expression that, of those given, best completes the statement or answers the question. Some questions may require the use of the *2011 Edition Reference Tables for Physical Setting/Earth Science Reference Tables.*

Base your answers to questions 36 and 37 on the diagrams below. The diagrams represent the events that occur when a large meteor, such as the one believed to have caused the extinction of many organisms, impacts Earth's surface. Diagram *A* shows the meteor just before impact. Diagram *B* represents the crater forming, along with the vapor and ejecta (the fragmented rock and dust) thrown into the atmosphere.

Diagram A: Before Impact

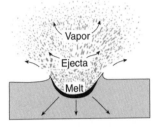
Diagram B: During Impact

36 Which statement best explains how global climate would most likely be affected after this large meteor impact?
(1) Large quantities of ejecta in the atmosphere would block insolation and lower global temperatures.
(2) An increase in vapor and ejecta would allow radiation to escape Earth's atmosphere and lower global temperatures.
(3) Ejecta settling in thick layers would increase the absorption of insolation by Earth's surface and raise global temperatures.
(4) Forest fires produced from the vapor and ejecta would raise global temperatures.

37 Many meteors are believed to be fragments of celestial objects normally found between the orbits of Mars and Jupiter. These objects are classified as
(1) stars   (2) asteroids   (3) planets   (4) moons

Base your answers to questions 38 through 41 on the diagram and data table below. The diagram represents the Sun's apparent paths as viewed by an observer located at 50° N latitude on June 21 and March 21. The data table shows the Sun's maximum altitude for the same two dates of the year. The Sun's maximum altitude for December 21 has been left blank.

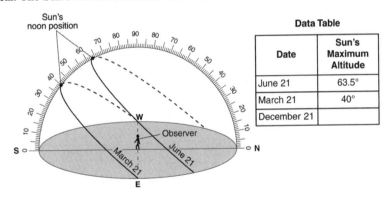

Data Table

Date	Sun's Maximum Altitude
June 21	63.5°
March 21	40°
December 21	

38 Which value should be placed in the data table for the Sun's maximum altitude on December 21?
(1) 16.5°   (2) 23.5°   (3) 40°   (4) 90°

39 Which graph best represents the relationship between the time of day and the length of a shadow cast by the observer on March 21?

(1)   (2)   (3)   (4)

40 Which statement best compares the intensity and angle of insolation at noon on March 21 and June 21?
  (1) The intensity and angle of insolation are greatest on March 21.
  (2) The intensity and angle of insolation are greatest on June 21.
  (3) The intensity of insolation is greatest on June 21 and the angle of insolation is greatest on March 21.
  (4) The intensity of insolation is greatest on March 21 and the angle of insolation is greatest on June 21.

41 Which diagram represents the approximate location of the Sun at 3 p.m. on March 21?

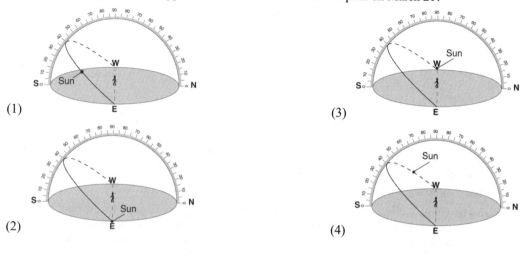

Base your answers to questions 42 through 45 on the laboratory experiment described below.

The weathering of four different rock samples with different masses was studied. Each rock sample was placed in a separate beaker containing 500 milliliters of a dilute acid for 10 minutes. Bubbling was observed in some of the beakers. The data table below shows the mass of each sample, in grams, before placement in the acid and after removal from the acid.

Data Table

Rock	Mass Before (g)	Mass After (g)
limestone	19.72	19.64
granite	20.77	20.77
gneiss	26.83	26.83
marble	20.81	20.73

42 Which Earth process is being modeled in this experiment?
  (1) physical weathering in the hydrosphere
  (2) physical weathering in the mesosphere
  (3) chemical weathering in the hydrosphere
  (4) chemical weathering in the mesosphere

43 Which table correctly shows the classification of the rock samples based on the amount of weathering during this experiment?

(1)
Group A	Group B
limestone marble	granite gneiss

(2)
Group A	Group B
limestone granite gneiss	marble

(3)
Group A	Group B
limestone	granite marble gneiss

(4)
Group A	Group B
limestone granite	gneiss marble

44 Approximately what percentage of the marble sample remained after the experiment?
  (1) 0.4%   (2) 8.0%   (3) 20.7%   (4) 99.6%

45 Which property of the gneiss sample prevented it from weathering?
  (1) crystalline texture   (2) mineral composition   (3) density   (4) cleavage

Base your answers to questions 46 through 48 on the topographic map at the right. Points A, X, and Y are reference points on the map.

Contour interval = 50 meters

0 1 2 3 4 5 km

46 What is a possible elevation of point A?
 (1) 575 meters
 (2) 600 meters
 (3) 655 meters
 (4) 710 meters

47 In which general direction does Flint Creek flow?
 (1) southwest
 (2) southeast
 (3) northwest
 (4) northeast

48 What is the approximate gradient along the straight dashed line between points X and Y?
 (1) 50 m/km
 (2) 100 m/km
 (3) 150 m/km
 (4) 300 m/km

Base your answers to questions 49 and 50 on the diagram at the right, which represents the current locations of two planets, A and B, orbiting a star. Letter X indicates a position in the orbit of planet A. Numbers 1 through 4 indicate positions in the orbit of planet B.

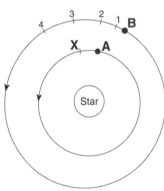

(Not drawn to scale)

49 As planet A moves in orbit from its current location to position X, planet B most likely moves in orbit from its current location to position
 (1) 1   (3) 3
 (2) 2   (4) 4

50 If the diagram represents our solar system and planet B is Venus, which planet is represented by planet A?
 (1) Mercury   (3) Earth
 (2) Jupiter   (4) Mars

Answer all questions in this part.

Directions (51–65): Record your answers in the spaces provided. Some questions may require the use of the *2011 Edition Reference Tables for Physical Setting/Earth Science Reference Tables.*

Base your answers to questions 51 through 53 on the magnified views shown at the right of the minerals found in an igneous rock and in a metamorphic rock. The millimeter scale indicates the size of the crystals shown in the magnified views.

51 Identify the environment of formation of this igneous rock based on the size of its intergrown crystals. [1]

_____

52 Based on the minerals present, identify the relative color and density of this igneous rock compared to mafic igneous rocks with the same crystal size. [1]

Color: _____

Density: _____

53 Describe the texture shown by this metamorphic rock that indicates it could be schist. [1]

_____

_____

Igneous Rock   **Metamorphic Rock**

Scale
0   2   4 mm

Key

Amphibole	Plagioclase feldspar	Quartz
Biotite	Potassium feldspar	

Base your answers to questions 54 through 58 on the passage below.

Dinosaur Skull Offers Hints About Africa's Past
　　A fossil skull was found in Africa among many dinosaur bones from the Late Cretaceous Epoch. This skull came from a dinosaur named *Rugops primus*, or "first wrinkle face." This meat eater, believed to have been about 30 feet long and to have lived 95 million years ago, belonged to a group of dinosaurs called abelisaurids.
　　This fossil skull, unearthed in the Sahara Desert in 2000, provides new evidence that Africa split from other southern continents at a later time than previously thought. Before this discovery, abelisaurids from that period had been found only in South America, Madagascar, and India, but not in Africa. This new fossil, *Rugops primus*, found only in Africa, indicates that Africa was still connected to the other southern landmasses, at least by a land bridge, 100 million years ago.

54 During which geologic era is Rugops primus inferred to have lived? [1]

_____ **Era**

55 What evidence suggests that Africa was still attached to South America 100 million years ago? [1]

_____

_____

56 State the type of rock in which *Rugops primus* was most likely preserved. [1]

_____

57 *Rugops primus* is *not* a good index fossil. Describe *one* characteristic of a good index fossil. [1]

_____

58 Identify the type of tectonic plate movement that caused Africa to separate from South America. [1]

_____

_____

Base your answers to questions 59 through 61 on the map in your answer booklet, which represents two bridges that cross the Green River. Letters *A*, *B*, and *C* represent locations in the river. A ball was dropped from bridge 1 at location *A* and the distance and travel time to location *B* were recorded. The results are shown in the data table at the right.

Travel from A to B	
Distance (cm)	Time (s)
12,000	240

59 On the map at the right, place an **X** at the location between the bridges where the greatest amount of deposition is most likely occurring. [1]

60 Determine the rate at which the ball traveled, in centimeters per second, from location *A* to location *B*. [1]

_____ **cm/s**

61 After a thunderstorm, the velocity of the river at location *C* was 100 centimeters per second. What was the largest type of sediment transported by the river at this location? [1]

_____

Base your answers to questions 62 through 65 on the diagram at the right. The diagram represents daytime and nighttime on Earth. Point *X* is a location on Earth's surface. Earth's rotational surface velocity is shown in miles per hour (mi/h) at specific latitudes.

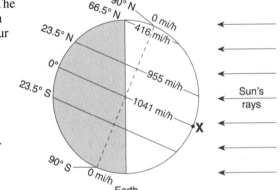

62 What is Earth's rotational surface velocity, in miles per hour, at 23.5° south latitude? [1]

_____ **mi/h**

63 Record, to the *nearest hour*, the duration of insolation at location X for one Earth rotation. [1]

_____ **h**

64 On the grid below, draw a line to show the general relationship between distance from the equator and Earth's rotational surface velocity. [1]

65 Identify the Northern Hemisphere season that is just beginning when Earth is at the position represented in this diagram. [1]

_____

Part C
Answer all questions in this part.

Directions (66–85): Record your answers in the spaces provided. Some questions may require the use of the *2011 Edition Reference Tables for Physical Setting/Earth Science Reference Tables.*

Base your answers to questions 66 and 67 on the world map at the right. Points *A* through *H* represent locations on Earth's surface.

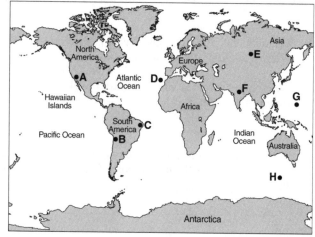

66 Identify the *two* lettered locations from the map that are *least* likely to experience volcanic activity or earthquakes. [1]

_____ and _____

67 Identify the tectonic feature responsible for the formation of the Hawaiian Islands. [1]

_____

Base your answers to questions 68 and 69 on the data table at the right and on the partial weather station model for Oklahoma City, Oklahoma, below.

Data Table	
Visibility	7 miles
Dewpoint	48°F
Wind Direction	from the south
Wind Speed	25 knots

68 On the partial weather station model for Oklahoma City below, add the correct weather map symbols to indicate the weather conditions shown in the data table. [1]

62 ⬭ 134

69 State the actual barometric pressure at Oklahoma City. [1]

_____ **mb**

Base your answers to questions 70 through 72 on the geologic cross section at the right, which represents a portion of Earth's crust. Some rock units contain index fossils. Box *A* indicates a missing portion of the cross section.

70 In the box that represents box *A* on the cross section at the right, draw both the volcanic ash layer and the basaltic intrusion to clearly show their relative age. [1]

71 Describe *one* piece of evidence which indicates that the horizontal rock layers are younger than the tilted rock layers. [1]

_____

_____

72 The meteor impact debris was deposited at the time trilobites became extinct. State the age, in million years, of this debris layer. [1]

_____ **million years**

Base your answers to questions 73 and 74 on the map at the right, which represents the center of a low-pressure system indicated by **L**. The 1000-millibar (mb) isobar is drawn around the center of this low-pressure system.

73 On the map at the right, draw *two* additional isobars around the outside of the 1000-mb isobar in a way that indicates that the strongest winds are west of the low-pressure center. [1]

74 Identify *one* factor that usually causes many low-pressure centers to generally move from west to east across the United States. [1]

_____

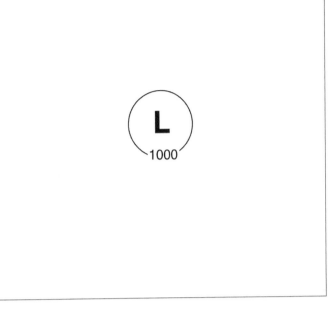

Base your answers to questions 75 and 76 on the map at the right, which represents the geographic source regions of two air masses, X and Y. The arrows represent the convergence of these air masses, which may result in tornadoes.

75 Use the standard two-letter air-mass symbols to identify air-masses X and Y. [1]

Air-mass X: _____

Air-mass Y: _____

76 A tornado watch or warning is issued for a location in the area labeled Tornado Alley. State *one* safety precaution that should be taken to avoid possible injury from this tornado. [1]

_____

_____

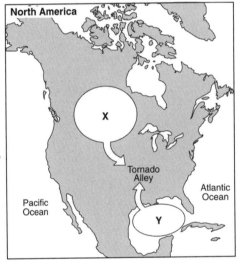

Base your answers to questions 77 through 82 on the calendar at the right and data table below. The calendar shows the month of February 2007, indicating the dates when some lunar phases occurred. February 24 lists only the name of the Moon phase that occurred on that day. The data table shows the highest and lowest tides (in feet) recorded for the Hudson River at Kingston, New York, over a 2-day period in February 2007.

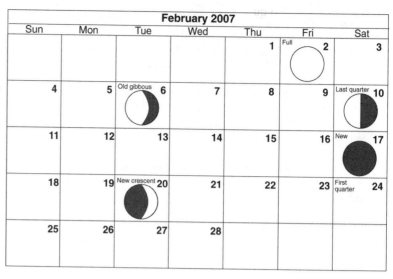

High and Low Tides for Kingston, New York

Date	Time of Day	Tide Height (ft)
Friday, February 2	1:30 a.m.	3.5
	7:30 a.m.	−0.2
	1:30 p.m.	4.1
	8:00 p.m.	−0.4
Saturday, February 3	2:00 a.m.	3.6
	8:30 a.m.	−0.2
	2:00 p.m.	4.0
	9:00 p.m.	−0.4

77 On the grid at the right, plot the tide height for *each* time of day listed in the data table. Connect the plots with a line. [1]

78 Predict the time of the first high tide on Sunday, February 4. Include a.m. or p.m. in your answer. [1]

_____

79 On the diagram below, draw a small circle (**O**) on the Moon's orbit to show the position of the Moon in its orbit on February 2. [1]

(Not drawn to scale)

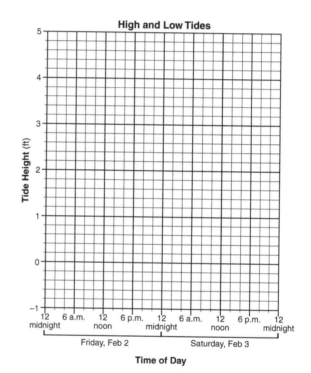

80 State the date of the next full Moon that occurred after February 2. [1]

_____

81 In the circle at the right, shade the part of the Moon that appeared dark to an observer in New York State on February 24. [1]

82 Determine the altitude of *Polaris* at Kingston, New York, to the *nearest degree*. [1]

_____ °

Base your answers to questions 83 through 85 on the passage below.

Mount Manaro Erupts!

Mount Manaro is a volcano on Ambae Island, about 1400 miles northeast of Australia. Ambae Island is located in the South Pacific Ocean at 15° south latitude, 168° east longitude.

After Mount Manaro had erupted in 1995, Ambae Island residents developed an evacuation plan. When Mount Manaro began erupting gas, steam, and ash on November 27, 2005, scientists and residents watched the volcano carefully.

The eruption became more severe on December 9, 2005, when steam and gases rose 1.8 miles up into the air. Rocks and ash began to fall on nearby farms and homes. Thousands of people left their homes, making it the largest evacuation ever on Ambae Island.

83 Name the highest layer of the atmosphere into which the steam from the volcanic eruption rose on December 9, 2005. [1]

_____

84 Identify the ocean current off the northeast coast of Australia that most affects the climate of Ambae Island. [1]

_____

85 On the diagram below, draw *one* arrow through point *X* and *one* arrow through point *Y* to indicate the direction of tectonic plate motion near Mount Manaro. [1]

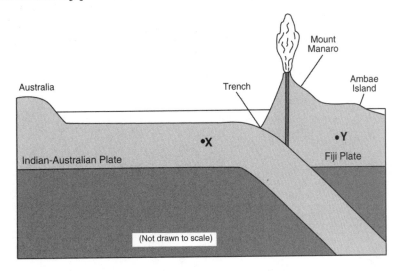

_____